RE-VIEWING
THE COLD WAR

RE-VIEWING THE COLD WAR

Domestic Factors and Foreign Policy in the East-West Confrontation

Edited by
Patrick M. Morgan and Keith L. Nelson
Foreword by Georgi Arbatov

Westport, Connecticut
London

Library of Congress Cataloging-in-Publication Data

Re-viewing the cold war : domestic factors and foreign policy in the
  East-West confrontation / edited by Patrick M. Morgan and Keith L.
  Nelson ; foreword by Georgi Arbatov.
      p.   cm.
    Includes bibliographical references and index.
    ISBN 0–275–96636–4 (alk. paper).—ISBN 0–275–96637–2 (pbk. :
  alk. paper)
    1. Soviet Union—Foreign relations.   2. Cold War.   3. World
  politics—20th century.   I. Morgan, Patrick M., 1940–   .
  II. Nelson, Keith L.   III. Arbatov, G. A.
  DK266.45.R48   2000
  327.47—dc21   99–16056

British Library Cataloguing in Publication Data is available.

Library of Congress Catalog Card Number: 99–16056
ISBN: 0–275–96636–4
        0–275–96637–2 (pbk.)

First published in 2000

Praeger Publishers, 88 Post Road West, Westport, CT 06881
An imprint of Greenwood Publishing Group, Inc.
www.praeger.com

Printed in the United States of America

The paper used in this book complies with the
Permanent Paper Standard issued by the National
Information Standards Organization (Z39.48–1984).

10 9 8 7 6 5 4 3 2 1

This study was supported by
the Institute on Global Conflict and Cooperation
of the University of California.

To our wives
Marilyn and Paddy

Contents

Foreword

Georgi Arbatov

The necessary research, writing, and editing have finally been completed, and we have before us an impressive volume, which I, before writing this foreword, have read carefully. And, in truth, I have read it with great interest. I hope this interest is shared by a broad audience of readers after the publication of the book.

Still, my task, as I understand it, is not to evaluate the quality of the work done by this group of distinguished American, Russian, West European, and Israeli scholars, nor to introduce the readers to the process and results of their investigations. My challenge, I think, is rather to discuss the "grand design" of the study and the importance of its topic, as well as to highlight its main dimensions. In addition, I should offer a point of view on how the major events described in the book can be evaluated today, given our present knowledge and experience. I am not sure I can accomplish all of this, but I shall do my best. To begin with, I would like to say a little about the phenomenon of the Cold War itself and, in particular, to address the question of whether we should consider it to have been a more or less usual state of international relations or an aberration, a deviation from whatever can be defined as normal in our far-from-perfect world.

Violence and war are ancient institutions, actually inherited from the period prior to recorded history. The famous British philosopher Thomas Hobbes described the most primitive stage of human society as a war of all against all. Of course, he had in mind primarily the internal state of affairs in each society, not interrelationships among them. He was suggesting that domestic chaos played a large role in the birth of law and legal institutions, of the governments and codes of behavior that made possible the preservation of societies. Very rarely was the result real peace, much less perfect law and order, but more often than not societies could at least survive.

Much more complicated than the internal life of societies was their relationship with each other. Those who say that human history was mostly a record of wars are deplorably close to the truth. Even within and among highly developed civilizations, in international relations the law of the jungle prevailed. To be sure, international law existed for centuries, but it was born as a law of war, designed to decrease the losses and the sufferings of peoples and to introduce a few rules into this dirty game. Violence, killing noncombatants, and destroying cities, property, and institutions remained a "legitimate" mode of behavior.

World War II was a watershed in this sense. After it ended, quite a few of its perpetrators were tried as criminals, sentenced, and punished. But neither war as a continuation of policy nor violence in international relations was outlawed. And even after the most bloody and criminal war in history, new military conflicts were waged in such places as Korea, Vietnam, Hungary, the Middle East, Afghanistan, Yugoslavia, and Chechnya. What was especially sad was that, long before the wounds of World War II were healed and those who lost their lives were buried, preparations for a new all-out war, with more-destructive and really ultimate weapons, had begun.

Yet I believe that in contrast with the "hot" wars in the millennia-long experience of mankind, the Cold War was not normal but abnormal and irrational. I would say more. Despite serious differences among the victorious allies in their fight against the common enemy, despite natural suspicions deriving from their opposing ideologies, and despite the character of some of these nations' leaders—including symptoms of paranoia in Stalin—the leaders of the major nations of the anti-Hitler coalition had almost certainly not intended to gravitate from alliance to bitter hostility, suspicion, and preparation for another even bloodier war.

Of course, the alliance could not have been sustained on a permanent basis after the common enemy had disappeared. The breakup of such alliances is a usual consequence of victorious wars, and one cannot suspect Roosevelt, Churchill, and Stalin of being so naive that they hoped for an exception in this case.

But this does not mean that the wartime alliance had to be immediately succeeded by cold war and an intensive arms race. There were other alternatives, and the leaders of the United States, USSR, and Great Britain thought about them and even prepared for them. If not, why did they worry so much about creating the United Nations organization? And why did they think so much about the postwar world order in general? Remember that these leaders expected such a substantial increase in trade and economic cooperation that, to service it, the American government established a new Export–Import Bank. Even Stalin anticipated such expanded contacts and cooperation with the outside world (mainly with the West) that at the end of the war he established a special, and by our standards unprecedentedly privileged and lavishly financed, Foreign Literature Publishing House (where I worked from 1949 to 1953).

So, though the end of the war meant also the end of the Grand Alliance, we were not at all condemned to fight the Cold War. Given somewhat less hysteria, relations could have developed along other lines, not in an idyllic sense but in a more or less peaceful way, with many problems and difficulties but without decades of balancing on the brink of nuclear war. I hope that in future years historical scholars will be able to demonstrate this more and more clearly.

In any case, whether we could have avoided the Cold War is not the issue at hand. We did have it. Indeed, we had it for almost half a century. And now *new* questions about the Cold War have become interesting and important. One is how the Cold War really came to a close, and with what results? In other words—who won, and who lost?

In the West, and among quite a few people in Russia, the conventional wisdom is that the Cold War ended with a clear victory on the part of the United States. Nevertheless, I am absolutely sure that, like much conventional wisdom, this is mistaken.

I understand why this view has become widespread. The main reason is that the end of the Cold War coincided with the collapse of the Soviet Union and of Communism as a political system and ideology. Yet it is important to realize that these deep crises were connected mainly with internal shortcomings and seeds of self-destruction in the Soviet system and not with the course of events in the Cold War.

Those who defend the opposite view often claim that it was the policy of President Reagan that, by scaring the Russians and compelling them to follow the American lead in a new and expensive round of the arms race, undermined the Soviet economy and Soviet willingness to compete. I do not agree.

As for "scaring" the Russians, new weapons or the threat of their creation could hardly add anything to the terror that for years had remained—for Russians and Americans alike—the basis of deterrence and the cornerstone of strategic relations. The economic arguments are even less convincing. Soviet leaders could hardly have been led to reform by a more expensive arms race because they themselves did not know the whole truth about the economic condition of their country. This was largely because they were constantly misled by their own bureaucracy, which did not dare report on how difficult the situation was and did not want to tell the truth about the staggering cost of military hardware. The armed forces dared not frighten the political leaders so much that the military appropriations they asked for would be denied.

Moreover, one should not forget that Cold War military expenditures were a double-edged sword, impacting on both sides. Even if the Americans did plan to bleed the Soviet economy white (and this is not yet proved), the fact is that, being not only richer but also greater spendthrifts, they transformed themselves during Reagan's years from being the biggest creditors in the world into being its biggest debtors.

I think in general that the Cold War was a lose-lose game. Nobody could win it; both sides lost. Therefore the question of who won is the wrong one. A more correct one is: Who contributed more to putting an end to the Cold War? And here I can say, with considerable direct knowledge, that it was the Soviet Union, its leadership, and in particular Mikhail Gorbachev that played the largest role.

What were the motives behind Gorbachev's policy and the changed Soviet behavior on the international scene? I think they were mainly of an internal nature and were rarely directly connected with the Cold War. One of them was the obvious fact that all Moscow's plans and hopes for the "great leap" forward had failed. We had neither reached the "paradise" promised for 1980 by the Party Program nor overcome the painful economic, social, and political difficulties that nagged at us and even became aggravated as time went on. Furthermore, the victorious and glorious march of Communism across the globe had not hurried to manifest itself. In the countries where Communists came to power great achievements remained absent or at least invisible.

So the principal way the domestic situation helped to end the Cold War was by generating the hope that if we managed to throw from our shoulders the heavy burden of continuing international conflict, this would make it easier for us to handle our internal challenges.

An added consideration was that thoughtful people in my country (and it was lucky that the future president turned out to be among them) as well as some in other countries had come to the conclusion that the Cold War was not only dangerous and expensive but also futile and without the prospect of positive results.

The end of this gloomy and dangerous period in the history of modern international relations was a tremendous blessing. Of course, for those who had illusions that the end of the Cold War would bring an immediate solution to all our problems—that it would bring us a peaceful and harmonious world—there were to be bitter disappointments. Still, for such heartbreaks we should blame not the end of the Cold War but the naïveté and political ignorance of the "disappointed ones." The Cold War and the danger of a nuclear holocaust obscured other problems for a time but could not and did not eliminate them.

In this connection I have found the latest book of the British historian Eric Hobsbawm (*Age of Extremes: The Short Twentieth Century, 1914–1991* [New York: Pantheon Books, 1994]) particularly helpful. He points out that the Cold War had transformed the international scene in several respects:

First, it had entirely . . . overshadowed all but one of the rivalries and conflicts that characterized world politics before the Second World War. Some disappeared because the empires of the imperial era vanished and with them the rivalries of colonial powers over dependent territories under their rule. Others went because all the "great powers" except two . . . were no longer autonomous, or indeed of more than local interest. . . .

Second, the Cold War had frozen the international situation, and in doing so had stabilized what was an essentially unfixed and provisional state of affairs. . . . The combination of power, political influence, bribery, and the logic of bipolarity and anti-imperialism kept the divisions of the world more or less stable. . . . The shadow of the mushroom cloud guaranteed the survival not of liberal democracies in Western Europe, but of regimes like Saudi Arabia and Kuwait. (253–254)

And then the British historian comes to *post*–Cold War realities:

The end of the Cold War suddenly removed the props which had held up the international structure and, to an extent not yet appreciated, the structures of the world's domestic political systems. And what was left was a world in disarray and partial collapse, because there was nothing to replace them. . . .

The consequences of the end of the Cold War would probably have been enormous in any case, even had it not coincided with major crises in the world economy of capitalism and with the final crisis of the Soviet Union and its system. . . . The end of the Cold War proved to be not the end of an international conflict, but the end of an era. . . . (255–256)

Aside from the inevitable reasons for disappointment, there were also factors of another kind connected with the policies of the major international actors and, in particular, of both superpowers. It is astonishing but the end of the Cold War caught both countries—to use a well-known American expression—"flat-footed," without a well thought out and long-term policy.

Such planning was badly needed. A whole period of international attitudes came to an end with the end of the Cold War. As a result the very approach to foreign policy should have been changed. At first this was vaguely felt by the leaders. President Bush talked about a "new world order," President Gorbachev about "new political thinking." But it was not quite clear what they had in mind. And soon even these weak attempts to face up to the new realities and new opportunities faded without leaving recognizable traces in the theory and praxis of foreign policy.

Up until now neither country has had a coherent *post*–Cold War program. And without suitable strategic goals and concepts, policy is doomed to be a series of reactions to events, reactions that tend to revive old suspicions and distrust, especially if they are accompanied by behavior that can be interpreted by the other side as hostile (as, for instance, the expansion of NATO to the East).

I will be more emphatic: The dialogue between the two countries has declined in substance and importance. Russian-American relations and diplomacy today do not have a clear and really adequate agenda regarding major problems. Granted, this is a separate and important topic that requires separate consideration and discussion. I shall offer, therefore, only a few comments.

One set of present-day problems involves the vast legacy of the Cold War. This is a serious inertial force that will always tend to pull us back, if not into a renewed Cold War, at least to a revival of suspicion, rivalry, and hostile attitudes. It will poison our relations even if we do not do anything particularly bad or harmful.

What do I have in mind? First of all, mountains of redundant weapons left over from the East-West conflict. These weapons are not simply heaps of old, corroding hardware. They have a peculiar ability to spread: by being sold, stolen, lost, forgotten during movement of troops, and the like. And they can easily get into the wrong hands—inside the country or abroad. Meanwhile, the international arms trade continues to be a favorite and profitable pastime, one that can create serious dangers, sow distrust, and serve as an excuse to drag one's feet with regard to conversion of the defense industry.

Another part of the legacy of the Cold War is a tremendously big defense establishment, together with the related defense-science partnership. In the Soviet Union this sector constituted roughly half of the economy of the country. Often a defense enterprise was so dominating as to form a whole town around itself. To shut down the factory now means real disaster for this town and many thousands of its inhabitants. One can imagine what an albatross around the neck of Russia this arrangement becomes.

And not only economically. It is in fact an embodiment of the military-industrial complex, the danger of which President Eisenhower warned us in his farewell address. We know now from first-hand experience that it constitutes a lobby not only for arms racing and militarism but also for a militant foreign policy, backed by every antidemocratic, nationalist movement in its area.

Besides liberating ourselves and the world from the after-effects of the Cold War, we must have on our agenda another very important item—to construct a system of international ties that guarantees peace, security, equality, and human rights. This will require an effort by many nations to enlarge the scope of multilateral policies and their implementing instruments. Starting, obviously, with the United Nations, but also with regional organizations and an adequate system of international treaties, we must provide the international community with a solid legal basis for cooperation.

There is an even more basic point, however. To surmount the legacy of the Cold War and build a truly new world order, we must, first of all, fortify and secure the democratic processes of our own countries. One thing we have surely learned: No foreign policy can be reasonable, flexible, and stable unless the system and leaders behind it are open, responsible, and just—unless, that is, they are open to their people and responsive to their wishes. Foreign policy inevitably reflects domestic politics, for better or for ill.

Introduction

Patrick M. Morgan

This book is the end result of a lengthy project about a complicated subject. The project was initiated by members of the Global Peace and Conflict Studies Program (GPACS) at the University of California, Irvine, as the first stage in a research program on the "foreign-domestic nexus." It is obvious that foreign and domestic affairs interact and that foreign policy decisions are made with both domestic and external considerations in mind. The problem is sorting out the relative and often reciprocal influence of domestic and external factors, and perceptions thereof, in explaining foreign policy making. It is also clear, though this often receives less attention, that the same applies to domestic policy decisions—both international and internal considerations apply, but just how is uncertain. The foreign-domestic nexus program is devoted to the further exploration of this subject.

Work on this volume was initiated when GPACS faculty members suggested that the Cold War was a potentially interesting subject for collaborative research because it could now be tackled by a research group that could include Russian scholars who could draw, and help the others to draw, on the wealth of material becoming available from Russian and other East European archives. This turned out to be feasible. In the end several Russian scholars, others from Germany, Sweden, and Israel, and three GPACS faculty members at Irvine joined in the effort. This was a disparate group in terms of field, specialty, nationality, age, gender, and methodological persuasion, making management of the project sometimes akin to herding cats. Cohesion was initially supplied by the fact that the members have a significant professional (and often personal) interest in the history of the Soviet Union and particularly in its relations with the outside world. Many have also long had an interest in American foreign and national security policy during the Cold War. All were attracted by the idea of reexamining the Cold War in the light of how it ended and, where appropriate, by utilizing the new information now available.[1]

This desire to explore the links between domestic politics and foreign policy as well as the broader relationship between domestic systems and the international environment was stimulated by the same factors that have been inciting renewed interest in this aspect of foreign policy on the part of both historians and political scientists during the past decade. While over the years historians had more often than not remained sensitive to the interplay between the two sectors, by the 1980s political scientists had turned from earlier explorations of this in comparative foreign policy to neo-Realism's primary emphasis on the international system, particularly in the form of systemic constraints on state behavior. In security-oriented studies, although the neo-Realist perspective readily admitted that a theory of foreign policy must include domestic factors, neo-Realists and neo-Liberal institutionalists pressed theories and other analyses that modeled the impact of the international system on actor behavior. In international political economy studies, rising interdependence incited particular emphasis on the penetration of domestic systems by external actors and the global economy.

For both historians and political scientists the end of the Cold War has invited a return to seeing foreign policy as made from the inside out. Its demise seemed to have derived from the Soviet Union's domestic situation, the impact of a particular leader, and the surprising shift in foreign policy he introduced. The pressures from the global system were relentless at the time, but the responses to them seemed to have been clearly shaped by the peculiarities of that political system and its remarkable leader. Even before the end of the Cold War there had been a shift in international political economy studies toward "bringing the state back in" through a focus on the impact of state structures on foreign economic policy and by an insistence that substate actors were playing an increasing role in shaping state preferences and policies in foreign affairs. The participants in our project agreed with this perspective—we were particularly interested in the domestic roots of much that went on in the international politics of the Cold War.

If the project was clear in terms of its general outlook, the question remained as to what analytical framework might be employed to bring coherence to the individual studies. The members of the project considered this question at length. In particular the group explored the utility of the "two-level-game" framework developed by Robert Putnam at Harvard.[2] In the end there was no consensus on adhering rigorously to that framework. Nevertheless, the impact of Putnam's framework pervaded the group discussions by clarifying the existence of multiple layers of the "domestic" arena for policy making and highlighting the reciprocal interaction between international and domestic politics as opposed to thinking about them in sequential or additive terms. Thus it is useful to say something further here about Putnam's approach.

Putnam claimed that although many analysts had detected a constant interplay between the foreign and domestic levels of analysis in shaping policy making, they had found no consistently effective way of conceptualizing this that could facilitate more rigorous, less impressionistic, research and generate reliable findings. He suggested that progress could be made by viewing the chief political official (the person responsible for international negotiations) as seeking an agreement with a similar actor in another state and as having to engage in two simultaneous political games to bring the agreement into effect. In pursuit of a satisfactory agreement the first political game (level one) is the interaction in which the two sides bargain to achieve a mutually acceptable deal. This involves exchanges of information, efforts at persuasion, even attempts at coercion. The key to what results at level one is whether the "win-sets"—the collection of what would be acceptable agreements—of the two parties overlap or can be adjusted so that they overlap. If they overlap, a mutually acceptable agreement can be concluded. If they do not overlap and they cannot be adjusted to make them do so, then one or both parties will refuse any tentative agreement proposed.

One implication is that the chief political official, or CoG (Chief of Government), must try to ascertain whether the win-sets do indeed overlap, and thus whether the prospective agreement he or she has in mind is feasible. A second is that when the ascertainable win-sets do not overlap, the CoG must either find a way to shift the win-set of the other side, such as by offering additional inducements on other issues or by threatening an unfavorable reaction on other issues, and the like, or adjust his own side's win-set so that he settles for less than planned but still gets an agreement. Finally, the CoG naturally seeks the best bargain that falls within the overlap. With this in mind it should be possible to characterize the various strategies available to the CoG and to explore which ones work or do not work under various conditions, developing hypotheses that could be tested against case studies to tighten our understanding of the foreign-domestic nexus. For instance, at times it may be advantageous to make one's win-set very clear, at other times it will be better to leave it ambiguous.

Within such a framework we can hypothesize that the larger the win-sets of the two parties, the higher the likelihood of reaching an agreement. However, each party will normally press for an agreement that falls at the margins of the other's win-set so as to maximize its own benefits. For this purpose it may seek bargaining leverage by suggesting that it has a narrow win-set, and it will therefore benefit when this is manifestly true. Hence the final shape of an agreement does not necessarily reflect the overall political (or other) strength of the two sides; bargaining leverage is not simply a function of power measured in a standard way. This makes it important to explore how ongoing negotiations or other developments may affect the parties' win-sets and enhance or diminish the chances of reaching an agreement.

Putnam then suggested that the CoG plays in a second political game (level two), one equally important for achieving a workable understanding. Normally, someone at home must approve of the CoG's negotiated agreement. This is a domestic "ratification" game. Domestic elements—key leaders, or the legislature, or major interests, or public opinion—must accept the agreement, or it cannot be sustained and implemented. This is easy to see in the legislative ratification of a treaty—the agreement must command the required majority. However, it readily applies to other kinds of ratifiers. In a cabinet system, the treaty could require majority support in the cabinet. If the support of key bureaucracies is needed for effective implementation of an agreement, then they become ratifiers. It might be that if there is little public support, the agreement will not be significant even if formally ratified, and thus the public is a ratifier. For example, the agreements on détente in the Nixon years became of less import when elite and public support for détente began to fade in the United States.

This is also a problem shaped by win-sets. To the ratifiers there is a range of acceptable international understandings. The CoG must either come up with an agreement that falls within their collective win-set or find a way to shift its boundaries. Once again, the CoG has a variety of options, from seeking renegotiation of an agreement to trying to alter an unfavorable domestic win-set through a variety of tactics. Here also, Putnam contended that his framework can facilitate the development of hypotheses about the behavior of states and leaders that is involved.

Ultimate success results from a conjunction of two groups of win-sets, while CoG tasks and tactics concern getting such a conjunction and then determining where, within the overlap, the eventual resting point is to lie. This overall perspective can help us work through the many layers of political activity usually required and thereby facilitate taking into account in a systematic way, via a common approach to both games, the interplay between foreign and domestic factors in shaping foreign policy regardless of the differences in the nature of the systems involved, differences that have greatly complicated arriving at reliable cross-national generalizations in the past.

To this Putnam added further speculations. One was that the CoG need not be merely a mouthpiece for state or ratifier interests, but that he would have interests and preferences, perceptions, and skills of his own that would play a role in determining the kinds of agreements sought, the tactics used, and the degree of effort mounted. This inserts the CoG as a player in his own right, not just on behalf of others, as various analysts of foreign policy decision making have often urged.

Putnam also suggested that the interplay between the two games sometimes produces an agreement that would not have been possible before the games started and thus not intended when the process began. The process could have a synergistic element, in which exploring win-sets and trying to adjust them leads to discovery of an unanticipated type of agreement or of bundles of agreements. In extending this point beyond Putnam's argument, we might anticipate some manifestations of negative synergy as well—in which the process of seeking agreement uncovers previously unexplored barriers or complications, leading to little or no agreement when prospects initially seemed good or even leading to the cancellation of existing agreements.

EXPLORING REFINEMENTS

With this understanding of a two-level-game approach in hand,[3] we secured the assistance of Professors George Breslauer (Berkeley), Jack Snyder (Columbia), and Putnam himself in conducting what amounted to a lengthy tutorial on the options and pitfalls in employing a two-level game framework for the American-Soviet relationship. Those intensive discussions were extremely beneficial in focusing the group's periodic reexaminations of the thrust of the individual studies.

For instance, consideration was given to features of the U.S.-Soviet relationship that seemed to require adjustments in the two-level game approach. For one thing, the approach emphasizes the search for agreements, implying that this is a central objective of the parties, but in the Cold War the superpowers often behaved as if agreement was not very probable or desirable and thus not a high priority. Obviously there were occasions when the two sides sought agreement and when, presumably, the two-level-game framework should apply. But often agreement seemed quite unlikely, proposals for agreements seemed designed to serve as political ammunition, and even official negotiations were *pro forma* in nature. The question was whether the two-level-game approach could be applicable to a relationship characterized by intense political conflict.

Another possible problem lay in the applicability of the framework to the Soviet political system. It is easy to see how to apply the concept of domestic ratification to a democratic system, particularly when there are institutionalized requirements for the ratification of foreign affairs agreements. But its relevance is less obvious for a highly centralized and authoritarian system that accepts no serious limits on the leaders' ability to conduct the regime's foreign policy largely as they saw fit.

In the end we agreed that Putnam's framework could indeed be relevant. It was possible to broaden the notion of an agreement. In many cases the United States and USSR sought informal understandings on rules for limiting their conflicts, mutual understandings that appeared to have been subject to two-level-game negotiating. Détente, for example, quite apart from specific agreements reached, was often a subject of intense political debate in both countries and could not be undertaken without both the willingness of the two parties to move in this direction and a degree of ratification by key domestic elements. There were also many instances in which agreement appeared to be the goal of the two sides in spite of the difficulties involved. As for the applicability of the agreement to the Soviet political system, the Soviet Union was far less dominated by a single leader after Stalin's death, and collective leadership imposed constraints on potential deals with other governments that amounted to a ratification process.

Another refinement pertained to the levels of analysis. We noted that each superpower, as leader of a large international coalition, had to consider the wishes of its allies in shaping agreements with the enemy. Although the United States and USSR dominated their respective camps and could not be stopped if they were determined to reach an agreement with which their allies disagreed, considerations of retaining their legitimacy, bloc solidarity, and international image required that in most instances major agreements between them have at least a modicum of support from the allies. This was particularly true when they negotiated as a bloc with the allies (even though they were in charge of the specifics), as in the Mutual and Balanced Force Reduction (MBFR) talks, or where they were charged with negotiating on behalf of their allies, as in the Intermediate-Range Nuclear Forces (INF negotiations.

On occasion, the relationship between allies and superpowers was reversed, so that allies, individually or collectively, took the lead in pressing for agreements (intrabloc or on their own)—as West Germany did in pursuing Ostpolitik—which acted as an incentive to the superpowers to broaden their willingness to seek agreements and to expand their win-sets in the resulting negotiations.

The implication is that relations with allies concerning prospective agreements constituted an additional (third) political game for CoGs. As in the other games it was necessary to find (or create) an overlap in allied win-sets to make an agreement possible and to have that win-set coincide sufficiently with the other side's collective win-set to sustain a pact. One thinks, for example, of the preliminary discussions between Reagan and Gorbachev at Reykjavik about getting rid of nuclear deterrence capabilities and how the resulting uproar among U.S. allies (as well as critics at home) led to shelving the idea shortly after the President returned home. It seems clear that sometimes agreements acceptable in Moscow and Washington foundered due to the heavy opposition of important allies.

We also gave some consideration to including a fourth political game as well. Once the CoG is singled out as a player and as the person(s) responsible for seeking and designing a potential agreement, it is difficult to treat the entire government or administration as a single actor. Instead, the rest of the administration and relevant parts of the government become players in yet another ratification game. As often noted, presidents negotiate with Cabinet members and bureaucratic agencies to get the support necessary for a policy to be adopted and implemented, and when that support is not achieved, the president is severely handicapped. Arms control negotiations with the Russians sometimes involved far more elaborate negotiations *within* the U.S. government to hammer out the official position. To sell agreements in Congress often required a unified administration stance, so any agreement had to fall within the win-sets of key leaders and agencies. Judging by accounts of Kremlin politics, something similar occurred in many cases in the Soviet Union. Even with a dominant leader in the Politburo, sustaining sufficient political support among its membership for prospective agreements was often a necessity. In the same way, no agreement with Washington on arms control, for example, that was flatly opposed by the Soviet armed forces could be reached.

This invites us, in effect, to further adjust the concept of ratification. In the Putnam framework, "ratification" normally pertains to an approval *after* the agreement has been signed. It is clear, however, that in many important international agreements the approval is sought in advance, during the negotiations, so that once the agreement is signed, ratification is *pro forma*. This occurs so often, particularly when the agreement is a highly sensitive one, that it makes more sense to consider ratification as a functional step in a successful process without trying to specify specifically when in that process it occurs.

As a result, we learned to expect that in many cases in U.S.-Soviet relations the search for an agreement would have involved games on three or even four levels, each with win-sets relevant for success and therefore of concern to CoGs in managing the political processes involved. This enlarges the complexities involved in exploring efforts and agreement and assessing the factors that contributed to success or failure. One implication is that once the Cold War was up and running, many potential agreements were bound to be very difficult to achieve because so many levels were involved. An overlap in win-sets at the highest level could be readily undone by mismatches in win-sets at the alliance level, within each government, or within elements beyond the government whose support was essential.

THE RESULTS

It was inevitable that the great variety in backgrounds and perspectives of the participants in the project made close adherence to a common intellectual framework impossible. Though the two-level-game approach proved useful in stimulating discussions and helping orient each study, the participants ended up drawing on it unevenly. For several of us it was the primary basis for organizing both our research and the discussions in our chapters. For others it was employed as a useful broad metaphor and framework but not as a plan for analysis. For still others it served only as a stimulus to thinking and research. Thus this book is not meant to be used to draw conclusions about the analytical utility of the two-level-game approach, in particular its strengths and weaknesses. Rather it offers an opportunity to observe several different ways, Putnam's and others, of trying to encompass the foreign-domestic nexus while examining many different eras in Soviet-American relations.

Historian Jon Jacobson (UC Irvine) leads off with an extended exploration of the formative years of Soviet foreign policy in the 1920s, of the roots of what was eventually to become the Cold War. This period gave birth to Soviet perspectives on the threatening nature of the West and the need to hold it at arm's length even when interactions with it took place. Moreover, it was during this time that Stalin developed his unique attributes and attitudes as a statesman. Jacobson traces the ways in which the revolutionary imperative of the Soviet state contributed to its isolation and insecurity internationally, a pattern that continued throughout most of its existence. This was soon supplemented by an effort to curtail the previously presumed links between the necessities of regime survival on the one hand and developments in the international system on the other—to suspend the ideological insistence of that era that a socialist revolution in Russia could not survive without foreign assistance—so as to stimulate and legitimize the construction of socialism in one country. For the time being, international capitalism was stable, and there would be no revolutions in the West to come to the aid of the Soviet state. Instead, that state could use the period of stabilized capitalism to build its own economic and social system. Indeed, it was vital to do so because the inherent conflicts of the capitalist world and that world's inevitable antagonism toward the Soviet Union would soon recur. Thus the extensive debate on the proper route to development and rapid industrialization in the late 1920s was not a turning inward, dismissing foreign policy concerns, but was directly linked to—even driven by—such concerns. Soviet diplomacy was expected to exploit conflicts among capitalist states to keep them from interfering while national development proceeded. At the same time, Jacobson suggests, emphasis on capitalist hostility was used to sustain national unity and regime dominance by linking the external enemy to the class enemies at home.

Jacobson establishes the existence of a circular relationship operating in the foreign-domestic nexus of the Soviet system. The intense concern of Soviet leaders about present and future threats from outside, particularly on Stalin's part, drove their domestic policies in important ways. However, it was their initial, ideologically based, conception of their state's role in the international system, the domestic ideological basis of their rule, that established this way of viewing international politics.

Professor Victor Mal'kov (Moscow State University) continues the exploration of Soviet foreign policy by examining the Soviet approach to nuclear weapons in the early years of the Cold War. This is a daunting task because not all the pertinent archives are open, and on the basis of those that are, as the report of a recent conference about the Korean War puts it:

Historians of Russia cannot produce a study of relations between foreign and domestic policy under Stalin that is . . . comprehensive and sophisticated; we just do not know what that relationship was. In view of the new evidence, historians face a mammoth new task of synthesizing and analyzing Stalin's overall thinking.[4]

Mal'kov shares this view. He notes that in addition to incomplete access to the archives, the historian must contend with the unfortunate fact that Stalin and his major associates were often unwilling to put intimate discussions and private thoughts about foreign policy down on paper.

However, the parallels with the 1920s are striking. Once again, the Soviet leadership confronts the possibility of a more normal relationship with the West and cannot reconcile this with its ideological perspective and its domestic political requirements. As before, catching up with the West in a crucial national capability—this time nuclear weapons—is vital to lay the basis for a coming era of struggle and war. As before, the attempt to achieve complete national autonomy breeds isolation and culminates in justifying tighter controls at home. Once again, this is accompanied by efforts to play Western states off against one another because they are seen to be inevitable rivals. Mal'kov describes the interplay between domestic fears and the shaping of a foreign and national security policy in which the drive for nuclear weapons was paralleled by deliberately deepening the discord with the West. He traces the roots of this behavior partly to the stimulation of Stalin's insecurities, never difficult to do under any circumstances, provided by the atomic bomb and by evidence, via the Gouzenko case, of how contacts between his society and the West could readily spread damaging information about the Soviet Union.

Mal'kov goes beyond the impact of intense security considerations and the destructive effects of pervasive secrecy to show that this broad policy was not inconsistent with important aspects of the mass political culture of the nation. To this he adds a particularly innovative analysis that stresses the deficiencies of Soviet intelligence and the government's processing of intelligence information. Political intelligence was damaged by the totalitarian nature of the system and by the domination of politically derived analyses of the international system, while it also labored under the burden of Stalin's excessive confidence in his own intuition and judgment.

Patrick Morgan (UC Irvine) introduces the American side of the Cold War story to the volume by examining the Eisenhower years. He recounts the U.S. contribution to extending and deepening that conflict in the first years after Stalin's death, at a time when hope was widespread that the struggle could be sharply curtailed instead. Casting his analysis explicitly within a four-level-game approach, he tracks Eisenhower's rising determination and frustration as he sought to bring the relevant win-sets into sufficient alignment to permit various East-West agreements.

This leads to consideration not just of the president's efforts to reach a meeting of minds with Soviet leaders on such agreements but of the constraints imposed by the divergent views of the Allies, the resistance to possible agreements mounted within the administration by key officials and bureaucratic actors, and the problems raised by domestic political forces and considerations. The author finds that these daunting obstacles were magnified by the president's leadership style and the implications of his personal view as to how the nature of the Soviet Union limited the realistic chances for any fundamental breakthrough. Nevertheless, the president persevered, trying various tactical maneuvers to evade these constraints and achieve at least a partial mitigation of a conflict he viewed as too dangerous to be allowed to continue developing as it had been. The four-level game framework calls attention to how intricate the interrelationships were that sustained the Cold War, suggesting that relaxation of the conflict was perhaps never really a viable alternative politically and psychologically, just its collapse.

The study by Vladislav Zubok (National Security Archives) returns the volume to the Soviet side of the Cold War. He takes up Soviet-German relations as a way of tunneling into the larger matter of Soviet Cold War policy-making. Influenced by the four-level-game approach but not specifically applying it, Zubok depicts Soviet leaders as putting together their German policy out of legitimacy concerns in domestic elite politics, the desire to mobilize support from key bureaucracies, and the need to build consensus among their East European allies. He depicts the Soviet leaders in the 1950s as caught up not only in a power struggle but in a "legitimacy" struggle as well. Their fundamental dilemma with regard to Germany was that steps to consolidate the East German state and the Soviet position there alienated the West Germans and diminished Soviet influence with them—that is, with the more important Germany. Nevertheless, in a departure from explanations often found in the literature, Zubok sees Khrushchev's initiative vis-à-vis Austria as driven primarily by his domestic political competition with other top Soviet leaders and not by the desire to use a resolution of the Austrian problem as a stepping stone to agreement with the West on Germany. Though Khrushchev was not averse to the opportunities that the Austrian agreement gave him to lure Adenauer into improving relations with Moscow at little or no expense, his demarche was due less to Soviet strategic planning than to the power struggle over the succession to Stalin in Moscow.

This approach to the German problem then ran afoul of the rising strength of West Germany and its growing integration into the Western alliance, alongside the unrest in Eastern Europe in 1956. This led Khrushchev into abandoning overtures to Bonn in favor of a drive to squeeze the West on Berlin to force a settlement on his terms of the German Question, an initiative also spurred by Khrushchev's need to offset Chinese pressure to get tougher with the West (particularly on the problem of Taiwan) and bolstered by the spreading image of Soviet strength in the aftermath of Sputnik. Zubok draws a picture of Khrushchev as dominating the foreign policy process, repeatedly pursuing new initiatives with, apart from the Austrian breakthrough, only modest efforts to build a consensus at home or with the relevant Soviet bureaucracies and the allies. In the end he confronted a mounting list of failures due to backlash from the West and pressures from the German Democratic Republic and other allies. He was forced to retreat from plans for a final settlement of the German Question, forced into accepting the status quo. In effect, Khrushchev failed to find a way to shape the relevant win-sets so that they would accommodate a resolution of the German problem, in large part because he did not effectively play each of the political games in which this matter was decided.

Falling in the same time frame as the Zubok chapter is the study by Jasmine Aimaq, a Swedish scholar, which reflects many aspects of the multilevel-game approach. She traces the political considerations that helped shape the Soviet effort to weaken the Western alliance by courting the government of Charles de Gaulle from the late 1950s through the following decade, which in turn has an important impact on Soviet domestic politics. She thereby traces a circular relationship in the foreign-domestic nexus in a fashion that parallels the Jacobson study. Her analysis begins with Soviet leaders' appreciation of the gaps between French policies and those of other allies as displayed in the French rejection of the European Defense Community (EDC), gaps Moscow wished to exploit. However, she follows this by recalling the subsequent Soviet rocket rattling toward France and Britain during the Suez crisis, a policy that tended to drive the Western allies together. She links the latter, seemingly irrational, policy to a domestic political struggle among Stalin's heirs for legitimacy and effectiveness in the conduct of foreign policy, a struggle Khrushchev won by emphasizing the need for Soviet strength, particularly the military strength associated with nuclear weapons as opposed to counting on and exploiting divisions among the Western powers.

The subsequent effort to court de Gaulle stemmed in part, in her view, from Khrushchev's mounting domestic difficulties, particularly in trying to reform the economy. Emphasis on an active foreign policy resting on Soviet military strength now gave way to calls for putting greater resources into the consumer economy via cuts in defense spending. Politically, this could only be justified by citing an easing of the international situation and this was one of the attractive features of cultivating a relationship with France.

Professor Keith Nelson (UC Irvine) takes up the American side of the Cold War again in a close examination of the domestic aspects of Nixon's pursuit of détente. The question at hand is much like the one that animated the Morgan study: Were there opportunities to ease the Cold War in the 1970s that were lost for reasons best understood within a two-level-/four-level-game framework? Nelson begins by establishing the central foreign policy concern in the Nixon Administration as Vietnam, with détente with the Soviet Union and China seen by the president and Kissinger as the key to extracting America from the war. Such an approach required that any deals with Moscow and Beijing be linked to their help in ending the war. Their reluctance to provide that assistance made agreements difficult to obtain. At the same time public feelings against the war and in favor of détente, the desire of various agencies to pursue détente agreements irrespective of any linkage to ending the war, and pressures on both levels against Nixon's efforts to sustain or escalate military pressure on North Vietnam steadily undermined this grand strategy. The administration also had to confront the urge for détente in Europe (a third political game), something that was particularly reflected in the emergence of West Germany's Ostpolitik.

This background helps explain why, in important respects, the openings to Moscow and Beijing negotiated by Nixon and Kissinger were a reflection of the American government's weakness. Soon Nixon was seeking summit meetings as a way of deflecting domestic antiwar pressures and ensuring his reelection. With this in mind he significantly enlarged his win-set to promise the Soviet Union a loose-fitting agreement on strategic arms control and a lucrative trade arrangement. In seeking a deal with China he chose to abandon Taiwan. In each case, this fit well with the other side's wishes. The resulting summits and agreements were dramatic, but when these electoral and other considerations subsided and Third World turbulence resurfaced, support for the agreements in the nation, and support for détente itself, proved to have shallow roots. Contributing to this were Nixon's (and Kissinger's) own conceptions of international politics as inherently conflictual and the Cold War as impossible to resolve, conceptions that placed limits on what détente could be expected to accomplish. In this fashion, according to Nelson, détente was ambushed by a broad set of factors in the last years of Nixon's second term.

Taking our volume into the waning years of the Cold War, Professor Egbert Jahn (University of Mannheim) shows how the fundamental attitudes that dated back to the 1920s and to Stalin, along with the main policies that flowed from them, were finally unraveled in the Gorbachev era. Jahn's analysis traces the way in which, from a multilevel game perspective, the nature of Soviet foreign policy decision making shifted during the Gorbachev years. Domestic ratification of a policy initiative or agreement in the Soviet era involved securing a consensus among the ruling oligarchs, men driven by personal desires for power and personal relationships as much or more than by the general imperatives of their worldview or by explicit pressures from domestic "interests," even though these could not be ignored. Gorbachev came into office convinced that the foreign policy and international burdens of the USSR were standing in the way of the reforms desperately needed to save the Soviet system and socialism. A transformed foreign policy would clear the way for domestic revival, while domestic reform would win friends and secure agreements abroad to make the new foreign policy a success. But under *perestroika* the players in the domestic game, and the range of views represented, grew enormously. Domestic ratification now became a major effort, what with the opposition from old elites in the Party and state machinery, together with pressure from radicals to carry reforms much further. And soon, with the "New Thinking" on foreign policy, the old ideological framework began to collapse. Gorbachev sought to command the middle of the political spectrum and retain dominance for the view that a reformed Communist Party of the Soviet Union (CPSU) should run a liberalized socialism in the USSR within a reformed, almost Wilsonian international system. But domestic policy failures, minority group separatism, and the collapse of the Eastern European regimes ran events well past what his perspective could encompass or his power could control.

By 1991 this became a case of a leader losing control in foreign affairs not for lack of sufficient domestic and foreign support (Gorbachev had considerable success in his foreign policy and received plaudits, for the most part, for it at home) but because the turmoil in the domestic system and the interplay between that system and the foreign influences that had poured in led the political system into outcomes that outran his personal win-set. Indeed, the impact of the dissolution of the system at home on the Soviet position in Eastern Europe was far greater than he could handle. This reaffirms one of the themes of the book, the crucial nature of domestic politics and other domestic developments at many points in shaping Cold War foreign policies.

Galia Golan (Hebrew University) carries the discussion of the Gorbachev period and the last years of the Soviet Union into analysis of Soviet policies in the Middle East, particularly in its interactions with the West over Iraq's seizure of Kuwait in August 1990. Like Jahn, she emphasizes that Gorbachev's reforms called for shifts in policy at home and abroad, with each intended to reinforce the other and with each dependent on the benefits that would flow from a flourishing relationship with the West. She puts a bit more stress than Jahn on the complex external limitations on Gorbachev's policymaking. She delineates, both in general terms and in the specific circumstances of the Gulf crisis, what he needed for success or faced in the way of constraints from the international system, from relations with the United States, from the domestic system, and from intragovernmental politics inside the Soviet regime. The "new thinking" in foreign policy and the need for Western support on other matters required condemning Iraq's action, but this opened the door for domestic critics of *perestroika* to attack Gorbachev not only for domestic failures but for abandoning fundamental Soviet interests as a great power. She traces the ways in which President Bush's appreciation for Gorbachev's dilemma led to several adjustments that allowed him to stand somewhat apart from, without abandoning, the anti-Iraq coalition.

However, Gorbachev was soon squeezed between conservative pressures at home and the worsening situation in the Gulf, and there proved to be no effective way to reconcile the two. With little leverage over developments, Gorbachev was forced to accept an American decision for war, which demonstrated the collapse of Soviet influence, and this did nothing to ease the conflict with the conservatives over his policies. All this contributed to the 1991 coup against Gorbachev and the disintegration of the Soviet Union that was to follow. The Gulf crisis exacerbated the political contest at home first by offering conservative elements an additional opening for attacking the reformers and then by demonstrating that Gorbachev's efforts to build relations with the West could not be translated into the maintenance of significant international influence.

CONCLUSION

The variety of perspectives in this volume coalesces around several common beliefs. The most basic is that we need a rigorous consideration of the interplay of domestic and foreign elements, factors, and negotiating games if we are to refine our understanding of the Cold War. The second is that we need to place considerable emphasis on domestic political elements in explaining Cold War policies. This means that we need sophisticated notions of the action-reaction dynamics that were involved, whether in arms racing, propaganda, economic assistance, political posturing, or other areas. We must continue to explore how each side often posed problems for the other—setting problems or challenges not just in direct relations but also, and particularly, by inciting domestic political difficulties for the other superpower or within the other side's allied governments. We must continue to investigate the sources of positive initiatives to determine the extent to which they were driven primarily by less-than-obvious interests and concerns.

A third contention is that the influence of allies on the superpowers and on the course of the Cold War should be taken very seriously. Notions that the superpowers dominated everything and readily ignored the interests or inputs of their allies were common during the Cold War, but the richer understanding supplied by studies like these will set such views aside on a good many matters.

The Cold War is and will remain, just like the events that led up to and constituted the two world wars, a vast laboratory for the development, testing, and refinement of interpretations of foreign policy-making, and a compelling focus of historical analysis—particularly on how that remarkable conflict could flourish for so long only to disappear so quickly. Apart from addressing the specific subjects of these chapters, we hope we offer some useful considerations bearing on how studies to come will have to be designed and directed.

NOTES

1. On behalf of all the project participants, but particularly the editors, I want to thank the University of California Institute on Global Conflict and Cooperation (at UC San Diego) for its generous support. We also greatly appreciate the financial support extended to the project by the Global Peace and Conflict Studies Program at UC Irvine. We are grateful as well to our efficient and gracious typist, Mindy Han.

2. Robert D. Putnam, "Diplomacy and Domestic Politics: The Logic of Two-Level Games," *International Organization* 42 (Summer 1988), pp. 427–460.

3. The available literature on the two-level-game approach continues to grow and includes the following: Peter B. Evans, Harold K. Jacobson, and Robert D. Putnam, eds., *Double-Edged Diplomacy: International Bargaining and Domestic Politics* (Berkeley: University of California Press, 1993), which includes numerous detailed case studies; William P. Avery, ed., *World Agriculture and the GATT* (Boulder: Lynne Rienner, 1993); Howard P. Lehman and Jennifer L. McCoy, "The Dynamics of the Two-level Bargaining Game," *World Politics* 46 (July 1992), pp. 600–644; Jeffrey W. Knopf, "Beyond Two-Level Games: Domestic-International Interaction in the Intermediate-Range Nuclear Forces Negotiations," *International Organization* 47 (Autumn 1993), pp. 599–628; Frederick W. Mayer, "Managing Domestic Differences in International Negotiations: The Strategic Use of Internal Side-Payments," *International Organization* 46 (Autumn 1992), pp. 793–818; Keisuke Iida, "When and How Do Domestic Constraints Matter: Two-Level Games with Uncertainty," *Journal of Conflict Resolution* 37 (September 1993), pp. 403–426; Michael D. McGinnis and John T. Williams, "Policy Uncertainty in Two-Level Games: Examples of Correlated Equilibria," *International Studies Quarterly* 37 (March 1993), pp. 29–54; H. Richard Friman, "Side-Payments versus Security Cards: Domestic Bargaining Tactics in International Economic Negotiations," *International Organization* 47 (Summer 1993), pp. 387–410.

4. "Conference Report," Conference on the Korean War: An Assessment of the Historical Record, July 24–25, 1995, sponsored by the Korea Society, Georgetown University, and the Korea-America Society (The Korea Society, Washington, D.C.), p. 10.

CHAPTER 1

Internal and External Factors in Soviet Foreign Relations during the 1920s

Jon Jacobson

INTRODUCTION

This essay examines the internal and external factors behind the policies formulated and conducted by the party/state elite of the Russian Federation and the Soviet Union between the end of the Civil War in 1920 and the beginning of the First Five Year Plan in 1929. Domestically, this period is identified with the New Economic Policy (NEP); in foreign relations these were the years of what has been called "the first cold war." The party/state elite referred to here was composed of the somewhat overlapping membership of the Politburo and the Executive Committee of the Comintern (ECCI), as well as of the Sovnarkom and the Collegium of the Commissariat of Foreign Affairs (NKID). With the Commissariat of Foreign Trade these bodies made up the foreign policy-forming institutions in the Russian, and later All-Union, Communist Party, the Soviet state, and the international Communist movement. The foreign-domestic nexus is examined in four locations—in the relationship between national security requirements and the imperatives of "proletarian inter-nationalism," in the relationship between the international situation after 1923 and the formation of a doctrine of socialist development in Russia, in the relationship between foreign trade and the alternative strategies of industrialization propounded by the party/state leadership, and in the impact of the advent of Stalinism on foreign policy.

Reference is made only occasionally to the two-level-game approach, largely because this chapter is not focused on efforts by the fledgling Soviet government to reach any extensive agreement with foreign powers. However, the discussion clearly demonstrates how, in the 1920s, Soviet leaders struggled to reconcile the terms of possible agreements abroad with what was ideologically defensible and politically acceptable at home. It also traces the emergence of Stalin's distinctive approach to foreign relations, one that can be termed "the leader as hawk" in a two-level-game analysis. Stalin became preoccupied with economic autarky, military preparedness, and national self-sufficiency, rejecting the concessions required for major agreements and true rapprochement with the capitalist states. His motives (in addition to his desire to defeat Trotsky, Bukharin, and other rivals) included fear that the imperialists would, sooner or later, exploit any Soviet dependence that agreements had created, and the desire to use alleged machinations of the imperialists against Soviet socialism to justify greater repression and political control at home. This sharply limited the Soviet win-set for agreements with other great powers and characterized Soviet foreign policy for decades thereafter.

The theses put forth here include: (1) that efforts to sharpen social conflicts in Europe and nationalist conflicts in Asia, and thereby to promote the end of the imperialist dominated world order on which the security of socialism in Russia was presumed ultimately to depend, directly increased the isolation and insecurity of the Soviet state; (2) that the doctrine of socialist development adopted in 1924–1926 ("socialism in one country") was premised on a particular estimate of the post-1923 international situation ("international capitalist stabilization") in which the conditions for the development of socialism in Russia could be facilitated through a "prolonged respite" achieved by Soviet diplomacy; and (3) that the way in which Russia acquired the means of production for development was determined by its foreign relations as well as through intraparty political struggle. Soviet Russia's integration into the world economy or isolation from it mandated one or another strategy of socialist industrialization. It also determined whether the regime would be susceptible to the pressures of international opinion and to international democratic and humanistic norms.

A fourth thesis of the chapter is that the rhetoric of the "third period" ("a new era of wars and revolutions") that developed within the Comintern at the time of the USSR's "great turn" into the administrative-command economy in 1928–1929 was not consistent with the pursuit of "peaceful coexistence" that emerged at the same time. This contradiction is explicable primarily in terms of the requisites of the First Five Year Plan that included (a) gaining foreign technology, (b) maintaining social cohesion and national integration, and (c) sustaining deterrence against foreign interference.

NATIONAL SECURITY AND INTERNATIONAL REVOLUTION: THE PROBLEM OF "THE DUAL POLICY"

Soviet foreign relations were founded on twin principles. One was that the revolution that began in Russia in 1917 could be continued by forming an international Communist movement and aligning it with mass-based, noninsurrectionary proletarian organizations in Europe and with nationalist and anticolonial movements in Asia. The other was that the survival of the new Socialist Republics depended on protecting them against further intervention by foreign powers and on reconstructing and industrializing the Russian economy. To achieve the latter objectives, Soviet foreign policy sought to obtain up-to-date technology from the advanced industrial countries, construct zones of protection around the USSR composed of stable and independent states, and find a regular place for Soviet Russia within the capitalist international system. Thus those who made the October Revolution now sought conventional commercial and diplomatic relations with the capitalist governments of Europe and the authoritarian modernizers of Asia, none of which were at all sympathetic to the international Communist movement.

To achieve these ends, the Bolsheviks developed not one but two foreign policies. With one, they coordinated and assisted the efforts of national Communist parties in Europe and Asia that stood in revolutionary opposition to the metropolitan and colonial governments of the imperialists. With the other, they sought conventional diplomatic and commercial relations with those same governments. The international conditions for the latter were generally referred to as "peaceful coexistence;" those favoring the former were subsequently termed "the world revolutionary process." To those who made the October Revolution, both seemed essential.[1] World revolution was the means by which the regime would reproduce itself; "peaceful coexistence" would allow the regime to survive as it did. By 1921 the Bolsheviks were committed to both, and they could renounce neither.

Consequently, while the NKID announced that socialism and capitalism could exist side by side in mutual benefit, Comintern manifestoes proclaimed a coming civil war in Europe and the end of capitalism there. Such contradictory statements created difficulties both for the conduct of Soviet diplomacy and for internationalizing the October 1917 revolution. How could the governments of Europe and America feel confident about the reliability of diplomatic relations with Soviet Russia knowing that the ruling party affirmed the doom of the present system of international relations? On the other hand, how could Communist party members in Russia and in Europe maintain faith in the coming socialist revolution when the Bolsheviks reinforced capitalism with offers of industrial concessions, access to natural resources, and even payments on prewar Tsarist debts?

This has been termed "the dual policy." Justifiably characterized as the most fundamental contradiction in early Soviet foreign relations, two rather different explanations for it have been offered. During the most intense period of the Cold War, some scholars contended that the revolutionary drive of the Communist International was the central intention of Soviet foreign relations and that diplomacy and foreign trade were a facade behind which the USSR retreated temporarily at a time of vulnerability and weakness. But subsequent scholarship has emphasized Lenin's realism and pragmatism and depicted the survival and security of the revolutionary regime in Russia as the goals to which all forms of Soviet foreign relations were subject.[2] The common element in these two interpretations is the suggestion that the pursuit of revolution on the one hand and security on the other were integrated in early Soviet foreign relations and that this was achieved by prioritizing one or the other.

How much integration was there? Lenin himself did not regard the security of the Soviet state and the advance of international proletarian revolution to be contradictory. Speaking and writing in the three years after the end of the Civil War in late 1920, he articulated a concept of foreign relations with the capitalist powers in which security and revolution interacted dialectically. Without crediting him with a complete and coherent strategy of foreign relations, analysis of his statements on international relations uncovers the outlines of a foreign policy concept by which the class struggle would be advanced under conditions of "peaceful coexistence." Lenin suggested, for example, that assistance on the part of the proletariat of the major capitalist states (along with the ability of Soviet diplomacy to exploit contradictions among imperialist states) had prevented the success of allied intervention during the Russian Civil War, despite the vastly greater military potential of the intervening countries. "The massive sympathy of the working people all over the world," Lenin affirmed in December 1921, was "the decisive reason for the complete failure of all the attacks directed against us."[3] This success could be duplicated again if aggression by the imperialist states could be checked by exploiting diplomatically contradictions among them and if European workers could prevent their governments from launching a second war of intervention or from imposing another economic blockade on Russia. A Soviet state secured and defended in this manner, with access to industrial technology from America and Europe, would restore and develop the Russian economy. With the economy reconstructed, this "dictatorship of the proletariat" could be consolidated in Russia, and the example of successful socialism would encourage and inspire the workers of Europe to duplicate the Soviet experiment. The Soviets would in turn aid the newly victorious proletarian states "and protect them from strangulation by American capital," as Lenin phrased it.[4] Thus, in what might be termed "the foreign relations of late Leninism,"[5] international proletarian revolution and Soviet national security were not incompatible—theoretically.

In practice, the parties of the Communist International were informed in resolutions adopted by Comintern and Russian Communist Party (RCP) congresses that there was no distinction between the interests of Soviet Russia and those of the European working class. Indeed, the purposes of international proletarian revolution were formally subordinated to the imperatives of Soviet national security and economic reconstruction in June–July 1921 when the Third Congress of the Communist International resolved:

The unconditional support of Soviet Russia remains as before the cardinal duty of Communists in all countries. Not only must they vigorously oppose any attack on Soviet Russia, but they must fight energetically to clear away all the obstacles that the capitalist states place in the way of Soviet Russian trade on the world market and with other nations.[6]

This notion—that foreign Communist parties existed to protect Soviet Russia—was sustained for decades both as a central tenet of proletarian internationalism and of Soviet foreign relations.

Meanwhile, governments that entered into recognition treaties and trade agreements with Soviet Russia were assured that the Soviet government would not interfere in their domestic affairs, and when those governments subsequently protested against the propaganda and the subversive activities supported by the Communist International, they were informed that the Soviet government and the Comintern were separate organizations.

In actuality, the dialectic of "world revolution" and "peaceful coexistence" was clumsy, both in Lenin's era and after. At times, pursuing normal relations with the capitalist powers and preparing the proletariat of Europe and the oppressed of Asia for revolution complemented one another. But for the most part, attempts to sharpen social conflicts in Europe and nationalist conflicts in Asia in an effort to the promote the "proletarian internationalism" on which the national security of the Soviet Union was presumed to depend actually increased the immediate insecurity of the Soviet state.

The examples are many. The series of trade and recognition agreements negotiated by the Foreign Affairs Commissariat beginning in 1921 necessarily restricted the dissemination of revolutionary propaganda. Boshevik rhetorical commitment to global revolution posed a formidable obstacle for Soviet diplomacy to overcome in its attempt to establish economic and diplomatic relations with Europe and America. Trade and loan agreements with those countries presupposed a stable and prosperous system of states ready to transfer technology, grant credits, and make loans; however, internationalizing the October Revolution in Europe directly threatened what Comintern theses termed "international capitalist stabilization."

In Asia, Comintern strategy vested the Nationalist Revolution in China with momentous expectations. However, the ideological encouragement, the political advice, and the military assistance given to the Nationalist Revolution in China in 1923 to 1927 along with the financial aid given to the General Strike in England in 1926 was rendered at the expense of diplomatic and commercial relations with Great Britain, which severed both in 1927, only three years after recognizing the Soviet government. This was significant not only because Britain was the major foreign power in China but because it was the state from which most other governments took their lead in relations with the USSR. It was also important because it provoked Russia's most severe foreign relations crisis between the end of the Civil War and the German invasion of 1941—the war scare of 1927 with Britain.

The strategy for revolution in Europe articulated in Comintern theses and resolutions was designed to increase contradictions among the capitalist powers by supporting Germany in opposition to the victors of the World War, and to sharpen class antagonism by encouraging proletarian revolutionary opposition to the bourgeoisie both in the Allied Powers and Germany. Hence, Comintern rhetoric condemned the Treaty of Versailles as the instrument by which the German working class was exploited and the German people were oppressed. This effort to promote Soviet solidarity with the German proletariat in opposition to the reparations-collecting European bourgeoisie indirectly encouraged revanchist and nationalist forces in Germany, diminished the prospects for international stability in Europe, and put Russian national security at risk. Eventually it ruined the efforts of Soviet diplomacy to establish a security system in the years between the two world wars.

At the same time, Comintern strategists failed to recognize and grasp the opportunity for strategic, as opposed to tactical, "united front" collaboration with the forces of social democracy in Europe against the threat posed by Fascism. Instead, from 1924 to 1934 Comintern spokesmen from Radek, Trotsky, and Zinoviev to Stalin and Bukharin attacked both under the heading of "social-fascism".[7] Again, the effect was to undermine the political forces most favorable to the stability in Europe, essential both to the security of Russia and its construction of socialism.

Because Comintern-coordinated revolutionary activities created difficulties for the NKID, Foreign Minister Georgii Chicherin repeatedly petitioned the CP Politburo to disjoin the two levels of Soviet foreign affairs and to separate the activities, personnel, instruments, and policies of the Comintern from the Soviet government. He first did this at the start of the NKID's efforts at détente with Europe and America in 1921, and he continued this until the eve of his retirement in 1930. Lenin supported him by insisting in 1921 that the Politburo adopt an official ban on foreign policy statements by party leaders unless they had Chicherin's prior consent. Indeed, Lenin himself ceased to couple the policies of the government and the Comintern in his public speeches and directed that Soviet diplomatic representatives not engage in propaganda and agitation: "We have the Comintern for such purposes." Trotsky, however, was openly derisive of such principles on several occasions, including the Fourth Comintern Congress in 1922.[8] As it was, Politburo members sat on the Comintern Executive Committee; leading diplomats had Comintern connections; some Soviet embassies housed Comintern emissaries—all of which undermined the credibility of the campaign for "peaceful coexistence." While the Foreign Commissariat announced that socialism and capitalism could exist side by side in mutual benefit, Comintern manifestoes proclaimed the violent demise of capitalism and the inevitability of proletarian revolution.

Comintern rhetoric troubled Soviet diplomacy not only in relations with the victorious Allies but with "defeated and oppressed" nations. Soviet foreign relations under Chicherin's leadership were based on favorable ties with Weimar Germany and Kemalist Turkey. These states were the anchors of his foreign policy in Europe and Asia respectively, and good relations with them was the major achievement of his career. He was therefore particularly sensitive to damage caused by the Comintern to diplomatic relations with either country. Following a series of statements in 1926 and 1927 by Nikolai Bukharin, at that time the leader of the Comintern, Chicherin wrote to him directly: "Would you please stop equating Chiang Kai-shek with Kemalism. This is absolutely ridiculous and spoils our relationship with Turkey. Isn't spoiling our relationship with Germany enough for you? . . . Now you are definitely spoiling our relations with Turkey!"[9]

In the end, internationalizing the October Revolution while normalizing relations with European capitalists and Asian nationalists was no simple task. The two efforts complicated each other. No way was found both to participate in and to overthrow capitalist international relations. Nor, despite Chicherin's efforts to do so, were the two projects separated from each other within Soviet foreign relations, either institutionally or rhetorically.

Recalling the two-level-game perspective, we see that the steps needed to fully normalize Soviet relations with the other great powers carried a stiff price tag—in terms of abandoning revolutionary activities—that made them unacceptable in domestic (regime) politics. As a result the win-sets of the Western powers and the Soviet Union did not overlap sufficiently to make real bargaining possible. As Chicherin repeatedly discovered, the agreements he sought could not be ratified domestically. He himself had little leverage or political resources in the main centers of power for trying to adjust the domestic win-set, and he could enlist the aid of powerful domestic figures only intermittently. As the next sections demonstrate, the source of the problem of a very narrow win-set for such agreements lay in the internal battle over power and in political/ideological struggles over how to develop the country.

INTERNATIONAL RELATIONS AND THE DOCTRINE OF SOCIALIST DEVELOPMENT

The central theme of the doctrine of "socialism in one country" was that socialism could be constructed in the Soviet Union alone—in the absence of proletarian revolution in Europe, and on the basis of the social circumstances and economic resources of the USSR. Russia had, after all, achieved and consolidated proletarian power without the assistance of revolution in Europe. A secondary proposition was that although it was possible to construct socialism in the USSR independently, there would be no "complete victory" for socialism, and no guaranteed security for the revolution in Russia, until the threat of imperialist interference and intervention was banished by proletarian revolution in several European countries. Thus while "socialism in one country" apparently deprioritized international revolution and asserted the primacy of Soviet internal development, revolutionary internationalism was not ideologically renounced. It remained an integral feature of the Bolshevik theory of global history.

The doctrine of "socialism in one country" was implicit in elements of Bukharin's thought as early as November 1923, at the time of the failure of "the German October"—the second abortive Communist revolution in Germany within a two and one-half year period. Stalin first enunciated the idea formally in December 1924. Bukharin began to address the question publicly and explicitly in April 1925. Resolutions of the Fourteenth Party Congress the following December adopted the doctrine as the central principle of socialist construction. It was Bukharin who worked "socialism in one country" into a proto-program for the modernization, industrialization, and socialization of Soviet Russia, and who developed the theoretical basis for it. Stalin popularized the idea by proclaiming it in his speeches and writings during the two years extending from late 1924 to late 1926. Thereby he gained the political benefit that accrued from acceptance of the doctrine among the party rank and file. Together they utilized it to inflict a decisive political defeat not only on Trotsky but on Stalin's erstwhile partners in the post-Lenin triumvirate, Lev Kamenev and Grigorii Zinoviev.[10]

While in prison in 1906 for his activities during the 1905 Revolution, Trotsky had put forth the idea of "permanent revolution":

Without the direct state support of the European proletariat, the working class of Russia cannot remain in power and convert its temporary domination into a lasting socialist dictatorship. Of this there cannot for one moment be any doubt.[11]

Twenty years later Stalin, Kamenev, and Zinoviev perverted the meaning of "permanent revolution" by attributing to Trotsky three suppositions—that Russia was too backward to achieve socialism on its own, that genuine socialism could not be constructed in Russia until European proletarian revolution occurred, and that the USSR could not survive without the support of revolution in Europe. Trotsky, they maintained, had lost confidence in the Russian Revolution, and thereby they created "the myth of Trotskyism".[12] As of 1924–25, Trotsky no longer held those positions if he ever had (although he would reassert the doctrine of "permanent revolution" in 1929). Indeed, he maintained that the idea of "permanent revolution" was of strictly antiquarian significance and without present relevance. Moreover, he made no reply to "socialism in one country" until late 1926, after the political battle was decided and he was about to be removed from the Politburo and Central Committee. What opposition there was to "socialism in one country" in 1925 came from Zinoviev and Kamenev.[13]

"Socialism in one country" was a significant ideological innovation. Before 1924–1926 the transition from capitalism to socialism had been linked in Marxism-Leninism to transnational proletarian revolution, the result of a single process during one historical period lasting, the Bolsheviks thought at first, for weeks, then for months, and then perhaps for years. This was Lenin's original vision of "world revolution," and it was this conception rather than "permanent revolution" against which Stalin was really polemicizing in 1924–1926, although he obviously could not say so and still pose as "the best Leninist" among Lenin's successors.[14]

In contrast to the original Leninist vision, "socialism in one country" formulated the proposition that socialism could be achieved independently in separate nations at different times, that Soviet Russia could survive indefinitely in a world composed of nations as well as of classes, and that socialism's complete victory would be guaranteed only when revolution in one or more imperialist powers rendered capitalist interference with socialist construction in Russia impossible. Thus, the achievement of socialism became a national occurrence and its survival and ultimate triumph a matter of relations among states. It has aptly been termed "a theory of international relations *par excellence*."[15]

Indeed, the doctrine was accompanied by a thorough consideration of the matrix of foreign relations in which the Soviet experiment was set. In the mid-1920s that matrix began to be characterized both within the Comintern and the RCP as "the international stabilization of capitalism." This was no mere catchphrase. Rather it integrated ideologically the concept of foreign relations and the concepts of socialist construction and economic development adopted by the Central Committee majority in 1924–1926. It also had some basis in reality. Beginning in late 1924—within months after the diplomatic recognition of Moscow initiated the previous February by Rome and London—Soviet foreign policy sustained several serious reversals. First, Gustav Stresemann and the German Foreign Ministry engineered a rapprochement with Britain and France that undermined the "special" Soviet-German relationship symbolized by the Treaty of Rapallo (1922). Second, the Conservative government of Stanley Baldwin and Austen Chamberlain renounced the Anglo-Soviet Draft Treaty negotiated by their Labour predecessors and refused to discuss measures to improve or repair relations with Moscow. Third, as part of a reestablished Anglo-French entente in 1924, the British and French agreed to coordinate their policies toward the USSR. In effect, Germany, Britain, and France put relations with the USSR on hold while they resolved their differences and concluded agreements regulating reparations, war debts, trade, and security. It was in this context that the debates on the future of socialist construction and economic development took place in Moscow.

Stalin and Bukharin were impressed by the reversals of 1924: the fall of the Labour government, the rejection of the Anglo-Soviet Draft Treaty, the formulation of the Dawes Plan, the intervention of American capital in Europe, and the movement of Germany toward what Stalin called "the capitalist camp."[16] In these events they saw a decisive turning point in the international situation, one that would influence an entire phase of history. Bukharin first proclaimed—in June 1924—that a new stabilization in the history of capitalism was beginning, a notion he then vigorously defended in theoretical debates. Stalin explained the international situation to the party membership in a series of articles, interviews, speeches, and reports beginning in September 1924 and culminating in December 1925 with his Political Report of the Central Committee to the Fourteenth Party Congress.[17]

The conception of world politics held by the Central Committee led by Stalin and Bukharin began with the proposition that "world revolution" was not an event but a lengthy process. The "epoch of world revolution" begun in Russia in 1905 comprised "a whole strategic period, which will last for a number of years, perhaps even a number of decades." An equilibrium resulting from the ebbing of the revolutionary tide and the recovery of capitalism was now the characteristic feature of the international situation. The imperialist system had "succeeded in extricating itself from the quagmire of the postwar crisis" and had achieved a "partial" and "temporary" stabilization. The Soviet system had stabilized as well. The economy was growing; socialism was under construction; the exploited of Europe and the oppressed of Asia were rallying around the USSR. The result was "a certain temporary equilibrium between these two stabilizations." Although its duration could not be predicted, "there is no doubt," Stalin stated, that "it will be a long one." In 1918, Lenin thought the end of the war with Germany would be followed by a short "peace break;" after the Civil War he predicted a lengthier truce; in 1924–1925 Stalin announced "a whole period of respite." What had begun in 1920–1921 as a tenuous breathing space, Stalin told the Fourteenth Party Congress, "has turned into a whole period of so-called peaceful coexistence of the USSR with the capitalist states."[18]

The data for this analysis was collected from current events: With the failure of revolution in Germany in November 1923, "the period of revolutionary upsurge" had come to an end. A "new situation" existed in which Communist parties would have to find their bearings.[19] The stabilization of capitalism, although temporary and partial, was now definite. Postwar inflation had ended and currencies had stabilized. Agricultural and industrial production was increasing and international trade was expanding; all were approaching prewar levels. This financial-economic stabilization had been achieved "mainly with the aid of American capital, and at the price of the financial subordination of Western Europe to America."[20] Germany—once the locus of revolutionary upsurge in Europe—had been, Stalin said, "Dawesified" into an appendage of Anglo-American capital. The British, the Americans, and the French had reached agreement regarding "the scale on which [Germany] was to be robbed," and the United States had moved to the verge of financial hegemony in the capitalist world.[21] Simultaneously, the British, Americans, and Japanese had struck a deal over China (the Washington treaties of 1922), and the imperialists had promised to respect each other's colonial possessions. And there was one more arrangement in the works. "The stabilization of capitalism," Stalin forecast, "may find expression in an attempt on the part of the imperialist groups of the advanced countries to strike a deal concerning the formation of a united front against the Soviet Union."[22]

However, "the process of capitalism's 'recovery' contain[ed] within itself the germs of its inherent weakness and disintegration," according to the dialectic Stalin elucidated in 1925.[23] Stabilization had not settled the issues over which the First World War had been fought. The imperialists still struggled over markets. Anti-imperialist national liberation movements were "growing step by step" and "beginning in some places to assume the form of open war against imperialism (Morocco, Syria, China)."[24] And while "the capitalist world [was] being corroded by a whole series of internal contradictions, . . . the world of socialism [was] becoming more and more closely welded, more united." Soviet industry had revived and would continue to develop, giving the USSR's proletariat "a new way of life" and leading the workers of Europe to demand workers' states of their own. At the same time, the working class of Europe had come to regard the Soviet state "as its own child," Stalin asserted, and "having adopted our state . . . is ready to defend it and fight for it" against imperialism and its interventionist machinations.[25]

In predicting the eventual demise of capitalist stabilization, the Stalin-Bukharin duumvirate counted heavily on the Dawes reparation agreement destabilizing the Weimar Republic. Their hypothesis was that German workers would be required to bear the costs of reparations to France, Britain, and Belgium in addition to what was normally extracted from them by the German bourgeoisie, a "double yoke" of exploitation. "To think that . . . the German proletariat will consent to bear this double yoke without making repeated serious attempts at a revolutionary upheaval means believing in miracles." The Dawes Plan must inevitably lead to a revolution in Germany. As a result, the British, French, and Italian governments would have to increase taxes to make war debt payments to the United States, meaning that "the material conditions of the working people in Europe . . . will certainly deteriorate and the [European] working class will inevitably become revolutionized."[26]

Such conflicts were being covered over by what Stalin called a facade of "false and mendacious bourgeois-democratic pacifism." When the London Conference adopted the Dawes Plan in 1924, Prime Ministers Ramsay MacDonald of England and Eduard Herriot of France had envisaged a future of peaceful collaboration, reconciliation with Germany, and normalization of relations with the USSR. Stalin maintained that this camouflaged not only the contradictions among the victors of the World War, but also "the intense antagonism between Germany and the entente" and "the deadly enmity of the bourgeois states" toward the Soviet Union.[27] When the Locarno agreements regarding Germany's western frontier were concluded in October 1925, there was additional rhetoric from London and Paris lauding a "a new spirit" of international cooperation and peace. Stalin contended that international relations were now recapitulating the pre-1914 era. Like the treaties, agreements, and conferences that preceded the World War, Locarno was "an example of the matchless hypocrisy of bourgeois diplomacy, when by shouting and singing about peace [bourgeois statesmen] try to cover up preparations for a new war." "If the Dawes Plan is fraught with a revolution in Germany," Stalin maintained, "Locarno is fraught with a new war in Europe."[28]

Such was the concept of Soviet foreign relations and of world politics formulated by the Stalin-Bukharin duumvirate. It was linked closely to the doctrine of "socialism in one country" and was adopted by the Party Congress in December 1925 alongside that doctrine. This was of considerable significance for the history of post-revolutionary Russia.

The truth was that the Dawes Plan and Locarno Treaties called into question the fundamental precepts of Leninist foreign relations as formulated in 1920–1921: that the German problem was insoluble, that postwar crisis would bring proletarian insurrection to Europe, and, most of all, that interimperialist conflict was inevitable and could be counted on to protect the Soviet Union from a united anti-Soviet coalition. Reconciliation between Germany and the entente and the increasing stabilization of international relations made imperative a comprehensive and agonizing reappraisal of Soviet security policy.

Evidently, such a reappraisal took place both in the ECCI and in the NKID.[29] Nevertheless, doctrinally the party continued to assert Lenin's belief that antagonisms among the imperialist powers would benefit Soviet interests. Thus in speaking to the Moscow Party Organization Stalin counted "the struggle, conflicts, and wars between our enemies," as one of the three available "allies of Soviet power," the other two being the proletariat of the advanced capitalist societies and the oppressed colonial peoples.[30] This not only reaffirmed Lenin's belief that interimperialist conflict would protect the USSR, but raised relations among nations to the level of class conflict as a factor in deciding the contest between socialism and capitalism.

From these principles and the new situation the Stalin-Bukharin duumvirate derived the prognostication for the future that was then adopted by the Fourteenth Party Congress (December 1925). Both by diplomacy and through the activities of foreign Communist parties, it stated, the war-prone tendencies of the imperialists could be moderated and "peaceful coexistence" extended. This prolonged respite constituted an opportunity to construct an independent industrial economy. The notion that the imperialist powers posed a threat to the USSR was not discarded, however, and that threat, the resolution concluded, made imperative the creation of a modern military establishment.[31]

In the campaign to build up Soviet defenses, Stalin played a central role. Although he informed the Party Congress that the international situation was in a stable equilibrium, he had told a closed session of the Central Committee the previous January that "a radical change in the international situation has begun lately." On at least three occasions during the relatively tranquil 1925, he stated that the international situation resembled the one prior to the outbreak of the great imperialist war in 1914, with developing anticolonial movements and great power rivalries. There was another crisis in Morocco; the powers of Europe were again contesting for control of North Africa and the Balkans; a renewed postwar arms race was underway; the French were building a large air force; and the British, Americans, and Japanese were competing in naval power in the Pacific. "The conflict of interests among the victor countries is growing and becoming more intense," he argued; "collision among them is becoming inevitable, and in anticipation of a new war, they are arming with might and main." Differing notably from the "line" adopted by the party as a whole, Stalin maintained that a second imperialist war would break out "not tomorrow or the day after, of course, but in a few years time."[32]

And the USSR, Stalin contended, must prepare by building up its armed forces. Military preparedness was a national priority because, in his mind, war was inevitable and imminent. He distinguished between imperialist and interventionist wars, just as Lenin had done in 1916. He viewed both as inevitable and both as threats to the USSR. The central concern that he voiced was that conflict within the capitalist camp would develop into an anti-Soviet war as the imperialists, either as a prelude to or a consequence of war with each other, attempted to thwart the international socialist revolution. Because Stalin believed that war among the imperialists would be accompanied by intervention against the USSR, the threat to Russia was close at hand.

Thus, as Stalin emerged as spokesman for the party's conception of foreign relations, and as a member of the duumvirate, he carried a distinctive set of opinions about the international situation. Despite "temporary stabilization" capitalism was "ridiculously unstable," and a second imperialist war was inevitable and imminent. Moreover, the approach of that war would "intensify the internal, revolutionary crisis both in the East and the West," bringing revolution to Germany and uprisings to the colonies of the European powers. That revolutionary surge "is bound to turn the ruling strata of the Great Powers against us." Threatened with global revolution, they would attack its source. "The danger of intervention," Stalin concluded, "is again becoming real."[33]

Stalin's personal version of the international situation made significant inroads into the collective opinion of the Soviet elite. In May 1925 resolutions of the Third Soviet Congress noted: "The capitalist states are making preparations for new conflicts and new wars," preparations accompanied by "a hostile encirclement of our Union that takes the form of an entire system of military conferences, agreements, and support for the measures taken by different governments against the USSR." The Fourteenth Party Congress in December partially incorporated Stalin's perspective into resolutions it adopted that assailed the "blocks of capitalist states under Anglo-American hegemony [that are generating] the frenzied growth of armaments and therefore . . . the danger of new wars, including the danger of intervention." Both assemblies stressed the need for the USSR "to guard its frontiers from possible attack," to strengthen the country's defense capabilities, and "to intensify the power of the Red Army and the Red Navy and the Air Force."[34]

FOREIGN TRADE AND STRATEGIES OF INDUSTRIALIZATION

During the period that "socialism in one country" was introduced and adopted, what has been termed the "industrialization debate" was being conducted within the party/state elite. Contrary to some views, that debate was not a retreat from the international scene following upon the disappointing results of the attempts to export revolution in 1917–1923. Actually, the debate over industrialization was closely linked to foreign policy considerations, in particular to a worrisome conception of a world divided into two camps. As the camps stabilized, it was suggested, the contradictions between them would grow stronger and lead to new wars, both interimperialist and interventionist, preceded by efforts on the part of capitalist Europe to impose diplomatic isolation and economic blockade on the USSR. This scenario formed the basis for the conclusion that the Soviet Union must achieve economic independence from the capitalist states.

Bukharin was convinced that the capital required for economic development and socialist construction would not be coming from Europe. The collapse of the "German October" insurrection of 1923 made clear to him that the USSR could not count on a Communist Germany to be its technological and industrial provider. Nor, he realized, after the failure of the Genoa Conference (1922) and the Anglo-Soviet Conference (1924) to resolve the issue of Russian debts, could Moscow expect to receive large-scale loans from European banks. Subsequently, Bukharin hoped that the grain surplus held by prospering farmers might be sold abroad to finance imports of industrial equipment. However, the difficulties encountered by the government in procuring that surplus after the harvest of 1925 convinced him that the Soviet economy must not be dependent on an international market controlled by the bourgeoisie. He concluded that the capital for development could only be amassed from the increasing profitability of state industry, from a progressive income tax on entrepreneurs prospering under NEP, and from the voluntary savings deposits of the peasantry. These sources would not provide the necessary sums very soon, however, and Bukharin's protoprogram for socialist development included no real solution to the problem of capital accumulation. It was not a critical issue for him. Vast amounts of capital were unnecessary, he believed, because existing machinery could be used more intensively, enabling industrial socialism to develop in the USSR without substantial investment—slowly, gradually and "at a snail's pace," he stated in December 1925. Bukharin's contribution to the debate, therefore, was to transform the New Economic Policy that Lenin had introduced in 1921 (to partially integrate Russia into the capitalist system) by identifying it with building socialism slowly in isolation.[35]

Stalin, too, seems to have given little thought to how industrialization would be financed. During 1924–1925, when he first proclaimed that socialism could be constructed in Russia separately, he apparently believed that the funds simply could be borrowed from the state treasury. Of greatest importance, he thought, was the international political situation. Economic dependence on Europe must be avoided, primarily because it would lead "to a whole series of new dangers," in the phrase of the Fourteenth Party Congress or, in Stalin's words, make the USSR "vulnerable to blows from the side of our enemies."[36] The immediate challenge, he thought, was the Dawes Plan. Western observers from John Maynard Keynes to Stanley Baldwin had suggested that the best solution to postwar indebtedness would be for Germany to create the favorable balance of payments necessary to fund reparations to France and Britain by selling manufactured goods in the USSR in exchange for agricultural commodities and raw materials. Stalin objected strongly to such proposals, which were intended, he maintained, to "squeeze money out of the Russian market for the benefit of Europe." As he put it, "We have no desire to be converted into an agrarian country for the benefit of any other country whatsoever, including Germany."[37]

Stalin's own program for industrialization included a strong rhetorical commitment to economic independence, which to him included the notion that Russia would produce the various means of production rather than acquire them from abroad. The Soviet Union must be converted, he stated, "from a country that imports machines and equipment into a country that produces machines and equipment. . . . In this manner the USSR . . . will become a self-sufficient economic unit building socialism."[38] This contrasted sharply with the integrationist consensus that had formed in 1920-1921 under Lenin's auspices and had guided economic development and foreign policy since then. Moreover, it is significant that, in Stalin's concept of economic development, independence was not just the goal but the basis of industrialization. It was not just the way the USSR would become independent of capitalism; the USSR had to be independent to industrialize. Both the capital and the technology for industrialization could, should, and would come from Russia's own resources. Otherwise, the capitalist states would stifle or interrupt Soviet industrialization through the imposition of blockades. Autarky was the means as well as the end of economic development for Stalin.

The alternative was formulated by Trotsky, who of all the leading Bolsheviks, Richard B. Day has argued, examined the difficult and complex issues of industrialization most realistically.[39] After his dismissal as Commissar for Military and Naval Affairs in January 1925, Trotsky served on the Supreme Council of National Economy (Vesenkha) and as chairman of the Principal Concessions Committee, from which he observed firsthand the many problems of planning and managing the weak and undeveloped industrial sector. During the most intense period of the industrialization debate, Trotsky identified low labor productivity—rather than the threat of dependence on the capitalist camp—as the most critical problem of Soviet economic development. The solution, he decided, was to encourage foreign trade and capital imports, to transfer the advanced technology of America and Europe to the USSR, and to achieve thereby a rapid tempo of industrialization and a high level of industrial productivity. Bukharin's industrialization "at a snail's pace" simply perpetuated the misery of the masses. And Stalin's approach, based on Russia's indigenous engineering and metallurgy, would simply bind the USSR to a primitive technology, require an industrialization period of many years, and result in low-quality products. Importing the most sophisticated and expensive technology, on the other hand, would catapult the USSR into the future and create the basis for true economic independence. For these reasons, Trotsky argued, the Soviet Union could not isolate itself from the global economy. Industrialization required not a reduction but an increase in relations with the outside world and a temporary increase in dependence on the world market.

Accordingly Trotsky was in 1925–1926 the leading exponent in the party leadership of integration into the world economy and political accommodation with Europe and America. Russia, he noted, lacked not only advanced technology but also capital. It needed foreign concessions to develop its resources and foreign credits to purchase machinery. He announced this in a *Pravda* article in June 1925, and in August he told the British representative in Moscow of the terrible state of Soviet technology, stressed the crucial importance of machine building, and informed him that unless the British stopped insisting on cash-and-carry, they would lose out, in machine sales, to the United States.[40] Trotsky did not hesitate to follow the implications for diplomacy of his development strategy. He supported the debt/loan negotiations that opened with France in February 1926, seeing prospects for credits three times the size of what Vesenkha expected to invest in industry in

1925/1926, and he urged noninterference in the British General Strike the following May in order not to jeopardize prospects for loans from Britain and elsewhere.[41]

At the December 1925 Fourteenth Party Congress, the Central Committee committed the party to building socialism separately and to transforming the USSR into a self-sufficient industrial nation. Important issues were left undecided, however. At what tempo would socialism be constructed? With what technology would the USSR be industrialized? How would industrialization be financed? This irresolution was largely the result of intraparty politics. The commitment of Stalin and Bukharin to "socialism in one country" bound them in theory to industrializing the USSR with indigenous technology and capital. To deny this would have constituted a victory for Trotsky. On the other hand, to call for industrialization without designating sources of investment capital was to run the risk of economic crisis.

Unless capital was acquired through foreign loans, the available alternative was the one espoused by the leading party economist, Evgenii Preobrazhenskii. He advocated immediate and rapid industrialization paid for with capital mobilized by transferring to state industry what could be accumulated internally within the private sector, especially agriculture. At the center of his strategy was expropriation of agrarian surpluses, or "primitive socialist accumulation."[42] Preobrazhenskii's proposal represented a direct challenge to the *smychka*, the worker-peasant alliance on which NEP was based, and to Bukharin's gradualist, voluntarist, and harmonious concept of how socialism would be constructed. Bukharin ridiculed Preobrazhenskii's strategy as industrialization at any cost, or "super-industrialization." And he included Trotsky, who shared Preobrazhenskii's preference for rapid industrial growth, in his condemnation—even though Trotsky did not identify himself with the notion of peasant expropriation but favored rapid industrialization funded by foreign capital.[43] Stalin simply ignored the problem of investment, probably to avoid any dispute with his political ally, Bukharin.

Thus, one strategy (Bukharin's) posited during the "industrialization debate" envisioned social equilibrium, evolutionary industrialization, and the crisis-free construction of socialism. The other, based largely on Stalin's, Trotsky's, and Preobrazhenskii's ideas and adopted at "the great turn" of 1928–1929, took "a great leap forward" into rapid-tempo industrialization, collectivized agriculture, and intensified class conflict. What has sometimes been overlooked is that socialist industrialization by the latter strategy, even more than by the other, could be achieved most efficiently by importing advanced technology from America and Europe.

To fund the acquisition of advanced technology, two alternatives were considered. One was to acquire capital from Europe and America in forms ranging from short-term credits to what amounted to long-term development loans. London, Paris, Brussels, and Washington, however, set political prerequisites: The USSR had to recognize the debts of *all* past Russian regimes (although it was not asked to pay them in their entirety) and to behave both internationally and domestically as a "normal state." What stood in the way of this, of course, was Comintern/government involvement in "the anti-imperialist struggle" in Asia, the rhetorical encouragement given to civil disobedience within European armed forces, and repression of opposition and dissent within the USSR.

The other method of funding, the one eventually adopted, involved (1) state control over the production and distribution of grain and (2) compulsory loans extracted from the public. This had serious consequences for the long-term development of the Soviet polity. Whereas foreign loans depended on favorable world opinion, internal loans and state control of grain production freed socialist construction in the USSR from concern about attitudes overseas, allowing the regime to defy international norms and perpetuate the use of preemptive state terror. Thus, the way in which the first socialist society was to acquire the means of production was of grave importance for the future of Soviet foreign relations.

FOREIGN RELATIONS AND "THE GREAT TURN"

In his report on the international situation to the Sixth Comintern Congress (July to September 1928), Bukharin discussed the changes that had taken place since the 1924 congress. The era of "temporary capitalist stabilization" was coming to an end, he announced, and a "third period" in the history of the world since the October 1917 Revolution was beginning. The documents subsequently adopted by the congress on the international situation and world political economy reaffirmed the "general line" that Bukharin, with Stalin's support, had been formulating since late 1926: namely, that the contradictions to which imperialism was subject were sharpening at an accelerated rate, and that, as this happened, the masses of Europe and Asia were becoming increasingly radicalized while the security of the USSR was becoming increasingly threatened. The "third period" would be a time of crisis, characterized in the resolutions of the congress as systemic and international, that is, involving intensified class struggle and renewed imperialist war. In the "Resolution on the Measures of Struggle against the Dangers of Imperialist War," the future was defined in catastrophic terms, as a time of growing imperialist hostility toward the Soviet Union, a time when "two imperialist groups of states" would clash "in a struggle for world hegemony," and a time when "a mighty revolutionary movement" would come into being.[44]

Adoption of this general line within the Comintern was one of several interrelated developments taking place in 1928–1929. A "socialist offensive" was undertaken against both independent peasant agriculture and small business. The moderate Bukharin-Rykov-Tomskii group was defeated, and Stalin and his supporters gained control of the party Central Committee. They initiated what is often called "the great turn" in Soviet history, putting into effect the optimum variant of the First Five Year Plan and launching "Stalin's industrial revolution" with its "class war ideology." There was continued talk among the leadership of a mounting "foreign threat" as Stalin became a spokesman for the view that the Soviet Union was surrounded by foreign enemies, linked to "enemies" at home, who plotted the ruination of the industrialization drive and the downfall of the Soviet regime. These developments, along with Comintern resolutions forecasting a new imperialist war, seemed to suggest that the party majority no longer based its concept of foreign relations on an indeterminate period of "peaceful coexistence." Such momentous changes in party leadership, in strategies of economic development, and in the general line of the international Communist movement might well have been accompanied by a shift in policy toward the major capitalist powers. Yet there was none.

"People often forget," *Izvestiia* stated in May 1929, "that the Five Year Plan defines our foreign policy," and that the plan makes it necessary "to delay the war threat and make use of . . . world markets."[45] Aleksei Rykov, the perpetual integrationist and the last remaining member of Lenin's Politburo other than Stalin, stated the case for peaceful relations in his report to the Fifth Soviet Congress that same month:

Comrades, the fulfillment of the Five Year Plan is bound up with an enormous development in our exports and imports, the import of a vast mass of equipment for our industry, agriculture, and transport. Therefore we are not less, but more interested than before in the development of peaceful relations and trade agreements. The fulfillment of the Five Year Plan demands consistent and systematic work over a number of years. Therefore in international relations we are trying for such solidarity and firmness in relations with individual states that no setback or loss will occur from that quarter in carrying out the colossal schemes of works laid down in the plan.[46]

Thus, at the very time when Comintern resolutions proclaimed the entire capitalist system to be in catastrophic crisis, the First Five Year Plan was launched on the assumption that world trade would continue to flourish to the benefit of Soviet industrialization. In the face of this contradiction, official announcements stressed continuity in foreign policy. The search for trade agreements continued, and "the struggle for peace and disarmament" remained the key slogan of Soviet diplomacy, particularly at the World Disarmament Conference in Geneva. It was the continued dependence of Soviet economic development on peace and trade that determined that there would be no abrupt change in relations with Europe and America to accord with the catastrophic analysis of the international situation contained in the Comintern doctrine of the Third Period.

Nevertheless, the divergence between Soviet foreign policy and Comintern doctrine is striking. It has usually been presumed that by 1928 the Comintern was becoming increasingly the servant of Soviet national interests and foreign policy. However here we have an instance in which the Comintern proclamation of a new era of wars and revolutions could only conflict with efforts to present Soviet foreign policy as one based on peaceful agreements and expanded trade with the capitalist world. How is this contradiction to be explained? How is the shift from "capitalist stabilization" and "international equilibrium" to "a new era of wars and revolutions" to be understood?

Recent research[47] concludes that—as is the case with many issues in the history of the politics and foreign policy decision-making during the Stalin era—a definitive answer can only be made when archival sources are available. Provisionally it refuses to dismiss the apocalyptic statements appearing in the reports and resolutions of the Comintern as ideologically delusionary, or as meaninglessly rhetorical. It asserts that the "new era of wars and revolutions" doctrine was a key factor in the continuing struggle among the leadership of the Russian Communist Party. It originated with Bukharin as a response to the criticism directed by the Trotsky-Zinoviev United Opposition at Stalin and himself during the 1927 war scare with Britain,[48] and Stalin subsequently sustained it as a way of defining and defeating those whom he regarded as his enemies, including Bukharin, first of all within the party and then within the international Communist movement.

The slogan originated as Bukharin's way of understanding the international situation in terms of Communist ideology. Its importance for Soviet foreign relations does not end there, however. It can also be understood as a measure of national security and a means to national integration. At a time when the Soviet and foreign Communist Parties included those who sympathized with the Trotsky Opposition or with the Bukharin moderate group, solidarity could be forged in reaction to a supposed enemy threat to the socialist homeland. Indeed, the "foreign threat," along with domestic "class enemies," could be utilized as a new basis for social cohesion at a time when collectivization and industrialization were seriously disrupting Soviet society. While the USSR was without stable diplomatic alliances, the support of an international working class alerted to the supposed threat of an imperialist attack provided one of the few measures of preparedness available. And at a time when the Soviet defense establishment was unprepared, the slogan "a new era of wars and revolutions" stood as a warning to the capitalist powers and a deterrent against attack: "War against us will bring revolution to you."[49]

Stalin benefited from all this. It is doubtful, however, that he really believed that capitalism was on the eve of collapse in 1927–1929 or that war was imminent. He was nevertheless vitally concerned with security issues. The "policy program" he implemented in his "revolution from above" was shaped by his concept of Russia's situation in world politics. He believed that the international situation confronting the USSR made imperative the development of a modern arms industry. Well before 1928 he had decided that Russia's "backwardness" and isolation necessitated the construction of "socialism in one country." "To transform NEP Russia into a socialist Russia," Robert Tucker has stated, "was to construct an industrially and militarily powerful Soviet Russian state owning the instruments of production and capable of fending for itself in a hostile world." The requirements of national defense were primary for Stalin. "All else had to be subordinated to the one great task of amassing military-industrial power in a hurry."[50]

Constructing a military-industrial complex carried foreign relations imperatives of its own, namely a prolonged period of peace. Stalin stated this in 1927:

We can and must build socialism in the USSR. But in order to build socialism, we first of all have to exist. It is essential that there be a respite from war, that there be no attempts at intervention, that we achieve some minimum of international conditions indispensable for us so we can exist and build socialism."[51]

Preventing the formation of anti-Soviet coalitions and forestalling intervention by the imperialist states and their clients while socialism—and the heavy industry and the modern military capacity that accompanied it—was constructed in the USSR became the paramount issue of Soviet foreign relations as "the great turn" was taken. Termed "stretching out the breathing space," the task was assigned by Stalin to Soviet diplomacy.[52] Consequently, there was no pressure from him to give diplomatic relations with Europe and America the temper characteristic of Comintern proclamations during this period. In fact, dealing with whatever problems those proclamations might create for the relations of the USSR with the capitalist world was part of the assigned task.

CONCLUSION

By the time of the "great turn," the basic institutions of Soviet national security had been formed and the most important institutions and doctrines for Soviet foreign policy had been set on the course they would follow for decades. These institutions and doctrines were not inherent in the revolutionary origins of the regime nor taken directly from pre–World War Marxism-Leninism. They were formed in an interplay of internal and external factors in Soviet foreign relations between the Bolshevik and Stalinist revolutions.

First, by the summer of 1922, Soviet diplomacy had become discouraged on the prospects of a comprehensive peace settlement between the socialist and capitalist camps, and by 1926 the special relationship with Germany had been seriously eroded. Thereafter, NKID efforts were no longer aimed at dramatic breakthroughs with one or more of the capitalist powers. Thereafter, the search for a secure place in the world was concentrated instead on gradual improvements in the tenor of relations and on efforts at piecemeal agreements between the USSR and other countries.[53]

Second, a massive effort to create an industrial complex that would provide Soviet armed forces with weapons of current design was launched and given first claim on national income and other resources. Beginning with the war scare of 1927, this was justified by extreme overestimates of "the foreign threat," and with the Shakhty trial in 1928 it was linked to the use of preemptive state terror. Soon it would have priority above all other economic, social, human, and environmental requirements.

Third, the doctrine that informed foreign policy was synthesized from several sources: the capitalist world order was incapable of prolonged stabilization; the more coherence that order demonstrated, the greater the dangers that confronted the USSR; the Soviet Union would be made more secure by participating in capitalist world politics than by separating from them; any rapprochement between the USSR and the capitalist world could, however, go no further than a "peaceful coexistence" standoff.

As long as this perspective dominated Soviet foreign policy-making, and as long as the state was guided by a leader with such a profound disinclination to trade adjustments in his policies for foreign agreements, there was to be very little room for a true rapprochement with the capitalist states. Even the Molotov-Ribbentrop Pact and related agreements of 1939 can be seen as efforts by Stalin to preserve Soviet independence and bolster Soviet military capabilities. Stalin's win-set on most serious agreements was to remain very narrow indeed.

NOTES

1. L. N. Nezhinskii, "Vneshniaia politika sovetskogo gosudarstva v 1917–1921 godakh: kurs na mirovuiu revoliutsiu ili na mirnoe sosushchestvovanie?" *Istoriia SSSR* 6 (1991), pp. 3–27.

2. Jon Jacobson, "On the Historiography of Soviet Foreign Relations in the 1920s," *International History Review*, forthcoming.

3. Speech by Lenin to Fourth All-Russian Congress of Garment Workers, February 6, 1921, V. I. Lenin, *Collected Works* 32 (Moscow: Progress Publishers, 1960–1970), pp. 113–114; report by Lenin to Ninth All-Russian Congress of Soviets, December 23, 1921, Lenin, *CW*, 33, p. 145.

4. Theses and resolutions of the Third Congress, June 29–July 17, 1921, in Jane Degras, ed., *The Communist International, 1919–1943: Documents*, 1 (London: Oxford University Press, 1956–1965), p. 256; hereafter *Communist International*.

5. Jon Jacobson, *When the Soviet Union Entered World Politics* (Berkeley: University of California Press, 1994), pp. 39–45.

6. Theses and resolutions of the Third Congress, June 29–July 17, 1921, *Communist International* 1, pp. 255–256.

7. Fernando Claudin, *The Communist Movement: From Comintern to Cominform* (New York: Monthly Review Press, 1975), pp. 152–153; Fridrikh I. Firsov, in USSR Institute of Marxism-Leninism, "Nekotorye voprosy istorii Kominterna," *Novaia i noveishaia istoriia* 2 (1989), p. 89.

8. Vladlen Sirotkin, "Ot grazhdanskoi voiny k grazhdanskomu miru," in Iu. N. Afanas'eva, ed., *Inogo ne dano* (Moskva: Progress, 1988), p. 384; Lenin quoted in Lazitch, Branko, and Milorad Drachkovitch, *Lenin and the Comintern* (Stanford, CA: 1972), p. 534.

9. Chicherin quoted in S. Iu. Vygodskii, *Vneshniaia politika SSSR, 1924–1929* (Moskva: Gos. Izd-vo Polit. Lit-ry, 1963), p. 292.

10. Stephen F. Cohen, *Bukharin and the Bolshevik Revolution: A Political Biography, 1888–1938* (New York: Knopf, 1973), pp. 147–148, 162, 186–188; Robert C. Tucker, *Stalin as Revolutionary, 1879–1929: A Study in History and Personality* (New York: Norton, 1973), pp. 377–394.

11. Lev Trotskii, *The Permanent Revolution and Results and Prospects* (New York: Merit Publishers, 1969), p. 105.

12. The role played by the debate over the doctrines of "socialism in one country," "permanent revolution," and "revolutionary internationalism" in the Lenin succession is discussed in Richard B. Day, *Leon Trotsky and the Politics of Economic Isolation* (Cambridge: Cambridge University Press, 1973), pp. 3–16, 98–101, and in Anthony D'Agostino, *Soviet Succession Struggles: Kremlinology and the Russian Question from Lenin to Gorbachev* (Boston: Allen and Unwin, 1988), pp. 75–105. Both works correct the notion that Bolshevik intraparty politics of 1925 to 1927 are to be understood as a confrontation between Stalin and "socialism in one country" on the one hand and Trotsky and "permanent revolution" on the other.

13. Isaac Deutscher, *The Prophet Unarmed: Trotsky, 1921–1929* (London: Oxford University Press, 1959), pp. 157–163, 201–270, discusses Trotsky's absence from the debate during the important period from January 1925 to April 1926. For a discussion of Trotsky's writings and politics during these years, see Pierre Broué, *Trotsky* (Paris: Fayard, 1988), pp. 441–473.

14. R. Craig Nation, *Black Earth, Red Star: A History of Soviet Security Policy, 1917–1991* (Ithaca: Cornell University Press, 1992), p. 58.

15. V. Kubalkova and A. A. Cruickshank, *Marxism and International Relations* (Oxford: Clarendon Press, 1985), pp. 85–86, quotation, 82; also, Allen Lynch, *The Soviet Study of International Relations* (New York: Cambridge University Press, 1987), pp. 18–19.

16. For example, Report by Stalin to the Moscow Party Organization on the results of the Fourteenth Party Conference, May 9, 1925, Josef Stalin, *Works*, 7 (Moscow: Foreign Languages Publishing House, 1953–1955), p. 95.

17. "The International Situation and the Tasks of the Communist Parties," *Pravda*, March 22, 1925, Stalin, *Works*, 7, pp. 51–57; Report to the Moscow Party Organization, May 9, 1925, Stalin, *Works*, 7, pp. 90–134; Political Report of the Central Committee to the Fourteenth Party Congress, December 18, 1925, Stalin, *Works*, 7, pp. 267–403; Resolutions, Decisions, and Directives of the Fourteenth Party Congress, December 1925, in Richard Gregor, ed., *Resolutions and Decisions of the Communist Party of the Soviet Union: The Early Soviet Period: 1917–1929*, 2 (Toronto: University of Toronto Press, 1974), pp. 258–260, hereafter cited as *Resolutions and Decisions*. For Marx, Lenin, and Bukharin on the theory of "capitalist stabilization" and its implications for the doctrine of "socialism in one country," see Richard B. Day, *The Crisis and the Crash: Soviet Studies of the West (1917–1939)* (London: NLB, 1981), pp. 73–77; for the reaction of the party leadership to the stabilization of 1924, see pp. 77–81.

18. Stalin, *Works*, 7, pp. 51, 92–95, 302–304.

19. Ibid., pp. 51–52.

20. Ibid., pp. 272–73.

21. Ibid., p. 98.

22. Ibid., pp. 99–100.

23. Ibid., p. 52.

24. Ibid., p. 276.

25. Ibid., pp. 53–55, 290–294.

26. Ibid., pp. 98–99, 273–274, 278–279.

27. "Concerning the International Situation," *Bolshevik*, September 20, 1924, Stalin, *Works*, 6, pp. 289–299, 303.

28. Stalin, *Works*, 7, pp. 279–283.

29. Jacobson, *When the Soviet Union*, pp. 203–205.

30. Report by Stalin to the Moscow Party Organization, January 27, 1925, Stalin *Works*, 7, pp. 25–29.

31. Resolutions of the Fourteenth Party Congress, *Resolutions and Decisions*, pp. 258–260.

32. Speech by Stalin to the Central Committee Plenum, January 19, 1925, Stalin, *Works*, 7, pp. 9–14; "The Prospects of the Communist Party of Germany and the Question of Bolshevization," *Pravda*, February 3, 1925, Stalin, *Works*, 7, pp. 34–41; Speech by Stalin at a Plenum of the Central Committee and the Central Control Commission, January 27, 1925, Stalin, *Works*, 7, pp. 13–14; Political Report of the Central Committee to the Fourteenth Party Congress, December 18, 1925, Stalin, *Works*, 7, pp. 279–283, 287;

Robert C. Tucker, "The Emergence of Stalin's Foreign Policy," *Slavic Review* 36 (1977), pp. 563–564, 565–566.

33. Stalin, *Works*, 7, pp. 12–13, 34.

34. Resolutions of the Third Soviet Congress, May 16, 1925, *Soviet Documents*, 2, p. 45; Resolutions of the Fourteenth Party Congress, *Resolutions and Decisions*, p. 258.

35. Cohen, *Bukharin*, pp. 179, 246–247; Day, *Leon Trotsky*, pp. 101–104, 118–121.

36. Resolutions of the Fourteenth Party Congress, *Resolutions and Decisions*, p. 258; Stalin quoted in Day, *Leon Trotsky*, p. 120.

37. Stalin, *Works*, 7, p. 279; see also the statement by Ia. Rudzutak quoted from the Stenographic Report of the Fourteenth Party Congress in Vygodskii, *Vneshniaia politika SSSR*, p. 85: "The Dawes Plan is aimed at converting Russia into an agrarian appendage, even Germany's, . . . [and] at squeezing pennies (out of the Russian working people) to pay German reparations to the USA. That is not our way, comrades!"

38. Stalin quoted in Day, *Leon Trotsky*, p. 121.

39. Day, *Leon Trotsky*, pp. 126–178, and his "Leon Trotsky on the Dialectics of Democratic Control," in Peter Wiles, ed., *The Soviet Economy on the Brink of Reform: Essays in Honor of Alec Nove* (Boston: Allen and Unwin, 1988), pp. 17–24.

40. Hodgeson (Moscow) to Chamberlain, August 25, 1925, *Documents on British Foreign Policy*, ser.1, vol. 25, no. 326.

41. Day, *Leon Trotsky*, pp. 131, 169.

42. On Preobrazhenskii and the law of primitive socialist accumulation, see M. M. Gorinov and S. V. Tsakunov, "The Life and Works of Evgenii Alekssevich Preobrazhenskii," *Slavic Review* 50 (1991), pp. 286–296, and Alexander Erlich, *The Soviet Industrialization Debate, 1924–1928* (Cambridge: Harvard University Press, 1960), pp. 31–60.

43. Richard B. Day, "Trotsky and Preobrazhensky, the Troubled Unity of the Left Opposition." *Studies in Comparative Communism* 10 (1977), pp. 69–86.

44. Report by Bukharin on the International Situation and the Tasks of the Communist Parties, July 18–19, 1928, in Xenia J. Eudin and Robert M. Slusser, eds., *Soviet Foreign Policy, 1928–1934: Documents and Materials*, 1 (University Park: Pennsylvania State University Press, 1967), pp. 106–120; hereafter, *SFP, 1928–1934*; "Measures of Struggle against the Danger of Imperialist War and the Tasks of the Communists," Sixth Comintern Congress, July–September 1928, *SFP, 1928–1934*, 1, p. 128. On the origins of the Third Period, see Kevin McDermott and Jeremy Agnew, *The Comintern: A History of International Communism from Lenin to Stalin* (London: Macmillan, 1996), pp. 68–98, and Nicholas N. Kozlov and Eric D. Weitz, "Reflections on the Origins of the 'Third Period': Bukharin, the Comintern, and the Political Economy of Western Germany," *Journal of Contemporary History*, 24 (1989), pp. 387–401.

45. *Izvestiia*, May 23, 1929, quoted in *SFP, 1928–34*, 1, pp. 4–5.

46. Report by Aleksei Rykov to Fifth Congress of Soviets, May 20, 1929, in Jane Degras, ed., *Soviet Documents on Foreign Policy*, 2 (London: Oxford University Press, 1951–1953), p. 374.

47. See in particular McDermott and Agnew, *Comintern*, pp. 89–90.

48. Jacobson, *When the Soviet Union*, pp. 229–232. The United Opposition had been formed by Trotsky, Zinoviev, and Kamenev in April 1926 in response to the emerging Stalin-Bukharin alliance. See Ibid., pp. 202–205.

49. Antonio Carlo, "Structural Causes of the Soviet Coexistence Policy," in Egbert Jahn, ed., *Soviet Foreign Policy: Its Social and Economic Conditions* (New York: St. Martin's 1978), p. 65.

50. Robert C. Tucker, "Emergence of Stalin's Foreign Policy," pp. 563–575, in his *Stalin in Power: The Revolution from Above, 1928–1941* (New York: Norton, 1990), pp. 44–65, quotations p. 45, and his "Stalinism as Revolution from Above" in *Stalinism: Essays in Historical Interpretation*, edited by the author (New York: Norton, 1977), pp. 77–108.

51. Stalin quoted in Alfred G. Meyer, "The War Scare of 1927," *Soviet Union/Union Sovietique*, 5 (1978), p. 3.

52. "To stretch out the breathing space for as long as possible . . . is the foundation and the most essential formula of the foreign policy of the USSR." "Leninist Principles of Soviet Foreign Policy," *Izvestiia*, January 22, 1929, *SFP, 1928–1934*, 1, pp. 160–161.

53. Jacobson, *When the Soviet Union*, pp. 197–203.

CHAPTER 2

Domestic Factors in Stalin's Atomic Diplomacy

Victor L. Mal'kov

Nuclear diplomacy at the end of World War II turned out to be disappointingly complex. Operating in accord with a well-entrenched political mentality, Washington policymakers had developed a relatively clear picture of a new and better international regime and how they would achieve it. This world order would be assured, they believed, by the American (and later United Nations) possession of the atomic weapon, a generous American involvement in the world economy, and benevolent American support for a conciliation policy in Europe and around the world. One can imagine the Americans' surprise when this scenario did not come to pass due to what seemed perverse behavior on the part of Soviet decision makers in 1945–1949. They could explain this only by attributing it to Joseph Stalin's personal calculations and his misperceptions of U.S. policy, as well as to his commitment to expansionism. It did not seem rational from a Western perspective that the Soviet Union, with its demolished industrial and agricultural infrastructure, its losses in manpower and demographical "holes," and its seriously undernourished population, would push itself near bankruptcy by engaging in a defense-spending contest it could not win. Nor did it seem rational to the West that Moscow would try to achieve military parity in the most technologically sophisticated and economically demanding armaments of mass destruction.

Achieving a durable peace for at least two or three decades on the basis of international interdependence and an American deterrence capacity, an idea widely discussed by such political leaders as Franklin D. Roosevelt and Cordell Hull in 1941–1945, had a great influence in shaping the liberal/realist approach of postwar foreign policy planners. Unfortunately, the majority of them (in preaching the preeminent significance of power correlations in shaping the postwar settlement)[1] failed to foresee the increasing role of domestic factors and traditional values.

Thus, in the months after Roosevelt's death White House policy debates on the future of Soviet-American relations were carried out largely from the perspective of a "one level (international politics) game." Very soon, however, it appeared that the scenario anticipating "normal" reactions on the part of Soviet leaders to an extremely unfavorable and asymmetrical weapons situation did not materialize. The Soviet decision makers' response to the American atomic monopoly in 1945–1949 proved instead to be an example of a tactic (or a strategy) aimed at what some analysts call "a non-cooperative stalemate."[2] This tactic could be dangerously provocative in some cases, although we do not yet possess solid evidence as to what its real objectives were.

In truth, many historians argue that it is too early to treat this subject because the archival repositories of top governmental Soviet authorities dealing with this issue continue to be restricted. Melvyn Leffler, for instance, is in no hurry to achieve closure. "Scholars remain uncertain," he wrote recently, "about Stalin's aims and motives after World War II."[3] David Holloway, the author of the pioneer book on the history of Soviet nuclear policy (a volume that can be considered a real breakthrough in a field that is shrouded in secrecy), is also cautious. "A great deal of new material," he writes in his introduction, "became available while I was writing the book. . . . All of these sources have been extremely helpful. They remain nevertheless unsatisfactory by comparison with those which historians of American or British nuclear policy can use. I have been able to work in Russian archives but some of the most important archives remain closed. The records of the main nuclear policy-making bodies are not yet accessible."[4]

No doubt the essential sources are still scarce, fragmentary, and disorganized. But they do give enough information to go beyond the "conventional" themes and questions that produced the initial impetus for a great variety of studies of Soviet nuclear policy. Moreover, they provide sufficient evidence to refute the simplistic constructions of various professional storytellers (such as Pavel Sudoplatov and his coauthors),[5] constructions that derive from the needs of their own lives, ignore the social and historical context, and reduce the role of domestic politics to trivial assumptions about the nature of the totalitarian regime or Stalin's guilt. The personal factor is what very often makes these sensational stories irrelevant in assessing the conflict mentality and national-international linkages in the active stage of atomic diplomacy.[6]

To be sure, we may never achieve the final goal, stipulated by Leffler, of revealing "Stalin's aims and motives after World War II." Indeed, Stalin, the central actor in U.S.-USSR diplomacy during 1945–1949, remains more obscure today than any of the other main participants. Nikita Khrushchev's brief and general remarks about him, widely noted by scholars, only fortify the notion that, in the end, Stalin's reactions will not be verified by solid historical documents.

There are two main reasons for this pessimism. First, within the Soviet apparatus there was no working mechanism or analytical body to formulate or implement long-term tasks in foreign policy or to keep records of highly sensitive discussions or conversations among top-level officials, including Stalin and his closest associates. Together with the traditional "opacity" of Soviet politics, which made it impossible even for Stalin himself to discuss his limits and opportunities, this emptiness in the most sacred Kremlin files could plunge an historian into a state of genuine despair. Second, Stalin's practice was to avoid situations in which the decisions would be marked by personal "fingerprints" in the form of written remarks, notes, memos, or personal correspondence. He was, for example, absolutely sphinxlike during his meetings with leading scientists and engineers summoned to the Kremlin to report in person on the preparations for the first Soviet atom bomb test in 1949.[7] This was almost certainly a security precaution against his internal and external enemies, present and future. Stalin had converted his unique sense of history into a paranoia in which witnesses were always unwanted.

Nevertheless, historians can hope to be rewarded by diversifying their search for sources and focusing on untraditional "indicators" such as Academy of Sciences' Archives (which include scientists' reports on their foreign trips and conversations) or records of the subdivisions of the Communist Party and governmental bodies. These indirect or reflective data help us to understand the options that Soviet leaders faced in a potentially explosive situation shaped by erosion of the consensus built during World War II and by concern about the new military technology of mass destruction acquired by the "imperialistic" West. When one adds to this corpus Foreign Office documents, research institutes' manuscript collections, and the State Archives of the Russian Federation (i.e., the so-called Stalin, Beria, Malenkov "folders" of the Kremlin Archives), an historian has a "fighting chance" to master the Soviet decision-making environment in the early stages of the Cold War. Good examples of the successful use of such sources are recent volumes by Sergei Goncharov, John W. Lewis, and Xue Litai, and by Vladislav Zubok and Constantine Pleshakov.[8]

Yet difficulties remain. One can, for example, find materials prepared for the "eyes" of top-level party officials such as Viacheslav Molotov, Andrei Zhdanov, Georgi Malenkov, and Mikhail Suslov, but usually these documents do not bear remarks exposing the personal views of the recipient. They often contain only directions for distribution ("Attention Comrade Molotov," one reads). If one is lucky, one may find underlinings on documents that communicate the mood of a reader.

What was behind such super-discreet behavior? Was it a cult of collective irresponsibility? Was it a concern about (or fear of) finding oneself (as Russians used to say) "running before the engine"? Or was it the established tradition of forming a consensus by means of "irreversible" oral conversations, phone talks, or personal clearance with "the boss" himself? All these possibilities should be taken into account. But this reality leaves us, perhaps forever, with incomplete records regarding atomic energy and its political implications. We cannot be more than 50 percent sure that such records reflect the changing pattern of the Soviet elite's approach to nuclear issues.

Does this mean we should limit our conclusions to what can be completely verified? Or that we should be forced by our documentation into focusing primarily on the international ramifications of the bomb? I hardly think so. Scholars who disregard domestic cleavages and follow the postulate that one of the international actors—the Soviet leadership, in this case—cared only about international gains and faced no domestic constraints cannot make much progress.[9]

In the various chapters of this volume the attempt is made to show that both foreign and domestic factors impact on foreign policy. Demonstrating this is difficult but not impossible for the Soviet Union in the first years after the war. The evidence is far from satisfactory, but it indicates the existence of certain patterns, which we intend to examine.

However, this volume also includes efforts to apply versions of two-level-game analysis to decisions of the chief-of-government. Here our lack of detailed evidence is a more serious problem. Because we cannot fully ascertain the perceptions and calculations of the Soviet leader, whether in regard to his government's dealings with other states or in his work with his colleagues in the government and the party, use of two-level explanations is hard to justify. We will be content with a few comments about this at the end.

Although we still have no precise knowledge of what actually happened in Stalin's Kremlin after Hiroshima and Nagasaki (August 1945), the main outlines are clear. The seriousness of the questions produced a kind of disarray among foreign policy planners already stunned by the sudden stoppage of Lend-Lease in May 1945. It took almost two weeks for any policy of relevance to be generated, and what was produced seems to have been primarily motivated by domestic considerations.

The first indication of new thinking came on August 19, 1945, when the Soviet press announced to an exhausted Soviet people a five-year plan that envisaged a considerable increase in industrial production over the prewar level as well as complete restoration of the war ravaged territories.[10] There would be no breathing space, no shift in priorities; industrial production would remain the predominant goal; the tempo of development would be accelerated; sacrifices would be expected. Stalin himself offered no comment. Throughout the fall and early winter he made no public appearances and did not make any significant international statement. He did, however, receive numerous foreign emissaries in Moscow and at his vacation retreat in Gagra, among them some Americans.

The second indication of government policy came on November 7, 1945, when Foreign Minister Molotov delivered a speech commemorating the twenty-eighth anniversary of the Bolshevik Revolution. It was, in fact, the Soviet response to a speech by President Harry S. Truman on October 27 in which the President had repeated his previous assertion that America would retain the atomic bomb and secrets of its production until it could be safely outlawed forever.[11] On this occasion Molotov made it clear that the Kremlin had decided to pursue policies vis-à-vis the United States that would not neglect the popularity of the regime at home. Hinting at the Truman-Stalin conversation at Potsdam in July 1945, he argued that it was a mistake for anyone to try to exploit the atomic bomb in international affairs. No technical secret could long remain the exclusive possession of any one country or group of countries, he predicted. With peace restored, "we shall have atomic energy, and many other things too in our country."[12]

Stalin himself kept silent until February 1946, making a deliberate effort to avoid speaking on foreign policy issues. But the barrage of "vigilance" speeches and articles in the state-controlled press emphasizing the imminence of a new world war gave some indication of what he was thinking. Though there was no single statement that linked such a war to Soviet-American relations, it was commonplace, in speaking about the war danger, to hold that the uneven development of capitalism and contradictions of imperialism remained dominant within the world system, even after the defeat of Germany, Italy, and Japan. Such alarmist rhetoric targeted people's fears by implying that at almost any time the Soviet Union and the "new (socialist) democracies" could be converted into victims of attack by an imperialist military bloc. This was the central point of Stalin's message on peace and war of February 9, 1946, presented on the eve of elections to the USSR Supreme Soviet.[13]

The real intention of all these calls for vigilance (together with the discussion of pseudo-theoretical matters) was a very practical one: to render the Soviet people more willing to be mobilized, more immune to the appeal of imported goods (both material and spiritual), and less receptive to the moral and political values of capitalist society. More specifically, reestablishment of the "besieged fortress" mentality, although not fully consistent with current military policy (which entailed the demobilization of the army and the withdrawal of troops from Iran, Korea, and Austria), had two objectives:

1. To justify the cleansing of Soviet society (in Stalin's style) through mass deportations of "unreliable ethnic groups" and "collaborators with the enemy."
2. To prepare the country to make a large contribution to the rebuilding of Eastern Europe and the facilitating of revolution in the Colonial World.

To achieve these goals, an "atomic scare" was the ideal instrument. It made possible public approval of vast military expenditures, endorsement of heavy industry, and support for the concentration of human and material resources on official projects. And it did not require special cultivation. Indeed, it was the predictable result of continuing clashes between the Soviet Union and the United States at United Nations sessions and at Council of Foreign Ministers summits. It was reinforced by the apprehension the Soviet people quite naturally felt in contemplating the incredible destructive power of atomic weapons. In this context, Washington's determination to test and use the atom bomb as a conventional weapon seemed a warning of imminent air attack.

Still, some observers noted that the Soviet concern went beyond the popular level. The British chargé d'affaires in Moscow, Frank Roberts, in his cable to Foreign Minister Ernest Bevin in March 1946, reported:

The shadow of the atom bomb [has] darkened our relations, and behind every manifestation of Anglo-American solidarity, e.g. in Bulgaria or Romania, the rulers of the Soviet Union, until [now] confident of the overwhelming strength of the Red Army, [see] the menace of an Anglo-American block possessing this decisive weapon and therefore capable not only of depriving the Soviet Union of the fruits of the victories of the Red Army but even of endangering the security which the Soviet Union [has] so hardly won.[14]

Ambassador Averell Harriman in his cables described a "neurotic" Russian reaction to the American atomic monopoly.

George Kennan, on the other hand, speaking of Soviet insecurity in his "Long Telegram" (February 1946), did not touch on this subject. Instead, he wrote of Marxism as a "justification" for the Soviet leadership's "fear of the outside world." One can hardly disagree with analysts who suggest that this was the least satisfactory section of Kennan's telegram.[15] It is worth mentioning that a year later, during a discussion at the Council on Foreign Relations on "The Soviet Way of Thought and Its Effect on Soviet Foreign Policy," Kennan gave a brief, unimpressive answer when asked how "the Russians confront scientific problems, such as that of atomic energy."[16]

The historian Martin Sherwin is only half right when he describes the Soviet reaction to the bombing of Hiroshima and Nagasaki as a "soundless" maneuver aimed at downgrading the difference in military potentials between the USSR and the United States ("reverse atomic diplomacy"). To be sure, the Soviet press and radio made little or no comment about the atomic explosions, and foreign reports implying that the bomb was now the single most important factor in international relations were also censored. Yet despite this, Soviet citizens could see bomb shelters being rebuilt while they were being taught how to conduct themselves during an atomic attack. Thus a two-level tactic on the part of Moscow provided for public manipulation on the one hand and confrontational diplomacy (conducted in United Nations' gatherings, foreign minister and summit talks, exchanges of views through diplomatic channels, the mass media) on the other. The demonstration of coolness in connection with frightening disclosures of atomic destruction; the decision not to use unofficial contacts that had proved to be helpful during the war; the unwillingness to accept the idea of great power responsibility for nuclear security of the globe—all served as a message to the Soviet people confirming that the Soviet government, despite temporary delays, was on the right track for catching up with its adversaries. Meanwhile, the West's appeal for collaboration had to be rebuffed, with double alertness and preparedness for the contingency of war.[17]

This did not mean that the alternative option had not been discussed or that the Kremlin had come easily to the decision to meet the new challenge with its chosen policy. Maxim Litvinov's bold dissent from the official line is a good example of the disagreement among Soviet political leaders over the atom bomb during the short interregnum between August and November 1945. Archival sources reveal that in November 1945 Litvinov recommended that the Soviet Union agree to the American, British, and Canadian proposal for an international nuclear regulatory commission. He was in effect urging the Soviet Union to subordinate itself to the requirements of controlling and inspecting atomic energy production through the United Nations, endorsing what appeared to be the first draft of a non-proliferation treaty. He was proposing that Moscow follow "the Yalta formula."

Litvinov's recommendation was rejected. His two memos were read by Molotov and obviously discussed with Stalin and Lavrenti Beria (who was in charge of the Soviet atomic project), but his suggestions were not followed. Instead the decision was made (as evidenced by Molotov's Secretariat files) both to insist unconditionally on full Soviet participation in the "atomic club" and to "educate" the world as to America's improper and selfish disposition with regard to atomic energy secrets and control proposals. Andrei Gromyko (the young Soviet representative in the UN Atomic Energy Commission) was apparently one of the principal architects of this diplomacy of clumsy methods and strong words, diplomacy designed in retribution for the refusal of the United States and Great Britain to treat the Soviet Union as an equal in atomic matters.[18]

In any case, Stalin's view of world affairs at this time was strongly shaped by a revived sense of insecurity.[19] His anxiety and indignation in connection with the dramatic disclosure of the Soviet atomic espionage network (the "Gouzenko case" and "the May-affair") in Canada and the United States were intense.[20] And his ability to find a "conspiracy" can hardly be exaggerated: the Zhdanovshchina, the attack on "cosmopolitanism," and the "doctors' plot" were all in part by-products of the postwar "atomic scare" in the USSR.

The defection of Soviet cipher clerk/intelligence officer Igor Gouzenko in Ottawa in September 1945, which so shook Western public opinion, had enormous impact in Soviet domestic affairs as spy-hunting and secrecy spread to every facet of public life. Hundreds of well-known scholars—biologists, chemists, physicists, etc.—were accused of being negligent in their attitude to "state secrets." Even atomic scientist Petr Kapitsa was put under strict surveillance. In his memo to Zhdanov in August 1947, A. P. Aleksandrov, a high party official in charge of scientific development, suggested the special precaution with regard to Kapitsa. Aleksandrov recalled, in justification, Kapitsa's letter of September 1944 to the Central Committee of the Party on the "irresponsible" behavior of Klyueva and Roskin—two biologists who were under severe attack because of their contacts with Western scholars.[21]

The "Gouzenko case" dramatically changed the situation with regard to scientific and technological exchanges between the Soviet Union and the West. Reading the available documents, one receives the impression that Gouzenko's desertion (which was a major event to the intelligence community and public in America but was virtually unknown to people in the Soviet Union) was a central factor in the Kremlin's decision to stop all contacts between Soviet scientists and their Western colleagues. The object was to eliminate the leakage of information concerning the real state of nuclear research in the Soviet Union. The cipher clerk/intelligence officer seemed to become the universal symbol of the vulnerability of Soviet national secrets.

Until the end of 1945 the Soviet government had replied positively to proposals of the Academy of Sciences to maintain the prewar links between Soviet and Western scholars;[22] but in the spring of 1946 an official ban was put on all such connections.[23] One may suspect that this decision was based on a number of considerations, but the "Gouzenko case" and the atomic espionage panic of 1945–1946 contributed greatly to it. In the spring of 1946 the president of the Soviet Academy of Sciences, S. I. Vavilov, was ignored by Stalin, Malenkov, and Zhdanov in connection with his request to approve membership for the Academy in the International Council of the Scientific Union. The London session of the Scientific Union had appealed to the Soviet Academy in December 1945, and Vavilov sent his letter to the Politburo the following April, but there is no indication it was ever seriously read. Later, in August, Suslov, without giving any reasons, rejected the request of the well-known Soviet physicist G. Landsberg to visit Holland even though Landsberg had visited Paris in the spring of 1946.[24] In the summer of 1947 the Party leadership refused to approve visits by mathematicians L. Pontrjagin and P. Aleksandrov to the United States, although both had been invited by leading American universities.[25] Even before this, in September 1946 Beria, Molotov, Vavilov, and I. V. Kurchatov had formally agreed that contacts between Soviet and American scientists had to be reduced in number.[26]

Beyond Gouzenko's defection, the Kremlin leadership was also concerned with the wave of anti-Soviet propaganda in the West (such as spy movies and other mass-media efforts), which portrayed the Soviet position on atomic energy as sinister and untrustworthy. Especially disconcerting was the fact that stories of espionage reinforced American determination to retain a nuclear monopoly as long as possible. Intensive deliberations in the USSR Foreign Ministry and the CPSU Central Committee resulted in a decision in the winter of 1946–1947 to match this American "offensive" with countermeasures, both at home and abroad. The "provocation" of the Gouzenko affair, and the unyielding American demand for a veto on any new commission were cited as reasons for the counter attack and for Soviet rejection of the Baruch plan.[27]

As it happened, the combination of the propaganda effort with the deterioration in Soviet-American relations during the course of the debate over the Baruch plan actually brought substantial benefits to Stalin. It strengthened his image at home as a stubborn, tough, and wise leader resisting indecent and hostile Western pressure. It also made a special impression on Soviet scientists and senior government officials who considered participation in the "Uranium Project" their supreme patriotic duty. As a result, they more readily accepted supersecrecy in their everyday lives and isolation from the world scientific community, convinced that the Soviet nuclear project had acquired top priority in the eyes of the leadership of the country. They were guided by the belief that the Soviet Union at that moment had already reached the capability to undertake a crash program in the development of atomic hardware and possessed the necessary resources (intellectual and material) to accomplish this program. In that respect, one episode is particularly revealing and can be reliably reconstructed using the documents of the CPSU archives.

A certain Dr. Bernstein, a chemist and chief of a Red Army chemistry laboratory during the Berlin operation of April 1945, reported in February 1946 to party officials in charge of scientific affairs that he had personally searched through the ruins of the Kaiser Wilhelm Institute for Chemistry in Berlin-Dahlem for the German Scientist Otto Hahn. It seems that Bernstein's group was responsible for doing what the American Alsos team had been organized to do: namely, to locate major German scientific centers, to capture German nuclear physicists, and to collect their scholarly documents. But Dr. Bernstein was not as successful as his American counterparts, Samuel Goudsmit and Major Boris T. Pash, had been. In his memo Bernstein reported that, "Professor Otto Hahn had vanished while the Institute had ceased to exist, being ruined by bombardments."[28] The Alsos team, on the other hand, apprehended a number of key German scientists, men whom Goudsmit graciously referred to as "former enemy colleagues." It shipped ten of these scientists to England, including Otto Hahn,[29] the object of Bernstein's search. (Later Goudsmit himself was spirited out of Germany because Allied authorities feared that the Russians might capture him.[30])

This semi-detective story had a happy ending for all its major participants. Bernstein got a quick reply from the special Committee to whom he reported stating that there was no reason to worry, that Soviet atomic research was on the right track, and that the failure to capture Otto Hahn would cause little harm. This reply was astonishingly frank and self-confident in tone: "The evidence communicated to us offers nothing new. The location of the German research centers and scientific equipment has been rediscovered. German scientists able to be used have been registered and all measures necessary for their proper employment have been taken."[31] Here was an appeal to self-confidence and an expression of faith in the leadership's farsightedness.

On August 27, 1946, even informal links between the Soviet scientific community and industrial complex and their Western equivalents were severed by the government. The resulting isolation, enormously counterproductive for science, inflicted much harm on the moral climate of Soviet society. It generated a great deal of distrust towards the former Allies and undermined the prospects for people-to-people diplomacy that had resulted from the meetings on the Elbe, in Berlin, and in Vienna. Extreme secrecy was also translated into military uncertainty between the East and West, between the Soviet Union and the United States—and this was Stalin's intention. He obviously calculated on such uncertainty as an instrument in his moves and countermoves at the bargaining table. Uncertainty and frustration created uneasiness and fear. Prudent military intelligence analysts and science advisers in the West were supposed to assess uncertainty in favor of Soviet defensive capabilities. This could create important advantages for the Soviet Union, which in reality was much more vulnerable than the United States and its allies to a punishing atomic attack.[32]

This strategy had the probability of at least being workable, if not wholly successful. The American scientist I. I. Rabi, who contributed enormously to the Manhattan Project and was frequently praised for his broad vision regarding the moral and political aspects of atomic energy, wrote in *The Atlantic Monthly* (April 1949):

That the Soviets could not agree to this [Baruch Plan] has been held variously to result from the Original sin of Communism, the intrinsic inability of a totalitarian state to withstand impartial inspection from outside, ignorance in the Kremlin of the fatal power of the atomic bomb, and lastly to plain cussedness. The result in any event, has been a greatly heightened tension in the Western world, particularly here in the United States. The mounting fear and frustration have resulted in vastly increased military appropriations, a severe loyalty check to weed out all leftist elements from the important phase of American life, and in general an effort to put the country, and in fact the whole non-Soviet world, in a state of preparedness for war.[33]

Today we could reproach Rabi for neglecting the impact of the strategic climate of the 1940s. As David Holloway has suggested, Soviet nuclear weapons policy was from the very beginning rooted in the urge to compete with the United States and driven by a fear that a position of inferiority would have harmful military and political consequences for the Soviet Union.[34] After Hiroshima this posture on the part of Stalin and his colleagues was predictable. Professor Gerald Robinson, the head of the Soviet Department in the OSS, noted in his report on "USSR Policy and the Atomic Bomb," dated September 12, 1945:

It is . . . obvious that Soviet leadership, in considering its present security problems, must regard the following tasks as of primary importance:

a. To appraise the political and military intentions of the Western Allies, now that the latter are in exclusive possession of decisive military weapons.

b. To devise means to alter this unfavorable balance of military power, or at least to make the inequality less decisive.

c. To adjust the world political policy of the USSR in such a manner that, at least until the USSR has devised means to redress the unfavorable balance, there will be little likelihood of war between the Western Allies and the USSR.[35]

The phrase "to make the inequality less decisive" could be taken as a summary description of Soviet nuclear objectives in 1945–1949. Of course, in offering his analysis Robinson was not able to comprehend all the puzzles and anomalies in the East-West relationship during the early Cold War. Nor in September 1945 was it easy to say what might produce additional tensions or bring this relationship to the threshold of enmity. As Jack Snyder points out, "Tensions were often highest when statesmen on both sides were merely trying to consolidate their respective blocs."[36] Moreover, in this first postwar September, few recognized what George Orwell later described in stark terms in his *1984*: "War . . . is now a purely internal affair. . . .

The object of war is not to make or prevent conquests of territory, but to keep the structure of society intact."[37]

In truth, Stalin's uncertainty and his reluctance to search for a workable agreement on atomic energy with the West were determined as much by factors at home and in Eastern Europe as by a desire "to make the inequality less decisive." Though the security dilemma (especially concerning Germany) required a solution short of war, cooperation with former Allies, because it could damage the internal stability of the whole Eastern bloc, was *not* an option. Stalin needed hyperorthodoxy (Communism versus Capitalism) and the stereotypes of class struggle to justify a crackdown on pluralistic forces that had been allowed to emerge during the war years in the Soviet Union and had the potential to grow in eastern European countries.[38] Of course, Stalin could not be absolutely sure that in the long run he would not make a deal with pragmatic politicians in the West on a "non-ideological" basis. But such a deal was not on the priority list of his foreign policy goals.

In the end, thanks to an initiative by the Federation of American Scientists (probably acting at the solicitation of the United States government), the West got an emphatic, if indirect message from the Kremlin that the latter had decided to continue its efforts to become an atomic power, even at the cost of further complications with the West. The story of the Federation's questionnaire, which was mailed in September 1946 to individual Soviet scientists and produced a great deal of discussion at the top level of the Soviet government, illuminates this development of Moscow's strategy vividly.[39] Signed by Albert Einstein, Robert Oppenheimer, Leo Szillard, and others, the questionnaire included a request that each respondent explain his or her position with regard to atomic energy control and the "free exchange of information." It was an invitation to take part in the Atoms for Peace dialogue and in the process make a contribution to the United Nations agenda.

However, before individuals could act, the Soviet government decided to co-opt the matter. The first draft of an official response was ready at the end of December 1946 after extensive correspondence between Zhdanov, Molotov, and senior diplomats from the Foreign Ministry of the USSR. (Soviet scientists were deliberately excluded from this time-absorbing but important exchange.) The critical tone of the working paper exposed the established mode of strategic thinking. It charged the United States with initiating the atomic arms race and therefore having no moral right to judge any country directly or indirectly about the route it had chosen in the pursuit of its national interest.

This initial draft was severely criticized by V. Dekanosov—the deputy minister for foreign affairs and one of the closest of Beria's associates—mainly for wordiness and for too much stress on the control issue. An alternative draft proposed by him was short and completely nonobliging in tone. But it in turn was killed in February 1947 when A. P. Aleksandrov—the person on the Central Committee of the Party in charge of scientific research—wrote on the margins of the last draft, "The case has become obsolete. Send to Archives!"[40] Thus, there would be no response, and no international cooperation, until the Soviet Union had the atomic bomb.

OTHER OBSERVATIONS

It may be useful to offer a few further remarks with regard to ideological, political, and institutional dimensions of the problem. American intelligence sources pointed out just after Hiroshima that the new reality in the strategic balance—exclusive possession of atomic weapons by the West—might lead to negative Soviet appraisals of Western intentions and to fear that the West would use the atomic bomb to extract political concessions from the USSR.[41] This was a powerful insight. Yet there were certainly additional factors that contributed to the Soviet unwillingness to accept the new situation. There was, for instance, the standard "totalitarian" tendency of the Soviet state to keep its citizenry isolated from any information that might evoke dangerous or simply unpredictable responses. There were also the unusual personality characteristics of Stalin and his closest circle. Finally, and equally important perhaps, were the deep-rooted feelings and aspirations of the people themselves.

It is important to recognize that, traditionally and especially after victory in World War II, Soviet propaganda, both internal and external, emphasized that the Red Army was the world's strongest military force and that it was backed by the world's greatest military-industrial capability. The intention in making such a claim was to create the impression that, with Germany defeated, the USSR was now invincible. But it would be wrong to conclude that the image of invincibility was offered only to strengthen the regime's domestic base or to deter foreign encroachments on its sphere of influence. The perception of Soviet strength was an integral part of the Soviet leadership's worldview as well as a strong component of mass political culture. Or, to put it another way, Moscow stepped onto the path of the arms race with the West with considerable confidence that it could win it. Both elite and people were ready to make great sacrifices for a legitimate goal that they saw as well within their reach.

Let me add a few thoughts about Soviet perceptions of the atomic threat. Amidst many important questions related to this problem, the most crucial is whether information about American intentions received by the Kremlin through the channels of Soviet intelligence was adequate and comprehensive. The answer is surprising and paradoxical. In Stalin's postwar Soviet Union—with its government-controlled mass media, cult of censorship, ideological stereotypes, and anxiety about conflict—the government's intelligence sources can be seen as the most accurate and reliable factor in the process of decision-making by the Politburo as well as by Stalin himself. The primary reason is that, traditionally, Soviet foreign intelligence, including political intelligence, functioned more or less independently (at least in operational matters) from the Party bureaucracy. That is why this institution had the capacity to make realistic analyses of the situation abroad and of the adversary's intentions.[42]

Ironically however, in spite of its achievements during the war, Soviet intelligence during this period (in part because of the Kravchenko and Gouzenko cases)[43] lost both independence and respect among the interexecutive groups, key members of the Politburo, and the high party apparatus. Though it is still difficult to assess the full scope of Soviet intelligence activity and, above all, the character of the relationship between intelligence and the party leadership, one can argue without much fear of error that political intelligence was damaged severely. The reason was almost completely due to a domestic factor: that the guidelines for analysis set down by official ideology, and by Stalin himself, could not be ignored under any circumstances.[44]

In other words, while intelligence analysts were expected to describe what they saw and what they thought in assessing obtained information, they also had to be attuned to "the decisions," as reflected both in *Pravda* editorials and in the latest statements of leaders at official forums. Of course, in some matters, the intelligence agencies maintained a certain freedom of expression and the right to a degree of independent judgment. Yet as the 1940s wore on, Stalin's well-known preference for relying on his own intuition, imagination, and ability to foresee the future helped to render unorthodox opinion in the Soviet intelligence community more and more scarce.

Sometimes the ideological confrontation with the West completely shaped the analysis that was produced by "the brains." Thus in October 1947, a year of some accomplishment in achieving European settlements, academician Eugene Varga in a "Memorandum on World Policy" for the Party leadership argued that the West was preparing a new war against the Soviet Union in which it would use atomic weapons. No other interpretation of the situation was discussed in this document, which is remarkable for its assumption of the inevitability of war and its scenario of diplomatic relations helpless before the final crisis.[45] Another influential observer, T. A. Stepanjan (of course, while referring to Stalin), formulated a security doctrine that envisaged military buildup as the answer to geopolitical challenge anywhere beyond the Soviet Union's borders. The idea of unacceptable risk due to the possibility of atomic attack was not even considered in his discussion of possible developments.[46]

Perhaps more significant is the fact that Stalin was gradually losing touch with the mainstream of Western politics, social-economic development, and mood.[47] As a result, the Soviet leader was inclined to deny the possibility, for the foreseeable future, of a satisfactory *modus vivendi* with the capitalist world. His attitudes seemed to parallel those of the notorious German General Erich Ludendorff: "In the course of the so-called peace, politics . . . made sense [only] in so far as they prepared for a total war." To be sure, Stalin's politics can be described as defensive. Moreover, it is clear that, in following this particular logic, he believed that he could postpone a settlement of the atomic problem until the Soviet Union possessed the devastating weapon.[48]

It is still not certain what the decisive factors were behind this risky policy. Was it, for example, Stalin's desire not to give America the strategic initiative? Or was it the Soviet dictator's assumption that nation-state competition could not be transcended? Or was it perhaps the personal and collective mentality of a closed society cultivated in a besieged fortress and explicated by a pretentious ideology? To suggest precise conclusions or generalizations at this stage of research would be premature. Taking into account the limited accessibility of the Russian archives, as well as their volume, complexity, and incompleteness, any categorical judgment should be resisted.

In any case, a concluding comment relevant to the applicability of the two-level-game framework is in order. One of the central issues in any analysis of the dawn of the Cold War has been, and will continue to be, the degree to which the contest was unavoidable. Were there sufficient grounds for a more peaceful settlement, that is, did the win-sets of the two sides overlap so significantly that we can say the Cold War resulted from misperceptions and miscalculations? Or was the gap between the two sides too great to be bridged by agreements such as the Baruch Plan? The evidence available to this point on Stalin's decisions strongly suggests that there was little overlap. The "non-cooperative stalemate" that resulted was to last for many years.

It appears that domestic considerations played a dominant role in the outcome. Stimulated by the appearance of the atomic bomb, Stalin's insecurity promoted tighter political control and a progressive suspension of contacts with the West. It was not, therefore, that agreements with the West were unratifiable—Stalin faced no such problem—but that agreements, and indeed the contacts they would have required and inspired, were themselves something of a threat. With respect to possible agreements, the leader's and Party's win-sets, not the nation's, were too limited and inflexible.

NOTES

1. On January 7, 1947, George F. Kennan, speaking at the Council on Foreign Relations meeting on "The Soviet Way of Thought and Its Effect in Soviet Foreign Policy," gave a clear example of how this approach could be applied. The transcript reads: "As to the question of atomic energy, Mr. Kennan did not think that the Russians would take a rigid ideological attitude. . . . There is inescapable logic in our control plan and they will probably accept it (with a possible exception on the veto matter) but it will be a slow process and they will attempt to maintain the best possible bargaining position." (Meeting sponsored by the Council on Foreign Relations, January 7, 1947, Allen Dulles Papers, Box 30, Seeley G. Mudd Library, Princeton University.)

2. Jack Snyder, "East-West Bargaining Over Germany," in Peter B. Evans, Harold K. Jacobson, and Robert D. Putnam, eds., *Double-Edged Diplomacy: International Bargaining and Domestic Policy* (Berkeley: University of California Press, 1993), p. 113.

3. *New Republic*, October 3, 1994, p. 5.

4. David Holloway, *Stalin and the Bomb: The Soviet Union and Atomic Energy 1939–1956* (New Haven: Yale University Press, 1994), p. 6. The author of this chapter has come across the same situation while working on his own book. See Victor L. Mal'kov, *The Manhattan Project: Intelligence and Diplomacy* (Moscow: Publishing House "Nauka," 1995). In Russian.

5. See the discussion of Pavel Sudoplatov's memoirs [Pavel and Anatoli Sudoplatov, *Special Tasks: The Memoirs of an Unwanted Witness—A Soviet Spymaster* (Boston: Little, Brown, 1994)] in the American press: Hans Bethe, "Atomic Slurs," *Washington Post*, May 27, 1994, Eric Breindel, "The Oppenheimer File," *National Review*, May 30, 1994; William

J. Broad, "Charges Creators of A-Bomb Aided Soviets," *New York Times*, April 19, 1994; William Broad, "Physicists Try to Discredit Book Asserting Atom Architects Spied," *New York Times*, May 1, 1994; Roger Donald, "Dissenting Thoughts on KGB Memoirs," *Washington Post*, May 19, 1994; George Kennan, "In Defense of Oppenheimer," *New York Review of Books*, June 23, 1994; Amy Knight, "The Man Who Wasn't There," *New York Times*, May 3, 1994; Walter Laquer, "Red Herrings," *New Republic*, June 6, 1994; Priscilla Johnson McMillan, "They Weren't Spies," *Washington Post*, April 26, 1994.

6. C. Van Woodward has addressed the value of this kind of historical "evidence" in a recent review in which he notes that "the most conspicuous sources cited are interviews with participants and 'recollections' of witnesses of events that took place a quarter of a century or more ago. Such off-the-cuff testimony is notoriously unreliable and often self-serving" (*New York Review of Books*, 41 [20 October 1994], p. 52). One of the few positive results of encountering this sort of literature is that it strengthens our quest for authentic documents.

7. His most revealing comment dates from 1945, when he is reported to have told a group of physicists, "The balance has been broken. Build the bomb—it will remove the great danger from us" (Stephen J. Zaloga, *Target America: The Soviet Union and the Strategic Arms Race, 1945–1964* [Navato, CA: Presidio Press, 1993], p 29.)

8. Sergei N. Goncharov, John Lewis, and Xue Litai, *Uncertain Partners: Stalin, Mao and the Korean War* (Stanford: Stanford University Press, 1994); Vladislav Zubok and Constantine Pleshakov, *Inside the Kremlin's Cold War: From Stalin to Khrushchev* (Cambridge: Harvard University Press, 1996).

9. Evans, Jacobson, and Putnam, eds., *Double-Edged Diplomacy*, p. 437.

10. *Pravda*, August 19, 1945.

11. *Public Papers of the Presidents of the United States: Harry S Truman, 1945* (Washington: Government Printing Office, 1961), pp. 431–438.

12. At the September 1945 London foreign ministers' conference, Molotov had gone out of his way to show his disdain for the new weapons. "We had to set a tone," he recalls, "to reply in a way that would make our people feel more or less confident"; Albert Resis, ed., *Molotov Remembers: Inside Kremlin Politics: Conversations with Felix Chuev* (Chicago: Ivan R. Dee, 1993), p. 58. See also John Lewis Gaddis, *We Now Know: Rethinking Cold War History* (Oxford: Clarendon Press, 1997), pp. 96–97.

13. *Pravda*, February 10, 1946. Molotov's speech of February 6, 1946 was more explicitly anti-Western. See V. M. Molotov, *Problems of Foreign Policy: Speeches and Statements, April 1945–November 1948* (Moscow: Foreign Languages Publishing House, 1949), pp. 34, 39.

14. Kenneth H. Jensen, ed., *Origins of the Cold War: The Novikov, Kennan and Roberts "Long Telegrams" of 1946* (Washington, D.C.: United States Institute of Peace Press, 1991), p. 34.

15. Sean Greenwood, "Frank Roberts and the 'Other' Long Telegram: The View from the British Embassy in Moscow, March 1946," *Journal of Contemporary History*, 25 (1990), pp. 103–122.

16. Meeting Sponsored by the Council on Foreign Relations, January 7, 1947, Allen Dulles Papers, Box 30.

17. Molotov had not speeded up the negotiations on atomic energy after the establishment of the UN Atomic Energy Commission on January 24, 1946. Earlier, before attacking the Baruch Plan in an October 29 speech before the UN General Assembly, he had rejected an opportunity to discuss the issue with leading American politicians, including

Byrnes and Joseph Davies (Arkhiv Vneshnei Politiki [AVP] of the Russian Ministry of Foreign Affairs, Fond 6, opis 8, delo 756, papka 45, listy 52, 55, 59, 62–64). The U.S. plan and proposals had many drawbacks on which to build the Soviet diplomatic response and that served to strengthen the resolve of the Soviet people and its leaders. Andrei Gromyko called it an attempt to infringe on Soviet sovereignty. Walter Lippmann concluded that the Soviet representative's rhetoric had been justified by Baruch's maximalism. Baruch, Lippmann wrote to Chester Barnard, "has not only aroused the Russians more than is necessary, but he has hardened American opinion behind ideas that really, at bottom, make no sense" (Walter Lippmann to Chester I. Barnard, June 25, 1946, David E. Lilienthal Papers, Box 114, Seeley G. Mudd Library).

18. A. Gromyko to V. Molotov, November 22, 1946; AVP MID Rossijskoj Federazii, Fond 6, opis 8, delo 107, papka 8, listy 1. See also Andrei Gromyko, *Memories* (London: Hutchinson, 1989), pp. 137–141.

19. Sudoplatov's statement (p. 210) that Stalin knew he did *not* have to be afraid of the American nuclear threat has no serious basis in fact. All solid evidence points to the opposite conclusion. See Jaroslav K. Golovanov, *Korolev: Fakty I Mify* (Moscow, "Nauka" 1994), pp. 396–398.

20. The 1946 "spy scare" in the West, and its destructive effects, is well described in Gregg Herken, *The Winning Weapon: The Atomic Bomb in the Cold War, 1945–1959* (New York: Vintage, 1981), pp. 114–136. But see also Richard Rhodes, *Dark Sun: The Making of the Hydrogen Bomb* (New York: Simon and Schuster, 1995), pp. 94–132, 183–187.

21. Rossiskii Tsentr Khraneniia Dokumentov Noveishei Istorii (RTsKhIDNI), Fond 17, opis 125, delo 545, listy 65, 67.

22. Ibid., Fond 17, opis 125, delo 452, listy 1–5.

23. On a formal note from A. P. Aleksandrov recommending this, G. Malenkov inscribed: "I agree!" (Ibid., listy 5; Aleksandrov to Malenkov, April 10, 1946.) The role of Malenkov in the crisis episodes of the early Cold War must be reexamined. As an influential member of the top-level Party apparatus during and immediately after World War II, he had an extraordinary opportunity to supervise the governmental mechanism. Indeed, during this period, Malenkov accumulated more political power than any of his colleagues due to personal links with party officials at every level. Later, after the death of Zhdanov and the removal of the "Leningrad group" headed by A. Kuznetsov, Malenkov returned to authority as an able and respectable spokesman for the new generation of hard-liners. During the Korean War this group of militants made the question of nuclear weapons the central point of their discourse with the "traditionalists."

Moscow had been deeply involved in the decision-making with Pyongyang that brought war to the Korean Peninsula. However, new evidence has emerged which suggests that the abrupt turn in Stalin's policy in April 1950 was in contrast to his earlier cautious behavior in this area. (Kathryn Weathersby, "Soviet Aims in Korea and the Origins of the Korean War, 1945–1950: New Evidence from Russian Archives," Cold War International History Project, *Working Paper N 8*, pp. 23–24).

We also know that Stalin was not eager to test American resolve to defend Korea with atomic weapons. Apparently the Kremlin gave priority to the views of more-moderate political elements, individuals who saw disadvantages for the Soviet Union in pursuing extreme militancy within the "nuclear use zone." These included the party officials and the industrial administrators from the western part of the country who were involved in restoring the war-ravaged economy (and would later be counted by Khrushchev among his "thaw" supporters); the new generation of scientists and technology experts who did not hesitate to give negative assessments about Soviet capabilities to wage war on the sea and in the air without sophisticated offensive and defensive weapons; and the Soviet cultural and educational elite who, through some of its most influential spokesmen (like I. Erenburg, K. Siomonov, S. Kaftanov, A. Nesmejanov, A. Oparin, P. Kapitsa), maintained an officially approved "corridor" for communications with the pacifist groups in the West (*Bulletin of the Cold War International History Project* (Fall 1994), pp. 21, 60–61).

24. M. Suslov to A. Zhdanov, August 31, 1946; RTsKhIDNI, Fond 17, opis 125, delo 452, listy 35–37, 62–64.

25. Ibid., Fond 17, opis 125, delo 545, listy 26, 30.

26. AVP MID; Rossijskoj Federazii, Fond 6, opis 8, delo 101, papka 7, listy 66.

27. Ja. Lomakin to A. Vyshinsky, December 23, 1947; L. Iljichev to M. Suslov, February 9, 1948; B. Ponomarev to A. Zhdanov, January 7, 1948; V. Stepanov to M. Suslov, February 24, 1948; RTsKhIDNI, Fond 17, opis 128, delo 4408, listy 242–255, 256, 260, 261.

28. Bernstein to Litvin, February 9, 1946; ibid., Fond 17, opis 125, delo 452, listy 7.

29. Gerenc M. Szasz, "Peppermint and Alsos," *The Quarterly Journal of Military History*, 6 (Spring 1994), p. 46.

30. Ibid.

31. Special Committee at the Soviet government in Litvin, March 22, 1946; RTsKhIDNI, Fond 17, opis 125, delo 452, listy 12.

32. In a special report, prepared for the American Joint Chiefs of Staff in March 1946, the Joint Intelligence Committee concluded: "It is unlikely that the USSR will be able to develop an atomic bomb and produce a substantial number [of them] before 1949, but she may have done so by January 1952. In the future, Soviet developments in military technology will compare more favorably than in the past with United States and British developments but [they] will still lag behind them in 1952" (J.I.C. 342/2, March 27, 1946, "British Capabilities vs the USSR: Report by J.I.C.," OSS Archives, Folder 1562, Box 495, RG 226, National Archives).

33. I. I. Rabi, "Playing Down the Bomb: Blackett vs the Atom," *Atlantic Monthly* (April 1949).

34. David Holloway, "Lessons of the Arms Race," in L. Ackland and S. Mcguire, eds., *Assessing the Nuclear Age* (Chicago: University of Chicago, 1986), p. 141.

35. "USSR Policy and the Atomic Bomb, 12 September 1945," OSS Archives, Folder 2, Box 8.

36. Snyder, in Evans, Jacobson, and Putnam, eds., *Double-Edged Diplomacy*, p. 104.

37. George Orwell, *1984: A Novel* (New York: Signet, 1949), p. 151.

38. William O. McCagg, Jr., *Stalin Embattled, 1943–1948* (Detroit: Wayne State University Press, 1978), pp. 149–284. See also Werner G. Hahn, *Postwar Soviet Politics: The Fall of Zhdanov and the Defeat of Moderation, 1946–1953* (Ithaca, NY: Cornell University Press, 1982), pp. 44–93.

39. RTsKhIDNI, Fond 17, opis 125, delo 452, listy 85–114.

40. Ibid., listy 114.

41. "USSR Policy and the Atomic Bomb, 12 September 1945," OSS Archives, Folder 2, Box 8.

42. See Andrew and Oleg Gordievsky, *KGB: The Inside Story of Its Operations from Lenin to Gorbachev* (New York: Harper Collins, 1990). See also Allen Weinstein and Alexander Vassiliev, *The Haunted Wood: Soviet Espionage in America—The Stalin Era* (New York: Random House, 1999).

43. The reference is to Victor Kravchenko, an officer of the Red Army and an official of the Soviet Purchasing Commission in Washington, who asked for political asylum in the United States in April 1944. On this, see Thaddeus Wittlin, *Commissar: The Life and Death of Lavrenty Pablovich Beria* (New York: MacMillan, 1972), pp. 309–312.

44. Comprehensive and balanced political intelligence analyses were often replaced with short character sketches prepared by officials of the party Central Committee using stereotyped "ways and means" in describing leading American statesmen and their views on nuclear issues. Thus the Kremlin leadership's initial assessment of Bernard Baruch was probably informed at least in part by the sketch of him in "The Dictionary" circulated among the high party leaders. It described the veteran of American business and politics as an irreconcilable antagonist of the Soviet-American rapprochement and a Cold War-rior who had no desire to reduce the danger of nuclear war. This description simply repro-duced Moscow daily newspapers' standard way of thinking. (Dictionary of leading politicians of the USA prepared by Department of Foreign Policy of the CP, May 1947, RTsKhIDNI, Fond 17, opis 128, delo 229, listy 5.)

A year later Baruch was writing to David E. Lilienthal: "I do not think we are in for war because I do not think the Russians can have one. I think it is quite necessary that we should watch with great care what they are doing so that we will not exhaust ourselves but rather keep pace with them, all the time trying to find some method of trying to under-stand one another and help raise their standards of living and well being" (Baruch to David E. Lilienthal, April 19, 1948, David Lilienthal Papers, Box 129).

45. Eugene Varga to D. Shepilov, October 1, 1947, RTsKhIDNI, Fond 17, opis 125, delo 551, listy 99–100. See also Gavriel D. Ra'anan, *International Policy Formation in the USSR: Factional "Debates" during the Zhdanovschina* (Hamden, Conn.: Shoe String Press, 1983), pp. 62–74.

46. "Stenogramma zasedaniya Po obsuzhdeniyu v redaktsii zhurnala 'Voprosy Philso-phii,'" raboty V.S. Pankovoi, November 10, 1947; RTsKhIDNI, Fond 17, opis 125, delo 551, listy 161.

47. U.S. Intelligence sources received the following report on Harold Laski's two-hour conference with Stalin in 1946: "Stalin indicated that the Labor victory [in Great Britain] had been a great surprise to him. Mr. Laski then inquired what confidence he could have in his sources of information if he had been allowed to remain under misapprehensions in regard to this forthcoming event. Mr. Laski went on, as I remember it at second hand, to say that he could understand, of course, that the Embassies, tightly sealed up as they were, might fail in understanding the countries where they were situated, but he supposed Stalin would receive supplementary intelligence from the Communist parties abroad. Stalin re-plied only to the latter part of the question and said he was 'not interested' in foreign Communist parties—using a phrase conventional with him, which is, I understand, trans-lated in this way" (Allan Evans to Morrison, November 21, 1946, "Minor Intelligence," OSS Archives, Folder 7, Box 19).

48. On this, see Vojtech Mastny, *The Cold War and Soviet Insecurity: The Stalin Years* (New York: Oxford University Press, 1996), pp. 58–60, 74–79.

CHAPTER 3

Eisenhower and the Cold War: An Opportunity Missed?

Patrick M. Morgan

The end of the Cold War, with neither bang nor whimper, invites speculation that it could have ended earlier, specifically during one of those periods when the pursuit of détente came to naught.[1] This chapter focuses on such efforts in the Eisenhower Administration. There have long been suspicions that statesmen of that day missed a chance to either end the Cold War or avoid its worst excesses.[2] Events in this decade revive the issue.[3] After all, Mikhail Gorbachev's reforms had deep roots in the Khrushchev era. His attempts to link domestic reform with détente were foreshadowed by Soviet leaders in the 1950s; Gorbachev himself, personally and politically, was a child of "the thaw" after Stalin's death and its disappointing denouement. In the 1950s Moscow regularly proposed creation of a new European security system, something Gorbachev's policies finally made possible. Had the West responded to Khrushchev as it did to Gorbachev, might there have been no need for a Gorbachev?

Also intriguing, for purposes of this volume, is that those who claim an opportunity was lost often cite domestic factors in the United States as responsible, in a fashion tailor-made for a four-level-game analysis. Analysts have depicted Eisenhower as ready for a rapprochement but unable to overcome domestic resistance—lacking the necessary domestic ratification. Standing in the way? John Foster Dulles, right-wing Republicans, hawkish Democrats, the armed services, the military-industrial complex.... The same is frequently said of Khrushchev. He also wanted a détente but had to contend with unrepentant Stalinists, ideological dogmatists, and the military services, among others.

Another notable feature of the period is the prominence of phenomena treated in this volume as the second level in a four-level game. Eisenhower (and Khrushchev) had to cope with important allies with their own agendas. Bloc solidarity was a first order objective of theirs, but consensus was difficult to obtain, especially in treating with the enemy.

The picture that results is ideal for a four-level approach: Two leaders groped for agreements but could not simultaneously assemble the necessary allied and domestic support to exploit the occasional windows of opportunity available. Each maneuvered to enlarge the other's win-set not just to secure a more favorable outcome but to make it easier to resolve sticky ratification problems at home.[4]

The alternative view of the "lost" opportunity is that Eisenhower and Khrushchev themselves were responsible. The failure lay not in the dynamics of the multiple games they played but in the narrow confines of their thinking. They lacked the inclinations, the vision, and the daring needed. The Cold War remained because they remained Cold Warriors.

This chapter evaluates these competing explanations. For reasons of space only the American half of the relationship is examined. The questions posed are: (1) Did Eisenhower seriously desire agreements for a major improvement in East-West relations? (2) If he did, was his failure to achieve them due to insufficiently overlapping win-sets between the United States and the Soviet Union, or between the United States and its allies, or because of the narrow win-sets he faced at home?

AN OUTLINE OF THE OPPORTUNITY

If an opportunity to end or mitigate the Cold War existed in the 1950s, the following points about it apply. First, the Cold War was preeminently about the division of Germany and security in Europe, especially in the 1950s. Events and issues elsewhere were of secondary importance. Therefore, any opportunity to end it had to be concerned with the future of Germany, European security, and U.S.-Soviet relations in Europe. Second, the Cold War was profoundly political/ideological in nature, not inherent in the logic of the international system or the nuclear age or the result of broad misperceptions and communication gaps. If it was inherent, chances of ending or easing it would have been minimal. If misperceptions and poor communication were to blame, then the issues involved were not so serious, which seems silly given the enormous sustained efforts and risks involved.

Third, the opportunity must have been driven by an ample fear of war—what else might have overridden such a profound political conflict? Finally, the opportunity had to consist of a chance at a significant political rapprochement and not just a marginal easing of tensions. There were always two main ways to end the Cold War peacefully. The two sides could have practiced peaceful coexistence and over a lengthy period of increasing contacts seen the worst features of the Cold War eliminated. Or, one side could have quit and embraced the central values of the other, presumably due to exhaustion, revolution, or a legitimacy crisis. As things turned out, the second option prevailed.

What does this tell us about the "opportunity" in the Eisenhower Administration? First, what most critics have meant by the "lost opportunity" was option one, missed chances to improve communication, ease conflict and the arms race, and initiate a slow evolution of the dispute to a less threatening level. Second, although this is not how the Cold War ended, it might have. Perhaps in the 1950s significant steps could have initiated its gradual erosion, so that it didn't become so solidly entrenched and institutionalized. Third, only the first option fits a four-level-game framework—the collapse and termination of the opponent was hardly likely to have fallen within overlapping win-sets! Thus any "opportunity" that existed in the Eisenhower era must have consisted either of the chance for a rapprochement (option one), or of leaders dedicated to a rapprochement as a first step toward the collapse of the other side. Key leaders on both sides had to be strongly interested in a rapprochement, which meant they had to believe that bringing about the collapse of the other side in the near future was unrealistic.

Failure to achieve this rapprochement is what the Russians and various Western critics at the time (George Kennan, for instance) blamed on the Eisenhower administration.

THE OPENING

If there really was an opportunity, it started with Stalin's death on March 5, 1953. The new collective leadership was clearly more amenable to Western overtures or vulnerable to Western pressures than Stalin had been. Its initial decisions and rhetoric were relatively conciliatory domestically and in foreign policy. Georgi Malenkov, the new premier, announced a new emphasis on improving citizen welfare, shifting resources away from the military and heavy industry sectors. The secret police empire was pruned, and there was a deliberate erosion of Stalin's reputation and partial repudiation of his policies. Repression was relaxed. In foreign policy, Malenkov raised eyebrows by asserting that a nuclear war would mean catastrophe and not, as Stalin had insisted, the ultimate victory of socialism. The government called for peaceful coexistence via a relaxation of tensions, increased trade, and easing the arms race. Controls on Eastern Europe were reduced, the Korean War was allowed to end, the treaty ending Austria's occupation was signed, and the Soviets cooperated at the Geneva Conference on Indochina.

The second phase of the "opportunity" arose under very different circumstances, in the wake of Sputnik in 1957. (The prior two years had been a difficult time in East-West relations with the Suez Crisis, the Hungarian Revolution, and their aftereffects.) The West now confronted a Soviet leader with a firm political base. Sputnik had augmented Moscow's stature, and Khrushchev was eager to convert this into agreements with the West. Appealing to the West were his domestic reforms including more de-Stalinization, major cuts in military spending and the armed forces, and raised living standards. In foreign policy, he moved to slow or halt nuclear testing, resolve the problem of Berlin, and establish new European security arrangements. This phase continued to the collapse of the Paris Summit in 1960.

Both phases of the "opportunity" produced nothing. There was no rapprochement, no agreement on Germany or Berlin, no ban on nuclear testing, no curbing of the nuclear arsenals. And there were nasty consequences. No progress on Germany led ultimately to the Berlin Crisis in 1961 and the Berlin Wall. Stalemate on European security arrangements and in East-West relations meant that military forces in Europe, hurriedly enlarged as a result of the Korean War, were maintained indefinitely on an unprecedented peacetime scale. Nuclear arsenals reached staggering levels by the early 1960s and were married to prompt delivery systems ideal for surprise attack. Ahead lay deplorable developments: the Cuban Missile Crisis, the Vietnam and Afghanistan Wars, periodic confrontations in the Middle East, rampant competition elsewhere.

WAS EISENHOWER REALLY INTERESTED?

The following picture of the president and his administration emerges from the wealth of available sources.[5] Eisenhower had vast experience in international affairs but was not deeply reflective about the subject. Not a serious student of either the Soviet Union or communism, he had become a staunch anticommunist prior to his election campaign and remained so. He strongly mistrusted the Soviets and thus was consistently skeptical about summits unless prospects for agreement, ascertained in advance, were good. Not as pessimistic as John Foster Dulles, he shared Dulles's grim view of the Soviet bloc.

He was accordingly very concerned about the threat posed by the USSR, while only partially and selectively inclined toward any rapprochement. He adopted policies that made meaningful agreements with the Russians unlikely, in keeping with the threat and his view that agreements were not likely, and his efforts to ease tensions were motivated mainly by propaganda concerns until well into his administration. He counted heavily on American nuclear superiority and authorized a huge expansion in the nuclear arsenal;[6] he presided over development of a strategy for an enormous preemptive strike on the communist bloc in the event of a war;[7] he encouraged or authorized vigorous intelligence efforts against the communist world; he continually promoted West German rearmament and participation in NATO. All of these clashed profoundly with Soviet preferences and made rapprochement hard to achieve. Thus it is wrong to think of Eisenhower at this time as strongly committed to relaxing the Cold War but hemmed in by other American leaders and officials who were not. He shared their perspectives and did much to help cement the Cold War in place.[8]

Only late in his presidency did this change. By that point Eisenhower had developed a sophisticated view of national security in the nuclear age. He assumed that a major East-West war would escalate to the nuclear level and become total in intensity, bringing mutual catastrophe. Hence it was very unlikely, and the best way to keep it unlikely was to avoid illusions about limited wars and shape U.S. and NATO forces and war planning accordingly.[9] The prospect of mutual catastrophe made nuclear "superiority" meaningless; sufficiency would do. The real problem, he thought, was a strategic surprise attack and the fear of it, a primary concern to him even in his first term.[10] He eventually emphasized the need to halt vertical nuclear proliferation and displayed much anxiety about that.

The result was an evolving posture on disarmament and arms control. The administration initially embraced Truman's stance that serious disarmament could occur only with an overall resolution of political conflicts and that extensive verification would be required. Steps toward disarmament also had to be linked—no nuclear test ban without an end to production of nuclear weapons, no deep cuts in or elimination of nuclear weapons without conventional force cuts.

Over time, Eisenhower slowly shifted toward separating disarmament from arms control, toward detaching arms control from a general political settlement, making it valuable on its own, and toward detaching a test ban from other arms control measures. In the end he was willing to accept a test ban that was less than completely verifiable.[11] This reflected his unhappiness about prospects for the future because he viewed the ongoing nuclear arms buildup as increasingly dangerous. He felt that responsible statesmen should be able to provide people with hope and a less dangerous environment. In this regard he became, in time, more dovish than most of his administration, much of his party, and much of the country.

THE FIRST PHASE, 1953–1955

Eisenhower noted that Washington had no contingency plans for Stalin's death (in 1953) and no ideas on how to exploit it. His own reaction was to look for a way to steer the East-West relationship in a new direction.

One possibility was a summit conference, an idea strongly pressed by Winston Churchill (see later). This met with little approval in Washington. Eisenhower, Dulles, and others thought the timing bad, the prospects for success low. It was not clear that Soviet thinking on major issues had changed. And a summit was bound to raise serious difficulties with the McCarthyites, who would have compared it with Yalta.[12] When the first one was finally held in 1955, the administration had to assure Congressional leaders in advance that no binding executive agreements would be signed.[13]

Eisenhower turned, instead, to using a major speech to change the atmosphere, build public support for new initiatives, and make the United States look good. The initial goal was to provide a candid picture of the horrors of nuclear war and call for steps to ease the arms race. The result was a startling, well-received speech to the American Society of Newspaper Editors on April 16. It labeled military spending as the theft of resources from education, health care, housing, and welfare. The Russians displayed it as front page news.[14] However, it also listed steps Moscow had to take for improved relations: release of World War II POWs; settling the Austrian situation; armistice arrangements in Korea, Indochina, and Malaya; independence for Eastern Europe; moves toward unification of Germany. This was a bow to Dulles, who had opposed the speech out of fear that it would send the wrong message both to Moscow and the allies, and who insisted on these items being included.[15]

What happened was that nothing happened. One reason was that the Administration mounted the speech as a propaganda effort to offset Soviet détente proposals, reflecting the Eisenhower-Dulles view that a fundamental accommodation was impossible with the Kremlin.[16] In addition, there was as yet no obvious issue that lent itself to negotiation, no focal point around which to construct an agreement. Without a tentative agreement and overlapping East and West win-sets, there was no real basis for negotiations to shape a deal in Washington and the United States.

Was there a domestic constituency for détente? Putting one together would have been hard work. The worst problem was the Republican Old Guard, frantic about subversion at home and appeasement abroad. The Administration spent much energy beating back the Bricker Amendment and other right wing fears of presidential sellouts of U.S. interests. The Administration was also busy fending off McCarthyism. These elements could not just be dismissed, because the Administration needed broad support for large defense spending, keeping U.S. forces abroad, and the military assistance program, all of which many Republicans found repugnant. Being too far out front in pursuing agreements with the Soviets might have undermined efforts on these other matters.

Nevertheless, the speech was well received. There was evident public concern about the nuclear arms race. Nuclear testing was becoming a salient matter (Stevenson would try to exploit it in his 1956 campaign) as was the larger "peace" issue. There was also, as critics noted, Eisenhower's recent electoral mandate, his immense public stature, his credentials on security matters. He had a strong base on which to build support for reaching out to Moscow. On balance, it seems that various agreements would have commanded the necessary support.

But another political game Eisenhower had to play lay inside the administration. Any détente initiative had to get around the Secretary of State. His detractors then and since have called attention to his, readily admitted, unwillingness to seek accommodation, blaming him for the minimal U.S. responses to Soviet initiatives and for the failure to follow up vigorously on Eisenhower's speech. This appears to be inaccurate on two counts. Eisenhower was not particularly dovish or conciliatory about the Cold War at that point, and Dulles was not always rigid.

Dulles was not averse to negotiations with Moscow. What he wanted was negotiations from strength.[17] As he saw it, negotiations could come about through Western overtures or pressure. Dulles preferred pressure. The Soviet Union and other communist regimes were intrinsically illegitimate and immoral, and therefore fragile. They were also fundamentally, permanently hostile on ideological grounds.[18] Therefore, confrontation and pressure, based on superior Western strength and unity, made the most sense. Reaching for accommodation did not. First, it was futile; Soviet leaders could not readily accept a true accommodation. Second, it was ill advised; accommodation detracted from the only thing that really worked, which was pressure. When the Soviets were accommodating, it was a sign that pressure was working, not a reason to abandon it.[19] Third, it was dangerous. Steps toward accommodation would only strengthen elements in the United States or the allies reluctant to bear the burdens of containment: the military spending, aid programs, and other sacrifices. Fourth, it was a tactical windfall for the enemy because summits and disarmament conferences made fine platforms for communist propaganda and enhancing the Kremlin's stature.[20]

Dulles clearly worried about the durability and staying power of the West. Isolationist elements lurked in American politics, and socialist/communist elements in Western Europe were well established. Frictions among the allies seemed ample in the defeat of EDC, the Suez Crisis, and the rise of deGaulle. Dulles lacked the notion that accommodation could be deadly to the communist world. He felt that those regimes could exploit a relaxation of tensions in the West while effectively squelching its unwanted effects at home.

He had allies. Successive Secretaries of Defense and the Joint Chiefs were not in favor of reaching out to Moscow. The Atomic Energy Agency was unsympathetic. While Soviet specialists at the State Department supported a search for accommodation, other top officials there (Robert Murphy, for example) were in line with Dulles. Officials inclined toward conciliation included Harold Stassen (when he was Special Assistant on Disarmament) and Nelson Rockefeller (Special Assistant on Cold War Strategy), but Dulles worked assiduously to prevent them (or anyone else) from gaining a major role in foreign policy by having all access to the president on foreign policy go through him.[21]

The Eisenhower-Dulles relationship on this issue was not a struggle, as Dulles was not always an obstacle.[22] In a confidential memo on September 6, 1953, Dulles urged a "spectacular effort to relax world tensions" via a pullback of American and Soviet forces in Europe and agreements to reduce conventional and nuclear weapons. He wanted to take advantage of the United States' military superiority and its strong political position while playing to Moscow's desire to reduce arms spending. Eisenhower approved in principle but saw no way to implement it without evoking grave doubts about the credibility of American commitments.[23] Once West Germany entered NATO, ending a major threat to Western cohesion, Dulles displayed flexibility again,[24] such as on a test ban—he became a strong proponent of one later on. From 1956 on, Dulles supported various arms control measures and in his last year displayed flexibility on Berlin.[25] He sometimes agreed with Eisenhower that political considerations (appeasing allies or domestic opinion) and moral considerations (showing leadership in blunting the arms race) made pursuit of arms control appropriate.

The consistent opponents of these measures were in the Defense Department, the Joint Chiefs, and the Atomic Energy Agency.[26] Eisenhower's style of management magnified the impact of their views. The extensive delegation of responsibility Eisenhower practiced often also meant a reluctance to challenge subordinates' views and decisions as part of garnering their loyalty and best efforts. This was particularly true early in his administration—Eisenhower could hardly build a team if he readily dismissed the members' views and concerns. Later, he would grow restless with running things this way,[27] but he was seldom ready to simply take charge of an issue, impose his view of it, and disregard opposition. Even late in his second term, his style inhibited a more vigorous and compelling pursuit of his desire for restraint in national security matters,[28] contributing to his lack of success in building support for his view on strategic issues such as the missile gap.[29]

In terms of a four-level game, such a style leaves the leader with too little leverage on the win-sets of key subordinates and hands them too much leverage over his own. On many aspects of relations with Moscow, Eisenhower was often adjusting to the rest of the administration rather than having it adjust to him, which made success in negotiations quite unlikely.

The other relevant element in his leadership style was avoidance of a hierarchical approach to dealing with disagreements. Emmet John Hughes offers a composite of Eisenhower comments on leadership:

Now, look, I happen to *know* a little about leadership. I've had to work with a lot of nations, for that matter at odds with each other. And I tell you this: you do not *lead* by hitting people over the head. Any damn fool can do that, but it's usually called "assault"—not "leadership." . . . I'll tell you what leadership is. It's *persuasion*—and *conciliation*—and *education*—and *patience*. It's long, slow, tough work. That's the only kind of leadership I know—or believe in—or will practice.[30]

That approach can be ideal because it patiently shapes others' win-sets in ways likely to have durable results. It was how Eisenhower succeeded in slowly, patiently, winning acceptance of American internationalism among Republicans. But it is not good for responding to windows of opportunity because, with too much deference to others' views, it takes too long.

This helps sort out the paradox in the literature concerning Eisenhower's responsibility. While in office he was charged with having good intentions on improving East-West relations but little control over foreign policy. But revisionists later emphasized that his indirect approach to leadership hid his considerable involvement in foreign and defense policy, implying that if there was little improvement in East-West relations, it was really Eisenhower's fault.[31] In fact the Eisenhower style blended his involvement with deferring to subordinates even if he objected to the overall direction of policy that resulted. That was part of the price of leading in an indirect manner.

Then there was the political game with key European allies. Dulles and Eisenhower were immersed in alliance politics.[32] The Administration's objectives in Europe were to promote integration so that the allies' rising economic and military capabilities and political cohesion could be brought to bear in the Cold War, which in turn required maintaining European confidence in the American commitment to Europe. The objectives remained even when the derailing of the European Defense Community in August 1954 left U.S. policy in tatters.

The Administration had to carefully ascertain European views on, and then in, any talks with the Russians, and also worry about the potential impact any deal—or just showing interest in a deal—might have on American credibility. Enhancing allied capabilities was frequently interpreted in Washington as avoiding steps that would weaken a friendly government and, particularly for Eisenhower, showing sympathy for the allies' interest in either developing nuclear weapons or having them made available by the United States in the event of a war. (Thousands were stored in Europe for this purpose.) The administration worked to remove restrictions in the Atomic Energy Act on sharing nuclear information with the British, and the United States secretly aided aspects of the French nuclear weapons program.

The emphasis on healthy allies reflected Eisenhower's profound concern about the long-term effects of the Cold War. He opposed an indefinite American military presence in Europe, fearing adverse effects on the American economy and public opinion. He worried about the economic and political effects of a huge defense budget, and was always looking for Europeans to do more so that the United States could do less. Allies were also vital for the Massive Retaliation strategy, providing the overseas bases that put American bombers in reach of the Soviet bloc.[33]

Promoting European integration was American policy of long standing and had interested Eisenhower long before his election. (Dulles agreed completely.[34]) It was to make Europe strong not only through economies of scale and heightened efficiencies but by dislodging old enmities.

But if European integration and Western unity were vital then conciliatory moves by Moscow were potentially quite dangerous.[35] They might tempt allies into concessions and separate deals, unraveling unity. And American interest in negotiations could readily lead allies to expect an American withdrawal and thus to rush to make the best deal with Moscow. What was feared, in other words, was both the domino effect and Finlandization. Dulles also worried that Western accommodation might tempt the Soviet Bloc into war by miscalculation.[36]

A complication here was that Western unity was also needed for healing Europe itself, for absorbing Germany within a larger community. Hence to the extent that any Russian government had to object to Western unity, German rearmament, and thus to German reunification, American and Soviet win-sets could not overlap.

Because the allies were important, if they pressed for negotiations with the Soviets they could not readily or indefinitely be put off, whereas if they were unenthusiastic or opposed, negotiations could not easily be pursued. In 1953 the British (except for Churchill) were opposed to major conciliatory gestures, the French ambivalent, the Germans opposed—fearing a deal at Germany's expense. [37] But gradually these positions shifted, in part due to Russian reforms and efforts to improve the atmosphere. Adenauer remained consistently opposed to deals with the Russians, fearing a permanent freeze of the status quo in Central Europe. He insisted that no major arms control arrangement be undertaken without a clear link to progress on reunification.[38] And because the integration of West Germany into the West was of overriding importance, Adenauer had unusual leverage in Washington.

The strongest sentiments for détente came from Churchill.[39] After Stalin's death he began proposing a summit in cables and letters to Washington, and he continued this until just before retiring in April 1955.[40] He was particularly interested in going to Moscow himself to get a summit process underway.[41]

He had in mind rearranging Europe's security system. (Eden and Macmillan were later to feel the same way.) German unification would take place within a web of four-power guarantees, like the Locarno system of the late 1920s, that would circumscribe German military power and guarantee Russian security.

As noted earlier, the summit idea met with little approval in Washington. Churchill was seen as an old, and unhealthy, lion looking for one last roar as a global power broker. His own cabinet agreed, and they saw no benefit in pressing a summit on an unenthusiastic Washington. They wanted Churchill to retire (his energy was flagging, his mental acuity suspect)—something they thought, correctly, he would put off if a summit was possible. In addition, a Churchill trip to Moscow would have made Adenauer uneasy, and Eisenhower noted that it would look like Britain was trying to be an intermediary, not a staunch ally. Putting off Churchill became easy when he suffered a stroke. In a U.S.-UK-France Foreign Ministers meeting in July, the British and French suggested a careful probe of Russian intentions. Bidault informed Dulles and Lord Salisbury (sitting in for Eden) that negotiating with the Russians on Germany was a prerequisite for French ratification of EDC. (The idea that there was an alternative to German rearmament had to be squelched by unsuccessful negotiations!) Adenauer cabled that just the prospect of such negotiations would help him fend off the Social Democrats in the September elections. Dulles regarded Adenauer's political well-being as fundamentally important so he acquiesced and agreed to a big four Foreign Ministers meeting in the fall.

The meeting became, it turned out, the Berlin Foreign Ministers Conference in January 1954 on the future of Germany and Berlin. It was a spectacular failure. Russian determination to have some control over a unified German government and to prevent it from choosing to join NATO was unyielding. The Eden plan for multistage reunification capped off by a demilitarized zone either within Germany or to the east of it was rejected by Molotov.

Does this demonstrate that there was no way for Eisenhower to get any agreement past the ratification gauntlet of allies, administration, and the nation, and that this is why his speech had so little impact? On the first half of the question, ratification at home and in the alliance would certainly have been difficult but not impossible. On the second half of the question, the record suggests that securing ratification was not the main problem. Eisenhower may not have been a rabid Cold Warrior, but he was deeply suspicious of the Soviet leadership. He was not counting on a political settlement with Moscow as the basis of American and European security because one did not seem possible. That is why he stressed a "long haul" approach to national defense, preparing for a conflict of up to fifty years. He wanted to restrain the East-West rivalry because of its burdens and risks. But he saw Western superiority in nuclear weapons at the time as critical for offsetting Soviet bloc conventional capabilities. This put severe limits on any accommodation with the Russians, who consistently pressed for the abolition of nuclear weapons and foreign bases. Agreements that would threaten American nuclear superiority, erode the West's defense spending, or risk alliance solidarity on Germany were unacceptable.

In short, American responses to the death of Stalin do not offer a clear case of a leader eager to reach an agreement constrained by the high likelihood of failed ratification, of a dovish president bowing to political realities in Europe and at home. The president's worldview seriously limited his own win-set, and this was reinforced by most of his officials. Hence, "in 1954 the administration was not really interested in accommodation with the Soviets."[42]

However, the President had also tried another tack to take the edge off the Cold War. After his inauguration, Eisenhower had expressed strong interest in trying to turn attention to the peaceful uses of nuclear energy. Setting speech writers to work, he launched what became an eight-month search for the right formula. Cleared with allies at a summit (in December 1953), with Churchill adding last-minute corrections, Eisenhower's speech at the UN proposed an international agency for development of peaceful nuclear energy, using fissionable materials donated by the superpowers (the Atoms for Peace proposal).

The plan was enthusiastically received, then went nowhere for several years. The Russians refused to accept it (though not flatly rejecting it either), arguing that because it would not halt the production of nuclear weapons, it was a diversion from the real issue. This was both correct and self-serving. Atoms for Peace would have made no dent in American nuclear superiority; indeed, it might have constrained the fissile material available for the Soviet nuclear weapons program. The Russians had few operational nuclear weapons; the United States was approaching 1700 or more, and the President had approved production at a rate of one per day (with more increases to come). (See Table 3.1).

The Russian objections were not lifted until after Moscow's production capacity had increased considerably.

Once again, this looks like an insufficient overlap in leadership win-sets. Eisenhower had somehow managed to get the AEC's Lewis Strauss to back Atoms for Peace so domestic ratification was virtually assured. (I suspect Strauss agreed in order to have a freer hand in generating the numbers in Table 3.1.) But nothing could be done until the Russians were ready.

Still another track emerged in 1955 when pressure mounted for a summit. The British became steadily more interested once Churchill retired; eventually pressure from public opinion and the Labor Party made a summit a political necessity for the government. Eden's successful management of the Geneva Conference on Indochina, and his pulling the West together on West German rearmament and NATO membership, gave him more leverage. When he pleaded election necessities, Eisenhower was sympathetic.

The French also supported a summit. Rejection of EDC demonstrated how uneasy France was about German rearmament. But Washington and London were moving to make it happen anyway. The only chance to forestall this seemed to be a deal on German unification, and that would require a summit.

The major issue was Germany. Whether a deal was possible is uncertain but doubtful. Moscow was eager to prevent West German rearmament, dangling the prospect of unification but only if Germany would be neutral and unarmed. Not irrelevant was the fact that for Adenauer unification was not his foremost foreign

Table 3.1
U.S. Nuclear Weapons Stockpile[43]

Year	Number of Weapons
1945	2
1946	9
1947	13
1948	50
1949	250
1950	450
1951	650
1952	1000
1953	1350
1954	1750
1955	2250
1956	3550
1957	5450
1958	7100
1959	12,000
1960	18,500
1961	23,000

policy objective. His priority was partnership with the West, especially because he saw no possibility of unification on acceptable terms.

Dulles agreed. He was instrumental in having the President insist on no summit without a clear sign of Soviet good intentions, such as an Austrian peace treaty. Then when the Soviets signed that treaty, Dulles suspected that it was a ploy to lure Germany into neutrality in exchange for unification and move U.S. forces out of Germany (maybe out of Europe). Dulles also thought disarmament would go nowhere unless the German problem was resolved. Even the Open Skies proposal was not to his liking—it would only raise false hopes. All this in spite of the fact that the Russians had now implemented many of the prerequisites set down in Eisenhower's "chance for peace" speech: a truce in Korea, a settlement in Indochina, the Austrian peace treaty, the release of POWs from World War II.

Also striking was U.S. dismissal of a sharp shift in the Soviet position on arms control. On May 10, 1955, at a session of the UN Subcommittee on Disarmament, the Soviets suddenly announced that they would accept inspection posts on their territory plus an exchange of information on military establishments and budgets for an agreement to cut conventional forces, end nuclear testing and weapons pro-

duction, and close foreign military bases. The West was taken aback at this acceptance of the bulk of its arms control position. An answer was deferred until after
the impending summit, and then it was not serious. In September the United
States "suspended" its previous disarmament positions because of doubts that
ground inspection could be effective. Clearly the United States was not really
ready in 1955 to negotiate a major deal on disarmament.[44] The security establishment was basically wedded to the view later expressed by the Joint Chiefs: "There
is less risk to the security of the United States in the continuation of current armament trends than in entering into an international arms limitation agreement."[45]

The summit was such a modest success as to be a failure. Opening in Geneva on
July 18, 1955, it was notable only for its civilized discussion of differences (the
"Spirit of Geneva") and the Eisenhower "Open Skies" proposal for aerial inspection to forestall surprise attack plans. Discussions about Germany reached an immediate impasse. The West sought free elections leading to unification, and then a
German choice on neutrality, NATO, or the Warsaw Pact, with Soviet security
concerns handled by Western guarantees, limits on German forces, and a demilitarized zone. Then new European security arrangements could be taken up. The Russian view reversed the priorities: deal with general European security
first—agreements on peaceful settlement of disputes, an end to military blocs, the
withdrawal of foreign forces—and then settle the German question. At the
follow-up Foreign Ministers meeting in October-November, the tone was very
contentious. Molotov pressed all the standard Soviet positions, and there was no
progress. Clearly partition was acceptable to Moscow as long as West Germany was
reconciled to it.

Khrushchev rejected the Open Skies proposal almost at once (in 1956 the Russians would reject even a demonstration or test of Open Skies) as a transparent attempt to facilitate espionage. Khrushchev had several concerns. Given the Soviet
advantage in secrecy, it was hard to see what the West could trade to compensate
Moscow for sacrificing it. Also, Soviet military capabilities were weaker than the
West suspected and there was no profit, from Khrushchev's perspective, in having
this corrected.[46] The "bomber gap" and the "missile gap" concerns in the West enhanced Soviet deterrence and political leverage. Meanwhile, to offset Soviet inferiority in intercontinental bombers Khrushchev was pushing the rapid
development of ballistic missiles. That the West would now be better able to moni-
tor Soviet progress and energetically move to nullify it would have been very unacceptable. However, the Administration never expected him to accept the
proposal. Its primary purpose was public relations, including diverting attention
from the Soviet concessions on arms control offered in May. This was why it was
put forward in such a public fashion with no advance notice, not a realistic approach to getting an agreement.[47]

What went wrong? At home, Open Skies was popular in broad terms, except
with the Republican Old Guard. It is hard to believe that it could not have been
sold to Congress and the nation—breaching Soviet secrecy was clearly to the
American advantage. However, inside the government, Dulles was not happy

about the summit. Hopes would be raised, then dashed, which could hardly help the West. (When Soviet Premier Bulganin inquired about visiting the United States, Eisenhower's impulse was to agree, but Dulles objected, so the response was that the United States would study the idea.) He had little sympathy for Open Skies. The services and the CIA also objected—what was about to become a huge intelligence breakthrough would be negated. Another aspect of the proposal, exchanging "complete blueprints" of each military establishment, was uncomfortable to many officers. (This became clear late in the decade when the services looked at what a detailed inspection regime would involve.) Perhaps Eisenhower prepared the proposal in secret not only to surprise the Russians but to forestall opposition within the bureaucracy.

Apart from Adenauer, the allies were not averse to following up on the "Spirit of Geneva," and failure to move toward a rapprochement cannot be blamed on them. For the rest of the Cold War, European opinion was more comfortable than the United States with what Dulles would have termed "appeasement." Quite apart from the left's views on peace, nuclear weapons, and the Soviet bloc, there was general European unhappiness with being locked into a huge struggle over which Europe had little influence.

On balance, then, the Open Skies proposal was one for which top-level U.S. and Soviet win-sets did not sufficiently overlap. Failure can be traced to this rather than to the other levels in our model.

THE SECOND PHASE, 1958–1960

Little progress was made from the Geneva summit to Sputnik, but developments at the time had a bearing on what was to come, and these should be briefly summarized.[48] Inside the Administration there was an ongoing struggle over U-2 flights, nuclear testing, and defense spending. Within the country and abroad there was exploration of the possibilities of a nuclear test ban and other arms control steps. There were also rising complaints, greatly augmented after Sputnik, about administration neglect of the nation's security.

The U-2 flights began in the spring of 1956. Eisenhower repeatedly expressed concern about their provocative nature and the effect losing a plane could have. He consistently resisted having as many flights as the services and intelligence community wished. He also personally reviewed the plans for flights, altering routes and making other changes to meet his concerns.

Trying for a nuclear test ban had a long history in the Administration. In 1954 and 1955 the matter had been raised repeatedly, usually in proposed disarmament postures put forward by Harold Stassen.[49] Eisenhower was sympathetic, and consistently unhappy with the opposition from the AEC, DOD, and the Joint Chiefs. Public pressure for a test ban rose in 1956. But inside the government the pressure was to have far more tests. Demand for a ban eased for a time when it became evident that tests would be needed to develop ICBMs and because Bulganin wrote to Eisenhower proposing a test ban during the 1956 election campaign (in effect, supporting Stevenson, a kiss of death because it represented blatant interference in domestic politics). Still, Eisenhower was disappointed, and at times visibly angry, over resistance to a test ban, and Dulles was his most reliable supporter in all this.

A Russian test series early in 1957 was followed by a U.S series. At the London disarmament talks, Stassen presented the standard U.S. position—a test ban in exchange for a verifiable end to nuclear weapons production, plus other progress on disarmament. The Russians shifted to offering an immediate unconditional test ban or at least a test moratorium. They also accepted verification via monitoring posts, with backup inspections when monitoring turned up results of concern. But the U.S. got cold feet; Stassen was allowed to offer a moratorium on testing only with a nuclear weapons production cutoff (with verification). This was a direct result of AEC-DOD pressure for more tests, backed by the support of Senator Henry Jackson.[50] Both the verification and the fact that a cutoff would leave the Soviet Union with a much smaller arsenal than the U.S. made the proposal a nonstarter. The Russians denounced the whole business as indicating that the U.S. was not serious and moved to boycott the UN Disarmament Subcommittee.

Over the next several months debate in the Administration was strenuous. Stassen wanted to move toward a ban, most others did not. In June Eisenhower argued strongly against further tests as unnecessary, as a problem because of radioactive fallout, and as politically costly. Strauss, Edward Teller, Ernest Lawrence, and others from the AEC and the weapons labs strenuously objected.

Later in the year the debate resumed. The AEC and the DOD proposed far more tests than Eisenhower thought necessary—to find the ultimate h-bomb carrying capacity of a B-52, to develop a clean hydrogen bomb (eventually the neutron bomb), to find uses for peaceful nuclear explosions, to develop an ABM system. (At one point a Caribbean test off the Florida coast was proposed!) Eisenhower resisted, and toyed with adopting a moratorium. He had to take into account the British and French, who publicly supported a test ban but were privately eager to continue testing for their nuclear weapons programs.

In 1958, in the wake of Sputnik, the Administration had to respond to rising pressures for agreements with the Russians, particularly on nuclear testing. Eisenhower was ready to negotiate, and Dulles agreed, perhaps due to what they had learned about the immensity of the U.S. arsenal, SAC war plans, and the bottomless appetite of the services and AEC for more nuclear weapons.[51] They had to move forward over strenuous objections from the national security complex. They worked out a letter to Khrushchev that separated a test ban from a ban on nuclear weapons production and asked for a conference of scientific experts on the possibilities of verifying a test ban.

The talks began in early July and by late August had produced agreement that a control system was technically feasible: 160–170 seismic posts, plus sea and air monitoring, would detect tests down to five kilotons. Eisenhower ordered preparations for negotiations on a test ban and installed a test moratorium from October 31 to January 1 even though "some of my most trusted advisers . . . were against the suspension."[52]

Despite this opposition, and some from Britain and France, Eisenhower agreed to start the talks by October 31, compromising with the critics only in allowing many tests prior to that date. When Lewis Strauss had a frank discussion with Eisenhower:

Perhaps for the first time, Strauss saw the depth of Eisenhower's moral commitment to a nuclear test ban. Strauss conceded that the President's course was correct if the West could live in peace with communism. In contrast, Strauss regarded communism as he did sin—there could be no compromise with it. . . . As he left Eisenhower, Strauss realized that their ethical discussion had brought him to the brink of a 'permanent fundamental disagreement' with the President."[53]

In any event, the talks soon deadlocked over how the inspection regime was to operate (the Russians wanting a veto over on-site inspection teams), while test ban opponents vigorously developed evidence as to how tests might be hidden successfully from the proposed verification.[54] As a result, in early January 1959 the United States had to tell the Russians it wanted a more elaborate inspection system—generating more deadlock.

Steven Ambrose captures the struggle inside the administration:

Four days later, on January 16, McCone came to the President with a request that the AEC be allowed to build a new reactor, in order to produce more bombs, as required by the DOD. Eisenhower exploded that there were no "requirements" until he had approved them, and stated that he could see no point to building bombs at a faster rate than the current pace of nearly two per day. He said the Defense people were getting "themselves into an incredible position—of having enough to destroy every conceivable target all over the world, plus a threefold reserve." He said "the patterns of target destruction are fantastic." Just a few years ago, he said he had thought Defense agreed that there were only seventy targets inside Russia that they needed to hit in order to destroy the Soviet system, but now Defense came to him and said there were thousands of targets that had to be hit. So many ground bursts, Eisenhower said, would be certain to destroy the United States too from radioactivity. But then, as he almost always did, he reluctantly gave way to the AEC and DOD demands, and with a sigh "said he supposed that we have to go ahead with the construction of the reactor."[55]

Again, we encounter Eisenhower's leadership style. He found the arms race ugly but acquiesced, under strong pressure, in steps that exacerbated it.[56] This had lamentable consequences in terms of his own objectives.[57] As one analyst puts it, "Eisenhower clearly wanted to respond to growing international demands [in June 1957] for a test ban, but his own style of governing frustrated his best intentions."[58] Gradually, he began to try to escape the inconsistency. He moved away from the formal machinery of the National Security Council and the Cabinet in favor of informal consultations with particular officials. He had also appointed a science adviser, thereby getting information that conflicted with AEC and DOD assessments.[59] He continued to resist requests for more U-2 flights and more defense spending.

This was extremely difficult because of the "missile gap" and the immense gains Democrats were reaping from charges that the administration was not doing enough on defense. The pressure was so severe that Dulles had advised Eisenhower, in November 1957, to inform the nation in some (presumably oblique) way about the U-2 intelligence windfall.[60] In addition, in November 1958 Khrushchev had created a Berlin "crisis" via setting a deadline for the West to either leave the city or deal with the GDR. Eisenhower's low key response provoked complaints about too little being done.[61]

By spring, Eisenhower was hinting that he might consider a summit, with Berlin as the main topic, if a Foreign Ministers meeting showed that agreements could be reached. Convinced that the Russians did not want war over Berlin, he understood, like the British, that the situation there was very disturbing to Moscow and something had to be done. When Khrushchev insisted that West Berlin be turned into a free city, Eisenhower expressed interest. Pressure for a summit on this came from Harold Macmillan, citing both his convictions and domestic pressures.[62]

Eisenhower was also pressing for a test ban, suggesting just an atmospheric ban if the verification problem for underground tests could not be settled. In response, Khrushchev objected to a partial ban but said the Soviet Union would accept a fixed quota of inspections. This was potentially an important concession, abandoning a Soviet veto over on-site inspections. Eisenhower continued the American testing moratorium.[63]

Eisenhower also proposed that Khrushchev visit the United States and on August 5 announced that this would take place. (There was predictable opposition from conservatives.) The intent on both sides was that this would be followed by an Eisenhower visit to the Soviet Union.

With the test ban talks stymied by U.S. insistence on much more elaborate verification, the AEC and DOD had pressed for more tests. Eisenhower resisted and on February 12 described the projected numbers of U.S. nuclear weapons as "astronomical."[64] As spring passed, the slow dance toward a summit continued, Eisenhower still insisting on prior progress at a Foreign Ministers meeting. In the summer the AEC and DOD again sought authorization for more tests, and Eisenhower angrily refused. (They wanted to cram in as many as possible before a test ban.) In resisting pressure for more defense spending, on everything from the B-70 bomber to fallout shelters, the president was virtually isolated.[65]

As 1960 arrived, Eisenhower was still determined to get a test ban as a first step toward some kind of disarmament. In February he indicated he would settle for less than a comprehensive test ban, to get around the impasse on underground test verification. Soon he was meeting with officials to promote talks to end production of fissionable materials.

In March the Russians proposed an end to such production, plus a moratorium on underground testing, plus a test ban with some on-site inspection. But the verification system would not have been able to detect low-yield tests, so the moratorium on those would have had to be taken on faith. The Soviet position was now that any quota on inspections would be based on questionable seismic events but with a number chosen in advance (they suggested three; the United States and Britain insisted on twenty[66]).

Opponents of a test ban, and many others, strongly opposed any agreement not fully verifiable, but Eisenhower announced, at an NSC meeting on March 24, that he would accept a two-year moratorium on underground tests with no verification. Rejecting opposition from the AEC and DOD, Eisenhower said it was in the vital interest of the nation to pursue agreement with the Russians and thus worthwhile to take a modest chance for peace.

In pressing for talks on arms control, he had the support of deGaulle, Macmillan, and some Democrats. In opposition were many Republicans, influential Democrats, the services, the weapons lab scientists, and the intelligence community. The latter cited concern about prospective gaps in verification to press again for U-2 flights. Eisenhower limited them to one a month, with only one authorized in early April and none after that to avoid provocation on the eve of the summit. But bad weather pushed the last flight back to May 1. In the subsequent Congressional hearings on the U-2 debacle, the CIA insisted the May 1 flight was for vital but unspecified information. It appears that the object was to confirm the first Soviet deployment of ICBMs (four) and get a look at the site (Plesetsk).[67]

The President's efforts for a test ban collapsed with the U-2 incident and the non-summit. There was to be no test ban until 1963, and then it did not cover underground tests. The Berlin problem was left to smolder on into the next administration.

ASSESSMENT

What shall we conclude about these events? First, it is quite possible that Eisenhower and Khrushchev, left to themselves, would have reached agreement on both the test ban and Berlin. Eisenhower wanted a ban and was ready to ignore prior reservations about it that had shaped U.S. policy. He felt great frustration about the arms race and the Cold War, and sought a breakthrough, however modest, as a fitting end to his career. He was appalled at the scale of the American arsenal and the operational plans for a nuclear war, which called for casualties of 200 million or more in the Soviet Bloc on the first day. Equally appalling was that everyone around him wanted even more military hardware and defense spending.[68]

In his last months, Dulles joined Eisenhower in these objections, arguing that military spending was too high and the armed forces had forgotten that the point was simply to deter. He had long since abandoned massive retaliation, and at one meeting startled even Eisenhower by suggesting that military superiority was no longer a meaningful posture, a view Eisenhower was to display in his last months in office.

Khrushchev was similarly inclined. He knew better than anyone that his nation was in a race it could not win, with a minuscule ICBM force facing a coming flood of American missiles. His domestic reform program rested on restraining military spending, and his foreign policy rested on a bluff about the capacity of Soviet nuclear deterrence. He needed a deal to show that his gamble had paid off. He consistently signaled all this by a series of concessions—troop cuts, a testing moratorium, acceptance of on-site inspections.[69]

An agreement on Berlin was also negotiable. Though not conceding Western rights on Berlin, Eisenhower and Dulles were prepared to be conciliatory, as were the British only more so.[70] Dealing with the East Germans, perhaps as designated Soviet agents, was something Dulles had mentioned as a possibility, and it was certainly acceptable to London. For his part, Khrushchev told Macmillan, and later Eisenhower at Camp David, that he had no deadline on Berlin, which suggested that an agreement, not posturing, was what he sought.

If agreements were negotiable, were they ratifiable? On nuclear testing the British were strongly in favor. DeGaulle was also in favor, but it is difficult to see why. France was about to test its first nuclear weapons (in February 1960), and he could not have viewed a test ban with equanimity. Probably he planned to insist that a superpower ban did not bar French testing.

But a test ban would have faced opposition from the entire American security complex. How ratification could have been achieved under these circumstances is hard to see. The uproar in Congress would have been enormous, especially in an election year.[71] We can only speculate. Eisenhower had been happy to work behind the scenes on many matters, but by this time the effects of delegation, bureaucratic politics, domestic politics (especially in Congress), and Sputnik had resulted in the diminished responsiveness of the government to his leadership. He was looking for a way to offset this. It seems likely that he was prepared to make far more information available about nuclear arsenals, the strategic balance, and American intelligence capabilities to win the necessary support.[72]

This is the best explanation for the puzzle that still surrounds the collapse of the summit—Eisenhower's public acceptance of responsibility for the U-2 flights. It was strongly criticized then, and has been since, as unnecessary and as putting Khrushchev in an untenable position that forced him to abandon the summit. What seems plausible is that Eisenhower, while he misread the consequences for Khrushchev, believed that at least, and at last, he would be unraveling the myths and anxieties, the inertia, the political pressures in the United States that had given the arms competition such momentum. This is a president as dove, grasping for leverage in his domestic two-level game, seeking to expand domestic win-sets to get what he wanted.

As for Berlin, the key to domestic ratification would have been that no Western rights were given up and West Berliners were not subjected to communist rule. Kennedy settled for this under the circumstances of the building of the Berlin Wall, which suggests that it would have been an acceptable outcome of a more normal negotiation as well.

CONCLUSION

Was an important opportunity missed during the Eisenhower Administration? And if so, was this due to the dynamics of the four-level game in which Eisenhower was embroiled? The answer appears to be mostly "no." On a test ban and Berlin modest agreements were possible but were forestalled by Eisenhower's inability to secure a sufficient consensus. But for most of the possible steps toward détente and possible agreements on which negotiations ensued, failure was not primarily due to the impossibility of securing ratification. Eisenhower's worldview, his leadership style, his inhibitions based on what he believed containment required, when combined with the Soviet leaders' primary objectives, left win-sets too narrow at the highest level. Even on Berlin and the test ban the agreements sought late in his administration would have barely scratched the surface of the arms race and the Cold War—the damage had already been done and the "opportunity" to go in another direction had mostly passed. By then the United States had over 18,000 nuclear weapons with over 2,000 bombers, about 100 missiles, and contracts for almost 900 more.

Skepticism is also warranted because, as Dulles and other conservative critics of détente claimed, the breakthrough in the Cold War came only when the Soviet government quit. True détente between these highly competitive, conflictual systems was never permanently installed. That suggests that no fundamental breakthrough was possible earlier, which is precisely what Eisenhower believed at the time. Perhaps by the late 1950s the Cold War had become a seamless fabric that had to be unraveled only all at once, not piecemeal. If so, without a broad political accommodation little could have been done on the specific issues—Berlin, Germany, a test ban, the nuclear arms race. The conflict had developed this way during Eisenhower's presidency and in part through his efforts.

Any opportunity to get the nuclear arms under control was also severely circumscribed by the logic of massive retaliation. Eisenhower continually signed off on more nuclear tests and weapons because under massive retaliation an American lead was crucial for deterrence. Only late in his second term did he arrive at the true logic of the nuclear age—beyond a certain point superiority does not matter—and become appalled at the scale of the American arsenal and the Pentagon's war plans.

Eisenhower was also constrained by his leadership style. It left too much room for those in Congress and elsewhere who saw the administration as weak on defense to reinforce those inside the administration with a more hawkish view. As a result, only elaborate verification could have put even a test ban, much less a modicum of disarmament, in reach of ratification.

Where the dynamics of a four-level-game analysis clearly fit is the situation in the late 1950s, when there was a chance for some movement that, though not thawing the Cold War, would have been beneficial. A meaningful test ban might have curbed the huge refinements in nuclear arsenals that were in the offing, maybe slowing the missile buildups on each side in the next decade. A four-level-game analysis is useful for explaining why a meaningful test ban was only an outside possibility.

Inside the government, Eisenhower eventually stood virtually alone against more defense spending and nuclear weapons. He confronted virtually a phalanx opposed to meaningful arms agreements. He held the line where he could, grew steadily more interested in getting at least a test ban as a way to change the atmosphere, but never found a way to take back control of these issues. Though the collapse of the summit ensured that no test ban would emerge in his administration, the domestic opposition was as much responsible for this as the failure of the summit.

Eisenhower had put his ducks in a row at the first two levels but could not do so on the two domestic games. The profound commitment to the Cold War generated a domestic political environment poisonous for partial agreements—from the right's fear of appeasement to Cold-War-Liberals' exploitation of recurring fears about "gaps." The Cold War state provided an enormous organizational inertia behind the nuclear arms buildup and conflict with the Soviet Bloc. He said as much in his last speech.

NOTES

1. I am greatly indebted to the historian Jackelyn Stanke, who is working on the Eisenhower era in the Cold War, for research assistance on this chapter.

2. For example, Zbigniew Brzezinski suggested that after Stalin's death "a more active policy, combining a willingness to contrive a new European relationship (including perhaps a neutralized Germany) with a credible inclination to exploit Soviet difficulties in Eastern Europe, might have diluted the partition of Europe and maybe even transformed the rivalry into a less hostile relationship." Another opportunity was lost in the first two years after Sputnik, largely because of Khrushchev's bullying over Berlin. See Brzezinski, "How the Cold War Was Played" *Foreign Affairs*, 51 (October 1972), p. 205. Others who perceive opportunities missed include Deborah Welch Larson, *Anatomy of Mistrust: U.S.-Soviet Relations during the Cold War* (Ithaca: Cornell University Press, 1997); Mathew Evangelista, "Cooperation Theory and Disarmament Negotiations in the 1950s," *World Politics*, 42 (1990), pp. 502–528; and James G. Richter, *Khrushchev's Double Bind: International Pressure and Domestic Coalition Politics* (Baltimore: Johns Hopkins University Press, 1994), pp. 73–74. An early view to this effect: Charles E. Bohlen, *Witness to History, 1929–1969* (New York: W.W. Norton, 1973), p. 370.

3. Richard Immerman suggests that trying "reassurance" after Stalin's death might have provoked changes like the ones introduced by Gorbachev. Richard H. Immerman, "Confessions of an Eisenhower Revisionist: An Agonizing Reappraisal" *Diplomatic History*, 14 (Summer 1990), pp. 319–342, particularly p. 341.

4. George Bunn in *Arms Control by Committee: Managing Negotiations with the Russians* (Stanford: Stanford University Press, 1992) emphasizes that the pursuit of arms control involved the President in struggles on four levels: with the Russians, the allies, the government agencies concerned with defense and foreign policy, and the Congress. See pp. 7–8.

5. In addition to others cited in the notes, one can consult Blanche Wiesen Cook, *The Declassified Eisenhower: A Divided Legacy* (Garden City, N.Y.: Doubleday, 1981); William Brag Ewald, Jr., *Eisenhower the President: Crucial Days, 1951–1960* (Englewood Cliffs, N. J.: Prentice-Hall, 1981).

6. In this he was merely permitting a vast expansion, the groundwork for which had been laid since 1950 in a huge increase in the facilities for producing nuclear materials and weapons. See Richard G. Hewlett and Jack M. Holl, *Atoms for Peace and War 1953–1961: Eisenhower and the Atomic Energy Commission* (Berkeley: University of California Press, 1989), p. 18; Robert Bowie, "Bowie's Commentary" in Ernest R. May, ed., *American Cold War Strategy: Interpreting NSC 68* (Boston: Bedford Books, 1993), pp. 110–116.

7. Details are in David Alan Rosenberg, "The Origins of Overkill: Nuclear Weapons and American Strategy, 1945–1960," *International Security*, 7 (Spring 1983), pp. 3–71.

8. See Peter J. Roman, *Eisenhower and the Missile Gap* (Ithaca: Cornell University Press, 1995), pp. 198–200.

9. Campbell Craig, *Destroying the Village: Eisenhower and Nuclear War* (New York: Columbia University Press, 1998), pp. 41–89.

10. Hence his interest in détente was primarily focused on what are now termed "confidence-building measures" to promote transparency. See Michael B. Froman, *The Development of the Idea of Détente* (New York: St. Martin's Press, 1991), pp. 12–13.

11. On the sophistication of Eisenhower's national strategy see Charles C. Alexander, *Holding the Line: The Eisenhower Era 1952–1961* (Bloomington: Indiana University Press, 1975), p. 93; Fred Greenstein, "The Hidden Hand Presidency: Eisenhower as Leader, a 1994 Perspective," *Presidential Studies Quarterly*, 24 (Spring 1994), pp. 233–241; and Immerman "Confessions."

12. See Herbert S. Parmet, *Eisenhower and the American Crusades* (New York: Macmillan, 1972), pp. 276–283.

13. For details on the anticommunist crusade at home and its impact see Jeff Broadwater, *Eisenhower and the Anti-Communist Crusade* (Chapel Hill: University of North Carolina Press, 1992); and David Caute, *The Great Fear* (New York: Simon and Schuster, 1978).

14. However, the Presidium as a whole was skeptical about pursuing Eisenhower's proposals, according to Vladislav Zubok and Constantine Pleshakov, *Inside the Kremlin's Cold War: From Stalin to Khrushchev* (Cambridge, Mass.: Harvard University Press, 1996), pp. 154–157.

15. See, among others, Stephen E. Ambrose, *Eisenhower: Volume Two, The President* (New York: Simon and Schuster, 1984), pp. 94-96. Dulles toughened up an earlier draft of the speech.

16. Raymond L. Garthoff, "Assessing the Adversary: Estimates by the Eisenhower Administration of Soviet Intentions and Capabilities," Brookings Occasional Paper 1991, p. 7.

17. "He resisted any earnest search for accommodation or even for serious negotiation for his goal was not really coexistence based on a calculated balance of force; it was superiority and mastery based on a vague expectation that the West would maintain a permanent power preponderance" (Townsend Hoopes, *The Devil and John Foster Dulles* [Boston: Little, Brown, 1973], pp.488–489. This classic view of Dulles shapes the entire book.

18. Dulles was particularly attached to Stalin's *Problems of Leninism* as a guide to Soviet thinking during an era of extensive de-Stalinization. See Eleanor Lansing Dulles, *John Foster Dulles: The Last Year* (New York: Harcourt, Brace and World, 1963), pp. 96–103.

19. A content analysis of Dulles's speeches and writings demonstrated that when the Soviets were nasty Dulles saw his view of them, and the need for a tough stance in response, confirmed, and when they were milder, he saw this as victory for the tough stance and urged more of the same. Thus, any Soviet behavior was interpreted so as to reinforce the Dulles worldview. See Ole Holsti, "The Belief System and National Images: A Case Study," *The Journal of Conflict Resolution*, 6 (1962), pp. 244–252.

20. Often noted by biographers, this is confirmed by Eisenhower in his *The White House Years: Mandate for Change, 1953–1956* (Garden City, N.Y.: Doubleday, 1963), p. 504.

21. See, for example, Anna Kasten Nelson, "The 'Top of Policy Hill:' President Eisenhower and the National Security Council," *Diplomatic History*, 7 (Fall 1983), pp. 307–326 on Dulles's efforts to limit the role of the NSC.

22. Here I accept the more revisionist views of Dulles. In addition to Hoopes, *The Devil and John Foster Dulles*, other standard views of Dulles as not really interested in accommodation include Roscoe Drummond and Gaston Coblentz, *Duel at the Brink: John Foster Dulles' Command of American Power* (London: Weidenfeld and Nicolson, 1960); Frederick W. Marks III, *Power and Peace: The Diplomacy of John Foster Dulles* (Westport: Praeger, 1993)—even though Marks is eager to convey an image of Dulles as "flexible." More successful at this is Richard Gould-Adams, *John Foster Dulles: A Reappraisal* (New York: Appleton-Century-Crofts, 1962). Important revisionist views appear in several of the chapters in Richard H. Immerman, *John Foster Dulles and the Diplomacy of the Cold War* (Princeton: Princeton University Press, 1990). Recent works shows Dulles as having consistently (and unsuccessfully) struggled to shift Eisenhower's policy on massive retaliation toward what was eventually called flexible response. See Craig, *Destroying the Village*, pp. 41–89.

23. See James G. Hershberg, " 'Explosion in the Offing': German Rearmament and American Diplomacy, 1953–1955," *Diplomatic History*, 6 (Fall 1992), p. 533; and Hershberg, *James B. Conant* (New York: Knopf, 1993), p. 667. See also Marc Trachtenberg, "A 'Wasting Asset': American Strategy and the Shifting Strategic Nuclear Balance, 1949–1954," in Sean Lynn-Jones, et al., eds., *Nuclear Diplomacy and Crisis Management* (Cambridge, Mass.: MIT Press, 1990), pp. 69–113.

24. See Richard W. Stevenson, *The Rise and Fall of Détente: Relaxations of Tension in US-Soviet Relations 1953–1984* (Houndsmills, England: Macmillan, 1985), pp. 33–35.

25. See Michael A. Guhin, *John Foster Dulles: A Statesman and His Times* (New York: Columbia University Press, 1972), pp. 295–303; Richard G. Hewitt and Jack M. Holl, *Atoms for Peace and War 1953–1961: Eisenhower and the Atomic Energy Commission* (Berkeley: University of California Pres, 1989), pp. 274–276, 296–299, 362–363, 384, 397, 477–479.

26. See Hewlett and Holl, *Atoms for Peace and War*, for the repeated clashes between Eisenhower and both the AEC and DOD on arms control issues. Also Robert A. Divine, *Blowing on the Wind: The Nuclear Test Ban Debate 1954–1960* (New York: Oxford University Press, 1978).

27. Thus "Eisenhower increasingly came to regard government as an obstacle to effective defense and foreign policymaking" (Robert A. Strong, "Eisenhower and Arms Control" in Richard A. Melanson and David Mayers, eds., *Reevaluating Eisenhower: American Foreign Policy in the 1950s* [Urbana: University of Illinois Press, 1987], p. 261).

28. Fred Greenstein, "The Hidden Hand Presidency: Eisenhower as Leader, a 1994 Perspective," *Presidential Studies Quarterly*, 24 (Spring 1994), pp. 233–241, suggests: "The controversies of the late 1950s over whether the United States was falling behind the Soviet Union in missile strength and in other respects were an occasion for the bully pulpit, not the hidden hand" (p. 239).

29. See Roman, *Eisenhower and the Missile Gap*, pp. 200–207.

30. Emmet John Hughes, *The Ordeal of Power: A Political Memoir of the Eisenhower Years* (New York: Atheneum, 1963), p. 124. The traditionalist-revisionist debate concerns the degree of Eisenhower's involvement in policy making and his success in generating outcomes he wanted. The traditional criticism was that Eisenhower was uninvolved and grew frustrated with his inability to get what he wanted done. To revisionists he had a

profound and subtle conception of leadership, injected himself deeply into policy making without letting his hand show, and succeeded in achieving much of what he felt was important.

Criticism of Eisenhower at the time is illustrated by Marquis Childs, *Eisenhower: Captive Hero* (New York: Harcourt, Brace, 1958). Examples of revisionists: George H. Quester, "Was Eisenhower a Genius?" *International Security*, 4 (Fall 1979), pp. 159–179; Gary Wills, *Nixon Agonistes* (Boston: Houghton Mifflin, 1970); Herbert Parmet, *Eisenhower and the American Crusade* (New York: Macmillan, 1992); Robert A. Divine, *Eisenhower and the Cold War* (New York: Oxford University Press, 1981); Charles C. Alexander, *Holding the Line: The Eisenhower Era 1952–1961* (Bloomington: Indiana University Press, 1975); Fred I. Greenstein, *The Hidden-Hand Presidency: Eisenhower as Leader* (New York: Basic Books, 1982); Richard Immerman, "Eisenhower and Dulles: Who Made the Decisions?" *Political Psychology*, 1 (Autumn 1979), pp. 21–38.

31. Studies of the development of the revisionist view include: Stephen G. Rabe, "Eisenhower Revisionism: A Decade of Scholarship," *Diplomatic History*, 17 (Winter 1993), pp. 97–115; Richard H. Immerman, "Confessions of an Eisenhower Revisionist: An Agonizing Reappraisal," *Diplomatic History*, 14 (Summer 1990), pp. 319–342.

32. One gets a sense of how entangling the alliances were for U.S. policy-makers not only from the Eisenhower era papers and records but from the available materials on the Cuban Missile Crisis. See particularly Ernest R. May and Philip D. Zelikow, eds., *The Kennedy Tapes: Inside the White House during the Cuban Missile Crisis* (Cambridge, Mass.: Belknap Press, 1997).

33. On the perceived importance of allies for holding down the U.S. burden see Brian R. Duchin, "The 'Agonizing Reappraisal': Eisenhower, Dulles, and the European Defense Community," *Diplomatic History*, 16 (Spring 1992), pp. 201–221. The need for allies to provide bomber bases is noted in John Foster Dulles, "Policy for Security and Peace," *Foreign Affairs*, 32 (April 1954), pp. 353–364.

34. See Guhin, *John Foster Dulles*, pp. 212–218.

35. In Garthoff's words: "Soviet flexibility and moves toward more cooperative and less threatening policies were regarded not only with suspicion, but as an obstacle to American interests rather than steps toward accommodation" ("Assessing the Adversary," p. 9).

36. Guhin, *John Foster Dulles*, pp. 308–311.

37. On dealing with a wily and always uneasy Adenauer and his government see James G. Hershberg, " 'Explosion in the Offing': German Rearmament and American Diplomacy," *Diplomatic History*, 6 (Fall 1992), pp. 511–549; and Hershberg, *James B. Conant*.

38. This can be traced over the years in Roger Morgan, *The United States and West Germany 1945–1973* (London: Oxford University Press, 1974). The steady flow of correspondence between top U.S. officials and Adenauer can be traced in the Ann Whitman File, International Series, Boxes 13 and 14, at the Eisenhower Library in Abilene, Kansas.

39. Churchill's efforts are traced in detail in Martin Gilbert, *"Never Despair": Winston S. Churchill 1945–1965* (London: Heinemann, 1988), pp. 806–1111.

40. Churchill had actually been calling for a summit since 1950. See John Kentleton, "Eisenhower, Churchill, and the 'Balance of Terror'" in Melanson and Mayers, *Reevaluating Eisenhower*, pp. 173–181.

41. Churchill needed American approval, and pursuit of this led to a long series of letters and other exchanges between the two governments, which can be followed in the Ann Whitman File, International Series, Boxes 16 and 17. Or the interested reader can

draw on Peter G. Boyle, *The Churchill-Eisenhower Correspondence, 1953–1955* (Chapel Hill: University of North Carolina Press, 1990).

42. Alexander, *Holding the Line*, p. 93.

43. Thomas B. Cochran, William M. Arkin, and Milton M. Hoenig, *U.S. Nuclear Forces and Capabilities* (Cambridge, Mass.: Ballinger, 1984), p. 15.

44. See Alexander, *Holding the Line*, pp. 93–98, 202–203; Parmet, *Eisenhower*, pp. 399–401; Garthoff, "Assessing the Adversary," pp. 6–7; Bernard G. Bechhoeffer, *Postwar Negotiations for Arms Control* (Washington: Brookings Institution, 1961), pp. 290–315. The lack of response to this Soviet offer, and to the unilateral Soviet concessions accompanying it, such as a cut of roughly two million men in the Soviet armed forces in 1954–57, is usually taken as clear evidence that the United States really did not want nuclear arms reduction agreements, seeing its own and Soviet proposals as public relations exercises. See Larson, *Anatomy of Distrust*, pp. 65–70.

45. Matthew Evangelista, "Cooperation Theory and Disarmament Negotiations in the 1950s," *World Politics*, 42 (1990), p. 519.

46. Acceptance of aerial inspection grew very slowly. The Russians were ready, in principle, to accept it in 1957—much of Russia would be open to view in exchange for the United States west of the Mississippi plus Alaska. (See Bechhoeffer, *Postwar Negotiations*, pp. 382–385 for maps, and Alexander, *Holding the Line*, pp. 204–206.) Moscow was aware that the United States was overflying the USSR with the U-2, gaining unilaterally what it had earlier been prepared to pursue cooperatively. However, the U.S. response was quite guarded due to Pentagon and others' uneasiness about just what Soviet overflights of North America would mean, and strenuously expressed concerns from Europeans, especially West Germany, about overflights there. In the 1970s the Soviets accepted verification by "national technical means" (satellites) in the SALT agreements. Implementation of Open Skies by aircraft was not achieved until an agreement in the Bush Administration, ratified in the Clinton Administration, to add it to the CSCE process on arms cuts in Europe.

47. See Garthoff, "Assessing the Adversary," pp. 10–12, and Alexander, *Holding the Line*, pp. 96–97. Eden says, in his memoirs, that it came as a surprise even to him. Anthony Eden, *Full Circle: The Memoirs of Anthony Eden* (Boston: Houghton Mifflin, 1960), p. 337.

48. I have not attempted to summarize the elaborate communications at the highest level on various East-West issues, particularly on disarmament/arms control matters, that flowed between the President and Soviet leaders in 1955–1958, but the materials can be found in the Ann Whitman File, International series, Boxes 45–47.

49. Stassen was named the President's special assistant on disarmament in March 1955. His career as advocate for arms control arrangements with the Russians can be traced in many of the other sources cited as well as in the portrait of him provided in H. W. Brands, Jr. *Cold Warriors: Eisenhower's Generation and American Foreign Policy* (New York: Columbia University Press, 1988); and Harold Stassen and Marshall Houts, *Eisenhower: Turning the World toward Peace* (St. Paul: Merill/Magnus Publishing, 1990).

50. See George Bunn, *Arms Control by Committee*, pp. 18–23.

51. An illustration of the intense disagreement between Eisenhower and Dulles on one side and Strauss and Defense Secretary McElroy on the other: Robert A. Divine, "Eisenhower, Dulles, and the Nuclear Test Ban Issue: Memorandum of a White House Conference, 24 March 1958" *Diplomatic History*, 2, 2 (Summer 1978) pp. 321–330.

52. Dwight D. Eisenhower, *The White House Years: Waging Peace 1959–1961* (Garden City, NY: Doubleday, 1965), p. 477.

53. Hewlett and Holl, *Atoms for Peace*, p. 546.

54. Eventually the United States conducted numerous unannounced nuclear tests that were not detected by publicly announced monitoring. Whether they were successfully hidden from the Russians as well is not clear.

55. Ambrose, *Eisenhower*, p. 493.

56. On Eisenhower's deference to his officials and their advice, there are three options. The first, that he was not deeply involved, has been quashed by the revisionist literature. The second is that Eisenhower counted on professionalism and deferred too readily to in-house expertise. (For example, Kenneth Thompson, "The Strengths and Weaknesses of Eisenhower's Leadership," in Melanson and Mayers, *Reevaluating Eisenhower*, pp. 11–30; and Robert Griffith, "Dwight D. Eisenhower and the Corporate Commonwealth," *American Historical Review*, 87 (February 1982), pp. 87–122.) There is something to this, but it is clearly incompatible with his regular suspicion about CIA proposals, his pronounced skepticism about DOD views, and so on. That leaves the third option, adopted here, that it was the president's management style that continued to limit what he would do to make his views prevail.

57. See Rabe for a similar conclusion.

58. Divine, *Blowing on the Wind*, p. 152. A similar conclusion: Eisenhower was deeply interested in a test ban treaty, "Nevertheless, his style of administration and careful delegation of authority constrained his own convictions; he would not short-circuit the National Security Council or the special Committee of Principals in which John McCone could slow the progress of American bargaining." George B. Kistiakowsky, *A Scientist at the White House* (Cambridge, Mass.: Harvard University Press, 1976), p. iii.

59. The impact of this can be traced in James R. Killian, Jr., *Sputnik, Scientists, and Eisenhower: A Memoir of the First Special Assistant to the President for Science and Technology* (Cambridge, Mass.: MIT Press, 1977) and Kistiakowsky, *A Scientist at the White House*. Each provides details about the battles between Eisenhower and opponents of arms control in the administration.

60. Robert A. Divine, *The Sputnik Challenge* (New York: Oxford University Press, 1993), pp. 41, 47. The book details the pressures. Dulles's suggestion is reported in Eisenhower's memoirs. See Eisenhower, *Waging Peace*, pp. 223–225.

61. The elaborate moves of the crisis are traced in Jack M. Schick, *The Berlin Crisis: 1958–1962* (Philadelphia: University of Pennsylvania Press, 1971).

62. Eisenhower, *Waging Peace*, pp. 350–355, 397–409.

63. He would continue it until the end of his term, but was so unhappy with the lack of progress in test ban negotiations that he urged incoming President John Kennedy to resume nuclear tests immediately. See Alexander, *Holding the Line*, p. 210.

64. Ambrose, *Eisenhower*, p. 493.

65. For the best overview of Eisenhower's struggles in his second term for arms control, reductions in defense spending, and agreements with the Russians, see Ambrose, *Eisenhower*.

66. See Beckhoefer, *Postwar Negotiations*, pp. 497–500.

67. Garthoff, "Assessing the Adversary," p. 41. The pressures on Eisenhower to authorize more U-2 flights and his resistance are recounted in Michael R. Beschloss, *Mayday: Eisenhower, Khrushchev, and the U-2 Affair* (New York: Harper and Row, 1986), pp. 160–176.

68. In addition to the other sources cited in the notes, Eisenhower's resistance to strong pressures to spend more on defense are reviewed in Richard A. Aliano, *American Defense Policy from Eisenhower to Kennedy* (Athens: Ohio University Press, 1975), pp. 109–169.

69. Khrushchev's concessions make it hard to believe that he was not serious. Larson, *Anatomy of Mistrust*, pp. 72–107.

70. Details can be found in Schick, *The Berlin Crisis*, pp. 29–60.

71. See Alexander, *Holding the Line*, p. 210, where he writes that even with a test ban or arms limitation treaty signed, "ratification by the United States Senate would have been most unlikely."

72. The last U-2 flight, by covering the first Soviet operational missile site, would have helped considerably in any campaign to dispel the missile-gap charges. See Garthoff, "Assessing the Adversary," p. 41.

CHAPTER 4

The Multilevel Dynamics of Moscow's German Policy from 1953 to 1964

Vladislav M. Zubok

INTRODUCTION

A study of the politics that motivated Soviet foreign policy on the German Question must be preceded by a question: What were Soviet politics? Politics in general
are about groups and interests, but they are also about psychological motivations,
attitudes, and perceptions. Soviet Cold War mentality, to a degree, predated the
Soviet-American confrontation: It was based on the decades of Soviet isolationism, the ideologically motivated mistrust towards the outside world, and, first and
foremost, the experience of the Second World War, when the Soviet Union sur-
vived and triumphed in an epic struggle with the Third Reich. Therefore, although the geopolitical confrontation with the United States remained the main
generator of the Cold War, other important factors lay in the Soviet politics of insecurity and fresh memories of war. The fear of the Bolshevik revolutionary regime
that it would be crushed by its "imperialist hostile surroundings" meshed with a
fear that a loss of the firm grip on East Germany, on Germany in general, could ne-
gate the results of the Second World War and the "millions of lives" paid for it.

Soviet policy-makers, despite their monopoly on power, were part of this "politics"; sometimes it severely limited their ability to deal with the German Question
rationally and pragmatically. Domestic politics, in addition to geopolitical considerations, enhanced their determination to carry any burden and face any adversi-
ties, provided that the German Question was under control. During the first two
decades of the Cold War, the Soviet leadership considered the issue of guarantees
against a new German aggression as important for security as reaching a strategic
parity with Washington.

Most Western analysts in the 1950s–1960s, both policy-makers and scholars, tended to view Soviet policy towards the Federal Republic and West Berlin as a threat to the Western alliance. Later, in the 1970s, divisions inside the Western community of historians created schools of thought that began to look at Soviet German policy through the prism of "missed opportunities" for reunification (Stalin's note of March 1952, Beria's initiative in May 1953, the Austrian treaty of 1955) or of Soviet defensive needs (the Berlin crisis, 1958–1962). Some authors believed that the Soviet leadership was obsessed with nuclearization of Western Germany and construed its German policy on the basis of this obsession.[1] Robert Slusser argued on the basis of Soviet open sources that Soviet leaders, Nikita Khrushchev in particular, abetted the tension around Germany primarily to restore their sagging domestic authority and their prestige inside the communist camp.[2] Researchers with a European perspective emphasized the role of various forces and groups inside the Soviet leadership and Soviet empire, particularly the Kremlin "hawks," the hard-line faction of Walter Ulbricht in East Germany and the Mao leadership in China.[3]

Even before the archives of Moscow and East Berlin opened, Western research made impressive progress on the study of the Berlin crisis on the basis of public evidence, declassified Western documents, and oral histories.[4] Recent studies have benefitted from the access to Eastern archival sources.[5] There is even a joint research project by the senior analysts of American and Soviet intelligence that contains rich and intriguing evidence on bureaucratic perceptions and forces behind the policies of each side.[6] These works bring into focus the complex nature of Soviet foreign policy, driven in part by security concerns and by ideologically enhanced temptations to exploit "shifts in the correlation of forces." They confirm the predominance of defensive security motivations on the Soviet side and the absence of adventuristic plans to seize West Berlin. And pioneering research by Hope Harrison has brought to the surface the importance of "domestic politics" both inside the USSR and the German Democratic Republic (GDR)—a context that defined a convoluted interaction between the Kremlin and Ulbricht and constrained Soviet policy options with regard to the German Question.

Recent research, in other words, has borne fruit that, to use the expression of Alexander George, can provide "generic knowledge" about Cold War policies and politics.[7]

CONCEPTUAL REMARKS

The goal of this chapter is to peer into the "black box" of Soviet foreign policymaking from Stalin's death to the ouster of Khrushchev. A recent study of U.S. Cold War policy shows that the only way to uncover its overarching, strategic dimensions (or the lack thereof) is to explore the relationships inside the core policy making group (leadership); between the core and the key power and bureaucratic groups (elites); and between all of them and the alliance networks outside.[8] The need for a similar approach to Soviet security policy has guided this chapter.

The levels (or groups of factors) in Soviet foreign policy can be identified within a four-level-game framework, as follows:

a. The leadership level (the individuals and the *modus* or situation in which they operated, be it a one-man dictatorship under Stalin or several successors struggling for power in 1953–1955)

b. The bureaucratic level (sometimes involving rudiments of coalitions, but usually band-wagoning around a leader and a certain consensus with no alternatives; in the USSR, most bureacratic interests never became explicit and were always submerged in the tradition of complete subservience to the top leadership, usually a personality at the very top)

c. The alliance level (involving Soviet allies and followers abroad)

d. The interstate level (involving bilateral/multilateral relations with other great powers)

It is difficult to determine to what extent Soviet foreign policy-making was comparable or commensurate with that in America. The initial assumption of this chapter is that dynamics of power and international confrontation during the Cold War brought about similar reactions vis-à-vis the German Question by both superpowers even though their agendas on Germany were in fundamental conflict. Parallelism is especially striking on the C level (alliance), but also on the B level (bureaucratic). West Germany and West Berlin were the most important places where U.S. international credibility was tested and the hub of the American strategy of containment. Similarly, preservation of the Communist regime in East Germany was vital for the Soviet Union's international "legitimacy" and its overall strategy. From this central parallelism stemmed others: the comparable mixes of coercion and mutual dependence in relations with allies; the similar desires of various bureaucracies and groups motivated by more or less distinct professional duties and "dimensions" of national security; the related mechanisms of authority building by the top leadership in foreign policy under conditions of confrontation; the inertia within each superpower that developed behind once-adopted strategies and inhibited change; the informational problems both experienced in transition from bureaucratic fact-gathering to policy-making; etc. One common component in the behaviour of both the USSR and the United States was the response to being locked in a "prisoner's dilemma." It was no secret that behind the parity, peace, and disarmament initiatives of Moscow and Washington were tactical and strategic calculations aimed at achieving one-sided advantages. But gradually the bipolar regime created by the U.S.-Soviet confrontation began to reveal trends towards stability and even tacit cooperation. "Nuclear learning," an increasing awareness of the disastrous potential of strategic weaponry, led the elites in Washington and Moscow to a realization of their mutual interest in tacit cooperation on prevention of nuclear war. The same kind of learning took place with regard to the German Question, when the superpowers realized that they had to maintain the division of Germany as a part of the geopolitical status quo in Central Europe.

A second assumption is that there were special factors on each side that put the superpowers in asymmetrical positions—that forced the Soviet Union to take the initiative on the German Question while the United States posed as "status quo" guarantor. These special factors did not relate directly to the general security concerns that dominated the American-Soviet confrontation. Yet they were intimately related to the hegemony of each superpower within its respective sphere of influence (the alliance, or C level). The Americans' fear that West Germany would "go neutral," and skillful manipulation of this fear by Chancellor Konrad Adenauer, largely accounted for Washington's caution and rigidity with regard to talks with the Soviets on the German Question. This was paralleled by a Soviet fear, exploited by the SED General Secretary Walter Ulbricht, that a West German economic and political offensive would destabilize the GDR and put the Soviets in a dilemma: either having to "lose" East Germany or go to war in its defense.

The crucial asymmetry, of course, was the preponderance of West Germany over East Germany that was ever more formidable by the end of the 1950s. West Germany threatened "to swallow" the GDR, not the other way round. Even short of that, the Federal Republic of Germany (FRG) drained East Germany of hundreds of thousands of young and skilled workers and professionals every year. The position of West Berlin in the center of the GDR became, therefore, "a bone in the throat" for Soviet leaders, a Trojan horse inside their Communist fortress. Another major asymmetry was that all annexations of prewar German territory occurred in the East at the Soviet Union's initiative. Therefore, nonrecognition of these annexations by the West German government was regarded by the Soviets as a direct challenge to their "legitimacy," to their acceptance and prestige among the satellite-states in Eastern Europe.

A third assumption of this chapter is that Soviet policy on the German Question had unique features that made it look like a "black box," enigmatic at best and frightening at worst, for most observers. These features cannot be ignored or displaced to the margins even by modern adepts of *Realpolitik* or structuralist studies of international relations. They could mostly be found at the leadership (A) and bureaucratic (B) levels, but they also occcured on the alliance (C) level. First among these was the personality of the ruler. Both Joseph Stalin and Nikita Khrushchev left a unique imprint on Soviet strategies, and the motivations behind their actions were solely theirs. The second unique feature was the composition and functioning of the Soviet power elites, especially the relationship between them and the top leader, and the impact of this on the decision-making process. A third unique feature was the role of the communist ideology as the ultimate basis of the political "legitimacy" and "self-legitimacy" of the Soviet regime, state, empire, and security policies.

The peculiarities and unique attributes are more pronounced if one visualizes Soviet foreign policy across three dimensions. The first can be called the "state dimension" and is basically similar to what could be found in American administrations—namely, strategies and plans designed to build an international environment of some sort that would be optimal to Soviet interests and security.

The second can be designated "the military-industrial" dimension and had only a partial parallel in the United States, that is, subordination of all state interests to the task of accumulating military might and preparing for a future war. The third, uniquely Soviet, can be called "the party" dimension, related to the ideological roots of the Soviet empire, and was embodied in the networks of the former Comintern, and "fraternal" parties abroad, and so on.

I would argue that every Soviet leader had to base his foreign policy on some combination of these three dimensions, juggling among them. This juggling was particularly effective when it: (a) combined innovation and problem-solving with traditional "security" concerns; (b) mobilizied key bureaucracies while overcoming their parochial interests; (c) strengthened Soviet alliances and improved Soviet prestige in the Communist world and among the "progressive forces" abroad; (d) improved the Soviet position in relations with other great powers.

The dynamics and relative importance of these dimensions and their manifestation on various levels of "politics" that affected Soviet foreign policy will be shown in the Germany case. The analysis rests on fresh data from the Soviet archives, primarily of the International Departments of the CC CPSU.[9]

STALIN'S POLICY ON GERMANY: 1945–1952

Stalin's plans with regard to Germany, so important for the early dynamics of the Cold War, emerged even before the victory over the Nazis, as the Soviet leader abruptly shifted focus from war-winning tactics to peace-building ones. Stalin never doubted Germany's future resurgence, a development that would challenge Soviet domination and Soviet-imposed state borders in Central Europe. He told his subordinates that the Germans would be back on their feet "in fifteen-twenty years," and that might mean another war.

There is still no evidence on Stalin's strategy on Germany, and this fact led some researchers to conclude that there was none.[10] Patterns of Stalin's thinking and the new evidence on other aspects of Stalin's postwar foreign policy on Poland, Turkey, Iran, and Korea makes this inference highly doubtful. Germany and Poland were the two top priorities in Soviet planning for a postwar world.[11] Meeting with German communists on June 4, 1945, Stalin directed them to consolidate their positions in the Eastern zone with the help of Soviet occupational authorities. Stalin thereby sanctioned a division of Germany, but only as a stepping stone to a unified Germany where pro-Soviet forces (in a "popular front" of communists and "left" Social Democrats) would be predominant.[12] Stalin seemed to believe (and memoirs of his "German experts" stand on this point[13]) that a prolonged division of Germany would always pose a strategic threat to the status quo in Europe and to the Soviet Union. He wanted a new Germany to remain an ally of the USSR. There is little doubt that Stalin had in mind a quick withdrawal of U.S. power from Germany and envisaged subsequent steering of Germany's future by a combination of coercion, manipulation, and incentives—a sort of "hegemony" over Germany and thereby over the whole of Europe. In expectation of this moment he did not push for Bolshevization of the Eastern zone (in addition, that

would have cut it off economically from the rest of Germany, and Stalin still expected to profit from West German industrial resources), encouraging preservation of free enterprise and the creation of an all-German Social Democratic bloc in
the Soviet occupied area. "Quietly, bit by bit, we had been creating the GDR, our
own Germany," summed up Vyacheslav Molotov many years later.[14]

Between May 1945 and the summer of 1947 Stalin systematically tried to include in his current German program policies that could diminish or neutralize the
threat of German revanchism in the future. However, there were other circumstances and priorities that were even more urgent. First, there were the demands of
the Soviet economy, shattered by war, for German technology, equipment, and
other resources. Major defense projects, particularly the nuclear one and those involving the construction of aircraft and missiles, heavily depended on that. The
five-year plan and defense needs were sacred cows that in Stalin's eyes overshadowed German policy or any other policy. With Stalin's approval, the Soviet economic tsars, Malenkov and Beria, stripped East Germany of most of its industrial
potential, embittering the local population and undermining the inchoate legitimacy of Eastern Social Democrats. Molotov later referred to this predicament—
"We were taking from the Germans who wanted to work with us"—and admitted
that the Soviets could not resolve this dilemma. Military-industrial interests were
too strong, and they affected even Stalin's plans for Germany.

There was another set of powerful factors: huge obstacles to maintaining Soviet
control over the Eastern zone (and, by inference, over future Germany) by means
other than military occupation and Stalinist oppression. From the very beginning
it was clear that the Soviet influence could not be a benign hegemony: Occupation
was violent and brutal, its scars healed slowly. German Stalinists and other agents
of Stalin's will in Germany were never up to this task. According to Norman Naimark, "Soviet officers bolshevized their zone . . . because that was the only way they
knew to organize society. . . . By their own actions, the Soviet authorities created
enemies out of potential friends." The Social Democratic bloc was quickly transformed into a fig leaf for the Communist Party, run by the Soviet propaganda
branch of SVAG, the Soviet military administration in Germany.[15] For a while the
SVAG looked quite sincere in its efforts to avoid cloning Stalinism in East Germany,
but all "domestic politics" in the Zone precluded a victory of Social Democrats by a
majority vote in any elections. Gradually Soviet choices narrowed and eventually
they had to rely for their political control on a small group of die-hard German Stalinists, reimported into the Eastern bloc from Soviet exile. Walter Ulbricht became a
leader of the SED and, after November 1949, of the German Democratic Republic.
These factors, that could be designated "party/ideological" and "occupational," created another powerful corrective to Stalin's strategic plans for Germany.

The problems of implementation also hobbled Stalin's program. It required
ideal circumstances that did not exist: a withdrawal of the United States that
never took place, a better economic situation inside the Soviet Union and an absence of rearmament pressures on Soviet industries, better coordination of various

bureaucratic policies and informational flows. On the latter, Stalin tried to achieve such a coordination, but with mixed results.[16]

From the summer of 1947, when the United States started to build its security zone in Western Europe and decided that Western Germany should be its crucial component, Stalin had to place all his bets on the military-industrial might of the Soviet Union, on the one hand, and Stalinist methods of control ("party/ideological" factors) over the Eastern zone, on the other. Stalin never completely buried the program of Soviet domination over a reunified Germany, but after the breakout of the Korean war, the idea of German reunification became in his hands a powerful lever to influence politics in West Germany, as well as an additional means to build up legitimacy of the Ulbricht regime in the GDR. Stalin liked to alternate sticks (trying to kick the Western allies out of West Berlin during the Berlin blockade in 1948–1949) with carrots. All along, he hinted that he would grant a unified Germany broad concessions if Western powers backed off on their decision to build a separate Federal Republic.

In March 1952 Stalin used his carrot again. At this time the Soviet Union was at an enormous strategic disadvantage vis-à-vis the United States (due to American rearmament and its huge nuclear superiority). At this occasion Stalin sent to the United States, United Kingdom, and France a proposal to start talks on German reunification. As was correctly perceived in the West, Stalin's "March Note" was designed to thwart American plans to create a European army with a West German Bundeswehr as its backbone. It created confusion in West German politics and is still debated among historians as a possible "missed opportunity" for German reunification.[17] Stalin obviously wanted to gain time for better preparation for a future war. At the same time he gave a green light to the East German rulers' hurried program of further military mobilization.

By that time Soviet policy in Germany had become more centralized and monolithic than ever before or since. Stalin shaped it as he wished. On the surface there were no traces of any factional differences in the Soviet leadership on the German Question. Recent research in the documents in the Archives of Russian Ministry of Foreign Affairs confirms the total, one-sided dependence of the East German clique on Stalin's will.[18]

Yet, domestic politics on the German Question remained only dormant and suppressed. They came to the surface immediately and radically after Stalin's death on March 5, 1953, as the new Soviet rulers rushed to defuse the German "time-bomb" as part of their search for stabilization of their regime at home and internationally.

SOVIET GERMAN POLICIES DURING THE SUCCESSION CRISIS (1953–1954)

The death of the Soviet dictator created an enormous vacuum of "legitimacy" inside the Soviet Union and in the Soviet sphere of influence. Stalin alone could control (or pretend to control) all the strings and dimensions of Soviet domestic and foreign policy. None of his successors could fill his chair. Stalin's will and magic could no longer conceal the big holes in Soviet geostrategic and security positions worldwide. Also, nobody could squelch domestic political factors, the dissent among various bureaucratic groups, as ruthlessly as Stalin had.

A succession crisis, under Soviet conditions, made the power struggle among Stalin's lieutenants inevitable and opened room for "politics." Those with a leadership streak were bound to build their authority ultimately on distancing themselves from police terror and a permanent state of war mobilization. This, in turn, explains many of the foreign policy initiatives taken by Soviet rulers from March 1953 to spring 1955. The new head of government, Georgi Malenkov, and especially secret police chief Lavrenti Beria, took the lead in championing de-Stalinization. A very important part of this policy was a "peace initiative" towards the West, designed to end the war scare inside the Soviet empire and rationalize security strategies.

The German Question became one of the most important focal points in this effort. In the spring of 1953 it acquired a crisis dimension: in the first months of 1953 the flight of people to the West reached its all-time peak; East Germany was close to explosion.[19] In early April the Soviet leadership had discussed substantial economic assistance to the GDR.[20] It marked a momentous reversal: whereas in 1945–1947 the Soviet economy stripped East Germany of its resources, in 1953 it began to pump its own resources into the enfeebled GDR economy to bolster the faltering regime. This could have been done with a greater effectiveness back in 1945–1949, but then Stalin had other priorities.

Earlier, the Soviet leadership had received devastating accounts of the East German economic situation. Vladimir Semenov, the Soviet Political Adviser in East Germany in 1952–1953, had been recalled to Moscow for explanations.[21] Foreign Minister Molotov, who had been part of the earlier policymaking on Germany, proposed "the abandonment of the forced construction of socialism," to boost the popularity of the GDR regime. Beria and Malenkov, however, did not like the idea of the Soviet economy becoming a donor of the GDR. They also believed that part of a "peace initiative" should be another proposal on German reunification, perhaps even more radical than Stalin's "March Note." For Molotov, the GDR was both a strategic asset and a "socialist Germany." For Beria and Malenkov the East German regime was just an obstacle to the success of a new, post-Stalin foreign policy. They reflected "state" interests through stark *Realpolitik*, ignoring "party/ideological" considerations.[22]

On May 27 Beria, with a conniving Malenkov on the sidelines, came forward with a major initiative: He proposed to wind up "the construction of socialism" in the GDR and shift the focus of attention to building a unified, peaceful, and democratic Germany. Beria, more knowledgeable than the rest, blurted out the truth that East Germany was not "even a real state. It's only kept in being by Soviet troops." However, he met with frantic opposition from the majority of the Soviet rulers. Nikita Khrushchev supported Molotov's stand, and the rest of the Presidium[23] bandwagoned. Beria and Malenkov beat a hasty retreat.

The situation in the Soviet alliance relationships (the C level) and in dealing with the West (the D level) worked to the disadvantage of Beria and Malenkov.

The Soviet Union needed to keep its alliances intact in the difficult interregnum after Stalin's death. A "betrayal" of the GDR leadership would have been a terrible blow to the Soviet image among the satellite political elites and their foreign supporters. In addition, the Western governments, led by Adenauer and Eisenhower, were preoccupied with consolidating their alliance and therefore adopted a rigid line on possible negotiations on Germany, which discouraged the Soviet leaders from taking risks—particularly after the worker insurrection in East Berlin in June.

The Beria-Malenkov initiative had no chance domestically either (the A level and B level). Its radicalism threatened to destroy a shaky legitimacy of the ruling group in the eyes of bureaucracies and population. Khrushchev became the mouthpiece of this fear when he denounced Beria's initiative (after his arrest) as high treason. Reunifying Germany, Khrushchev argued, would not just strengthen imperialism but would place "18 million [East] Germans under the mastery of American imperialism."[24] Molotov, otherwise highly critical of Khrushchev, admitted late in his life that Khrushchev's gut feelings on the German Question reflected his Russian nationalism, which, in this case, coincided with "state interests." According to Molotov, Khrushchev expressed the opinion of many who thought: "Had our people shed our blood in vain [in the Second World War]? If the GDR had not followed the road of socialism, it would have been [the same] old Germany."[25]

From this moment until 1990 the attitude of the Soviet rulers towards the German Question was defined not only by the imperatives of the Cold War, or the considerations of *Realpolitik*, but by this domestic platform that, as they assumed, represented the consensus in Soviet society. The prospect of German reunification from a goal of Stalin's policy in 1945 became a nightmare scenario instead, a synonym for the worst geostrategic and ideological defeat.

As a result, Ulbricht, whose removal seemed imminent in June, consolidated his rule, with the direct support of Molotov and Khrushchev. For the first time the East German leader was able to profit from manipulating Soviet politics: He branded all his rivals as Beria's conspirators. He was no longer a political pawn in the Soviet game but the most important guarantor of the most important of the Soviet satellites.

Although the Politburo made decisions on foreign policy "collectively," Molotov became for a while a primary authority on the German Question. He conducted a duel of diplomatic notes with the West, attempting with only episodic success to define the settlement of the German Question as mutual recognition of "two German states." He reckoned on using France's fears of German rearmament to split the united Western front in favor of West Germany's integration into a "European Defense Union." He even undertook a secret attempt to establish bilateral contacts with the FRG. Indeed, the French National Assembly voted down the plan for a European army. However, the United States and Great Britain quickly recouped with a proposal to include the FRG in NATO. That discredited Molotov's foreign policy authority. Nikita Khrushchev challenged Molotov's position and began to look for ways to break the impasse and move toward accommodation with West Germany.

THE AUSTRIAN TREATY AND ADENAUER'S VISIT TO MOSCOW IN 1955

Khrushchev's struggle with Molotov and Malenkov for leadership in the party apparatus became the catalyst for change in policy toward Germany. As a party first secretary, he received information from all state bureaucracies, including Molotov's Foreign Ministry, and noticed among many problems one long-neglected issue—the future of Austria.

The Austrian dilemma repeated the German one of ten years before. Despite the tensions of the Cold War and its continued occupation this small country preserved its integrity and a central government that had consistently asked for an end to occupation and a neutral status. Since the formation of the two German states some Soviet diplomats, especially those stationed in the FRG, had advocated Austrian neutrality as a way to promote German neutralism and to build a wedge into NATO. In May–June 1953 Malenkov, then head of the state, asked Molotov to have another look at this problem. Andrei Gromyko, Molotov's first deputy, concluded in his analysis that "in the conditions of an appropriate international situation, a conclusion of a treaty with Austria would be more advantageous to the Soviet Union than an absence of this treaty and our sticking to our old positions." But Molotov deleted this phrase from his response to Malenkov's request. On June 3, 1953, he wrote that there was "no reason to change our stand on the Austrian issue."

By early 1954 there was no unanimity in the Politburo about an Austrian settlement. Meanwhile, Molotov vigorously objected to a withdrawal of Soviet troops, arguing that they should stay in Austria as an ultimate guarantee against another *Anschluss* of Austria to West Germany. He firmly linked an Austrian settlement to settlement of the German Question. Besides, he argued, the Soviets expropriated German property in their zone of Austria and that was another reason to keep a tight grip on it. Khrushchev, however, realized that there was a growing desire among Soviet bureaucracies to diffuse the prewar tensions in Europe; it helped him argue against the still strong "military-industrial" and "party-ideological" considerations. He decided to seek a neutralization of Austria and made sure that the Austrian Communist Party would not object to it.[26]

Khrushchev's initiative could not prevent the inclusion of the FRG into NATO—in response, the Soviet Union established the Warsaw Treaty Organization and included the GDR. But a new diplomacy did "unlock" negotiations with Western powers on the German Question. It cleared the road for a summit of great powers in Geneva, the first one since Potsdam. Simultaneously, the Soviet government opened its dialogue with West German Chancellor Konrad Adenauer, inviting him to Moscow to discuss diplomatic, trade, and cultural relations between the two countries.[27]

The existing evidence suggests that Khrushchev was also, if not predominantly, concerned with building his authority as a statesman, in competition with Molotov. He needed his own imprint on foreign policy, and he got it in Austria. This initiative increased his "self-legitimacy": He believed that his mixture of toughness and flexibility made him a better leader of Soviet foreign policy than Molotov. Already at the ceremony of the signing of the Austrian State Treaty Khrushchev let the Soviet diplomatic establishment know that he was now in control. In April–May 1955 he defeated Molotov's opposition to his other initiative, a reconciliation with Josep Tito in Yugoslavia. He sealed his victory on the elite level (B level) at the June 1955 Plenum. In Geneva in July 1955 Khrushchev was clearly the leader of the Soviet delegation.

Khrushchev's debut on the German Question achieved what neither Stalin nor Molotov could achieve. Khrushchev correctly acted as if the road to Bonn went via Vienna and Washington.[28] When the United States and other Western powers met with the Soviet leadership in Geneva, the Adenauer government could not afford to stay out of this process. The Kremlin learned that Adenauer's prestige was seriously undermined by the Geneva summit, and this pushed him to reassess his opposition to establishment of diplomatic relations with Moscow, under the pressure from the Social Democrats and the business circles interested in trade with the East.[29]

During Adenauer's visit in Moscow in September 1955 talks were difficult. In part, this was explained by the factors of alliance and domestic politics. The Soviets had to take into account the prestige of Ulbricht and the GDR who were not invited to the talks. Domestically, the talks evoked the bad memories of Soviet-German negotiations in 1939–1940, particularly Molotov's trip to Berlin followed by the Nazi surprise attack. The Kremlin leaders, particularly Khrushchev, were very nervous; they acted "tough" to show their bureaucratic constituencies and the general public that they would not give in on Soviet security interests. Molotov's ill-fated trip to Berlin in November 1940 and more recent denunciations of Beria's German initiative, fresh on their minds, also undoubtedly had an impact. The "good" part of the talks was publicized in *Pravda*; the contentious part remained hidden from the Soviet public. At one point Khrushchev produced one of his famous fits: "The German Federal Republic has signed the Paris Agreements, accepted the militarization and armament of Germany, and joined a NATO that is aimed against the Soviet Union. [NATO] is getting ready for war against the Soviet Union, and the Federal Republic is taking part in it."[30]

The results of the visit of Adenauer satisfied the Soviet leadership. A first encounter with Adenauer allayed the Kremlin's fears about West German designs to swallow East Germany. Soviet diplomats and intelligence sources had informed Khrushchev before that most West European politicians paid only lip service to the idea of German reunification. After the Moscow talks, he came to the same conclusion about Adenauer.[31] Until then, Soviet policy on the German Question stood only on one foot, the GDR. From now on the Soviets could build diplomatic and trade bridges to West Germany and hope to steer it away from the Western alliance.

Khrushchev and key German experts in the bureaucracies again, like Stalin in 1945–1946 and Beria in 1953, began to hope they could dramatically increase Soviet influence over West Germany by exploiting Bonn's interest in trade and economic relations as well as the antagonism between the SPD and the Adenauer government. The Soviets established direct confidential contacts with the SPD, first through "public diplomacy" in "neutral countries,"[32] and, after the establishment of diplomatic relations, through diplomatic channels as well. In December 1955 Valerian Zorin, first Soviet ambassador to the FRG, received instructions "to give necessary attention and support to the Social Democratic party and those bourgeois circles that stood in opposition to the policy of the Adenauer government."[33]

The diplomatic maneuvres in 1955 led to the first successes of the Soviet diplomacy in Germany. They developed, in part, because of the "politics" of the power struggle in Moscow. In 1953 nobody in the Politburo had enough authority to carry out changes. Two years later Khrushchev collected enough power and elite support (B level) to overrule Molotov on Austria and on Germany. But his initiative on Germany had its limits: He shared memories and fears of his generation, the party, and state *nomenklatura* who had experienced the Nazi assault and believed in a "socialist Germany." Neither he nor anybody around him was prepared even to discuss the possibility of German reunification; the maximum he hoped to achieve was the consolidation of the GDR as a part of the Soviet alliance and the weakening of the FRG as a key partner in the Western alliance. Because of these limitations, in the following years Khrushchev's strategies in Germany fizzled out. And Soviet foreign policy on the German Question remained in many ways a hostage to the health and stability of the Ulbricht regime in East Germany (C level), the situation that Beria and Malenkov had sought to change in vain in 1953.

THE AGGRAVATION OF THE SITUATION IN THE GDR AND THE DEADLOCK IN SOVIET-WEST GERMAN RELATIONS (1956-1958)

Khrushchev continued his unconditional support for a "socialist" German Democratic Republic. For him personally it presented an historic alternative to the "imperialist German state." Economically and politically, it remained a jewel in the Soviet imperial crown. The Soviet leader, along with Soviet economic planners and the military-industrial complex, expected to extract great benefits from combining high German productivity and technological mastery with Russian resources (a long-time dream of the Bolsheviks). And the existence of the GDR boosted the ideological claims of the Soviet regime in the communist world.

Thanks to massive Soviet aid, in late 1953 and early 1954 the economic situation in East Germany improved and the flight of young well-trained workers and professionals to West Germany diminished. But by the end of 1954 and during 1955, economic pessimism and the flight of population resumed with new force. As memoranda to the leadership stressed, this happened because of continuing attempts by the Ulbricht regime to increase "the socialist sector," and because the economic boom in the Federal Republic left the GDR further behind.[34]

The Soviet government recognized that the solution of this problem required enormous economic assistance and/or serious political reforms in the GDR. Top

Soviet economic leaders and some experts in the Foreign Ministry had doubts about the effects of the continuing pump-priming without major reforms and changes of leadership. They began to feel that the GDR could be a bottomless pit, swallowing resources desperately needed in the Soviet domestic economy. The strains over these problems grew. In the dispatches to the Foreign Ministry from the Soviet ambassador to the GDR G. Pushkin during 1955 and early 1956, criticism of Ulbricht policies and leadership was only thinly veiled.[35]

Ironically, it was Khrushchev's denunciation of Stalin at the XXth Congress of the CPSU (February 1956) and its consequences in the communist world that nipped in the bud all attempts at reforming the GDR. The "secret speech" evoked great anguish and protest from East Berlin. Ulbricht did not conceal his fear that sharp turns like this could throw him and his whole regime out of the saddle. This fear was remarkably confirmed in the fall of 1956 by the revolutions in Poland and Hungary. Suddenly Ulbricht's antireform wisdom became vindicated, and criticism in Soviet dispatches from East Germany was replaced by fraternal compassion. Instead of dwelling on what the GDR could do to improve its own (and Soviet) security, discourse, as in the summer of 1953, focused on what the Soviet Union could do to prop up its failing "asset."[36]

Another problem was a sudden revival of the "German threat" in Soviet politics. West German militarization took a serious turn. In January 1957 President Eisenhower announced plans to install medium-range nuclear weapons, targeted on the Soviet Union, in Turkey, Iran, Japan, and West Germany. Simultaneously, Washington strategists began to discuss the nuclearization of the Bundeswehr with weapons under American control in order to reduce the large number of U.S. troops in Europe. In the same weeks Bonn rejected the "Rapacki plan" to turn Central Europe into a nuclear-free zone.

On April 25, 1957, in a conversation with Soviet ambassador in the FRG Andrei Smirnov (who had replaced Zorin in October 1956), Chancellor Adenauer did not deny that West Germany might become a nuclear power. Foreign Minister Heinrich Brentano, present at the conversation, added: "If England and other powers have atomic weapons, why should the Federal Republic not have them?"[37] In retaliation, Moscow closed the confidential channel between Khrushchev and Adenauer. Smirnov continued to warn the Soviet leadership that the Adenauer government was deliberately stalling on negotiations with Moscow while building the position of strength from which it would resume its offensive with regard to the GDR and German Eastern borders.[38]

These developments (on the D level) were all the more painful to Khrushchev because they directly challenged his leadership in foreign policy. His debut in 1955 was in part nourished by a misplaced optimism that the days of NATO were numbered. As 1956 went on, Khrushchev was still confident that Soviet peace initiatives would undermine the Western convictions about a Soviet threat and this would be the end of NATO.[39] The split among Western great powers during the Suez crisis in November 1956 elated the Soviet leader. But in 1957 Smirnov's reports from Bonn contributed greatly to the worst-case mentality at the very top, at the time when a majority was bracing up for a direct assault at Khrushchev.

The instability in the Soviet alliance (the C level), a direct result of Khrushchev's policies, gave a menacing ring to the renewed "German threat." Even earlier, the impact of the series of revolutions in Eastern Europe was clear in an estimate of the Foreign Ministry and the Committee of Information to the Presidium CC CPSU on November 29, 1956 (the main author was Valentin Falin). The estimate indicated that, as a result of the Polish and Hungarian uprisings, the Bonn government expected to weaken the Soviet position by expanding bilateral ties to East European countries. The report even suggested that the FRG might recognize postwar Polish borders so that "the Polish government would no longer be interested in hosting Soviet troops on Polish territory." The Soviet Union would then have to pull the troops back "not to the Oder-Neisse line, but to the Soviet borders." Other studies created the impression that the Federal Republic was trying to entice Czechoslovakia to leave the Soviet-led alliance system. If Poland and Czechoslovakia "go neutral," they suggested, the Soviet strategic position in East Germany would be untenable. Beyond this, the reports said, the West German government had intensified efforts to destabilize the economic situation in the GDR and "to discredit and isolate" Ulbricht.[40] It speaks volumes that Soviet analysts at that time could discuss such worst-case scenarios.

In early 1957 the opposition to Khrushchev's leadership in the Politburo attempted to use against him the reversal in 1953–1956 from exploitation of East German economy to its pump-priming. Khrushchev's ally Anastas Mikoyan later, at the June 1957 Plenum, gave a revealing insight into this clash. He blamed Molotov, Malenkov, and Kaganovich for a narrow, purely budgetary, approach to the issue. "We believe we must create an economic base for our influence on Austria, to strengthen its neutral status, so that West Germany would not have a [economic and trade] monopoly in Austria." And, "if we leave East Germany and Czechoslovakia without [purchase] orders, then the entire socialist camp will begin to collapse. . . . After all, the issue stands as such: Either feed the workers of the GDR for free, or provide orders, or otherwise lose the GDR entirely."[41] Once again, Khrushchev beat the opposition by staying on the same platform as back in 1953 against Beria and Malenkov and claiming that the oppositioners had substituted petty politics for the issue of policy.

At first, the end of the power struggle in Moscow seemed to clear the ground for a less neurotic, less ideologically and domestically "tainted" policy on West Germany. Gromyko, the new Foreign Minister who replaced the member of the "antiparty group" Shelepin, considered Smirnov's reports from Bonn "too alarmist" and argued for giving Soviet-West German negotiations another chance. In January 1958 Anastas Mikoyan, obviously at Khrushchev's initiative, visited Bonn and tried to dissuade Adenauer from his military programs by stressing all the benefits (especially in trade) that an improvement of bilateral relations would bring. Mikoyan also, rather awkwardly, emphasized that atomic armament of the Bundeswehr would make German reunification impossible.[42] Nevertheless, in March

1958 the Federal Republic adopted the program of having American nuclear weapons stored in Germany for use by the Bundeswehr in a war. After that, Soviet relations with the FRG fell to the lowest point since 1955. The prevention of West German "nuclearization" became one of the top goals on Soviet foreign policy agenda.

As far as Khrushchev was concerned, the German situation needed another major push. Again, like in early 1955, the Soviet leader decided to put pressure on Western great powers in order to work around Bonn's intransigence and dark plots. His idea was to initiate an overall diplomatic settlement on the German Question before the Federal Republic could undermine the status quo in Central Europe. But this time Khrushchev lost his belief in winning the West over with unilateral Soviet concessions. Instead, he preferred to "kick the West in the balls" by threatening NATO positions in West Berlin. In the summer of 1958 the Soviet Union and GDR came up with a diplomatic offensive to promote a peace treaty between the two German states, with the great powers serving as guarantors. In November 1958 Khrushchev gave this a powerful twist by announcing his intention to recognize East Germany unilaterally in six months. That would in effect have given Ulbricht control over all access routes to West Berlin and forced the West to negotiate with his regime. To mark his peaceful intentions, Khrushchev proposed a special status of "free city" for West Berlin. The result of this diplomatic *tour de force* is well known: The Berlin crisis kept the whole of Europe and the United States in suspense and fear for more than three years.

KHRUSHCHEV BEGINS AND ENDS THE BERLIN CRISIS (NOVEMBER 1958–OCTOBER 1961)

After the defeat of the "anti-party opposition" (Molotov, Malenkov, Kaganovich) in June 1957 Khrushchev was the unchallenged ruler of the Soviet Union and centrally involved in foreign policy decision-making. His commitments as well as his perceptions therefore mattered a great deal in the Soviet line on Germany. The Berlin ultimatum was a product of his impatience and high personal stakes he felt he had in the resolution of the German Question. Also, considerations on various levels continued to define his choice of options. On the alliance level (the C level) his commitment to Ulbricht and the GDR regime made him inflexible on East Berlin and in negotiations about the status of West Berlin. Many times Western public figures had hinted that all of Berlin could become a neutral city, but Khrushchev rejected this outright. Also, Khrushchev did little to discourage Ulbricht and his people from hatching schemes for what amounted to the actual conquest and purge of West Berlin in case the West did retreat, and this East German belligerence made Khrushchev's proposal for a "free city" totally unappealing in West Germany, even in accommodationist circles. Soviet diplomats complained to Gromyko and the Party Central Committee, but Khrushchev did not want to intervene.

In another development on the alliance level, Khrushchev discovered that his "toughness" on the issue of Berlin helped him gain points in his difficult relationship with the Chinese communist leadership. Mao Zedong resented Khrushchev's denunciation of Stalin, did not recognize his leadership in the communist camp, and looked suspiciously at his foreign policy of "peaceful coexistence" with the West. Since spring 1958 Khrushchev-Mao relations had been in decline. At first, Mao accused Khrushchev of colonialist ambitions in China and later, without bothering to consult Moscow, unleashed an international crisis by threatening to invade Taiwan-held off-shore islands. The Soviet leadership was seriously upset but outwardly promised full support and a nuclear umbrella. Gromyko rushed to Beijing attempting to coordinate policy with the Chinese. The whole episode humiliated Khrushchev and further increased his determination to pressure the Western powers to negotiate over West Berlin and the German settlement.[43]

The impact of the Taiwan straits crisis for Khrushchev overlapped with the after effects of his clash with the "anti-party group" more than a year earlier. The party apparatus, KGB, the military and economic managers supported him. However, privately many agreed with the criticisms they heard at the June 1957 Plenum. Khrushchev was stung by Molotov's accusation that he had gone too far in making concessions to the West. Oleg Troyanovsky, who became Khrushchev's foreign policy assistant in 1958, recalls that this weighed heavily on his boss's mind as he plotted a showdown on Berlin. If so, then Khrushchev had indeed learned something from the struggle with Beria and Malenkov and was careful not to repeat the steps that had sealed their fate. For both realpolitik and domestic reasons he needed to conduct negotiations with the West from a position of strength.

At first, Khrushchev's risktaking seemed to have paid off: Eisenhower reluctantly decided to meet Khrushchev in the United States and to visit the Soviet Union. Such contact, from Khrushchev's perspective, could bypass Adenauer in the resolution of the German question. In a letter to the West German Chancellor he formulated the dilemma for him: either Adenauer reached a bilateral agreement with the Soviet Union on de facto recognition of the GDR and the Eastern borders, or the German Question would be settled without him, perhaps between Khrushchev and Eisenhower. Khrushchev made it clear that a bilateral deal with the FRG could make him shelve the idea of a separate treaty with the GDR.[44]

Subsequently, at Camp David, Khrushchev traded his deadline on Germany and West Berlin for Eisenhower's agreement to convene a four-power summit to discuss, among other issues, the German Question. For a brief moment, the Soviet leader must have felt that he was at the peak of his domestic and international career. Khrushchev's propaganda assistants orchestrated his return from the United States as a triumphal victory. To develop the effect of his "peace offensive," Khrushchev proposed a new military doctrine, relying on strategic missiles with nuclear warheads rather than on huge conventional forces for protection of Soviet security. He also proposed the most far-reaching unilateral reductions in Soviet military forces since 1945–1947 and announced them publicly in January 1960. In a longer-term perspective, these initiatives could have led to a drastic reduction of the Western forces stationed in Germany in response to the Korean war and

Stalin's decisions to turn East Germany into a beachhead for a *Blitzkrieg* in Western Europe in retaliation for a U.S. nuclear attack.

During these months (September 1959–April 1960) the rest of the Soviet political establishment (B level) lagged behind Khrushchev's pace. For a moment it seemed as if the innovative vigor of his leadership had pushed aside all the constraints imposed by domestic and alliance politics. The development of missile technology and the nuclear revolution reduced the importance of East Germany as a geostrategic asset. Marshals and generals may have disagreed with Khrushchev's "new look" and grumbled privately, but they obeyed his orders (in October 1957 Khrushchev dismissed Marshal Georgy Zhukov, the only military leader who could have resisted his reforms). Public opinion applauded Khrushchev's "struggle for peace," particularly from what seemed to be a position of strength.

In reality, Khrushchev's swinging from ultimatum and war threats to détente created serious strains on both levels, but particularly among the allies. In East Germany Ulbricht and his lieutenants viewed the plan for disarmament and the reduction of Soviet troops in Germany with open dismay. And Mao Zedong was extremely irritated by Khrushchev's visit to the United States and the high hopes he vested in Eisenhower.

The incident with the U-2 in May 1960 revealed the adventurist underpinning of Khrushchev's foreign policy. His perceptions of American politics and the relationship with the United States, with crude oversimplifaction, can be reduced to the following. He visualized the Cold War as a product of "dark forces": warmongers in the Pentagon and State Department, CIA, arms manufacturers. Distinct from them were "reasonable" elements, including Eisenhower. If one could neutralize "dark forces" by demonstrating Soviet power (nuclear brinkmanship) or by exposing their plots, then one could do business with Eisenhower. For that reason Khrushchev thought it would be a great idea to catch the CIA red-handed, make some heads roll, and "liberate" Eisenhower from its pernicious influence.

When the American President acknowledged his personal responsibility for spy flights over the USSR, Khrushchev lost the game: He was open to criticism back home and inside the alliance, from Mao to the Soviet high command. With alacrity Khrushchev fell back upon Cold War rhetoric and wrecked the Paris summit. He began to build up his revolutionary credentials neglected during the two years of his focus on Germany and relations with Washington. The wave of decolonization in the "third world," in the Congo, Laos, Cuba, and so on, provided the Soviet Union with a new field for expansion of its influence in the world. However, in the previous years Khrushchev had invested too much of his leadership credibility and had built excessively high domestic and alliance expectations around his scheme of German and West Berlin settlement. He could not simply back off and forget about his ultimatum of 1958. And the urgency of the German Question continued to aggravate, primarily due to the economic and social deterioration of East Germany.

In the summer of 1960 Ulbricht took revenge for the previous humiliation and began to push the Soviets toward a separate treaty. On October 17, 1960, Moscow learned that its East German "friends" were planning to close a sectoral border in Berlin. From documents in Moscow it is not clear whether it was just a provocation designed to stampede the Soviets into further action. What was obvious, however, was the new role of the GDR rulers: The tail attempted to wag the dog; the puppets learned to manipulate the puppeteer.[45]

Ulbricht played on his weakness: By threatening to collapse, he sought to extort massive new aid and concessions from the Soviets. This "tyranny of the weak," borrowing a phrase of historian Geir Lundestad, had parallels in the behavior of certain American allies at times. The difference was that the entire Soviet presence in Central Europe depended on the stability of the GDR. After the collapse of the Paris summit the flight of people from East to West Germany grew every week, depleting the East German economy. During 1960 Ulbricht repeatedly warned the Soviets that if they continued to alternate between crisis and détente, this would undermine his regime. He also surprised Moscow with the news that if Bonn chose to abrogate the existing trade relations with the GDR, its economy would collapse.

Khrushchev also had to react to the criticism of the Chinese who blamed him for naivete or, worse, for lack of guts in confrontation with the West over Germany. Unable to preserve the Sino-Soviet alliance and carry out his foreign policy in the West at the same time, Khrushchev moved in fits: In the summer of 1960 he suddenly withdrew Soviet technicians and terminated assistance programs in the People's Republic of China. But in the face of the Chinese criticism, he had to live up to his commitments to the GDR. So he forgave Ulbricht his plots and blackmail and promised massive assistance at the expense of the immediate needs of the Soviet economy. He also promised Ulbricht to sign a separate treaty with the GDR if the next President, Eisenhower's successor, refused to negotiate.[46]

The dialogue between John F. Kennedy and Khrushchev through diplomatic channels looked promising at first. However, after Kennedy's decision to take responsibility for the Bay of Pigs invasion of Cuba, Khrushchev decided to bully the young and inexperienced American leader into the same kind of bilateral talks on Germany that he had earlier carried on with Eisenhower. As a result, the summit meeting in Vienna (June 3–4, 1961) was another fiasco. Kennedy, encouraged by NATO unity after the U-2 episode, and particularly by deGaulle's support, emerged as a staunch defender of the status quo in Berlin. Despite rumors of bad chemistry between Kennedy and Adenauer, in Vienna Kennedy sounded even less flexible on a German settlement than had Eisenhower at Camp David. Khrushchev threatened war and soon after the summit published a Soviet *aide-memoir* with a new deadline for a peace treaty by the end of the year. But the logjam remained, and the interplay of forces, from American domestic politics to politics within NATO, pushed Kennedy into a "chicken game" with Khrushchev: The United States responded to a potential Soviet-GDR move on the allied positions in West Berlin with the threat of all-out war.[47]

After Kennedy announced this position on July 25, Khrushchev used John J. McCloy, who visited him on vacation the same day, to show he was not intimidated and ready to answer with a war threat of his own. Addressing his military and the leaders of the Warsaw Pact, Khrushchev vowed to continue a showdown with the United States. He stopped the program of unilateral reduction of the Soviet Army and authorized a test of a 100 megaton thermonuclear bomb to let "the sword of Damocles" hang over imperialists' heads. At the same time he supported Ulbricht's long standing request to close the border with West Berlin.[48] On August 13 the partition of Berlin became a fact: The city was cut into two parts by barbed wire, and later by the concrete Wall.

Khrushchev still expected to gain time and stabilize the situation in the GDR; after the showdown, he believed détente and agreement with the United States on Germany would follow. For that reason, he dragged out the Berlin crisis even after the construction of the Wall. But as he realized the impossibility of a headlong political offensive on the West, he allowed his deadline to lapse quietly. From then on Soviet German policy became "the diplomacy of attrition." Once Bonn learned East Germany could not be touched or reached, the logic went, it would formulate a more accommodating position. Soviet and GDR intelligence used penetration and large-scale "active measures" to expedite this development. This hope and these efforts became vindicated in the *Ostpolitik* of Willi Brandt and Egon Bahr. Tragically, the division of Berlin, a temporary move designed to bolster East Germany and the Soviet position in future negotiations on the German Question, became a permanent symbol of the division of Germany. The Wall collapsed only with the Cold War in Europe in November 1989.

Many claimed that the major factor that forced Khrushchev to rescind his plans was American strategic superiority and a series of failures in Soviet missile programs. Other analysts conclude that it was not superiority but the nuclear danger that put limits on Khrushchev's actions. Both sides assume that Khrushchev still wanted to sign a separate treaty, but then changed his mind after a speech of Undersecretary of Defense Roswell Gilpatrick that ended "missile gap" hysteria in the West and publicized U.S. strategic superiority.[49]

But, according to Khrushchev's closest foreign policy assistant, he did not think seriously about the danger of nuclear war during the summer of 1961.[50] What a contrast with Khrushchev's genuine fear during the Cuban missile crisis, and with the mood of the Kennedy administration during the same months in 1961![51] This serenity could only have come from the sense of control over the situation, and behind this sense was, I believe, Khrushchev's hidden shift to a minimalist, evolutionary policy regarding Germany.

This reflected the pressure of circumstances. The signing of a separate treaty with East Germany would have come into conflict with the important "military-industrial" coalition of interests and considerations, represented by numerous and angry voices: military and economic. Among high-placed military officers the fear was widespread that the Soviet army, weakened by hasty cuts, did not have enough firepower to impress the West in a showdown. GRU colonel and American spy Oleg Penkovsky reported to his CIA debriefers on July 18, at the height of Khrushchev's brinkmanship, that "the current belief" among the Soviet military was that, thanks to Khrushchev's militant speeches, Kennedy, Macmillan and de Gaulle have been forced to increase their armament programs by two or three times. If Stalin were alive he would do everything quietly but this fool is blurting out his threats and intentions and is forcing our potential enemies to increase their military strength. They dislike him and say that he is hurting his own cause and that he talks too much about Soviet military accomplishments in his effort to frighten the Western leaders.[52]

As for the economists and industrial planners in the Soviet government, they too would have been extremely unhappy about a separate treaty. So would most East European governments because Warsaw Pact leaders understood (and intelligence reports confirmed it) that the West would most likely retaliate with an economic blockade against the GDR and sanctions against the rest of the Communist bloc. The costs for Soviet and Eastern economies would have been staggering.

The erection of the Wall and the new time-gaining scenario on the German Question allowed Khrushchev to get off a dangerous hook, his commitment to the GDR, while regaining flexibility on German policy and bringing his ends closer to the means available. Immediately after August 13 he resumed personal correspondence with Kennedy and secret contacts with governing and opposition circles in the Federal Republic. The mild tension around West Berlin continued to serve Khrushchev's political needs in his relations with Washington and NATO. During the Cuban missile crisis, when the Deputy Foreign Minister suggested to him that overt threats on West Berlin could have made the Soviet position stronger, Khrushchev angrily dismissed this as "adventurism."

The crisis-ridden record of Khrushchev's foreign policy in general and German policy in particular became an important factor in creating the coalition of political-bureaucratic forces that overthrew him in October 1964. The consensus of "state," "military-industrial," "party-ideological," and other considerations turned against the aging and increasingly irrelevant leader. Khrushchev's successors did not want to reveal their frustrations and disagreements, so only now is documentary evidence coming to light that reveals the enormous tension that had accumulated between the leader and the elites (the A and B levels). An undelivered Presidium report[53] to the October Plenum reflected deep discontent by key elements of Soviet party and state apparatus, starting with economic and industrial management and including the KGB, Foreign Ministry, and the high military command.

The report singled out the Berlin crisis (along with the Cuban missile crisis and the Suez crisis of 1956) in accusing Khrushchev of reckless brinkmanship. It derided Khrushchev's ultimatum: "More than several deadlines have passed, and Berlin has not become a free city. True, the Wall was built, but one did not need an ultimatum to do this. However we may twist the truth, the result was not favorable for us. Comrade Khrushchev wanted to scare Americans, but they refused to be scared, and we had to back off, to sustain a sensitive blow on our authority and prestige of our country, our policy and our armed forces."[54]

In a telling recognition of the strain in GDR-Soviet relations produced by Khrushchev's German policy, the report severely criticized a visit by Khrushchev's personal emissary, his son-in-law Alexei Adzhubei, to Bonn earlier in 1964. It took seriously rumors that Khrushchev was getting ready for a breakthrough in relations with the Federal Republic. According to the report, the Adzhubei visit created "an impression that the Soviet Union was prepared, in the interest of improving relations with the FRG, to make some concessions to the militarists at the expense of the GDR and People's Poland. This produced justifiable discontent among East German and Polish comrades who have bluntly declared that they do not understand why the Soviet Prime Minister was going to visit West Germany at a time when there was a wave of revanchism there and when German militarists were openly threatening the security of the GDR, Poland, and Czechoslovakia.[55]

In 1964 once again, as after Stalin's death, domestic politics and alliance politics marched hand in hand in opposition to a perceived intent of the leader to break the deadlock on the German question. A coalition of people and interests, driven by anti-Khrushchev sentiment, came out in support of the Ulbricht regime in the same way Khrushchev and others had formed an alliance on the German issue while arresting and denouncing Beria.

CONCLUSION

The main conclusion of this chapter is that not only the bipolar logic of the Cold War but also politics on various levels prevented Soviet leaders from seriously pursuing German reunification in the 1950s and 1960s. Lined up against innovation were "domestic politics" of the power struggle after Stalin's death, the two-way relations with key Soviet allies, and personal inhibitions of the leaders themselves (particularly in the case of Nikita Khrushchev). In fact, all four of the levels mentioned at the outset (the A level to D level) dictated unflagging Soviet support for the GDR.

The consensus of state, military-industrial, and party-ideological motives and interests was remarkably strong in the case of Soviet policy regarding Germany. Indeed, the long-term Soviet consensus on the German question rested on a unique combination of military, economic, and ideological factors as well as profound "memories of the last war." In the case of the Beria-Malenkov option the attempt to put *Realpolitik* above politics backfired and cost the initiators dearly. In the years that followed, this direction in politics prevailed over *Realpolitik* (although Western intransigence provided "realist" grounds for the continued Soviet bolstering of East Germany), and this allowed the Ulbricht regime to rely on Moscow and even blackmail it.

Stalin was the only ruler in Soviet history who could willfully and abruptly change the course of German policy (as he had already demonstrated once in 1939), but he was perhaps the least willing to do so. Khrushchev never became an unchallenged ruler of the Soviet Union; he defeated his opponents and critics, but the power struggle after Stalin's death liberated politics on the elite level, and this factor more than anything else contributed to Khrushchev's ouster from power. Alliance politics continued to grow in importance as the Chinese leadership openly challenged the authority of Moscow in the communist world, and the Ulbricht regime exercised its "tyranny of the weak."

These pressures of politics, aggravated by Khrushchev's own mistakes and the fitful nature of his policymaking, muted and then deflected the impact of nuclear revolution and the growing costs of the empire on the Soviet economy. By the end of the 1950s, Khrushchev spasmodically attempted to put everything into proper place, initiating drastic cuts, a revision of Soviet security policy, and a "solution" for West Berlin—actions that, in a longer term, could have led to diminishing the GDR as a military-geostrategic asset and to stabilization of the "two states" situation in Germany. At the same time, Soviet industrial managers began to see pump-priming the GDR as futile. If it was too soon for a new combination of interests to give rise to a new policy on the German question from inside the Soviet establishment, those at least were the first important chinks in the monolith.[56] Tragically, Khrushchev's risk-taking and ideological excesses, his inconsistent attempts to short-circuit the route to a settlement of the German question, and his mishandling of the Berlin crisis left a lasting imprint on the Soviet establishment; even after Khrushchev's fall, the memory of his risky zigzags contributed to the coalition of political interests inside the country, allied with Soviet clients in Central Europe, that hindered the reappraisal of Soviet policy on Germany.

The fact that politics played a predominantly negative role and exacerbated Cold War rigidity and tensions in Central Europe does not change main elements of the "realist analysis" but adds some important nuances. In the Soviet Union, even with all the pressures of politics at various levels, the need for policy innovation, reforms, and economic relief from the costs of the empire continued to build up over time. In the early 1960s the construction of the Wall helped the Kremlin to gain some time and postpone reconsideration of its German policy. Ten years later the emergence of *Ostpolitik* gave the Kremlin a long-awaited way out of the logjam and transformed the German question from the most burning issue of the Cold War into a permanent nuisance, tolerable for all, even to some Germans. Only in the late 1980s, in a pervasive domestic crisis and reformist tailspin, did Mikhail Gorbachev have to face again the dilemma that his predecessors had resolved for themselves many times before: continue to support the ossified conservative regime in East Germany at any cost or to sacrifice it in the name of ending the Cold War in Europe. To his credit he chose the latter, erasing in a moment the grip of old politics and old memories on Soviet (and Russian) foreign policy towards Germany.

NOTES

1. Adam Ulam, *Expansion and Coexistence: Soviet Foreign Policy, 1917–1973*, second edition (New York: Praeger, 1974); Jack M. Schick, *The Berlin Crisis, 1958–1962* (Philadelphia: University of Pennsylvania Press, 1971).

2. Robert M. Slusser, *The Berlin Crisis of 1961: Soviet-American Relations and the Struggle for Power in the Kremlin, June–November 1961* (Baltimore: Johns Hopkins University Press, 1973).

3. Honore M. Catudal, *Kennedy and the Berlin Wall Crisis: A Case in U.S. Decision Making* (Berlin: Berlin Verlag, 1980); Michel Tatu, *Power in the Kremlin: From Khrushchev to Kosygin* (New York: Viking Press, 1968).

4. Michael Beschloss, *Kennedy and Khrushchev: The Crisis Years* (New York: Harper-Collins, 1991); Marc Trachtenberg, *History and Strategy* (Princeton: Princeton University Press, 1991); Peter Wyden, *Wall: The Inside Story of Divided Berlin* (New York, Simon and Schuster, 1989).

5. See, for example, James G. Richter, *Khrushchev's Double Bind: International Pressures and Domestic Coalition Politics* (Baltimore: Johns Hopkins University Press, 1994); by the same author "Reexamining Soviet Policy towards Germany during the Beria Interregnum," *Europe-Asia Studies* 4 (1993); Hope M. Harrison, "Ulbricht and the Concrete 'Rose': New Archival Evidence on the Dynamics of Soviet-East German Relations and the Berlin Crisis, 1958–1961," Working Paper 5, Cold War International History Project, May 1993; Gerhard Wettig, "Zur Stand der Forschung der Berijas Deutschland-Politik im Fruehjahr 1953," *Deutschland Archiv*, 26 (1993); Gerhard Wettig, ed. *Die sowjetische Deutschland-Politik in der Aera Adenauer* (Bonn: Bouvier, 1997); Wilfried Loth/Rolf Badsttuebner, eds., *Wilhelm Pieck—Aufzeichnungen zur Deutschlandpolitik 1945—1953* (Berlin: Akademie Verlag, 1994); Christian Ostermann, "Soviet Deutschlandpolitik and the SED: New Evidence from Russian, German and Hungarian Archives," *Bulletin of the Cold War International History Project* (CWIHP), March 1998, no. 10; Vladislav Zubok, "Khrushchev and the Berlin Crisis," Working Paper 6, Cold War International History Project, May 1993.

6. David E. Murphy, Sergei A. Kondrashev, and George Bailey, *Battleground Berlin. CIA vs KGB in the Cold War* (New Haven: Yale University Press, 1997); on the role of intelligence services in the Cold War in Germany see also Guenter Tutzing, *Spionieren fuer den Frieden? Nachrichtendienste in Deutschland waehrend des Kalten Krieges* (Olzog Verlag: Munchen, 1997).

7. Alexander George, *Bridging the Gap: Theory and Practice in Foreign Policy* (Washington, D.C.: The U.S. Institute of Peace Press, 1993).

8. Melvyn Leffler, *A Preponderance of Power: National Security, the Truman Administration, and the Cold War* (Stanford: Stanford University Press, 1992).

9. Diplomatic correspondence, KGB and GRU analysis and various other sources, information from "interparty" and other channels, flowed after 1945 into the CC International Deparment, the organization that inherited some functions of the disbanded Comintern and later claimed a role in discussing and even working out policy guidelines and documentation related to Soviet foreign policy. After 1956 the Department was split into two: the International Department dealing with communist parties and "progressive forces" in the capitalist countries, and the "Department" [Otled] focusing on relations with socialist countries. Boris Ponomarev was head of the International Department during the whole post-Stalin period until 1986. Among the most visible heads of the "Department" was Yuri Andropov, who was there between 1957 and 1967. Ponomarev's Department received information on the FRG and Soviet-West German relations; Andropov's Department was in charge of the GDR and Soviet-East German relations. Many issues, including West Berlin, were under jurisdiction of both institutions. Currently the files of the International Department under Stalin are stored at the Russian Center for Preservation and Storage of Contemporary Documentation (RTsKhSDNI) in Moscow. The files for post-Stalin years are at the Storage Center for Contemporary Documentation (TsKhSD) in Moscow. Most of these files were available to the author as a result of a

1991–1992 project involving TsKhSD, RTsKhIDNI, the Institute for General History of the Russian Academy of Science, and the Cold War International History Project (CWIHP) at the Woodrow Wilson International Center for Scholars. The author is very grateful to the staff of the RTsKhIDNI and the TsKhSD who helped him find his way. In 1993, when a proper declassification system was established in Russia, some of these files, particularly for the post-1953 period, turned out to be not properly declassified; to date they have not been available to researchers.

10. Norman Naimark, *The Russians in Germany: A History of the Soviet Zone of Occupation, 1945–1949* (Cambridge, Mass.: Harvard University Press, 1995), pp. 467, 469; for more critical evaluation of Stalin's plans see Vojtech Mastny, *The Cold War and Soviet Security: The Stalin Years* (New York: Oxford University Press, 1996), pp. 19–20. Mastny concludes that Soviet plans for Germany were "incoherent" and "Poland, rather than Germany was for Stalin the key to Soviet security."

11. It is impossible to cite all the relevant publications; reference to most of them can be found in the *Bulletin* and other publications of the Cold War International History Project. Particularly recommended is T. Volokitina, T. Islamov, G. Murashko, A. Noskova, and L. Rogovaia, eds., *Eastern Europe in the Documents of Russian Archives, 1944–1953*, Vol. 1 (Moscow-Novosibirsk: "Sibirskii khorograf," 1997). On Stalin's planning and mistakes see Vladislav M. Zubok and Constantine Pleshakov, *Inside the Kremlin's Cold War: From Stalin to Khrushchev* (Cambridge, Mass.: Harvard University Press, 1996), especially pp. 45–52; for more critical evaluation of Stalin's plans see Mastny, *The Cold War and Soviet Security*.

12. Loth/Badsttuebner, *Wilhelm Pieck—Aufzeichnungen zur Deutschlandpolitik 1945–1953*, S. 50–51; R. C. Raack, "Stalin Plans His Post-War Germany," *Journal of Contemporary History*, 28 (1993), pp. 62–63; Manfred Wilke, "Nach Hitler kommen wir: Die Planungen der Moskauer KPD-Fuehrung 1944–45 fuer Nachkriegsdeutschland," a research paper, September 1994.

13. For example, Wladimir S. Semjonow, *Von Stalin bis Gorbatschow: Ein halbes Jahrundert in diplomatischer Mission, 1939–1991* (Berlin: Nicolai, 1995), pp. 200–201, 206; Valentin Falin in a letter to the author, November 11, 1993.

14. Albert Resis, ed., *Molotov Remembers: Inside Kremlin Politics. Conversations with Felix Chuev* (Chicago: Ivan Dee, 1993), p. 60.

15. Naimark, *Russians in Germany*, p. 467, 469. To make matters worse, there was an issue of mass rape of German women by the Red Army personnel in 1945–47, ibid., p. 107. On reparations see ibid., pp. 132–33, 169; on the significance of these factors, John Lewis Gaddis, *We Now Know: Rethinking Cold War History* (Oxford: Clarendon Press, 1997), pp. 45, 286–287.

16. In August–September 1947 Stalin centralized all Soviet intelligence under the aegis of the Committee of Information, reportedly because he was exasperated with confusing reports from Germany. See Murphy, Kondrashev, and Bailey, *Battleground Berlin*, pp. 38–50; and Vladislav Zubok, "Soviet Intelligence and the Cold War: The 'Small' Committee of Information, 1952–1953," *Diplomatic History*, 19 (Summer 1995), pp. 454–455.

17. Rolf Steininger, *The German Question: The Stalin Note of 1952 and the Problem of Reunification* (New York: Columbia University Press, 1990); the German original appeared in 1985.

18. Gerhard Wettig, "Die Deutschland-Note vom 10. Marz 1952 auf der Basis diplomatischer Akten des russischen Aussenministeriums." *Deutsche Archiv*, 7 (1993), pp. 803–805.

19. Christian Ostermann, "Soviet Deutschlandpolitik and the SED," *Bulletin of the CWIHP*, 10 (March 1998), pp. 62–63.

20. James Richter, "Re-examining Soviet Policy towards Germany in 1953," *Europe-Asia Studies*, 45 (1993), p. 676.

21. Richter, *Khrushchev's Double Bind*, p. 677.

22. This is a reconstruction of the diverging positions, based on still sketchy evidence, but the subsequent polemics at Plenary Sessions of the CC CPSU help reconstruct the still secret debates at the Politburo; see Vladislav Zubok, "CPSU Plenums, Leadership Struggles, and Soviet Cold War Politics," *Bulletin of CWIHP*, 10 (March 1998), pp. 28–29; Pavel and Anatolii Sudoplatov with Jerrold L. and Leona Schecter, *Special Tasks: The Memoirs of an Unwanted Witness* (Boston: Little, Brown, 1994), pp. 363–364; Zubok and Pleshakov, *Inside the Kremlin's Cold War*, pp. 160–162; and Gerhard Wettig, "Zum Stand der Forschung ueber Berijas Deutschlandpolitik" pp. 672–682.

23. The Presidium of the Council of Ministers, largely overlapping with the Party Presidium (Politburo) in 1953.

24. "Delo Beria" [Beria's affair], June 1953 CC CPSU Plenary meeting, in *Izvestiia TsK KPSS* (1990), no. 1, pp. 157, 159.

25. Felix Chuev, *Sto sorok besed s Molotovim: Iz dnevnika FOND Chueva* (Moscow: TERRA, 1991), p. 336.

26. *Memuari Nikiti Segeevicha Khrushcheva* (original text of Khrushchev's memoirs), *Voprosy Istorii*, 8 (1993), pp. 75–77, 83.

27. Faina Novik, "Establishment of Diplomatic Relations between the USSR and the FRG," *Otechestvennaia istoriia*, 6 (November–December 1995), pp. 107–109.

28. For shrewd Western guesses on Moscow's intentions, see Rold Steininger, "1955: The Austrian State Treaty and the German Question," *Diplomacy and Statecraft*, 3 (1992), pp. 512–515.

29. See typical estimates in G. Pushkin, Soviet Ambassador in the GDR to Yuri Andropov, the CC CPSU, 7 June 1955, TsKhSD, fond 5, opis. 28, delo 327, pp. 147–148; "Voprosy normalizatsii otnoshenii mezhdu SSSR i Zapadnoi Germaniei" (The issues of normalization of relations between the USSR and West Germany), prepared by Soviet chargé d'affaires in the GDR A. Orlov on August 23, 1955; a report of Dimitry Shepilov, editor-in-chief of *Pravda*, to Suslov, TsKhSD, fond 5, opis 28, delo 328, pp. 16–25, 159–220.

30. AVP RF, fond 06, op. 15, papka 14, delo 206, l. 75; cited in Faina Novik, "Establishment of Diplomatic Relations," p. 115.

31. G. Pushkin to the Secretariat of the CC CPSU, March 7, 1955, reported on a suggestion received from Ilya Ehrenburg and Georgi Zhukov, SCCD, collecton 4, series 9, file 1242, p. 186. The suggestion was approved by the Secretariat on March 9.

32. The Committee of Information report on the possible positions of Western powers on the major international issues at the summit in Geneva, AVP RF, fond 595, opis 52, papka 780, pp. 96–104.

33. Instructions to the Soviet ambassador in the FRG, December 17, 1955, Archive of Foreign Policy of Russian Federation (AVP RF), coll. 06 (Molotov), series 14, file 201, vol. 14, pp. 15–18.

34. A. Gromyko to M. Suslov and all Presidium members, "A memo of the Committee of Information about the exodus of some citizens of the GDR to West Germany," 28 December 1955, SCCD, coll. 5, series 28, file 325, pp. 396–408.

35. Hope M. Harrison, "Ulbricht and the Concrete 'Rose'."

36. Ibid.

37. Smirnov's report to Moscow on this conversation, AVP RF, coll. 082, series 49, file 335, vol. 3, pp. 12–15.

38. Among Smirnov's many reports see, "Otchet posolstva SSR v FRG za 1958" [The annual report of the Soviet embassy in the FRG, 1958], TsKhSD, fond 5, opis. 50, delo 70, p. 72.

39. Khrushchev said this frankly in the presence of Bulganin, Mikoyan, and Molotov during his talks with Prime Minister Hansen of Denmark, March 5, 1956, TsKhSD, fond 5, opis 30, delo 163, p. 33.

40. "Rasschety i plany praviaschikh krugov FRG po germanskomu voprosu v sviazi s sobitiami v Polshe i Vengrii" [The plans and designs of the ruling circles of the FRG on the German Question in connection with the events in Poland and Hungary], AVP RF, fond 595, opis 77, papka 789, pp. 437–442.

41. June 1957 Plenum of the CC CPSU, *Istoricheskii arkhiv*, 5 (1993); excerpts published in translation in *Bulletin of CWIHP*, 10 (1998), p. 54.

42. A. Gromyko to the CPSU, the draft of the directives to Mikoyan's delegation, 11 April 1958; Mikoyan's report on the results of his talks, AVP RF, coll. 0757, series 3, delo 18, vol. 16, pp. 4, 6–8, 24–26.

43. Zubok and Pleshakov, *Inside the Kremlin's Cold War*, pp. 220–226.

44. For the text of the letter see, AVP RF, coll. 0757, series 4, file 22, vol. 9, pp. 22–34.

45. Hope Harrison, "Ulbricht and the Concrete 'Rose'."

46. Memorandum of conversation of N. S. Khrushchev with W. Ulbricht, November 30, 1960, AVP RF, fond 0742, opis. 6, papka 42, delo 4.

47. See details in Honore Catudal, *Kennedy and the Berlin Wall Crisis*, pp. 168–184; McGeorge Bundy, *Danger and Survival: Choices about the Bomb in the First Fifty Years* (New York: Random House, 1988).

48. The documentary evidence on the instruction from Moscow to close the border has not been yet discovered.

49. Bundy, *Danger and Survival*, p. 381.

50. Oleg A. Troyanovsky, interview with the author in Moscow, May 28, 1993.

51. McGeorge Bundy was not the first to quote from Robert Lowell that they "have talked our extinction to death," *Danger and Survival*, p. 363.

52. The transcripts of Penkovsky's debriefings were released by the CIA in August 1993. Copies are on file at the National Security Archives, Washington, D.C.

53. This Presidium report was discovered in the Archive of the President of the Russian Federation, fond 3, op. 67, pakage no. 223. The report was a team effort. The team leader was Dmitry Polyansky, Deputy Chairman of the Council of Ministers and Politburo member.

54. The Presidium report, p. 33.

55. The Presidium report, p. 45.

56. Interview with Oleg Troyanovsky, March 23, 1993, Washington, D.C.

CHAPTER 5

Domestic and Foreign Roots of Khrushchev's Policy toward France

Jasmine Aimaq

INTRODUCTION

In June 1966, amidst much pomp and circumstance, General Charles de Gaulle became the first Western statesman to be the guest of Leonid Brezhnev in the USSR. He was greeted with what have been described as unprecedented honors.[1] In a display of trust and friendship, de Gaulle's hosts took him to the Soviet space-launching center in Baikonur in Central Asia. Ten years earlier, Moscow had issued France an ultimatum threatening nuclear attack if Paris did not desist in trying to regain control of the Suez Canal. The same warning had been issued to Britain and Israel. But no British leader would be the honored guest of Brezhnev a decade later, nor would any Israeli be taken to a national security site.

Although this is often neglected, France holds a unique place in the history of postwar Soviet-West European relations. France remained one of Europe's major powers and was Germany's largest neighbor, and was thus of greater interest to the Soviets than were smaller Western European countries. Moreover, with a prominent Communist party and the deeply nationalistic platform of the Gaullist Right, the *Rassemblement du Peuple Francais* (RPF), France's position in postwar Europe and the Western Alliance was not readily defined.[2] Unlike West Germany, which sought only closer ties with Washington and whose population was heavily anti-Communist, and unlike England, which remained America's unquestioned European consort, France's role was ambiguous, vividly reflected by the withdrawal of French military forces from NATO in March 1966. In similar fashion, Soviet behavior toward France fluctuated, sometimes radically. Moscow would alternate between condemning France's actions in the colonial world on the one hand, and cultivating good relations on the other. Khrushchev would in one moment warn of nuclear attack and in another applaud the special French-Soviet friendship.

Why did the Soviet Union go from threatening nuclear attack in 1956 to demonstrating unprecedented friendship to de Gaulle ten years later? What factors molded Soviet foreign policy toward France during the first decades of the Cold War? And how did this foreign policy both reflect and influence the evolution of domestic Soviet affairs? The international part of the story is clear. After the fall of the Fourth Republic in 1958 and the rise of the Fifth under a defiantly nationalistic de Gaulle, France appeared to be withdrawing from the American umbrella. Although he championed independence from both superpowers, de Gaulle was explicitly distancing himself from Washington. This made France an obvious object of Soviet courtship. Even so, to better understand the contradictory Soviet diplomacy toward France, we must get beyond the international. With insights from a two-level game approach, derived from Robert D. Putnam, and with an analysis based on studies using Soviet material, we can trace the domestic factors behind Soviet foreign policy formulation *and* analyze how external developments in turn influenced domestic Soviet politics.

The years under study are bounded by two critical moments in French-Soviet relations: the Suez Crisis of 1956, and the French-Soviet détente of 1963–1964 which culminated in de Gaulle's visit in 1966. The period from the early 1950s to the mid-1960s saw real change in Soviet behavior toward France. During this time Moscow's initially vacillating approach toward Paris crystallized into détente. Within the Soviet Union profound leadership and structural changes took place, with Khrushchev rising to power at the expense of Malenkov and other rivals, and with Brezhnev and Kosygin subsequently taking the reins of power from a disgraced Khrushchev. Profound changes in French politics and in that country's role in the world also occurred during this period. It is in this multifaceted context that the zigs and zags of Moscow's behavior toward Paris must be understood. Thus, although this article talks of specific moments in Soviet relations with France, the reader should recall that our story is primarily one of context, of background, connections, and relationships.

Putnam has captured the complexity of this context, suggesting that rather than saying "the state, it" we say "the state, they."[3] This draws attention to the multitude of actors and pressures in the domestic and international arenas, and to the fact that significant disunity may exist among central decisionmakers. A heuristic device rather than a systemic theory, Putnam's approach invites us to probe both domestic (internal) and foreign (external) pressures, considerations, and constraints that together generate policy, and how internal and external dynamics influence one another. But what exactly distinguishes Putnam's approach, and how is it applicable to our purposes here?

THE TWO-LEVEL GAME

Putnam's Response to Previous Approaches

According to Putnam, the bulk of existing literature on the relationship between domestic and international affairs consists either of "ad hoc lists of countless 'domestic influences' on foreign policy or of generic observations that national and international affairs are somehow 'linked.'"[4] A glance at the historical literature suggests that his point is well taken. The body of scholarly studies on the foreign-domestic nexus remains fragmentary. Although recent efforts have sought to confront this issue more systematically these also are limited, and theoretical development has been limited since Putnam's work.[5] Most research has remained state-centric despite endeavors to recognize a wider spectrum of actors. One prominent effort, the so-called interdependence school of Joseph Nye and Robert Keohane, sought to draw the discipline away from a unitary actor perspective but ultimately allowed the domestic dimension to fade. The importance of an internal/external dynamic was never fully developed by scholars in subfields.[6] Models focused on bureaucracy, often dated back to Graham Allison's study of the Cuban Missile Crisis, also stopped short of rigorous, systematic analysis of the domestic-international dynamic.

Structural factors and their role in foreign policy have been highlighted by Peter Katzenstein and Stephen Krasner. In early works they made a point Putnam expands on, that those who formulate foreign economic policy, or "the state," face the perpetual challenge of making domestic policies compatible with the international economy.[7] Yet Putnam points out that these approaches are limited insofar as they identify "state strength," that is, the opposite of governmental fragmentation, as the most important variable. The simplistic strong state/weak state argument implies that the identity of the governing coalition does not matter.[8] It ignores the fact that shifting coalitions over time are crucial to fluctuations in "state strength" or "weakness." Conceptualizing state structure as a phenomenon that varies little from year to year, or from issue to issue, is not in accordance with empirical reality.[9] While this approach comes closest to appreciating the inseparability of the internal-external dimensions, of a foreign-domestic nexus, it remains state-centric and thus an "uncertain foundation for theorizing about *how* domestic and international politics interact."[10] Putnam's approach is more flexible, as discussed here.

Applicability of the two-level game

Putnam's analysis is founded on a classical bargaining scenario. Accordingly, the win-set and chief negotiators are central to his discussion.[11] Most foreign policy, however, does not result from bargaining between heads of governments. When Moscow intimates the possibility of a nuclear reprise against France, this does not involve a formal meeting, nor a bargaining situation in the classic sense. The present chapter deals with varying trends in the Soviet approach to France, ranging from threats of nuclear attack to general "flirtation," to détente, to formal meetings between heads of state. This involves everything from the intimation of war to an official show of goodwill, but no explicit bargaining scenario. How, then, can a two-level-game approach contribute to the study?

Although the concept of "diplomacy" is associated with formal, sit-down interactions between statesmen, it actually denotes much more than active bargaining.

Formal deliberations constitute the public and explicit manifestation of negotiation over a set of defined issues—for example, disarmament and arms control, or trade and tariffs. In such situations the win-set is important. But "diplomacy" also covers broader intergovernmental interactions. It is based on the recognition that any state exists in relation to all other states in the international system, and, as such, devises an approach to these states. One scholar aptly describes diplomacy as "a process of strategic interaction in which actors simultaneously try to take account of and, if possible, influence the expected reactions of other actors, both at home and abroad."[12]

In fact, much of Putnam's discussion, which deals largely with the win-set in bargaining decisions, should be understood as a specific application of the essential stipulations of a broad approach. Though several of Putnam's conclusions pertain specifically to bargaining—e.g. the distinction between voluntary and involuntary defection from international agreements, and the divergences of interest between a national leader and those on whose behalf he is negotiating—most of the stipulations encapsulate the wider world of international interaction.

First, at a general level, Putnam's two-level game approach rejects the notion of the state as a unitary actor and challenges the view of the state structure as rigid over time and across issues. Different coalitions do matter and must be taken into consideration in each case. The approach is valuable in examining situations of domestic unrest involving shifting ties among political actors and changing policy programs. *Second*, unlike state-centric theories, the approach highlights any domestic conflict that exists about what the "national interest" requires. In this chapter, for example, it leads us to emphasize that there were diverging visions regarding both domestic problem-solving and Soviet foreign relations in the political debate within the Kremlin. *Third*, it demonstrates that central decisionmakers must simultaneously seek to reconcile internal and external imperatives.[13] This conceptual tenet leads us to examine the degree to which this "double bind" existed in the evolution of Soviet policy toward France. And *fourth*, the approach emphasizes the reciprocal dynamic inherent to the two-level scenario. The causal links are not unidirectional from domestic factors to the formulation of foreign policy; external developments also affect the evolution of domestic politics.[14] This theoretical stipulation invites analysis of the way foreign interactions in turn influenced the course of political life in the Soviet Union.

THREATENING FRANCE WITH THE BOMB

The Birth of Soviet Missile Diplomacy

In September 1954 France was commended in *Pravda* for its rejection of the European Defence Community (EDC). By not allowing the EDC to come to a vote, the National Assembly had effectively defeated this long-pending proposal for an integrated European defense force, including a German contribution, under a supranational authority.[15] The EDC had been a "cornerstone of American foreign policy,"[16] and the French rejection despite intense American pressure was hailed in Moscow as "an important event in the political history of Europe."[17] Paris was asserting its independence from Washington and also delivered a blow to the momentum of European integration. Not surprisingly, this was welcomed by the Soviets, for whom preventing the rearmament of West Germany was a basic foreign policy objective.

Indeed, even before the era of de Gaulle and the Fifth Republic, France's position vis-à-vis the United States was ambiguous. Although the Communists had been removed from the French government in 1947, they remained a force in the National Assembly and led the struggle against the government's long and unpopular Indochina War.[18] The non-Communist Left, which included Socialists and left-leaning Radicals, was also a significant element in French political life, much to the concern of Washington. Paris pleaded for and received American assistance in Indochina after 1950, but insisted on controlling the allocation of all resources and rebuked American advice.[19]

In June 1954, Radical leader Pierre Mendès-France, whose campaign promises emphasized an end to the Indochina quagmire and resolution of the EDC question, assumed the offices of both Prime Minister and Foreign Minister. Relations with the United States deteriorated over sharpening disagreements regarding Indochina. Paris charged that Washington had let the French down, while an incensed Eisenhower lamented that the French refused American help except on their own terms.[20] And with the defeat of the EDC just a few months after the end of the Indochina War, "the whole of Washington's postwar policy in France seemed to be in ruins."[21] France was, as one scholar describes it, a "troubled ally."[22]

Tensions between France and the United States escalated. Analysts in Washington also feared that Mendès-France was not sufficiently anti-Communist.[23] As Paris distanced itself from Washington and NATO, some felt that lessened interest in the Alliance would result in a "feeling of a less close community of interest with the United States."[24] To make matters worse, by 1956, a Socialist, Christian Pineau, occupied the Foreign Ministry. In March, Pineau allegedly advised Moscow that Paris wanted to persuade the British and Americans to revise the foreign policy of the West.[25] Incidents such as this indicate that as early as the death of Stalin in 1953, France's loyalty to the United States was questionable. It would have seemed unwise and unnecessary for Moscow to alienate Paris under these circumstances. But within two years of the EDC defeat, the Soviets would threaten France with atomic reprise.

In late 1955 a Soviet-approved arms transaction between Egypt and Czechoslovakia granted Egypt a substantial number of modern weapons.[26] Nasser thus effectively established himself as an element hostile to Western "imperialism" in the Middle East, and manifested his connection to the Communist world. Furthermore, he supported radical governments in Africa and actively assisted the FLN movement in Algeria, to the detriment of French rule. Nasser, backed politically by the USSR, blocked the passage of Israeli vessels in the international waterways of the area of the Suez Canal.[27] It was in conjunction with this development that Egypt and England negotiated the withdrawal of British troops from the Suez Canal Zone, and Nasser approached both the United States and the Soviet Union for financial support to construct a dam on the river Nile above Aswan. Angered by the simultaneous negotiations, the United States withdrew its offer to finance the dam. Nasser replied by nationalizing the Suez Canal on July 26, 1956, seizing control from the Suez Canal Company in which the British government was the major shareholder.

Confronted with what they saw as a threat to their strategic and oil-related interests, the French and British began devising plans for military action after meeting with Israel at Sèvres between October 22 and 24.[28] In October Israel launched an attack in the Sinai peninsula. At the end of the month the French and British delivered an ultimatum calling for the withdrawal of Egyptian forces from both sides of the Suez Canal, but tensions only escalated. Efforts within the UN Security Council to bring about a cease-fire were vetoed twice by the British and French, who began sending troops to the area.

On November 5 the Kremlin warned France and Britain that it was foolish to provoke a nuclear power, and intimated the possibility of nuclear attack if London and Paris did not immediately cease their offensives. The next day, Washington replied that a Soviet attack would be answered in kind.[29] The French and British withdrew, more as a result of Washington's pressures than Soviet threats, which were generally considered noncredible in Western capitals.[30] But what is important for our purposes is that Soviet missile diplomacy was introduced to the world. The threat may not have been believable—would Moscow risk nuclear war for Nasser and uncertain political connections in the Middle East?—but it reflected emerging Soviet military capabilities. The Soviets had tested their first atomic bomb in August 1949, much earlier than Washington had expected. More surprises were in store for 1953, when the Soviets exploded a thermonuclear device, and 1955, when Moscow tested a true hydrogen bomb.[31] This "superbomb" had a yield of 1.6 megatons, not nearly as ominous as the American 15-megaton device tested a year earlier, but it nonetheless signaled that the Soviets had the necessary technology.[32]

These developments made it possible for the Kremlin to issue the threat, but the threat was also a bit of a bluff. The Soviets had only just begun to deploy a few medium-range missiles in the western USSR, and had not yet tested their first ICBM.[33] Indeed, missile diplomacy was not introduced just because of the obvious authority a nuclear threat could command, nor because Moscow felt this was the only, or most efficient, way to expel the French and British from the Suez area. Soviet policy in the Suez affair was also rooted in the internal political web of post-Stalinist Russia. To delineate the interplay of the external and the internal factors, we must explore what Khrushchev was trying to achieve in the USSR; the manner in which his objectives were greeted by key domestic actors; and how these realities shaped the decision to employ the nuclear threat in 1956.

Competing World Visions

Rivalry for power and authority is a perpetual trait of politics, and the USSR was no exception. Throughout its existence the Soviet Union was characterized by tension between the CPSU and the government even though the Party wielded immense, and final, decision making powers.[34] In 1953–1956 this tension was embodied in the persons of Khrushchev and Malenkov, who sought to bolster the power of the Party and the government respectively. Diverging doctrinal and policy lines also divided key actors from one another within the two institutions. This was especially true in the early years of the Stalin succession and is critical to understanding the course of events that led to Soviet nuclear diplomacy.

When Stalin died in March 1953, he left behind a small squadron of possible successors: Georgy Malenkov, Lavrenty Beria, Vyacheslav Molotov, and Nikita Khrushchev. None could wield the absolute power Stalin had enjoyed. They wrestled with defining the Soviet Union's global role and had to fashion new approaches to the foreign and domestic problems it confronted. Malenkov rose first to power, both as leader of the Central Committee (CC) of the CPSU and Chairman of the USSR Council of Ministers.[35] This meant that he was both Head of the Party and Prime Minister, at the top of the hierarchy in both Party and government. However, he was almost immediately compelled by his rivals to relinquish one or the other post, and stepped down as Head of the Party, choosing to remain Prime Minister.[36] Malenkov's foremost opponent was Nikita Khrushchev, whose power base was the Party. Khrushchev was appointed to the newly created post of First Secretary of the CPSU in 1953, and his efforts to make the Party the dominant organ became a consistent element of his political maneuvering. Between 1953 and 1955 the power struggle between Malenkov and Khrushchev escalated, and the aftermath influenced the course of Soviet politics until the fall of Khrushchev. The Stalinist succession would be wrought with political tension.

The fall of two of the principal contenders, Beria and Malenkov, was crucial to Khrushchev's ascent. Beria, Chief of the Secret Police, was early on removed from political contention, arrested in 1953 on charges of treason. His downfall is said to have been prompted in part by his lack of identification with any legitimizing principle, at a time when one of the major issues was legitimacy. Beria's foreign policy preferences, to the extent that they are known, reflected what James Richter has called a "marked lack of ideology."[37] In policy questions, Beria's fatal error was his controversial suggestion that the construction of Socialism in East Germany be abandoned and that Germany be united as a "peace-loving," neutral, and democratic state. His outlook implied an absence of commitment to Soviet ideology and world socialism. As a result, he encountered adamant opposition from both Khrushchev and Molotov. In June 1953 an uprising erupted in East Germany, and Soviet troops were dispatched to quell the revolt. Beria was arrested one week later. The arrest may have been prompted by rumors that he wanted to establish a dictatorship, seizing authority and establishing the rule of the secret police, but his decline was also related to his policy stance. In fact, his position on the German Question was specifically cited as evidence of his betrayal of Communism. From that point on, no Soviet leader could espouse policy lines similar to Beria without risking being branded a traitor.[38]

With Beria removed, Malenkov emerged as the most visible Soviet leader. Malenkov emphasized the supremacy of the government over the Party, a position that both reflected and exacerbated his rivalry with Khrushchev. In Washington, analysts noticed that although Khrushchev did not hold a bureaucratically key position, he was already acting "as though he occupied one and participated increasingly in governmental affairs."[39] Khrushchev visited the three most important countries in the Soviet orbit—Communist China, Czechoslovakia, and Poland.

Although Malenkov subscribed to the orthodox notion that the Soviet Union existed in a state of perpetual tension with the capitalist world, he downplayed the idea that war was inevitable. With the recent explosion of a Soviet thermonuclear device it was unreasonable for the imperialists to attack the USSR, he argued. But unlike Khrushchev, Malenkov did not have great confidence in Soviet strength. He hoped that Moscow's nuclear capability would suffice to deter the West but was not confident that Soviet strength could compete in war. Malenkov's foreign policy accentuated the isolation of the USSR. He downplayed not only the question of war but also the centrality of the global class struggle and the need to ally with foreign revolutionary movements. Malenkov was drawing dangerously close to the views of the disgraced Beria. Indeed, much like his former colleague, he not only called for a reduction in defense spending but also opposed the compulsory imposition of Socialism in East Germany.[40]

Malenkov's ideas were opposed by many of his colleagues. Was the West indeed "realistic" and comparatively benign? Could the USSR exist without strong ties to world revolutionary movements? Unfortunately, the external environment did little to reinforce Malenkov's vision. President Eisenhower reaffirmed American commitment to the European Defence Community in 1953, demanded a reduction of Soviet troops in Eastern Europe, and warned that any change in Washington's policy would have to be preceded by visible concessions from Moscow. In addition, while Malenkov argued that Western "realism" would appreciate the danger of Soviet nuclear retaliation and refrain from open warfare, Eisenhower pressed the swift deployment of American tactical and strategic weapons. Even worse, the President declared that tactical weapons would soon be treated like conventional arms by American forces.[41] These developments suggested that Malenkov's worldview and policy proposals were untenable.

When, in October 1954, the Allies signed the Paris Agreements providing for a German military contribution to NATO, Malenkov's foreign policy doctrine virtually collapsed. *Pravda*, which as the party organ was closely associated with Khrushchev, pointed to the Paris Treaty as evidence that the USSR needed to increase, not reduce, defense spending. Malenkov resigned as Prime Minister in February 1955 and was succeeded by Nikolai Bulganin, a Khrushchev ally. This propelled Khrushchev into a position where he could wield far greater influence than before. He became Commander in Chief of the military services, and one of his supporters, Marshal Georgy Zhukov, assumed the post of Defense Minister.[42]

In Khrushchev's worldview, global class struggle occupied a central position. The USSR could *not* exist in isolation and conduct an insulated foreign policy but must further its bonds with revolutionary movements worldwide. Furthermore, according to Khrushchev, the USSR must rely on its strength, particularly its new-found nuclear strength, rather than attempt to exploit divisions in the West. This fact is critical for understanding the 'reversal' of policy toward France in 1956. The French had displayed some vacillation vis-à-vis the Atlantic alliance, but Khrushchev did not count on divergences within the Western camp.[43]

Yet before Khrushchev's approach could prevail, a fourth contender, Molotov, had to be eliminated. Though as foreign minister Molotov did not wield the same influence Malenkov had as premier, he remained a respected conservative force who had been closely associated with Stalin. In accordance with an orthodox Leninist model, Molotov depicted the world in terms of class struggle and saw the Soviet Union as surrounded by dangerous and aggressive enemies.

Like Molotov, Khrushchev saw the world as characterized by class struggle. But in contrast to the other contenders, he pointed to Soviet strength and deterrence, rather than internal conflict among the Western states, as the means to prevent the capitalists from waging war. Thus, his posture was unlike Molotov's orthodox perspective, which contended that war among the capitalist states was inevitable. The Allied Agreements on rearming Germany had proven that contradictions among the capitalist countries were not greater than those between socialism and capitalism. They had also subtly weakened Molotov's prestige.

Khrushchev's vision was soon legitimized through two international achievements. The first of these was the creation of the Warsaw Pact, the East European alliance system established in 1955 in response to the Paris Agreements. The second was Khrushchev's success in bringing the West to the negotiating table at the Geneva Summit in July of that year, the first summit since Potsdam in 1945. The symbolic value of these events far outweighed any concrete advantages derived from them.[44] With the formation of the Warsaw Pact, Khrushchev signaled that he was intent on and capable of solidifying the bonds of the Socialist bloc. With the Summit, Khrushchev demonstrated that Moscow could induce negotiations and deal with the West on equal footing. Not surprisingly, *Pravda* applauded Khrushchev's model of foreign policy.[45]

Meanwhile, Khrushchev and Bulganin conducted an extensive tour of India, Indonesia, Burma, and Afghanistan, and openly challenged the West to an economic competition in such areas.[46] This reflected their conviction that the world was divided along ideological lines in which newly independent countries and revolutionary "progressive" forces were natural allies. In other words, Khrushchev was implementing his own approach while further discrediting those of the other political contenders. By the end of 1955 Khrushchev had consolidated his authority in foreign policy and assured the primacy of the Party's ideological authority.[47]

Khrushchev's famous denunciation of Stalin at the 20th Party Congress also contributed to the evolution of his foreign policy and the introduction of missile diplomacy. By condemning the Stalinist slaughter of loyal Party members, he implicated Malenkov and Molotov, both of whom were closely linked to Stalin.[48] In the process, Khrushchev officially proclaimed three innovations: *First,* war between the capitalist and communist camps was not inevitable; *second*, peaceful co-existence was to be the main line of Soviet foreign policy; *third*, the transition to socialism could proceed by means other than violent revolution. He also secured his position among the orthodox elements by arguing that the victory of world socialism remained certain, although it would not require violent revolt.

On this occasion, Khrushchev received a number of guests from overseas, most notably from the Third World and from France: Leaders from North Korea, Cambodia, Iran, and Indonesia all paid visits to Moscow, as did French Prime Minister Guy Mollet.[49] Khrushchev was well on his way to consolidating his authority. In June 1956 Molotov was replaced as Foreign Minister by D. T. Shepilov, a Party secretary loyal to Khrushchev. Even before his removal, Molotov commented that the Party was involved in foreign affairs to a greater extent than at any previous time.[50]

In these same months, Khrushchev had to prove that peaceful coexistence was both possible and necessary and that war with the West was unlikely. He began employing nuclear deterrence in international diplomacy. In April 1956, six months before the Suez Crisis, he advised London that if Britain tried to "to extort us, to demand the impossible from us, nothing will come of it." He let his Western counterparts know that the USSR had no need for others' rocket technology, "cannons, planes and ships," since the Soviets were not behind in this area. Indeed, he warned, Western armaments would soon become obsolete due to Soviet military innovations.[51] But back home, the situation was not so rosy.

Socioeconomic Crisis

A catastrophic consumer situation was one of the legacies of Stalinism. In 1953, the government had the budgetary priorities of a war economy, with military and heavy-industrial production retaining a monopoly over scarce resources. Mass poverty had spread throughout the country, which suffered dangerous shortages in food, housing, and consumer services. Agricultural output was a serious problem. Grain production was lamentable and the country was suffering a severe lack of foodstuffs. Stalin's successors would perpetually struggle with these dilemmas.[52] While Malenkov and Khrushchev struggled for primacy, the prevailing feeling was that an increase in consumer goods and improvements in agriculture were imperative.

Malenkov's attempts to improve living conditions met with much criticism from his colleagues, particularly Khrushchev. Malenkov spoke of slashing the defense budget and offered a long-term consumer-oriented program that had virtually no short-term payoff. His plan involved the transfer of as much capital investment as possible to light industry, which required an abundance of foodstuffs and raw materials. Khrushchev demonstrated not only that his opponent's calculations were off, but that the situation required immediate results, which had to be achieved without slashing military expenditures. Unlike his rival, Khrushchev emphasized the unsatisfactory nature of agricultural management and vehemently criticized the Ministry of Agriculture and Procurement as well as the Ministry of Sovkhozes.[53] He devised a new plan that capitalized on the vulnerabilities of Malenkov's abortive efforts.

Khrushchev submitted his proposal to the Presidium of the Central Committee on January 22, 1954. A direct challenge to Malenkov, the plan aimed at making use of 13 million hectares of land that were previously untilled, or that earlier had been cultivated and abandoned. Much of the land was located in dry farming zones, requiring special—read, costly—techniques for rendering it fertile.[54] But Khrushchev's proposal appeared to save millions of rubles compared to Malenkov's. It was comparatively low-cost and promised major near-term payoffs.[55] Moreover, Khrushchev provided added incentives. He aimed to raise grain production by encouraging peasants to grow more on their private plots. Taxes and compulsory delivery quotas were reduced; peasants were granted more pastureland and fodder for their own livestock; farms were better compensated for their deliveries to the state; and payments in kind for work on the kolkhoz (collective farm) and sovkhoz (state farm) increased.[56]

In 1954 a Central Committee plenum approved Khrushchev's proposal to plough up the Virgin Lands, which were expected to yield 20 million tons of grain in 1955. A conference of agricultural specialists in Moscow reported, in most cases, excellent experimental field results. The Virgin Lands were to be, as one scholar puts it, the Eldorado of the Soviet Union.[57] Khrushchev bet heavily on the success of this program to discredit his opposition, and gave no less than six official speeches on the agriculture problem between September 1953 and January 1954.[58]

Agriculture was also the sector with the most pressing labor shortage.[59] Khrushchev addressed this by releasing most of the political prisoners from Stalin's labor camps, and, more significantly, by launching a dramatic reduction in Soviet armed forces in 1955. Demobilized soldiers were to be integrated into the civilian economy. Recent studies suggest that Khrushchev's decision to cut troop numbers was linked to the targets of the (6th) Five Year Plan of 1956–1960. An anticipated shortfall in the non-state sector of the economy made the army a principal source of supply. Khrushchev thus planned the release from the army of some 1.2 million men in 1956, hoping that the entry of these men into the non-state labor force would stimulate economic growth.[60] Defense would become increasingly "nuclearized"; men would become almost superfluous. Unfortunately for Khrushchev, archival material and memoirs suggest that the armed forces resisted and opposed the troop cuts. Forces designated for demobilization were unhappy and demoralized.[61]

But Khrushchev was intent on expressing his control over military policy. Accordingly, the Soviet press emphasized the superiority of the Party over the Army.[62] By November 1957 the American Embassy reported home that Khrushchev had secured the domination of the police by the liquidation of Beria, of the government bureaucracy by the elimination of the "anti-party group," and of the armed forces by removing Zhukov. The Communist Party, it disclosed, under the "strong hand of Khrushchev," had clearly established its supremacy over all elements of power in the Soviet Union.[63] But despite the troop reductions, most analyses of Soviet military spending during 1957–1960 show that Soviet defense spending rose sharply, with heavy emphasis on nuclearization at the expense of conventional forces.[64]

In fact, when an anti-Khrushchev coalition pressed for reform of the Five Year Plan to reduce budgetary strain by lowering the targets for heavy-industrial production, Khrushchev's riposte was to scrap the entire Five Year Plan and supplant it with a new Seven Year Plan. At the same time, several heavy-industrial plants were converted to production of consumer goods, and investment was raised in the soft goods, food-processing, and consumer-durable industries.

The essence of Khrushchev's agricultural program was that production be further rationalized and existing reserves tapped to the maximum potential. The key lay in modernization, which would allegedly prove less costly than the current state of affairs or Malenkov's plan. The principal distinction between Khrushchev and Malenkov was that whereas Malenkov argued that deep cuts in defense were necessary if the grain and foodstuff situation was to be remedied, Khrushchev argued that modernization was the answer. He claimed that he could bring about both satisfied consumers and increased national security: modernized, rationalized agriculture would go hand in hand with modernized, rationalized defense. What did all this mean to Khrushchev's threat of nuclear attack in 1956?

Understanding the Threat

The defense budget had been increased in 1955, in accordance with Khrushchev's plans. But it was not until a year later that he was presented with a golden opportunity to provide evidence of the benefits, and indeed the necessity, of focusing on nuclear strength. The Suez affair was a chance for Khrushchev to demonstrate that modernization of the Soviet military posture had been justified. This in turn showed that the low-cost Virgin Lands Program had been a better option than other higher-cost proposals, since it had allowed the intensive modernization of the military that had deterred France and Britain. Khrushchev could claim to have killed two birds with one stone, to have satisfied two major aims, domestic and foreign, at once. The Suez Crisis allowed Khrushchev to show the effectiveness of his own foreign policy, which rested both on strength and on extending support to friendly international forces, in this case, Egypt.[65] Years later, in his memoirs, Khrushchev would continue to maintain that his use of deterrence against the French and the British influenced their decision to withdraw their forces from Egypt.

The threat reflects Khrushchev's attempt to validate nuclear deterrence as the core of his approach to the West. Since Paris had asserted independence from Washington on EDC and had allegedly sought to persuade the British and the Americans to revise Western foreign policy, Khrushchev could have portrayed the intervention in Suez as a largely British-led gambit. This would have been ideal for emphasizing internal divisions within the Western camp, for underlining that there were "reasonable" elements in the West, i.e. France, compelled into unreasonable actions by the Western alliance. Malenkov might have adopted this approach, whereas Molotov would probably have highlighted capitalist collusion and stressed the need to provoke divisions in the Western bloc. Khrushchev's innovation was in recognizing that nuclear diplomacy, rather than divisions within the Western camp, could assure him of a strong negotiating position, and Suez allowed him to implement this insight.

However, the eruption of the Suez Crisis also damaged Khrushchev's credibility at home. It undermined his argument that the West included reasonable elements, and it challenged the notion that working-class parties could prevent "imperialist aggression." The French decision to intervene had been taken by a Socialist premier, Guy Mollet, and a Socialist foreign minister, Christian Pineau. The timing could not have been worse. The Socialist bloc in the East was threatening to disintegrate, with Hungary at the fore, while Socialist forces in the West were behaving aggressively. The dual crises suggested that there were weaknesses in Khrushchev's foreign policy model. His rivals reentered the foreign policy debate. After Suez, Molotov and Malenkov became active voices again. By winter 1956, the Presidium strengthened the role of the government apparatus in economic affairs in an effort to reduce the First Secretary's authority.[66] In 1957 Shepilov argued that the "Eisenhower Doctrine" for the Middle East, as well as Washington's stand on French and British behavior during the Suez Crisis, revealed that America sought to undermine the interests of Paris and London.[67] This suggested a return to exploiting divisions within the West rather than reliance on nuclear deterrence. On the other hand, Khrushchev's emphasis on rocket development and heavy industry did result in a major triumph on October 4, 1957, when the Soviet Union stunned the world by launching *Sputnik*.[68]

Suez had challenged Khrushchev's worldview. He needed to salvage his legitimacy, and in this effort France would play a key role once again. He had subjected France to a nuclear threat in 1956, but changes in the French government and its foreign policy, plus shifts in his own domestic priorities, would soon lead him to court France. The Fourth Republic had fallen victim to Moscow's first use of missile diplomacy. The Fifth Republic would be the object of Moscow's most flagrant flirtations.

THE FRENCH-SOVIET DÉTENTE

Flirtation and "Rapprochement"

In 1958 the French Fourth Republic fell and de Gaulle returned to power as President of the new Fifth Republic. The Fourth Republic had been plagued by foreign policy dilemmas and internal political strife. The Indochina War and the EDC had been sources of great division. In 1954 the Premiership of *Radical* Pierre Mendès-France tipped the political balance left, away from the moderate *Mouvement Républicain Populaire* (MRP), the party that had heretofore dominated government. However, by 1958, the non-Communist Left, composed of Socialists and left-leaning Radicals, was internally divided; the *Gaullist Rassemblement du Peuple Francais* (RPF) had become a major force in the National Assembly; and the parties and public were divided over the role of the State as well as over the war in Algeria. Rising dissidence in public service and the military prompted a search for an authoritative political figure with sufficient prestige to bring some solution to these problems. It was in this context that General de Gaulle returned to the presidency.[69] The General understood that the psychological wounds inflicted by the Nazi occupation were still unhealed and that the people suffered from a "national lassitude," which he attributed to the awareness that France was no longer a great power.[70] Defeat in the Indochina War and the escalating dilemma in Algeria tore at what remained of dreams of a "Greater France." De Gaulle's wish to return pride and status to his people would permeate the foreign relations of the Fifth Republic. And this would contribute to a new interaction with the Soviet Union.

De Gaulle's principal foreign policy objective was to maximize France's autonomy, encapsulated in his *politique de grandeur*. But the American nuclear umbrella was a dark reminder of France's dependence on one actor in a bipolar world. The development of a separate French nuclear force, the *force de frappe*, was thus one of de Gaulle's highest priorities. Already in 1945 de Gaulle had commissioned the establishment of the Commissariat à l'énergie atomique (CEA), and in succeeding years the French had invested considerable effort in acquiring atomic raw materials, training scientists and technicians, and building laboratories. By 1952 the National Assembly had approved the first Five Year Plan for atomic development.[71] During the Fourth Republic, the nuclear force had been seen mainly as a way of enhancing France's military position within NATO; during the Fifth it was to support the evolution of an independent French foreign policy, to remind the world that France determined its own destiny and commanded the strength to do so.[72] In 1958 de Gaulle resolutely told Washington that France should, and would, have its own nuclear bomb.[73] On November 3, 1959, at the Institut des Hautes Etudes de la Défense Nationale, he insisted that "France's military defense must be French. . . . Her effort must be her own effort. . . . It is indispensable that France defend herself on her own, for herself, and in her own way. . . ." "Obviously," he said, "we have to be able to acquire, during the next few years, a force capable of acting on our behalf. It is evident that a nuclear arsenal will be at the base of our force." De Gaulle's objectives had serious consequences for French-American relations, triggering several crises over nuclear armament, the organization of NATO command, and the question of consultation.[74]

In March 1960, while tensions were escalating between de Gaulle and the Americans, Khrushchev paid a visit to France. On this occasion *Pravda* cheered the advent of a new era in Soviet-French relations, and Khrushchev waxed eloquent about the flourishing relationship, announcing that the "path to peace in Europe lies in the alliance and friendship between the Soviet Union and France."[75] Suez now seemed far away. Yet, if one looked closely, one could still detect Soviet ambivalence. De Gaulle's estrangement from Washington was welcomed, but his vision involved independence from bipolarity itself, and this was less acceptable. The true thaw began three years later, in 1963, when the Khrushchev era was drawing to a close. That year, France vetoed Great Britain's application to the Common Market, much to the frustration and dismay of both London and Washington. Another blow had been dealt to European integration, again by France. And in 1964 France became the first member of the European Economic Community to break with its five-year limit on credits to the USSR, extending Moscow a seven–year credit for $356 million for financing chemical plants and equipment.[76] In March, Khrushchev sent Nikolai Podgorny on a goodwill mission to Paris. Several weeks later, Khrushchev's son-in-law, Alexei I. Adzhubei, showed up in the French capital for discussions regarding economic and cultural cooperation.[77] These talks would lead to concrete agreements later, under Brezhnev. Was all this simply a response to the attractiveness of de Gaulle? What was happening on the home front?

The Virgin Lands Defeat

In 1960, when de Gaulle was enjoying his second full year as president of the Fifth Republic, Khrushchev experienced a turning point in his own political fortunes. We have noted how the international after-effects of de-Stalinization had underscored some of the weaknesses in Khrushchev's world vision. But his success in putting down the "anti-party group" in June 1957 testified to his continued dominance in Soviet political life. It was not until the failure of his domestic initiatives, especially the Virgin Lands program, that the local implications of his strategic vision came to be seen as problematic too.

Khrushchev's agricultural policy had been a triumph at first. The 1954 crop from the virgin lands turned out to be even larger than expected, and although 1955 proved disappointing, 1958 witnessed a record harvest.[78] Nevertheless, 1959 marked the beginning of a steady agricultural decline. Although Khrushchev told his American colleagues that "the virgin lands have been a complete success" and boasted that "even the skeptics are becoming ashamed," the facts were otherwise.[79] Prices for meat, milk, and butter procurements did not cover the cost of production, with the result that farmers made little effort to produce and sell these commodities to the state. Local party officials confiscated produce as well as seed supplies. The incentive structure for farms and farmers collapsed, and this was directly traceable to Khrushchev's policy. Ironically, the urban-industrial sector was producing according to plan, a fact that served only to accentuate the gap between industry and agriculture.[80]

Expected shortfalls in the Seven Year Plan (1959–1965) made labor scarcity an important issue once again.[81] Sensing that the new age of rocket missilery could provide him a solution to this problem, Khrushchev in 1960 announced a planned reduction of Soviet armed forces by one-third over the next two years. In a speech to the Supreme Soviet on January 14 Khrushchev explicitly linked troop reductions to a new military framework based on missile technology.[82] A month before, the Strategic Rocket Forces (SRF) had been created as a separate branch of service, to be the country's primary arm of defense.[83] In this modern age, Khrushchev argued, an army was not about soldiers but about nuclear and rocket technology. Indeed, armed forces were to be reduced by another 1.2 million, despite continued opposition from the military high command. Shortly thereafter, the body responsi ble for the development of nuclear weapons hired 3,600 soldiers, including 600 officers, demobilized in the 1960 army cuts.[84] Meanwhile, setbacks in the Virgin Lands program were compounded by problems in other plans. Khrushchev's claim that the USSR would catch up to the United States in meat and milk production per capita did not even come close to target.[85] And, as we shall see, international developments compounded Khrushchev's dilemma, contributing to the decline of his authority. No wonder that after 1960, "the First Secretary's pronouncements sounded like those of a politician who was on the defensive politically."[86]

Khrushchev's Bluff

A consummate gambler, Khrushchev consistently exaggerated his estimates of Soviet military strength, boasting that the Socialist bloc now enjoyed a preponderance of power.[87] Despite the strong American response to Khrushchev's threats against Britain and France in 1956, he continued to try to intimidate Washington with grandiose reports of Soviet technological progress. In 1959 he boasted to Governor Harriman: "We developed the hydrogen bomb before the US. We have an intercontinental bomb which you have not." Furthermore, he added, it was foolish for the West to forget that a few Russian missiles could destroy all of Europe. One bomb, he warned, was sufficient for Bonn, and three to five would knock out France, England, Spain, and Italy. Under these circumstances, it was unrealistic to threaten the Soviets. "Within five to seven years, we will be stronger than you. . . . If we spend 30 billion rubles on ballistic missiles in the next 5–6 years, we can destroy every industrial center in the US and Europe. Thirty billion rubles is no great sum for us. . . . Let us keep our rockets loaded and if attacked we will launch them."[88]

On May 5, 1960, ten days before Khrushchev was to meet with President Eisenhower in Paris to discuss the German Question and a possible test ban, the Soviets shot down an American U-2 plane over Soviet territory. The incident only further discredited Khrushchev's leadership, undermining his claims that Eisenhower was realistic and could successfully be negotiated with, especially when the American President accepted personal responsibility for the flight and refused to apologize for his violation of Soviet airspace.[89] Back in the Kremlin, the political elite concluded that the incident was evidence of Western irrationality.[90] At the same time, the Soviets were increasingly aware that the United States knew Khrushchev was bluffing about the superiority of Soviet missile technology.[91]

By the fall of 1960, Khrushchev was trying to undo the damage. In fact, he spent the next two years trying to recover from the U-2 affair, resorting to brinkmanship to affirm that nuclear deterrence could bridle Western ambitions. To maintain his legitimacy, he had to return to a rhetoric that emphasized the untrustworthiness of the capitalist world, the need to enlarge the nuclear deterrent, and his continuing resistance to "imperialist threats."[92] He also called for reprioritizing the connection between heavy industry and agriculture and a retreat from modernization and rationalization, as well as renewed concentration on agricultural machine-building. Over the next three years he withdrew from a number of other principles espoused in his agricultural reform program.[93] Meanwhile, as Khrushchev put ever greater emphasis on the importance of a nuclear arsenal, the Kennedy administration initiated a strategic doctrine, Flexible Response, which required a massive buildup of strategic and conventional forces. In fact, during the Kennedy years, America's defense expenditures increased 13 percent,[94] and NATO's conventional forces were steadily improved.[95] While Washington was preparing NATO for different levels of armed conflict, all major Warsaw Pact exercises were still conducted under the assumption of a war begun with massive missile strikes. Even in the field, it was believed that the "basic force" of Soviet ground troops would lie with operation-tactical and tactical nuclear weapons.[96] However, Washington's new program left Khrushchev open to attack by his political rivals because it challenged his claim that Russia needed only nuclear technology to deal with the West. Kennedy's doctrine undermined the plausibility of Khrushchev's worldview, and the Berlin Crisis and the Cuban Missile Crisis would definitively expose his bluff and help shatter his authority in the Kremlin.

In May 1961, Khrushchev renewed his ultimatum of 1958, warning that if steps were not taken to turn West Berlin into a "demilitarized free city" within six months, Moscow would give the East German government control over Western access to Berlin. But Kennedy was undeterred. Asking Congress for supplementary military funds, he warned that any unilateral Soviet action against West Berlin would trigger war with the United States. Khrushchev replied that he would not be pushed around. In July the Soviet leader suspended his planned troop reductions and ordered an increase of 3.14 billion rubles in defense allocation. In September he initiated a new series of nuclear tests.[97] Still, Kennedy's actions frightened him enough that he did not make good his threats about Berlin. Instead, when it was clear that the Americans would not respond as desired, Khrushchev decided to build a wall dividing Berlin.[98] In effect, Washington had exposed Khrushchev's bluff, confirming suspicions that the United States enjoyed significant nuclear superiority over the Soviet Union and had "a second strike capability which is at least as extensive as what the Soviets can deliver by striking first."[99]

While the crisis over Berlin was escalating, Khrushchev and Kennedy had also begun what became a lengthy and increasingly tense exchange over Cuba. In part to offset American superiority in ICBMs, in part to protect Cuba, and in part to salvage what remained of his foreign policy model, Khrushchev moved in the spring of 1962 to position intermediate range missiles in Cuba. Washington had warned that it would not accept the placing of "offensive weapons" in the Caribbean. Indeed, after the half-emplaced missile force was discovered by the Americans in October, Kennedy advised Khrushchev not to underestimate the "will and determination of the United States" in removing "this threat to the security of this hemisphere."[100] Khrushchev was determined to resist. It was imperative that he demonstrate both to the world and his rivals at home that he could negotiate with Washington from a position of strength, particularly after the Berlin affair. On October 24 he rebuffed Kennedy and accused him of "setting forth an ultimatum and threatening that if we do not give in to your demands you will use force." "Such folly can bring grave suffering to the peoples of all countries, and to no lesser degree to the American people themselves, since the United States has completely lost its former isolation with the advent of modern types of armament." In a final show of force in this battle of wills, Khrushchev warned Kennedy that he would not let the Americans threaten him out of Cuba: "We will then be forced on our part to take the measures we consider necessary and adequate in order to protect our rights. We have everything necessary to do so."[101] But on October 28, in return for minor concessions, Khrushchev capitulated to Kennedy's terms, promising a unilateral withdrawal of "all Soviet offensive arms" from the island.[102]

By the end of 1962, international developments had taken a serious toll on Khrushchev's authority at home. The U-2 incident, the Berlin Wall, and the Cuban Missile Crisis, not to speak of the related breakdown in relations with China, all revealed the weakness of his position. He had repeatedly been unable to gain American concessions on the basis of Soviet nuclear strength. The nuclear deterrent seemed a bluff. And the importance of American naval superiority in the Cuban Missile Crisis contradicted Khrushchev's claim that conventional weapons no longer mattered and discredited his policy of curtailing naval development.[103] Indeed, the Cuban confrontation devastated Khrushchev's foreign policy vision and ended his "coercive campaign against the West," which had seemed only to stimulate further American military buildup.[104] His bluff had been called; revisions were in order.

New Visions and Policies

Bolstered by Khrushchev's recent, repeated setbacks, his rivals began expressing their dissent more openly. National security based wholly on nuclear deterrence had been a core aspect of Khrushchev's strategic view. He had presented himself as the man who could strengthen both the international status and the internal resilience of the USSR. However, the first- and second-quarter results of 1963 suggested that the year's grain harvest would be a catastrophe and that current consumption would continue to drop. Economic problems plagued the country while Khrushchev's foreign policy staggered. Moreover, demographic disaster continued to take its toll. The deaths of so many men in World War II had resulted in a massive fall in expected births, with the number of males reaching age nineteen falling from 2,300,000 in 1960 to 960,000 in 1963.[105]

In April 1963 Khrushchev threw himself into a new tack. He now lamented the waste and inefficiency in heavy industry and defense and warned that the Soviet economy could not go on producing "nothing but rockets."[106] Warning of the follies of nuclear war, Khrushchev called for a change in policy direction. He spoke of détente and espoused a policy of conciliation with Washington. The struggle against imperialism was no longer the core of his approach. Worldwide liberation movements were suddenly not as important as the avoidance of thermonuclear conflict.[107] In a letter to Kennedy, Khrushchev went as far as speaking of a comprehensive test ban agreement, but was rebuffed. Kennedy's rejection undermined Khrushchev's new policy of conciliation, and his domestic authority continued to erode. However, despite this setback, the superpowers signed the Limited Test Ban Treaty on August 5. Khrushchev could argue that his conciliatory stance had brought the United States to the negotiating table. Washington and Moscow reached several additional agreements over the next few months, including a hot-line protocol and a treaty prohibiting orbiting nuclear weapons.[108] Khrushchev used these developments to justify a plan to reduce defense spending. He also turned his attention to the chemical industry, touted as a field that would solve a multitude of problems including agricultural shortages.[109]

The defense budget of 1964 was to be slashed. The cuts necessitated an international thaw. How else could Khrushchev justify the change in defense policy? He hoped improved relations abroad would make it possible for him to continue playing the champion of both national security and a healthier economy. In this context France could play a key role. Khrushchev now moved to exploit the growing tension between Paris and Washington. This indicated that his opponents and critics, who championed playing the capitalists off against each other, had reentered the foreign policy debate, and that his foreign policy model, which downplayed divisions within the West and emphasized nuclear deterrence, had been to some extent discredited. Relying on divisions among the Western states was a call back to the orthodox foreign policy models of Molotov and Malenkov; it signaled that Khrushchev's worldview had lost considerable legitimacy.[110]

Khrushchev and the "Force de Frappe"

Khrushchev's position had become shaky, tenuous. The contradictions in his policies had been exposed by events. Meanwhile, de Gaulle was not only pulling away from Washington, making exploitation of divisions easier for Moscow, but was also developing a nuclear arms program. France had also just joined the nuclear club. Some months after his return to power, de Gaulle publicly announced that France had the means to equip herself with nuclear weapons and would soon conduct her first nuclear test.[111] In February 1960 Paris detonated its first atomic device; and less than two months later, and one month before the U-2 incident, the French government announced the explosion of a second bomb, a far smaller plutonium device of some 20 kilotons. This indicated that France was moving toward miniaturization, which implied the eventual production of tactical atomic weapons.[112]

What did the advent of French nuclear power mean for Khrushchev? Clearly, the proliferation of nuclear arms suggested a possible increase in international tensions, the creation of another danger in Western Europe. But more importantly for Khrushchev, it also indicated that the nuclear medium was not restricted to the superpowers. If France had a separate nuclear force, other countries could follow suit. This could eventually strip the superpowers of their diplomatic trump card, deterrence. In the political struggle at home, Khrushchev's image was so closely linked to his doctrine of deterrence that any disruption could damage his legitimacy. But as long as Khrushchev boasted and blustered about Soviet nuclear superiority, France's development of nuclear arms did not seriously disturb his status. It was after 1962, when Khrushchev entered the post–Cuban Missile Crisis phase of his tenure, that détente with the new nuclear power became crucial.

As we have seen, in 1963 Khrushchev advocated cuts in defense and a heavier concentration on rectifying economic ills, policies that necessitated détente with Washington. As Khrushchev began pursuing the thaw, however, differences between de Gaulle and Washington were escalating. And when Kennedy and Khrushchev signed the Limited Test Ban Treaty, de Gaulle refused to join them, again demonstrating his commitment to an independent defense policy. Khrushchev could ill afford enmity with an autonomous nuclear power on the flank of Eastern Europe. He was losing authority among his colleagues, and the world needed to be reinterpreted as more accommodating, benign. By bettering relations with Paris, Khrushchev could thus not only pursue a general détente with the West but could prevent an independent nuclear power from becoming more hostile to the USSR. In addition, since Moscow was back to capitalizing on divisions in the West, France could become an important consort. Washington had few nuclear-armed, vocal critics within the Western bloc. Courting de Gaulle could perhaps lend some legitimacy to Khrushchev's new world vision, which envisaged two hierarchies riddled with dissent. It was the combination of de Gaulle's independence from Washington, France's development of a nuclear arsenal, and Khrushchev's domestic and foreign policy dilemmas that generated the "rapprochement" between Moscow and Paris.

However, Khrushchev's efforts to recoup his declining authority failed. His domestic plans and projections had proved faulty, and consumer satisfaction remained low. His foreign policy model was unconvincing. By mid-1964, the cut in defense spending was reversed, and the First Secretary came under heavy fire from increasingly vocal critics. Even his long-time allies argued forcefully in favor of increased defense spending. And the Defense Minister publicly complained of interference by Party leaders in military affairs.[113] Khrushchev was forced to concede that America's continued military buildup made it impossible to transfer funds from defense to the domestic economy. It had become obvious that his policies were unworkable.[114] Détente with France was supposed to support his foreign model—but why didn't it? The decline in Khrushchev's authority that started with the Suez crisis was finalized with failures over Berlin and Cuba. He had twice counted on France to bolster his power at home—once by threatening her and once by trying to make France his best friend in the West. On neither occasion could France save Khrushchev.

CONCLUSIONS

The power vacuum that emerged after Stalin's death generated an often bitter power struggle among his successors. Khrushchev, with his new foreign policy model and novel plans for the economy, sought not only power abroad and stability at home but also legitimacy in a leadership context marked by competing world visions, doctrinal interpretations, and domestic policies. The international arena finally discredited both his world vision and his domestic policies, and economic quagmire undermined his programs. Khrushchev used the Suez Crisis to impress upon colleagues that the Soviet nuclear arsenal was enough to intimidate the West, but the crisis also discounted Khrushchev's estimates of Western intentions. By threatening France, Washington's "troubled ally," Khrushchev also wanted to show his colleagues that exploiting divisions within the West was not the optimal way of dealing with the enemy; deterrence was the central component of an effective strategic policy. In fact, he had negotiated his domestic plans, most prominently his much-touted Virgin Lands Program, partly with the argument that his calculations preserved resources for expansion of the nuclear arsenal. When the Berlin Crisis and, more dramatically, the Cuban Missile Crisis suggested that this deterrent was not enough to bend Washington's will, his foreign policy model lost potency, and his legitimacy declined. Tensions with the United States prompted an acceptance of détente, and failures in domestic planning meant that finances had to be moved away from nuclear development into the consumer economy. Thus, internal dilemmas also suggested that an international thaw was necessary. France, which was moving toward separation from both superpowers, clearly sought autonomy from Washington and developed an independent nuclear force. The internal and external dilemmas that plagued Khrushchev, the dynamics of the foreign-domestic nexus, drove Khrushchev to seek détente with France, as it once had driven him to threaten her with a nuclear bomb.

Khrushchev cultivated de Gaulle enough to pave the way for good relations going forward. Building on the foundation laid by his predecessor, Leonid Brezhnev appointed a more prestigious ambassador to France in 1965. That same year the USSR agreed to adopt the French system of color television, affirming an economic relationship between the two powers while paying a compliment to French technology. International developments contributed to the persistence of Moscow's drive for closer ties with France. In March 1966, de Gaulle delivered a symbolic blow to the Atlantic Alliance by withdrawing French forces from NATO. And in June he paid his famous visit to the Soviet Union. The meeting resulted in agreements for mutual consultation as well as scientific-economic cooperation.[115]

Domestic factors also sustained Brezhnev's pursuit of French-Soviet détente. Brezhnev inherited the problems that had so frustrated Khrushchev—inefficient agriculture, dissatisfied consumers, and the poor state of the economy in general—and tried to devise new means of dealing with them. Khrushchev's grandiose investments in the chemical industry were cut back. A new agricultural program devoted an unprecedented 71 billion rubles to agriculture over the next five years and offered increased incentives to peasants.[116] Khrushchev's entire industrial-administrative structure (which dated from 1962) was dismantled, and authority returned both to the central ministries in Moscow and the factories themselves (in the so-called "Kosygin reforms"). Such measures held some promise, but it was only promise. For the first two years, while the regime was consolidating its position, relatively few foreign policy changes from the Khrushchev era were initiated.

In the second phase, beginning in summer 1966, foreign policy was again mobilized to exploit divisions between Western Europeans and Washington, although

Bonn was not included in Moscow's promotion of closer relations with the Western European states.[117] The culmination of French-Soviet détente in 1966 must be understood as just that—a culmination. It was a Khrushchevian policy inherited by Brezhnev, and as such must be examined against the background of domestic affairs, foreign policy concerns, and a continuing quest for political legitimacy. Meanwhile to avoid his predecessor's miscalculations, Brezhnev not only revised Khrushchev's domestic programs in a renewed effort to raise the standard of living but also accelerated an across-the-board military buildup, expanding missile as well as conventional defenses.

The 1970s and 1980s witnessed a return to closer relations with France, but a relaxation of tensions eventually characterized Soviet relations with all Western European powers, especially Germany. In fact, by the early 1980s, the Federal Republic had become the USSR's most important trading partner—followed distantly by France. But that is a story beyond the province of this chapter.

NOTES

1. Thomas W. Wolfe, *Soviet Power and Europe 1945–1970* (Baltimore: Johns Hopkins Press, 1970), p. 290.

2. An excellent treatment of France's position in the Western Alliance is provided by Georges-Henri Soutou in "France," in David Reynolds, ed., *The Origins of the Cold War in Europe: International Perspectives* (New Haven: Yale University Press, 1994), pp. 96–120. For France's role in Europe and the Cold War immediately following World War II, see William Hitchcock's *France Restored: Cold War Diplomacy and the Quest for Leadership in Europe, 1944–1954* (Chapel Hill: University of North Carolina Press, 1998). Whereas the relationship between England and the United States is often described as "the special relationship," books devoted to French-American relations and France's position in the Atlantic alliance have titles such as *The Troubled Ally* and *The Reluctant Ally*. See Edgar J. Furniss, *The Troubled Ally: De Gaulle's Heritage and Prospects* (New York: Harper and Brothers, 1960); Michael M. Harrison, *The Reluctant Ally: France and Atlantic Security* (Baltimore: Johns Hopkins University Press, 1981). See also Frank Costigliola, *France and the United States: The Cold Alliance since World War II* (New York: Twayne Publishers, 1992).

3. Robert D. Putnam, "Diplomacy and Domestic Politics: The Logic of Two-Level Games," 1988, reprinted in Peter B. Evans, Harold K. Jacobson, and Robert D. Putnam, eds., *Double-Edged Diplomacy: International Bargaining and Domestic Politics* (Berkeley: University of California Press, 1993), p. 435.

4. Putnam, "Diplomacy and Domestic Politics," p. 434.

5. Among the more prominent recent works are Jack Snyder, *Myths of Empire* (Ithaca: Cornell University Press, 1991); and Bruce Bueno de Mesquita and David Lalman, "Domestic Opposition and Foreign War," *American Political Science Review*, 84 (1990), pp. 747–765.

6. See Robert Keohane and Joseph Nye, *Power and Interdependence: World Politics in Transition* (Boston: Little, Brown and Company, 1977); Keohane and Nye, "Power and Interdependence Revisited," *International Organization*, 41 (1987), pp. 725–753. For discussions on the domestic element in foreign affairs, see also Wolfram Hanreider, "Dissolving International Politics: Reflections on the Nation-State," *American Political*

Science Review, 72 (1978), pp. 1278–1287; Edward Morse, "The Transformation of Foreign Policies: Modernization, Interdependence and Externalization," *World Politics*, 22 (1970), pp. 371–392; and W. Wagner, "Dissolving the State," *International Organization*, 28 (1974), pp. 435-466.

7. Putnam, "Diplomacy and Domestic Politics," p. 434; see also Peter J. Katzenstein, "International Relations and Domestic Structures: Foreign Economic Policies of Advanced Industrial States," *International Organization*, 30 (Winter 1976), pp. 1–45; and Stephen D. Krasner, "United States Commercial and Monetary Policy: Unraveling the Paradox of External Strength and Internal Weaknesses," in Peter J. Katzenstein, *Between Power and Plenty: Foreign Economic Policies of Advanced Industrial States* (Madison: University of Wisconsin Press, 1978), pp. 51–87.

8. Putnam, "Diplomacy and Domestic Politics," p. 435; see also Peter Gourevitch, "The Second-Image Reversed: The International Sources of Domestic Politics," *International Organization*, 32 (Autumn 1978), pp. 881–911.

9. Putnam, "Diplomacy and Domestic Politics," p. 435.

10. Ibid. My italics.

11. Putnam, "Diplomacy and Domestic Politics," pp. 438–459.

12. Andrew Moravcsik, "Introduction: Integrating International and Domestic Theories of International Bargaining," in Evans, Jacobson, and Putnam, *Double-Edged Diplomacy*, p. 15.

13. The features of the two-level game figure in Putnam, "Diplomacy and Domestic Politics," p. 460.

14. See also Moravcsik, "Introduction."

15. For a discussion on the background and evolution of the European army plan, see Edward Fursdon, *The European Defence Community: A History* (London: Macmillan Press, 1980); Raymond Aron and David Lerner, eds., *La Querelle de la CED* (Paris: Armand Colin, 1956); Armand Clesse, *Le project de la CED du plan Pleven au 'crime' du 30 août: histoire d'un malentendu européen* (Baden-Baden: Nomos-Maison, 1989); Irwin Wall, *The United States and the Making of Postwar France, 1945–1954* (Cambridge: Cambridge University Press, 1991), Chapter 7. On the connection between the EDC and the French Indochina War, see Jasmine Aimaq, *For Europe or Empire? French Colonial Ambitions and the European Army Plan* (London: Chartwell-Bratt, 1996).

16. Robert McGeehan, *The German Rearmament Question: American Diplomacy and European Defense after World War II* (Chicago: University of Illinois Press, 1971), p. 187; Robert R. Bowie and Richard H. Immerman, *Waging Peace: How Eisenhower Shaped an Enduring Cold War Strategy* (New York: Oxford University Press, 1998), pp. 206–207; Klaus Schwabe, "The United States and European Integration: 1947–1957," in Clemens Wurms, *Western Europe and Germany: The Beginnings of European Integration 1945–1960* (Oxford: Berg Publishers, 1995), p. 127.

17. *Pravda*, September 9, 1954, cited in Wolfe, *Soviet Power*, p. 76. See also James Richter, *Khrushchev's Double Bind: International Pressures and Domestic Coalition Politics* (Baltimore: Johns Hopkins University Press, 1994), p. 64.

18. On the Fourth Republic, see, for instance, Jean-Pierre Roux, *The Fourth Republic, 1944–1958* (Cambridge: Cambridge University Press, 1987); and Philip M. Williams, *French Politicians and Elections 1951–1969* (Cambridge: Cambridge University Press, 1970).

19. English-language studies on the French Indochina War include Philip B. Davidson, *Vietnam at War: The History, 1946–1975* (London: Sidgewick and Jackson,

1988); Joseph Buttinger, *Vietnam: A Dragon Embattled*, volumes I and II (London: Pall Mall Press, 1967); R. E. M. Irving, *The First Indochina War* (London: Croom Helm, 1975); and Jacques Dalloz, *The War in Indo-China, 1945–1954* (Savage, Md: Barnes and Noble, 1990). An outstanding treatment of French-American relations in Indochina appears in Philip Spector, *Advice and Support: The Early Years of the US Army in Vietnam, 1941–1960* (New York: Collier Macmillan, 1985).

20. United States Department of State, *Foreign Relations of the United States, 1952–1954*, Vol. XIII, 2 (Washington: Government Printing Office, 1982), pp. 1636–1639, 1675–1679; and 1687–1689. On the Geneva Conference that ended the French Indochina War, see James Cable, *The Geneva Conference of 1954 on Indochina* (Basingstoke: Macmillan, 1986).

21. Wall, *Making of Postwar France*, p. 286; see also pp. 281–288.

22. Furniss, *Troubled Ally*, (1960).

23. For an excellent treatment of American relations with Mendès-France, see Wall, *Making of Postwar France*, pp. 275–296.

24. Dispatch from the Embassy in France to the Department of State, January 17, 1956, United States Department of State, *Foreign Relations of the United States, 1955–1957*, Vol. XXVII, (Washington: Government Printing Office, 1992), p. 27.

25. Richter, *Khrushchev's Double Bind*, pp. 82–83.

26. Nasser obtained an estimated 530 armored vehicles, 500 artillery pieces, and up to 200 fighter, bomber, and transport aircraft as well as destroyers, motor torpedo-boats, and submarines. See Chaim Herzog, "The Suez-Sinai Crisis Campaign: Background," in Selwyn Ilan Troen and Moshe Shemesh, *The Suez-Sinai Crisis 1956: Retrospective and Reappraisal* (New York: Columbia University Press, 1990), p. 4. See also Richter, *Khrushchev's Double Bind*, p. 71.

27. Herzog, "Suez-Sinai Crisis Campaign," p. 5.

28. See André Martin, "The Military and Political Contradictions of the Suez Affair: A French Perspective," in Troen and Shemesh, *Suez-Sinai Crisis*. See also Csaba Békés, "The 1956 Hungarian Revolution and World Politics" (Working Paper, Cold War International History Project, Woodrow Wilson International Center for Scholars, September 1996); and Herzog, "Suez-Sinai Crisis Campaign," p. 12.

29. See, for instance, Wolfe, *Soviet Power*, pp. 80–81; David Holloway, *The Soviet Union and the Arms Race* (New Haven: Yale University Press, 1983), p. 84; Nikita Khrushchev, *Khrushchev Remembers* (New York: Bantam Books, 1970), p. 480.

30. Richter, *Khrushchev's Double Bind*, p. 93.

31. Holloway, *Soviet Union and Arms Race*, pp. 23–24.

32. See Matthew Evangelista, "'Why Keep Such an Army?': Khrushchev's Troop Reductions" (Working Paper, Cold War International History Project, Woodrow Wilson International Center for Scholars, December 1997). Washington knew that Moscow had the basic capability, but also knew the Soviets were not nearly as advanced as the United States. See Memorandum of Discussion, February 7, 1955, *Foreign Relations of the United States, 1955–1957*, Vol. XXIV, p. 24.

33. See Wolfe, *Soviet Power*, p. 81.

34. See Martin McCauley, *The Khrushchev Era 1953–1964* (London: Longman Group Limited, 1995), p. xiv.

35. The principal features of the Party-government state are described in McCauley, *Khrushchev Era*, p. xv. The controlling organization of the Party was the CPSU Presidium (known as the Politburo after 1966 and before 1953), while the Presidium of the USSR

Council of Ministers was the top government organ. The CC, or Central Committee, was the second major institution of the Party, its equivalent in government being the Council of Ministers.

36. McCauley, *Khrushchev Era*, p. xiv.

37. Richter, *Khrushchev's Double Bind*, p. 36.

38. Ibid., pp. 36–37; Vladislav Zubok and Constantine Pleshakov, *Inside the Kremlin's Cold War* (Cambridge: Harvard University Press, 1996), pp. 154–163. On Beria, see Amy Knight, *Beria: Stalin's First Lieutenant* (Princeton: Princeton University Press, 1993).

39. Intelligence Report Prepared by the Office of Intelligence Research, February 19, 1955, *Foreign Relations of the United States, 1955–1957*, Vol. XXIV, pp. 28–29.

40. Richter, *Khrushchev's Double Bind*, pp. 37–40; Zubok and Pleshakov, *Kremlin's Cold War*, pp. 154–169. For a discussion of Malenkov's approach to the development of Soviet society, see also George Breslauer, *Khrushchev and Brezhnev as Leaders: Building Authority in Soviet Politics* (London: George Allen and Unwin, 1982), pp. 23–27.

41. *New York Times*, December 9, 1953.

42. In Washington, analysts recognized that Malenkov had fallen not because he was responsible for policy failures but simply because he had lost "the second round of a great power struggle." John Foster Dulles concluded that the removal of Malenkov meant that Khrushchev was now "clearly in the dominant position in the Soviet hierarchy." Memorandum of Discussion at the 236th Meeting of the National Security Council, Washington, February 10, 1955, *Foreign Relations of the United States, 1955–1957*, Vol. XXIV, p. 26. See also Intelligence Report Prepared by the Office of Intelligence Research, February 17, 1955, ibid, pp. 28–29.

43. See, for instance, Richter, *Khrushchev's Double Bind*, pp. 67–68.

44. Ibid., p. 71.

45. *Pravda*, November 7, 1955, cited in ibid., (1994), p. 71.

46. See, for instance, Vladislav Zubok and Constantine Pleshakov, "The Soviet Union," in Reynolds, *Origins of the Cold War*, p. 71. For more on the Soviet Union and the Third World, including the Khrushchev tour, see Elizabeth Kridl Valkenier, *The Soviet Union and the Third World: An Economic Bind* (New York: Praeger Publishers, 1983).

47. Richter, *Khrushchev's Double Bind*, p. 72 and p. 75.

48. Khrushchev was able to downplay the fact that he also had participated in Stalin's crimes; ibid., p. 80. See also Vittorio Vidali, *Diary of the Twentieth Party Congress of the Communist Party of the Soviet Union* (Westport, Conn: L. Hill, 1984).

49. McCauley, *Khrushchev Era*, pp. 45–46. See also Raymond Garthoff, *Deterrence and the Revolution in Soviet Military Doctrine* (Washington: Brookings 1990), p. 19 especially.

50. From the Twentieth Congress minutes, in Richter, *Khrushchev's Double Bind*, p. 84. See also Vladislav M. Zubok, "The Soviet Challenge," in Diane B. Kunz, ed., *The Diplomacy of the Crucial Decade* (New York: Columbia University Press, 1994), pp. 149–182.

51. *Pravda*, April 24, 1956, cited in Richter, *Khrushchev's Double Bind*, p. 82.

52. Breslauer, *Khrushchev and Brezhnev*, p. 23; and Martin McCauley, *Khrushchev and the Development of Soviet Agriculture 1953–1964* (New York: Holmes and Meier Publishers, 1976), pp. 44–45 especially. On the factors behind the Soviet agriculture problem, see G.A.E. Smith, "Agriculture," in Martin McCauley, ed., *Khrushchev and Khrushchevism* (Macmillan Press, 1987), pp. 95–117. See also Arcadius Kahan, "Soviet Agriculture: Do-

mestic and Foreign Policy Aspects," in Seweryn Bialer, *The Domestic Context of Soviet Foreign Policy* (Boulder:Westview, 1981), pp. 257–268.

53. McCauley, *Soviet Agriculture*, pp. 47–48.

54. Breslauer, *Khrushchev and Brezhnev*, p. 28; McCauley, *Khrushchev Era*, p. 33; and McCauley, *Soviet Agriculture*, p. 54.

55. Breslauer, *Khrushchev and Brezhnev*, p. 29.

56. McCauley, *Khrushchev Era*, p. 32; and McCauley, *Soviet Agriculture*, p. 50. In 1959 Khrushchev told his American colleagues that the Soviet Union was changing the incentives structure to once and for all alleviate the agriculture problem. "Our chief problem," he said, "is to change the psychology of the farmers not only by reorganization but by improving management and leadership. Up to now we have given too many directives to farms." Conversation Between N. S. Khrushchev and Governor Averill Harriman, Dispatch from the Embassy in the Soviet Union to the Department of State, June 26, 1959, United States Department of State, *Foreign Relations of the United States, 1958–1960*, Vol. X (Washington: Government Printing Office, 1993), p. 270.

57. McCauley, *Khrushchev Era*, p. 33; see also McCauley, *Soviet Agriculture*, p. 55.

58. A list of the speeches appears in McCauley, *Soviet Agriculture*, p. 57.

59. Kahan, "Soviet Agriculture," pp. 257–258. On the broader question of labor shortage in the Soviet Union see, for instance, Warren W. Eason, "Demographic Trends and Soviet Foreign Policy," in Bialer, *Domestic Context*, pp. 203–226. For a discussion on other solutions to the labor problem, see, for instance, D. Filtzer, "Labor," in McCauley, *Khrushchev and Khrushchevism*, pp. 118–137.

60. Evangelista, "Why Keep Such an Army?" A table on the average annual growth of the Soviet work force, 1956–1958, appears on p. 23. See also Richter, *Khrushchev's Double Bind*, pp. 107–108.

61. See Evangelista, "Why Keep Such an Army?"; Sergei Khrushchev, *Khrushchev on Khrushchev* (Boston: Little, Brown, 1990); and Richter, *Khrushchev's Double Bind*, p. 109. For an analysis of the military's impact on Soviet society and politics, see Timothy J. Colton, "The Impact of the Military on Soviet Society," in Bialer, *Domestic Context*, pp. 119–138.

62. See the Memorandum of Discussion at the 342d Meeting of the National Security Council: Significant World Developments Affecting U.S. Security, October 31, 1957, *Foreign Relations of the United States, 1955–1957*, Vol. XXIV, p. 177.

63. Telegram from the Embassy in the Soviet Union to the Department of State, November 3, 1957, *Foreign Relations of the United States, 1955–1957*, vol. XXIV, p. 178.

64. Richter, *Khrushchev's Double Bind*, pp. 107–108.

65. Khrushchev, *Khrushchev on Khrushchev*, p. 56.

66. See, for instance, Alec Nove, "Industry," in McCauley, *Khrushchev and Khrushchevism*, pp. 63–64.

67. "Questions of the International Situation and Foreign Policy of the Soviet Union; Report by USSR Minister of Foreign Affairs D. T. Shepilov," *Pravda*, February 13, 1957, cited in Wolfe, *Soviet Power*, pp. 82–83.

68. McCauley, *Khrushchev Era*, pp. 50–51.

69. On the formation and features of the Fifth Republic, Dorothy Pickle's *The Fifth French Republic* (New York: Praeger Publishers, 1960) remains a classic.

70. Memorandum of a Conversation between General Charles de Gaulle and the Minister in France (Achilles), Paris, April 20, 1955, *Foreign Relations of the United States, 1955–1957*, Vol. XXVII, p. 10.

71. Wilfrid L. Kohl, *French Nuclear Diplomacy* (Princeton: Princeton University Press, 1971), p. 18; see also Lawrence Scheinman, "Euratom: Nuclear Integration in Europe," *International Conciliation*, No. 563 (May 1967).

72. Andrew J. Pierre, "Conflicting Visions: Defense, Nuclear Weapons, and Arms Control in the Franco-American Relationship during the De Gaulle Era," in Robert O. Paxton and Nicholas Wahl, *De Gaulle and the United States: A Centennial Reappraisal* (Oxford: Berg Publishers, 1994). De Gaulle's speech excerpt is cited on p. 280.

73. Telegram from the Embassy in France to the Department of State, June 20, 1958, *Foreign Relations of the United States, 1958–1960*, Vol. VII, p. 36; and Memorandum of Conversation, July 5, 1958, ibid., pp. 58–59.

74. See, for instance, Pierre Messmer, "De Gaulle's Defense Policy and the United States," in Paxton and Wahl, *De Gaulle and the United States*, pp. 351–352; Frank Costigliola, "Kennedy, De Gaulle and the Challenge of Consultation," in ibid., pp. 169–194; and Richard Challener, "Dulles and De Gaulle," in ibid., pp. 152–155. See also Frank Costigliola, "The Pursuit of Atlantic Community: Nuclear Arms, Dollars, and Berlin," in Thomas G. Paterson, *Kennedy's Quest for Victory: American Foreign Policy 1961–1963* (New York: Oxford University Press, 1989), pp. 24–56. The problem worsened during the Kennedy administration. Eisenhower had been more amenable to de Gaulle's desire to develop an independent nuclear force.

75. *Pravda*, March 23, 1960, cited in Wolfe, *Soviet Power*, p. 116.

76. Alvin Z. Rubinstein, *Soviet Foreign Policy since World War II: Imperial and Global* (2nd edition, Boston: Little, Brown, 1985), p. 119.

77. Wolfe, *Soviet Power*, p. 116.

78. McCauley, *Soviet Agriculture*, pp. 59–60 and pp. 90–92.

79. Conversation between Khrushchev and Harriman, Dispatch from the Embassy in the Soviet Union to the Department of State, June 26, 1959, *Foreign Relations of the United States, 1958–1960*, vol. X, p. 270.

80. Breslauer, *Khrushchev and Brezhnev*, p. 81. It was the gap between agricultural and industrial output that had prompted the Khrushchev reform in the first place.

81. Evangelista, "Why Keep Such an Army?" pp. 24–26.

82. "Disarmament is the path toward strengthening peace and ensuring friendship among peoples—N. S. Khrushchev's report at the USSR Supreme Soviet Session," *Pravda*, January 15, 1960, pp. 3–4, cited in Raymond L. Garthoff, "Estimating Soviet Military Force Levels: Some Light from the Past," *International Security*, 14 (Spring 1990), pp. 93–113.

83. Michael McCGwire, *Military Objectives in Soviet Foreign Policy* (Washington, D.C.: The Brookings Institution, 1987), p. 24; Thomas M. Nichols, *The Sacred Cause: The Civil-Military Conflict over Soviet National Security, 1917–1992* (Ithaca: Cornell University Press, 1993), pp. 65–67.

84. Evangelista, "Why Keep Such an Army?" pp. 13–15. It has later been argued that actual numbers were somewhat different than Khrushchev claimed. For the CIA's evaluation, see Garthoff, "Estimating Military Force Levels."

85. Werner G. Hahn, *The Politics of Soviet Agriculture, 1960–1970* (Baltimore: Johns Hopkins University Press, 1972), p. 11, and pp. 33–42.

86. Breslauer, *Khrushchev and Brezhnev*, p. 108.

87. Speech to Polish Delegation, cited in Richter, *Khrushchev's Double Bind*, p. 118.

88. Conversation between Khrushchev and Harriman, Dispatch from the Embassy in the Soviet Union to the Department of State, June 26, 1959, *Foreign Relations of the United*

States, 1958–1960, Vol. X, p. 273, p. 277, and p. 279. See also Report on the Khrushchev Visit of September 1959, Washington, undated, ibid, pp. 486–487.

89. The U-2 Airplane Incident, Editorial Note, *Foreign Relations of the United States, 1958–1960*, Vol. X, p. 513.

90. See, for instance, Richter, *Khrushchev's Double Bind*, p. 126 and p. 131.

91. They were confirmed in this awareness in the fall of 1961, when the United States released information about its new satellite surveillance of the USSR.

92. Richter, *Khrushchev's Double Bind*, p. 132.

93. See Breslauer, *Khrushchev and Brezhnev*, p. 83.

94. Costigliola, in Paterson, *Kennedy's Quest*, p. 5.

95. See, for instance, MccGwire, *Military Objectives*, pp. 22–25; and Costigliola, in Paterson, *Kennedy's Quest*, p. 5, pp. 31–32. See also Aleksandr Fursenko and Timothy Naftali, *One Hell of a Gamble* (New York: W.W. Norton, 1997); James Richter, *Khrushchev's Double Bind*, pp. 144–145, and Keith L. Nelson, *The Making of Détente* (Baltimore: Johns Hopkins University Press, (1995), p. 15 and pp. 49–50.

96. This did not change until 1967. See, for instance, Nichols, *Sacred Cause*, p. 69.

97. Richter, *Khrushchev's Double Bind*, pp. 145–146.

98. See Vladislav M. Zubok, "Khrushchev and the Berlin Crisis (1958–1962)" (Working Paper #6, Cold War International History Project, Woodrow Wilson International Center for Scholars, May 1993); Zubok and Pleshakov, *Kremlin's Cold War*, pp. 194–202; Wolfe, *Soviet Power*, pp. 89–96; and Zubok, in Kunz, *Crucial Decade*, pp. 160–161.

99. October 21, 1961, Deputy Roswell Gilpatric, Defense Department, cited in Michael R. Beschloss, *The Crisis Years* (New York, 1991), pp. 330–331; see also Thomas Alan Schwartz, "The United States and Western Europe," in Kunz, *Crucial Decade*, pp. 115–148.

100. Letter from President Kennedy to Chairman Khrushchev, October 22, 1962, United States Department of State, *Foreign Relations of the United States, 1961–1963*, Vol. VI (Washington: Government Printing Office, 1996), pp. 165–166.

101. Letter from Chairman Khrushchev to President Kennedy, October 24, 1962, ibid, pp. 169–170.

102. Letter from Chairman Khrushchev to President Kennedy, October 28, 1962, ibid, p. 183.

103. Khrushchev emphasized the development of SLBMs, but halted development in conventional naval forces. See Nichols, *Sacred Cause*, p. 65.

104. Fedor Burlatsky, *Khrushchev and the First Russian Spring* (London: Weidenfeld and Nicholson, 1991), pp. 168–183; Zubok and Pleshakov, *Kremlin's Cold War*, pp. 266–271. On the origins and American handling of the crisis see also Thomas G. Paterson, "Fixation with Cuba: The Bay of Pigs, Missile Crisis, and Covert War against Castro," in Paterson, *Kennedy's Quest*, pp. 140–155.

105. Nichols, *Sacred Cause*, p. 65.

106. *Pravda*, April 26, 1963, cited in Breslauer, *Khrushchev and Brezhnev*, p. 96.

107. See, for instance, *Pravda*, January 17, 1963, cited in Richter, *Khrushchev's Double Bind*, p. 158.

108. Ibid., p. 164.

109. Breslauer, *Khrushchev and Brezhnev*, p. 95.

110. Wolfe, *Soviet Power*, pp. 116–117.

111. Charles de Gaulle, Press Conference, October 23, 1958, *Major Addresses, Statements and Press Conferences of General Charles De Gaulle, May 19, 1958—January 31, 1964* (New York: Ambassade de France, Service de presse et d'information, 1964), pp 27–28.

112. For further discussion, see Kohl, *French Nuclear Diplomacy*, pp. 103–106.

113. Richter, *Khrushchev's Double Bind*, p. 168.

114. Breslauer, *Khrushchev and Brezhnev*, p. 120.

115. See, for instance, Wolfe, *Soviet Power*, p. 289 and p. 290.

116. Ibid., p. 242.

117. Ibid., pp. 280–281. The third phase, with which we are here not concerned, is dated from the invasion of Czechoslovakia in 1968. For a detailed discussion on domestic changes made by the Brezhnev regime in the years immediately after the fall of Khrushchev, see Breslauer, *Khrushchev and Brezhnev*, pp. 137–178.

CHAPTER 6

Nixon, Kissinger, and the
Domestic Side of Détente

Keith L. Nelson

"You needed to devise a strategy that was politically sustainable at home and effective abroad," I said. "Right," he agreed. "Consider what you did and what Gorbachev has done. He has tried to serve his interest abroad through accommodation and cooperation until he could get his domestic situation under control or until he could get the domestic support he needed to take a more traditional approach to the West. Of course, his whole ideology and system are collapsing, but both of you designed foreign policy to take into account your domestic situation. Both of you were trying to stall." He looked at me and smiled. "Of course, I'm a democrat—small d," he said, "and Gorbachev is a Communist. But foreign policies are almost always related to how things are going at home. And sometimes," he said, "they are used as diversions."[1]

Richard Nixon's foreign policy has been widely praised as the principal redeeming feature of his five years as president of the United States. In the conventional view, his domestic policies are seen as nothing special and Watergate as a disaster, but his foreign policy is described as a great success. The opening to China, détente with the Soviet Union, international agreements to control arms, and the final American withdrawal from Vietnam—these are generally seen as achievements both unprecedented and substantial.[2]

Yet there have been serious criticisms of Nixon's foreign policy as well. "Nixon's diplomatic legacy is weaker than he and many others have maintained," writes Joan Hoff in her recent volume *Nixon Reconsidered*. "[T]he pursuit of 'peace and honor' in Vietnam failed; his Middle Eastern policy, because of [Henry] Kissinger's shuttling, ended up more show than substance; he had no systematic Third World policy (outside of Vietnam); détente with the USSR soon floundered in the hands of his successors; and likewise, the Nixon Doctrine has not prevented the use of US troops abroad."[3]

Other observers have been even more severe. Tom Wicker, for example, argues that "no matter how [Nixon] and the country he led adapted . . . [he] remained a creature of the Cold War he had helped to make a reality. . . . In pursuing détente he was not trying to *end* the Cold War or retreat from world competition with Communism. He sought [rather] to *strengthen* the U.S. for the race."[4] Raymond Garthoff contends that neither side in this contest understood the other. "It became increasingly evident," he says, "beginning even in the early 1970s when détente was at a high point, that Washington and Moscow had very different conceptions of what a détente policy entailed, and had had from the outset."[5] These authors suggest either that Nixon's goals were too limited or that the relationships he built were simply not well constructed.

Whichever historian one prefers, the question inevitably remains: Why was the détente that Nixon espoused and created *not* a more thorough-going reform and/or a more stable condition? Could it be that his endeavors were subtly transformed or undermined by America's allies abroad? Or was he blocked from achieving his real objectives by the situation at home? by the governmental bureaucracy? by the Congress? by the public? Or did Nixon's own beliefs and/or techniques put limits on what he strove for and accomplished? Or did he simply find himself constrained by what he could persuade his various Communist opponents to accept? Such queries cry out for a careful multilevel analysis.[6]

It is the intention of this chapter, then, to scrutinize Nixon's foreign policy toward the Communist world, especially during his first term, to see how domestic and foreign games interacted so as to determine its shape and to establish its results. Such an examination will serve to demonstrate that domestic and personal factors have been undervalued in most explanations of détente and that they played a crucially important role both in driving Nixon to action and, ultimately, in limiting the nature of his initiatives. This was the moment of the Cold War when there was perhaps the greatest chance for breaking through to real peace, when the public (at home and abroad) was probably more receptive to radical change than ever before, but Nixon, sadly, was unable fully to seize the opportunity. [7]

In the beginning, one must underline the centrality of the Vietnam War to the development of Nixon's posture vis-à-vis the international situation. This is not to say that his ideological predispositions were insignificant in shaping and structuring his reactions. But the impact of the war on American society was so severe, the resulting trauma and political polarization so extreme, that extricating the United States from the conflict had to be the foremost foreign policy concern of this era. Not only was the war costly, bloody, and futile, it was also undermining the anti-

Communist alliance system and destroying the consensus at home on which the policy of Containment had been mounted and maintained.

Moreover, Nixon had promised to end the war. In the rather vague presidential campaign of 1968 this was the one pledge Nixon made that had stood out.[8] Indeed, his narrow victory over Hubert Humphrey was almost always interpreted as a mandate for making peace. His reelection hung on his ability to achieve this.

All through Nixon's first presidential term he struggled to fulfill this promise. He did so by pursuing several war-ending and war-minimizing strategies simultaneously, seemingly in hopes that one or another, or all together, would succeed in reducing the nation's pain and in facilitating an agreement that allowed the United States to escape with what the president valued most—its "great power" image intact.

The first Nixon strategy, underway by June 1969, entailed a gradual and phased withdrawal of American ground forces. Dubbed "Vietnamization" by Secretary of Defense Melvin Laird and championed by him as a way to strengthen the Saigon regime, the policy had been criticized and resisted by Henry Kissinger, who believed that it weakened Nixon's hand in negotiations with the North Vietnamese. Nevertheless, the withdrawal continued steadily over three years, until by August 1972 the last American combat troops had left the theater of active warfare.[9]

In the interim, in a second effort, Nixon tried in every way possible to "invisibilize" the war for the American people. Not only was the scale of offensive military action reduced, but on occasion entire operations, like the Cambodian bombing, were hidden.[10] Draft calls were cut, a selective service lottery introduced, and finally, in September 1971, at the president's urging, a law enacted paving the way for an all-volunteer army.[11] United States battle deaths during the last half of 1971 were only 3 percent of the totals during Nixon's first six months in office.[12] There was a strong correlation between the declining personal threat to young Americans and the waning strength of the antiwar movement.

A third strategy employed by the Nixon leadership was to negotiate directly and secretly with the North Vietnamese, and, as it turned out, to offer them increasingly significant concessions (combined with an occasional threat). In May 1969, Nixon had publicly proposed a plan for mutual withdrawal of U.S. and North Vietnamese forces from South Vietnam over a twelve month period. This was not as fair as it appeared, but, after Hanoi had sharply rejected it, the two sides did agree to undertake the secret talks which occurred in Paris from time to time in the months that followed.[13] The next step came in October 1970 when Kissinger, as the American representative, proposed an internationally supervised cease-fire in place.[14] Eight months later, in June 1971, the Americans made clear that they no longer required the withdrawal of North Vietnamese troops from South Vietnam.[15] Finally, at the Moscow summit of 1972 Nixon and Kissinger conveyed to Hanoi through the Soviets their readiness to back a tripartite electoral commission in South Vietnam (with representatives of the Saigon regime, Viet Cong, and neutralists) that would organize and run post-armistice elections.[16] Little by little, the Americans inched closer to Hanoi's views and to what would become the settlement of January 1973.

In the early years of the Nixon presidency, however, no one dreamed that it would ever require such concessions. In fact, in 1969 Nixon had supreme confidence in the fourth strategy he employed, which envisaged manipulation of the major Communist powers—the Soviet Union and China—to bring pressure on the North Vietnamese to make peace. This idea flowed from Nixon's hierarchical notions of the international order—from his sense that the Communist world, like international relations generally, was organized from the top down—that is, from Moscow, or, depending upon one's view of the Sino-Soviet split, from Moscow and Beijing.[17] By making progress in Vietnam a *sine qua non* for future cooperation with the U.S.S.R. (and, hopefully, China), Nixon hoped to create leverage with the Communist giants that could be used to force Hanoi to stop fighting. He might even be able to play the two nations off against each other as they competed for America's favor!

All this presupposed that Russia and China were more ready and eager for cooperation with America than it was with them. In fact, Nixon and Kissinger were convinced that the Soviet Union was so desirous of agreements on weapons and trade that they did not hesitate at first to practice an extreme form of what Kissinger called "linkage," that is, linking the possibility of agreement on other issues to prior concessions regarding the war.[18] At Nixon's first press conference, on January 27, 1969, the president explictly linked strategic arms limitation talks with the Soviets to "progress on outstanding political problems."[19] Three days later, in a meeting with a prominent Soviet journalist (Yuri Zhukov), Kissinger "clearly and distinctly let [me] understand that Nixon will make development of Soviet-American relations directly dependent on how things will be going with [a] Vietnam settlement."[20]

And so it went, on into the summer. In his March 4 news conference Nixon expressed the hope that Russia would "play . . . a peacemaking role in the Mideast and even possibly in Vietnam."[21] On July 12, as Ambassador Anatoly Dobrynin was leaving Washington for Moscow, Kissinger impressed on him how important he considered the Soviet Union's assistance in overcoming the deadlock in the Paris peace talks.[22] As late as October 20 the president himself warned Dobrynin that improvement in bilateral relations depended on the desire of the Soviet Union "to do something in Vietnam."[23]

Nevertheless, by midsummer the Nixon version of linkage was faltering badly. Not only did the Soviets refuse to be "used" in connection with the war ("His Government leaders couldn't understand how it would be possible to tie political settlements with nuclear questions," Dobrynin told Averill Harriman in February[24]), not only did the North Vietnamese cling stubbornly to their previously announced demands for a coalition government in the South, but, as the weeks wore on, voices outside and within the administration were raised on behalf of negotiations that allowed individual issues "to stand on their own two feet."[25] The public and bureaucratic levels of the domestic game that any democratic leader plays started to assume significance. Even in the spring of 1969 Nixon had received a barrage of advice from those impatient to move forward rapidly in improving Soviet relations. Newspapers like the *New York Times* and *Washington Post* had asked the president to "stop dawdling."[26] Leading senators like Frank Church (D-Idaho) and Albert Gore (D-Tenn) and public figures like Clark Clifford had demanded an early opening date for SALT.[27]

To Kissinger's consternation, such views soon found resonance within the government, particularly within the State and Commerce departments, whose experts he believed were committed to negotiations and to trade as ends in themselves.[28] The worst offender was undoubtedly Secretary of State William Rogers, who may have had more than one axe to grind in openly speculating, and encouraging his subordinates (like Llewellyn Thompson and Gerard Smith) to speculate, that SALT would probably get underway during the summer. "The cumulative impact of all the bureaucratic indiscipline," Kissinger noted, "with media and congressional pressures added, was that we had to abandon our attempt to use the opening of the SALT talks as a lever for our other negotiations."[29] He and the president had lost a round to the public and to the bureaucracy. Their response was to play their cards even closer to their vests.

Still, when the SALT talks, ostensibly "de-linked" from Vietnam, opened in Helsinki in November 1969, all was not what it seemed. In the first place, American SALT negotiators had been explicitly directed to go slow, to listen, and not to offer proposals of any kind.[30] Secondly and simultaneously, the administration had inserted new teeth into linkage by blocking the requests of State and Commerce to sell computers to the USSR.[31] Nixon had also continued to hang tough with the North Vietnamese. Frustrated by Hanoi's refusal to bargain seriously, the president and his national security adviser had not only developed plans for a "savage, decisive" autumn attack against North Vietnam but had also begun to drop hints that, if by November there had been no major progress toward a settlement, they might have to make use of greater force.[32]

Once again, however, elements of the bureaucracy and the public rose up to alter Nixon's foreign policy. In September, upon learning of the actions the president was contemplating, Secretaries Laird and Rogers immediately made known their personal objections to such escalation.[33] This time opposition reached as far as Kissinger's NSC staff—William Watts warned Kissinger in a top secret memorandum that an attack on Hanoi could provoke widespread domestic violence; Roger Morris and Anthony Lake took the occasion to argue that the administration should propose a "caretaker government in Saigon acceptable to both sides"; Laurence Lynn suggested that air raids over the North would lead to heavy B-52 bomber losses without substantially diminishing Hanoi's capacity to continue the war.[34]

But the decisive factor was the antiwar movement. On October 15, 1969, 250,000 Americans, a much larger number than expected, marched in Washington in a "Moratorium" to protest the war. Few of the protestors had any sense that it was a crucial moment; they were protesting policies already adopted by the government, not those under consideration.[35] Yet the impact on the president's plans was profound. "I knew," he later wrote, ". . . that after all the protests and the Moratorium, American public opinion would be seriously divided by any military escalation of the war."[36] It was at this point that Nixon backed down and turned to the formulation of a "temporizing" speech, the "silent majority" speech of November 3. Vowing to continue the war until Hanoi accepted a "just" peace, he appealed on this occasion for patience and for the support of "you, the great silent majority of my fellow Americans."[37] To judge from the response, most Americans *were* willing to give Nixon more time. "The public," Seymour Hersh remarks, "seemed to believe that Vietnamization would end the war."[38]

The trouble was that Nixon could not let well enough alone. In his desire to prod North Vietnam off dead center, to demonstrate his ability to act forcefully, and perhaps in part to obscure the rejection of two controversial Supreme Court nominations, he succumbed to the temptation to go on the offensive in regions bordering South Vietnam, with disastrous results. Thus in February 1970 his authorization of bombing raids by B-52s in northern Laos was leaked to the press and led to serious protests in the Senate.[39] Even worse, at the end of April, six months after the neutralist regime of Prince Norodom Sihanouk had been overthrown by rightists in Cambodia, Nixon's decision to send South Vietnamese and American troops into the Communist "sanctuaries" within that country produced a hugely negative public reaction. The killing of students at Kent State University only compounded the outrage and roused the peace movement to its last great wave of anger and of protest.[40] When Senators John Cooper (R-Ky) and Frank Church introduced an amendment to a sales bill that prohibited American military activity in Cambodia after June 30, Nixon quickly announced that United States forces would be withdrawn before that date.[41]

The second half of 1970 was even more difficult for Nixon. In the Paris talks the American offer of a cease-fire in place (generated under the impact of the Cambodian affair) received practically no response from the North Vietnamese.[42] Equally disappointing was the fact that Nixon's efforts to achieve reconciliation and leverage with China appeared to be going nowhere. Indeed, despite vigorous signaling by Washington of its interest in better relations, Beijing displayed a pro-Soviet tilt throughout the year and especially after the American Cambodian invasion. Not until the triumph of the "moderate" faction at the Central Committee plenum of September 1970 were alignments created for an opening to the United States, and it was December before Nixon and Kissinger became aware of this.[43]

Indicative of Nixon's discomfort throughout 1970 was the way in which he repeatedly dreamed of silencing his critics by arranging an early summit meeting with party leader Leonid Brezhnev or Premier Alexei Kosygin. This was true even in the spring, but by the summer, deeply concerned about the approaching congressional elections, Nixon could hardly contain his desire for a summit. According to Kissinger, the president was so desperate that he would have accepted an "ABM only" agreement just to see the Russian leaders before November.[44] Brezhnev and Kosygin, however, who were still feuding over foreign policy precedence, narrowed their "win-sets" and attempted to drive a hard bargain. In addition to an ABM treaty, they wanted the promise of a European security conference and a protocol on "accidental war."[45]

So no summit occurred, and during September and October Nixon showed not only his irritation with the Russians but his hierarchical perspective and electoral opportunism by allowing such matters as hostilities between Syria and Jordan and crew stops by Soviet submarines in Cienfuegos (Cuba) to be magnified into ostensible clashes between the superpowers.[46] Kissinger too was anxious and cynical, describing the period as an "autumn of crises" involving "probes and challenges aimed by Moscow at the United States."[47] Small wonder that the Soviets, who during these same weeks (1) backed down on the Cienfuegos dispute, (2) dismantled eighteen of their most recent ICBM silo starts, and (3) displayed a new flexibility regarding Berlin, were puzzled and perplexed by the administration's behavior.[48]

In November the voters fired a warning shot across the bow of the administration in the congressional elections. Despite the president's having campaigned personally against "pot, permissiveness, protest, and pornography," Democrats increased their already large majority in the House by nine and maintained a comfortable majority in the Senate despite losing two seats. Apparently, a sluggish, inflating economy and lack of progress regarding peace were what really mattered to the voters. Raymond Price, the president's speech writer, complained that Nixon badly needed something more "elevating" to talk about, "something that would speak to the hopes, to the goodness, to the elemental decency of the American people."[49]

Within a month a warning shot of a different kind was provided in another of the presidential games—that involving America's relations with its European allies. Washington's concern here, at least since the 1950s, had been to maintain and strengthen the ties within NATO, that is, to counteract the centrifugal forces within the system. In the Kennedy-Johnson years Charles de Gaulle had provided the primary challenge, although the Vietnam War had strained relations between the United States and most of its European friends.[50] Then, in 1969 the election of Willy Brandt to the West German chancellorship and his introduction of a more accommodating Ostpolitik raised the possibility of a radically improved Soviet-West German connection. Extended negotiations between Moscow and Bonn led in August 1970 to a renunciation-of-force treaty that promised to achieve détente and proclaimed the acceptance of all present frontiers. Bonn expressed a willingness to conclude similar agreements with East Germany, Poland, and Czechoslovakia, and to treat East Germany as a second German state within one nation. Moscow, by implication, agreed to pressure East Germany into accepting less than full diplomatic recognition. The Soviet government also acceded to a West German stipulation that the treaty would not be submitted to the Bundestag for ratification until four-power negotiations on the status of West Berlin had been satisfactorily concluded.[51]

Kissinger exulted that the Soviet-German treaties had been "linked" to the Berlin question, putting Washington in a position both "to encourage détente and to control its pace."[52] Still, linkage could work in the other direction as well, and in December 1970 a six-week recess in the Berlin talks touched off a minor crisis in German-American relations. Impatient with the delay, Brandt wrote to the American and French presidents and British prime minister asking that the Berlin negotiations be put into "continuous conference." He also disclosed that his government saw no reason why discussions with East Germany or ratification of the German-Polish treaty of December should have to wait for a Berlin agreement.[53] In January 1971 Brandt backed down on both these threats but not before they had caused Nixon and Kissinger considerable concern.[54] "A prolonged stalemate over Berlin," Kissinger later recalled, "could [have damaged] U.S. German relations severely."[55]

Thus in December and January a number of factors from different games came together—increased anxiety about Nixon's reelection, growing worry about stagflation and negative balances of trade, new pressure from West Germany, an encouraging overture from China, and, above all, continuing failure to achieve peace in Vietnam—to push the president into a renewed attempt to achieve a partnership with Moscow. As it happened, he was not at all certain what the response would be. "[Some] Kremlinologists," he wrote Kissinger in November, "may be encouraging the Moscow leaders to wait out the '72 election on the theory that having any kind of détente between now and '72 would come up against a very tough bargainer and help to get him re-elected, whereas waiting [until] after '72 might reduce his chances of getting re-elected and thereby increase the chance for them to make a better deal after '72."[56]

Fortunately for Nixon, the Soviet rulers had almost simultaneously concluded that the time had come to press for understandings with the United States. On the eve of the new year Foreign Minister Andrei Gromyko and Yuri Andropov, head of the KGB, had drafted a memorandum for the leadership in which they urged, despite the "ideosyncracies and tactical delays" of Nixon's first two years, that the Soviet government increase its efforts to work with the president. The Politburo reportedly adopted this policy with little dissent, confident that for political reasons Nixon would want a Russian summit even more in 1972 than in 1970.[57]

By the end of January 1971 the confidential channel involving Kissinger and Dobrynin had been reenergized, the two men now concentrating their attention on the issues that seemed ripe for settlement—SALT and Berlin. To this point arms control negotiations had been characterized by confusion and lack of achievement. Under pressure from the Joint Chiefs of Staff and Melvin Laird, and despite the Senate's explicit opposition, Nixon had proceeded to test and deploy the new MIRV (an ICBM with independently-targeted warheads) while offering the Soviets an intentionally unacceptable "MIRV ban" as part of two more general disarmament proposals introduced at SALT.[58] The Soviet delegation had quickly turned down both arrangements, although it astonished the Americans by accepting a (later much-regretted) offer to restrict ABM systems on both sides to capital cities.[59] This cleared the way in August 1970 for a third American initiative that stipulated a ceiling of 1710 for ICBM and SLBM launchers as well as *no* limits on MIRVs and an absolute ban on ABMs (Kissinger hoped the last would be rejected and thus reopen the ABM matter).[60] It is not surprising that the negotiations remained deadlocked for the remainder of the year.

The fundamental issues were three: (1) Whether or not, as the United States wanted, an ABM treaty would be "tied" to an agreement on offensive weaponry; (2) What level of completeness a ban on ABMs would entail; and (3) What degree of comprehensiveness would be achieved in an understanding on offensive arms. In the end, in May 1971, the Soviet ambassador accepted the "simultaneity of [offensive/defensive] negotiation" and abandoned his insistence that ABMs be confined to the defense of national capitals,[61] but Kissinger paid for this in a number of significant ways: first, by allowing the future freeze on offensive weapons to be defined without reference to SLBMs; second, by accepting language that permitted the Soviets (and Americans) to continue modernizing and replacing strategic weapons without restraint; and third, by secretly promising the Soviet Union access to the American corn and wheat market.[62]

The third concession was undoubtedly prompted by Soviet needs (and Nixon's desire to enlarge the Soviet win-set), but it also reflected a political calculation on the part of the administration concerning the American economy. With U.S. corn production near an all-time high and its balance of trade increasingly anemic (American abandonment of the gold standard was only three months off), it clearly seemed the proper time to bring this factor into play.[63] Such trade also meant increasing prosperity for the farm belt in the months before the presidential election of 1972. Here was a case where the domestic and foreign policy games could be played synergistically. The arrangement was kept secret at the time partly to make the SALT agreement appear more advantageous to America but also because the administration needed the permission of the maritime unions to ship the grain in Soviet bottoms and believed it could more easily obtain this quietly.[64]

On May 20, 1971, Nixon and Brezhnev simultaneously and proudly announced the "breakthrough" that they had achieved in SALT. This accomplishment *was* a valuable lift to American morale at a difficult point, and it *did* in all likelihood constitute the key to a future Soviet-American summit.[65] Nevertheless, because it was negotiated from weakness as much as strength, Kissinger would have to spend much of the next year attempting to recapture what he had given away to get it.

Contributing significantly to the situation that made these agreements possible were political developments in the Soviet Union. At the Twenty-fourth Communist Party Congress (March–April 1971) Brezhnev established his leadership of the Politburo in foreign affairs and enunciated his "peace program," with its attendant opening to the West. Having publicly attacked Kosygin's stewardship of the economy and identified himself with Moscow's response to Brandt's *Ostpolitik*, Brezhnev had put himself in a position where he could plausibly argue that Western capital and technology were the answers to Soviet economic problems and that he was the man to manage the necessary collaboration.[66]

It was not only with regard to SALT and economic matters that Brezhnev demonstrated his new attitudes and power. In May he announced his interest in outlawing biological weapons and his readiness to accept NATO's proposal for talks with the Warsaw Pact on mutual and balanced force reductions (MBFR).[67] He also acceded to (and perhaps instigated) the resignation of Walter Ulbricht, the 77 year-old East German party leader who had dragged his feet on the Berlin question throughout the spring.[68] On June 7 the Soviet negotiator in the four-power talks, moving sharply toward the Western position, not only abandoned his refusal to guarantee West German access to Berlin but also accepted the continuation of Bonn's "official presence" in the former capital.[69] In mid-June Brezhnev, speaking in Berlin, emphasized that the Soviet Union was prepared "to make efforts to bring this matter [the Berlin Question] to a successful conclusion."[70]

Yet he was not willing to give away the store. The previous March, when Kissinger had approached Dobrynin with Nixon's suggestion for a summit in the late summer of 1971, Moscow had *not* been receptive. At a Politburo meeting in April Kosygin had endorsed Dobrynin's argument for such a summit, but Gromyko insisted that Moscow take advantage of the president's eagerness by requiring progress on Berlin *first*, and, supported by Brezhnev, he had carried the day.[71] Obviously Brezhnev had wanted Nixon's desire for a dramatic accomplishment to grow. By August he was more agreeable (both on Berlin and on a summit invitation), primarily for two reasons: because Brandt's governing coalition in Bonn was showing signs of coming apart (thereby endangering ratification of the Soviet-West German accords), and because Kissinger's surprise visit to Beijing had generated a Chinese invitation to Nixon.[72]

Nixon's intent, of course, was still to "use" the major Communist powers to manipulate North Vietnam, but if this was not possible he clearly hoped that at least a summit and a SALT bargain (now supplemented with a Berlin agreement) would demonstrate his statesmanship to the American public. As the president had told Bob Haldeman the previous November: "[It] now fits with politics. . . . Hold the summit until *we* want a big story and [until] it will be very big—with results."[73]

Now Nixon was going to have *two* summits, not one, and both in an election year! As a result he exerted every possible effort to guarantee success. To balance off the U.S. move to China, Washington acceded to a long-standing Soviet request and agreed to the immediate signing of SALT agreements on avoiding accidental war and improving hot line communications.[74] In addition, the administration not only worked out arrangements with the maritime unions to facilitate the wheat sale it had promised Moscow but also freed American business to enter into a variety of commercial transactions with Soviet economic ministries.[75] To assist the businessmen Secretary of Commerce Maurice Stans was sent on an exploratory visit to Moscow in November.[76] By January governmental experts were designing a Soviet summit agenda that included such items as a lend-lease agreement, a trade treaty, short-term financial credits, cultural and scientific cooperation, and a European security conference.[77] If American preparations for the Beijing summit were not quite as comprehensive, they were equally unprecedented. Among the more unusual was that Nixon and Kissinger stood aside in October as a majority of states voted to expel a long-time ally, the Republic of China (Taiwan), from the United Nations and give its seat to the People's Republic.[78]

The only real setback during the fall and winter grew out of the war that broke out in December between India and Pakistan. On this occasion the president and Kissinger persuaded themselves that Indira Gandhi's government was prolonging the conflict not only to assist East Pakistan (Bangladesh) in attaining its independence but also to attack and dismember West Pakistan.[79] Viewing these events hierarchically, that is, as part of the ongoing struggle among the great powers, they felt obligated to prevent India and its "ally," the USSR, from humiliating Pakistan and its "ally," China (not to speak of the United States). They attempted therefore to limit Indian objectives by applying pressure directly on the Soviet government, using the hot line to threaten military action and hinting that, unless Russia cooperated, they might cancel the summit.[80] They did this in spite of impressive evidence that Moscow did not favor the war and was itself trying to bring about a cease-fire.[81] Their behavior, understandably, left a bad taste in Soviet mouths and is possibly best understood as a reflection of their own nervousness at losing credibility with Beijing, even to the point of having to forfeit the Chinese summit.[82]

The Soviets were irritated as well, of course, by the prospect of Nixon's February 1972 visit to Beijing. They saw immediately that this strengthened the president's hand vis-à-vis both Hanoi and Moscow, just as it ensured that there would be no Soviet-American collaboration against mainland China. They also knew that the Beijing summit fortified Nixon at home and made him less dependent on Russian good will. Brezhnev tried to put a good face on the new situation by pretending that nothing special had occurred, but it is revealing that for about a month before Nixon's departure, and throughout his visit, the Soviet press and radio waged an unusually vigorous campaign to undermine China's international prestige.[83]

The strain of coping with China's opening to America was compounded for Brezhnev as a consequence of Hanoi's spring invasion of South Vietnam and Nixon's energetic reaction. Nixon and Kissinger had repeatedly warned Moscow and Beijing that the United States would respond strongly to a major attack in the South.[84] Nonetheless, and despite the fact that the Soviet Union had been advising Hanoi for weeks to negotiate and compromise, the North Vietnamese were not about to pass up the chance for a last, all-out effort to overthrow the Saigon regime.[85] The ensuing offensive and the savage American air attacks it provoked put the Soviets on the horns of an excruciating dilemma: Should they proceed to hold a summit with a nation that was pummeling their Asian ally?

Nixon himself was never in any doubt about what to do. Every political bone in his body cried out that he had to respond to a military challenge in kind, even if it cost him the upcoming summit. "No negotiation in Moscow is possible unless we come out all right in Vietnam," he confided to his diary. "Both [Bob] Haldeman and Henry [Kissinger] seem to have an idea—which I think is mistaken—that even if we fail in Vietnam we can survive politically."[86] Clearly, the president believed that he understood better than his advisers the interrelations of the multiple games he was playing. The only question in Nixon's mind was whether he should cancel the summit before the Soviets did. This became a critical issue in early May after Kissinger's meeting with the North Vietnamese in Paris failed to slow their offensive operations and the president felt compelled to bomb farther north as well as to mine Haiphong.[87] Nixon's first inclination had been to call off the summit, but Secretary of the Treasury John Connally and Kissinger's assistant Alexander Haig persuaded him that such an action would only arouse domestic dissent and hand the Democrats a campaign issue. If anyone cancelled, it should be Brezhnev, Connally argued.[88]

The Soviet leaders, despite several days of acrimonious debate, opted *not* to cancel. Peter Rodman, another Kissinger assistant, attributes this to the success of linkage, suggesting that (due to prior American management) Brezhnev and his colleagues simply had too much to lose to call off the summit.[89] In a sense this is true, although it is worth noting that by this time the process had become "de-linked" from Vietnam and that the most important "benefit" for Moscow—ratification of the Soviet-West German treaty—had been placed in the equation largely by Bonn, not Washington. Still, Kissinger had played a significant role in preserving the summit, especially during his April visit to Moscow when he had largely disregarded Nixon's instructions (to focus on Vietnam) and devoted himself to creating attractive compromises on pending summit issues.[90] He had made it clear, for example, that he had no serious difficulties with the Soviet reworking of his earlier draft of the Declaration of Basic Principles, a pronouncement the Russians had suggested and to which they attached considerable importance.[91] He had also proved accommodating on SALT, accepting (1) a Brezhnev plan to resolve the ABM dispute by permitting each side to protect its capital and one ICBM site,[92] and (2) a Soviet proposal (that had originated with Kissinger) to reintegrate SLBMs into the offensive agreement but with a cap of 950, the upper limit of what the CIA estimated the Soviets could conceivably build in the next five years.[93] Finally, Kissinger appears to have made substantial oral commitments to Brezhnev in the realm of economic relations, particularly with regard to the grain trade and financial credits.[94] Once again, American negotiators assumed that the international game and the domestic game could be made mutually supportive.

In any case, the Moscow summit took place as scheduled in the last week of May 1972. As Joan Hoff points out, "in terms of sheer complexity and scope, this summit meeting . . . was an unprecedented contrast from the previous five summits following World War II."[95] It produced, among other things, an ABM treaty and an interim five year "freeze" on offensive missiles, a Declaration of Basic Principles that provided an explicit endorsement of "peaceful coexistence," a bargain on European security issues granting Moscow the security conference it desired in return for participation in talks on force reductions, a new American overture to Hanoi (conveyed by Moscow and proposing a tripartite electoral commission), and a protocol establishing a joint Soviet-American commercial commission.[96]

It had been intended that matters of commerce would bulk larger than they actually did at the summit (an assortment of economic understandings having been scheduled for approval),[97] but at the last minute indispensable pieces in the negotiations had not fallen into place. Part of the problem arose from continuing disagreements over lend-lease repayment and over the interest rate on credits being provided,[98] but the greatest difficulty derived from the Nixon administration's inability to achieve a bargain in the domestic game with American longshoremen. "The maritime deal was screwed up by the unions," Kissinger informed William Safire shortly after the summit, "and that must be handled first before we can conclude the grain deal."[99] What he was saying was that the maritime unions had refused to accept his plan to abandon the requirement that half of all exports to the Soviets be carried in American-flagged ships (which were more expensive).[100] It took the better part of the summer to achieve a compromise stipulating that one-third of the grain purchased by Moscow would be shipped in American ships, one-third in Soviet vessels, and one-third in third country carriers.[101] (Interestingly, a few days before the agreement was made public in October, the International Longshoreman's Association—115,000 strong—announced that for the first time in its history, it would support the Republican candidate for president. It was the only major American union aside from the Teamsters to do so.)[102]

The irony was that, despite all the effort involved in making these arrangements (and in concluding a commercial accord and a trade treaty as well), the sale of wheat to the USSR backfired badly for Nixon politically. Warning no one, the Soviets plunged into the American market in July and August and bought more grain than anyone had expected—almost a billion dollars worth, or nearly the entire stored surplus. These purchases, combined with the Department of Agriculture's slowness in withdrawing export subsidies to grain companies, led to noticeably higher bread prices in the United States and strong resentment on the part of consumers.[103] By September George McGovern, the Democratic nominee for president, was complaining bitterly of farmers being victimized by grain traders,[104] while liberal journalists were writing of the great "wheat steal."[105] Nixon's domestic and foreign games had gotten badly out of "synch."

Yet at just this moment the administration received an unexpected political windfall. North Vietnam, militarily overextended and sensing that Nixon was winning his campaign for reelection, realized that it would be more advantageous to negotiate with him *before* November than after. Accordingly, Hanoi carried out a diplomatic retreat in Paris between August and October, gradually dropping its demands for a coalition government and President Nguyen Van Thieu's replacement while expressing willingness to accept a cease fire in place and a council of reconciliation to administer elections.[106] Strangely, Nixon was none too sure that he wanted a pre-election armistice, but Kissinger had no such doubts, and, after strenuous negotiating, felt able on October 26 to make his dramatic announcement that "peace is at hand."[107] He had not reckoned with President Thieu's capacity to impede the agreement, and it was not until January 1973, after renewed American bombing, that a revised version was finally signed. But the advent of peace obviously worked to the president's electoral advantage.

In the end, Nixon achieved his political dream—summits in Beijing and Moscow, peace in Vietnam, and a triumphant reelection with the third largest plurality in history (60 percent). As much as any recent president, Nixon had used his foreign policy accomplishments to political advantage in winning a second term. Yet it had not been simple. His options had been seriously constrained from the outset by public weariness with the war and by his own refusal to have the United States abandon that effort unilaterally. Thus he needed (and had promised) a certain kind of peace—a peace that preserved American credibility—and it was his inability to attain that objective (at least until the last weeks of his first term) that drove him to offer the electorate the substitutes of rapprochement with China and détente with Russia. The voters had demanded peace; Nixon gave them a safer, less expensive Cold War. In so doing he preserved the sinews of the forces he assumed would be needed in the future. As we praise his resourcefulness, we should not forget both that he had deviated from the majority's wishes and that *they* had provided the impetus for change.

This was to be the high point of Soviet-American détente, the months between the enthusiasm of the Moscow summit in May 1972 and the onset of doubt and distrust in November 1973 following the overthrow of the Allende government in Chile and the misunderstandings of the Yom Kippur War.[108] At the next summit, in Washington in June 1973, Nixon and Brezhnev ostensibly basked in a second triumph, but the president's ability to fulfill his promises on trade was already hobbled in the Senate, and his willingness to collaborate with Moscow in the Middle East was surprisingly limited. The two leaders were reduced to pledging a speedup in the SALT talks and to signing a vague agreement not to threaten or use force against the other.[109]

By 1975 the spirit and momentum of détente had declined severely. Watergate had weakened the capacity of both the Nixon and Ford administrations to initiate and defend policy. The Jackson-Vanik Amendment (requiring Jewish emigration from the USSR) to the Trade Act of December 1974 had prompted Moscow to reject the entire economic package Brezhnev had negotiated with the United States.[110] In April the military collapse of South Vietnam raised questions in the public mind about Soviet sincerity, and by the end of the year Soviet-Cuban intervention in Angola produced added tension.[111] At Nixon's last summit with Brezhnev, in Moscow in June 1974 (two months before his resignation), the participants had found themselves largely going through the motions. Their sole accomplishment was a reduction in ABM deployment sites on each side from two to one.[112] In Gerald Ford's only summit with Brezhnev, in Vladivostok in December 1974, the new president and the general secretary established a SALT II framework that put equal (but high) limits on each other's launchers and bombers.[113] Little could they have guessed that it would be almost four years before that treaty would be signed, and that it would never be ratified.

In Richard Nixon's last months as president, as he lost control of the domestic situation, he became ever more enamoured of détente and the improvement he had wrought in Soviet-American relations. From his point of view, the only thing wrong with détente was that because of Watergate, he was being increasingly deprived of the tools and power needed to defend and preserve it, the ability to use the "sticks" and dispense the "carrots," to bomb in Vietnam for instance, or to offer a "most favored nation" commercial privilege.[114] Today, twenty-five years later, it seems more accurate to conclude that there were other problems with détente as well, substantial weaknesses that contributed to its eventual unraveling. Why did SALT I include no MIRV agreement, for example? Why were the caps on SLBMs placed so high as to be a virtual incentive to build more? Why were the constraints on missile "modernization" so inadequate? Why was so little thought given to the dangers of superpower competition in the Third World? Why was there so little American interest in cooperating with the Soviet Union to reduce tensions in the Middle East? Finally, why did Nixon and Kissinger not warn the American people more forcefully that détente was a fragile accomplishment that needed to be deepened and extended?

The answers to these questions are generally to be found at home and not abroad. We can see that there were vested interests in the military, for example, as well as among its congressional allies, which opposed relinquishing the advantages *both* of being the first nation to MIRV *and* of continuing to exploit our technological advantages. Nixon and Kissinger were under tremendous pressure from Laird and the Joint Chiefs of Staff in this regard, and the president made a conscious decision to MIRV because he believed that giving up the ABM was all that the political and military markets (two levels of the domestic game) could "bear."[115] Yet we must also note that Nixon and Kissinger were ideologically predisposed to believe that international relations do not really change and that the Cold War would continue indefinitely. It followed logically that the United States must remain physically the stronger of the superpowers.

Similarly, Nixon and Kissinger were heavily influenced (despite the president's superficial anti-Semitism) by their perception that they dare not abandon the longstanding American pledge (a promise in the domestic game) to protect and assist Israel. Moreover, to keep oil flowing they knew that they must make sure that no war broke out in the Middle East, especially between Jews and Arabs. The peculiarly hierarchical (and suspicious) nature of their thinking is underlined by the fact that they sabotaged the projects of their own Secretary of State in order to keep the reins of Middle-Eastern peace-making entirely in American hands. During both the Jordan "crisis" of 1970 and the Yom Kippur War of 1973 it became clear that they would not share leadership with any other country, and especially not with the Soviet Union, whom they suspected of trying to "Communize" the Arabs. Their assumption seems to have been that the Third World has a natural tendency to become "pro-Western" (history was on our side, despite Vietnam), and that *any* Soviet involvement there should be seen as illegitimate. Besides, why stir up the tired American electorate with visions of U.S. collaboration and/or intervention in far away places?[116]

Traces of electoral considerations can be found in other sins of omission and commission committed by the Nixon leadership. Kissinger's decision to concede what Admiral Elmo Zumwalt later called "the appalling [excessively large] SLBM numbers" grew directly out of his eagerness for a summit meeting at the best possible time politically. Indeed, one can plausibly argue that the Nixon administration, over four years, went from one extreme to the other—from paying too little for a relationship with Moscow (i.e., assuming that Russia was the most eager for a partnership) to paying too much for a summit (i.e., ignoring vital issues and operating from an unnecessarily large win-set) just before the election. This seems also to have been the case when the administration allowed the Soviets to buy up the entire U.S. grain surplus.

There *had* been a genuine and unique opportunity for change in international relations during this period. The protracted struggle in Asia had fractured the Cold War consensus in the United States, dulling hawkishness and arrogance, and leaving large sections of the public with pronounced symptoms of withdrawal. The spiraling dangers and costs of the arms race, in league with declining economic growth in the Soviet Union and the United States, had made cooperation between the two countries unusually attractive. Nixon's domestic game, plus the frustration of his hopes for an acceptable peace in Vietnam and the unexpected success of Willy Brandt's *Ostpolitik* (not to mention the impact of the China "card" in Moscow) had made American initiatives to the Soviets increasingly necessary. By 1972 the win-sets on both sides were as broad and overlapping as they had ever been.

Yet, giving due credit for everything accomplished regarding arms control, Germany, East-West trade, and Vietnam, the fact remains that the progress made was not sufficient to prevent the relationship between the superpowers from sliding backward (thereby eroding the "ratification" of détente) once they encountered the major problems that had not been addressed. And for this, not only vested interests and ideological predispositions must be held responsible, but also the propensity of the major players to focus on the short-term game (in America, on reelection). Thus the final irony, especially in the United States, is that although the feelings of the citizenry had made a far reaching revision of the Cold War imperative, the leadership's *extraordinary* self-consciousness about how the people (and the world) would evaluate its actions resulted in these efforts not being radical enough.

Let it be emphasized, then, that matters internal to the nation, especially the electorate's condition and desires, played an immense role in the creation and definition of détente. It was the public's despair about the Vietnam War and its demand for peace that led the president to try to develop leverage with the Soviets (Vietnam's primary source of military supplies) in the first place, and it was his inability to end the war that led him to offer the voters the substitute of superpower détente as timely proof of his sincerity and statesmanship. China was brought into the equation for the same reasons and to reduce the cost of this new and more "relaxed" Containment. Nixon's hope, of course, was to heal the nation and to re-create the prewar foreign policy consensus, only at a less costly and more realistic level. As in the case of Dwight Eisenhower, it was to be a Containment for the "long haul." With such ideas Nixon forfeited a great chance seriously to challenge the Cold War.

NOTES

1. Monica Crowley, *Nixon in Winter* (New York, 1998), pp 27–28.

2. See, for example, Jonathan Aitken, *Nixon: A Life* (London: Weidenfeld and Nicholson, 1993), pp 457–466.

3. Joan Hoff, *Nixon Reconsidered* (New York, 1994), p.273.

4. Tom Wicker, *One of Us: Richard Nixon and the American Dream* (New York, 1991), p. 657.

5. Raymond L. Garthoff, *Détente and Confrontation: American Soviet Relations from Nixon to Reagan*, rev. ed. (Washington: Brookings Institution, 1994), p. 27.

6. In employing Robert Putnam's "two level game theory" I have found it helpful to discuss the evidence as if there were, in effect, *four* presidential games: (1) international with adversaries, (2) international with allies, (3) domestic within the executive branch, and (4) domestic with legislature and public. See Peter B. Evans, Harold K. Jacobson, and Robert D. Putnam, eds., *Double-Edged Diplomacy: International Bargaining and Domestic Politics* (Berkeley, 1993), pp. 431–468.

7. A contrasting view denies that it was possible to resolve the Cold War through gradually improving relations and argues that the only way it could have ended was with the collapse of one of the antagonists. For such scholars Nixon's foreign policy was misguided because it was too "friendly" to the Soviets. See Robert Kagan, "Disestablishment," *The New Republic* 219 (August 17 and 24, 1998), pp. 29–34.

8. Stephen E. Ambrose, *Nixon: The Triumph of a Politician 1962–1972* (New York, Simon and Schuster, 1989), pp. 190–191.

9. Henry Kissinger, *White House Years* (Boston: Little, Brown, 1979), pp. 271–288; Semour M. Hersh, *The Price of Power: Kissinger in the Nixon White House* (New York: Summit Books, 1983), p.121.

10. William Shawcross, *Sideshow: Kissinger, Nixon and the Destruction of Cambodia* (New York: Touchstone, 1981), pp. 91–95; Richard Nixon, *RN: The Memoirs of Richard Nixon* (New York : Touchstone, 1978), pp. 380–382.

11. Melvin Small, *Johnson, Nixon, and the Doves* (New Brunswick, N.J.: Rutgers University Press, 1988), p. 219; Ambrose, *Triumph*, pp. 467–468; Martin Anderson, "The Making of an All-Volunteer Force," in Leon Friedman and William F. Levantrosser, eds., *Richard M. Nixon: Cold War Patriot and Statesman* (Westport, Conn.: Greenwood, 1986), pp 171–177.

12. Small, *Johnson, Nixon, and the Doves*, p. 220.

13. Kissinger, *White House Years*, pp 270–280, 436–448, 968–984.

14. Tad Szulc, *The Illusion of Peace: Foreign Policy in the Nixon Years* (New York, 1978), pp. 338–341.

15. Szulc, *Illusion of Peace*, pp. 390–392; and Walter Isaacson, *Kissinger: A Biography* (New York: Simon and Schuster, 1992), pp. 331–332.

16. Szulc, *Illusion of Peace*, pp 571–573; Nixon, *RN*, p. 617; and Kissinger, *White House Years*, p. 1251.

17. Keith L. Nelson, *The Making of Détente: Soviet-American Relations in the Shadow of Vietnam* (Baltimore, John Hopkins University Press, 1995), p. 77.

18. Kissinger, *White House Years*, pp. 129–130, 132–133; William G. Hyland, *Mortal Rivals: Superpower Relations from Nixon to Reagan* (New York: Random House, 1987), p. 20.

19. Richard Nixon, *The Presidential Press Conferences* (New York E. M. Coleman, 1978), pp. 4–5; and Nixon, *RN*, p. 415.

20. Memo of Conversation Zhukov-Kissinger, January 31, 1969, in Storage Center for Contemporary Documentation (TsKhSD), f. 5, op. 61, d. 558, p. 18, as cited in Ilya Gaiduk, *The Soviet Union and the Vietnam War* (Chicago: Ivan Dee, 1996), p. 203.

21. Szulc, *Illusion of Peace*, pp. 68–69.

22. Anatoly Dobrynin to Andre Gromyko, July 12, 1969, *Bulletin of the Cold War International History Project* (Washington: Fall 1993), pp. 63–67.

23. Nixon, *RN*, p. 407.

24. Memo of Conversation, Anatoly Dobrynin-Averill Harriman, February 19, 1969, Averill Harriman Papers, Special Files, Box 455, Library of Congress, as cited in Gaiduk, *Soviet Union and the Vietnam War*, p. 205.

25. Kissinger, *White House Years*, pp. 130–138. Gerard Smith, interviewed by the author, April 12, 1983. The phrase is from Dobrynin.

26. *New York Times*, February 18, 1969; *Washington Post*, April 5, 1969.

27. Kissinger, *White House Years*, p. 134.

28. Ibid., pp. 134, 153.

29. Ibid., pp. 135–138.

30. Ibid., p. 149; and Gerard Smith, *Doubletalk: The Story of SALT I* (Garden City, N.Y.: Doubleday, 1980), pp. 75–80.

31. Kissinger, *White House Years*, pp. 152–154. This was done in spite of considerable pressure from the Congress to liberalize trade with the Soviet bloc; see Philip J. Funigiello, *American-Soviet Trade in the Cold War* (Chapel Hill: University of North Carolina Press, 1988), pp. 179–180, and Michael Mastanduno, *Economic Containment; CoCom and the Politics of East-West Trade* (Ithaca: Cornell University Press, 1992), pp.140–145.

32. Szulc, *Illusion of Peace*, pp. 149–157; and Hersh, *The Price of Power*, p. 123. See also Kissinger, *White House Years*, pp. 282–305.

33. Ambrose, *Triumph*, p. 301.

34. Hersh, *The Price of Power*, pp. 127–128

35. Small, *Johnson, Nixon, and the Doves*, pp. 182–187.

36. Nixon, *RN*, p. 404.

37. William Bundy, *A Tangled Web: The Making of Foreign Policy in the Nixon Presidency* (New York: Hill and Wang, 1998), pp. 80–83.

38. Hersh, *Price of Power*, p. 133.

39. Hersh, *Price of Power*, pp. 168–174; and Kissinger, *White House Years*, pp. 448–457.

40. Shawcross, *Sideshow*, pp. 128–160; and Ambrose, *Triumph*, pp. 343–363.

41. Henry Brandon, *The Retreat of American Power* (New York, 1972), pp. 146–147. See also Bundy, *Tangled Web*, pp. 153–161.

42. Szulc, *The Illusion of Peace*, pp. 337–341; and Kissinger, *White House Years*, pp. 968–980.

43. James W. Garver, *China's Decision for Rapprochement with the United States, 1968–1971* (Boulder, Colo.: Westview, 1982), chaps. 3 and 4; See also Harrison E. Salisbury, *The New Emperors: China in the Era of Mao and Deng* (Boston: Little, Brown, 1992), pp. 289–295, and Robert S. Ross, *Negotiating Cooperation: The United States and China, 1969–1989* (Stanford: Stanford University Press, 1995), pp. 17–54.

44. Kissinger, *White House Years*, pp. 552.

45. Ibid., pp. 554–558; and Garthoff, *Détente and Confrontation*, pp. 198–204.

46. The President's views are presented in Nixon, *RN*, pp. 483–490. For interpretations that play down the gravity of these events, see Szulc, *Illusion of Peace*, pp. 321–331, 364–366; Hersh, *Price of Power*, pp. 234–256; and Garthoff, *Détente and Confrontation*, pp. 87–100. William Bundy takes them more seriously in *Tangled Web*, pp. 179–204.

47. Kissinger, *White House Years*, pp. 594–652.

48. Hersh, *Price of Power*, pp. 300–303. The Soviet actions are discussed in Garthoff, *Détente and Confrontation*, pp. 206–207; Lawrence Freedman, *U.S. Intelligence and the Soviet Strategic Threat* (Houndmills, England: Macmillan 1986), pp. 13–19; and Honore M. Catudal, Jr., *The Diplomacy of the Quadripartite Agreement on Berlin: A New Era in East-West Politics* (Berlin: Berlin-Verlag, 1978), pp. 124–130.

49. Ambrose, *Triumph*, pp. 394–396.

50. See Frank Costigliola, *France and the United States: The Cold Alliance since World War II* (New York: Twayne, 1992).

51. Lawrence L. Whetten, *Germany's Ostpolitik: Relations between the Federal Republic and the Warsaw Pact Countries* (London: Oxford University Press, 1971), pp. 93–151. See also Werner Link, "Aussen- und Deutschland Politik in der Aera Brandt, 1969–1974," in Karl Dietrich Bracher, Wolfgang Jager, and Werner Link, *Republik in Wandel, 1969–1974: Die Aera Brandt* (Stuttgart: Deutsche Verlags-Anstalt, 1986).

52. Kissinger, *White House Years*, p. 416.

53. Catudal, *Quadripartite Agreement*, pp. 139–141.

54. Ibid., pp. 141–145, 152–153; and Hyland, *Mortal Rivals*, pp. 32–33.

55. Kissinger, *White House Years*, p. 800.

56. Box 229, Haldeman Chronological File, Special Files, Nixon Papers. Nixon and Kissinger were also encouraged by the food riots that had broken out in Poland in December 1970, which suggested to them that the Soviet Union could not continue to pursue détente in Europe without the collaboration of the United States.

57. Anatoly Dobrynin, *In Confidence* (New York: Times Books, 1995), p. 214.

58. Kissinger, *White House Years*, p. 540; Smith, *Doubletalk*, p. 161. Laird argues, in retrospect, that "MIRVs were the only feasible option available for response to an expanding Soviet threat, given the hostile attitude of many members of Congress toward defense spending;" Melvyn Laird, "A Strong Start in a Difficult Decade: Defense Policy in the Nixon-Ford Years," *International Security* 10 (Fall 1985), 5–26.

59. Smith, *Doubletalk*, pp. 124–125.

60. Kissinger, *White House Years*, pp. 549–550.

61. Ibid., pp. 813–819.

62. Garthoff, *Détente and Confrontation*, pp. 179–182; and Dobrynin, *In Confidence*, p. 220. But see also Isaacson, *Kissinger*, pp. 326–327.

63. See Peter G. Peterson to Richard Nixon, July 7, 1971, regarding East-West trade; Box 12, President's Handwriting file, Nixon Papers. See also Diane B. Kunz, *Butter and Guns: America's Cold War Economic Diplomacy* (New York: Free Press, 1997), pp. 201, 217–218; and Allen J. Matusow, *Nixon's Economy: Booms, Busts, Dollars, and Votes* (Lawrence: University of Kansas, 1998), pp. 222–224.

64. Roger B. Porter, *The US-USSR Grain Agreement* (Cambridge: Cambridge University Press, 1984), pp. 11–12; and Hersh, *Price of Power*, pp. 343–348.

65. Kissinger, *White House Years*, pp. 819–823. See also John Scali to Richard Nixon, May 26, 1971, President's Handwriting File, Nixon Papers.

66. Peter M. E. Volten, *Brezhnev's Peace Program: A Study of Soviet Domestic Political Process and Power* (Boulder, Colo.: Westview, 1982), pp. 58–87. See also George Breslauer, *Khrushchev and Brezhnev as Leaders* (London: Allen and Unwin, 1982), pp. 184–87.

67. Garthoff, *Détente and Confrontation*, pp. 114–17.

68. Michael J. Sodaro, *Moscow, Germany, and the West from Khrushchev to Gorbachev* (Ithaca: Cornell University Press, 1990), pp. 207–212.

69. Catudal, *Quadripartite Agreement*, pp. 166–71; and Willy Brandt, *People and Politics: The Years 1960–1975* (Boston: Little, Brown, 1976), pp. 292–293.

70. Catudal, *Quadripartite Agreement*, p. 173. Brezhnev's speech is reprinted in *Neues Deutschland*, June 17, 1971.

71. Dobrynin, *In Confidence*, p. 223.

72. Valentin Falin, *Politische Errinerungen* (Munich: Droemer Knauer, 1993), p. 172.

73. Haldeman Handwritten Notes, November 7, 1970, Haldeman File, Nixon Papers. Haldeman recorded on March 22, 1972, in an unpublished part of his diary, that the President "wants to be sure that I go to work on [Alexander] Haig and Henry [Kissinger], through him, to make the point that some of the decisions have got to be made on the basis of the effect they'll have on the election. For example, [the President] feels strongly we should go to Poland after the Russian trip, while Henry is equally strongly opposed to that, so we have got to convince Henry."; Haldeman Diaries, CD-ROM, 1994.

74. The texts of the two agreements, signed September 30, 1971, are in Smith, *Doubletalk*, pp. 517–523. See also Dobrynin, *In Confidence*, p. 233.

75. Much, if not all, of the shipping arrangement is spelled out in Peter Flanigan to Richard Nixon, November 3, 1971, Box 68, Charles Colson Files, Special Files, Nixon Papers. The mix of Nixon's motives becomes very clear in his remark to Haldeman on November 6 that he wanted "to really pour into the Farm Bill our initiatives to China and Russia, which are really farm policy-oriented and also get credit for our corn agreement with the Russians" (The Haldeman Diaries, CD-ROM). See also Hersh, *Price of Power*, pp. 346–348; and Lester A. Sobel, ed., *Kissinger and Détente* (New York: Facts on File, 1975), p. 88.

76. Maurice Stans, interviewed by the author, July 21, 1992.

77. Nixon's instructions were conveyed in NSDM 150 (February 14, 1972), Next Steps with Respect to U.S.-Soviet Trading Relationship, and NSDM 153 (February 17, 1972), Review of US-Soviet Negotiations; Box 10, Peter Flanigan File, Special Files, Nixon Papers.

78. Kissinger, *White House Years*, pp. 770–774, 784–787. See also Rosemary Foot, *The Practices of Power: US Relations with China since 1949* (Oxford: Clarendon Press, 1995), pp. 47–48.

79. Robert Jackson, *South Asian Crisis: India, Pakistan, and Bangladesh: A Political and Historical Analysis of the 1971 War* (New York: Praeger, 1975), pp. 224–228. Nixon offers a relatively brief discussion in *RN*, pp. 525–528.

80. Christopher Van Hollen, "The Tilt Policy Revisited: Nixon-Kissinger Geopolitics and South Asia," *Asian Survey*, 20 (April 1980): 350–361. See also William Burr, ed., *The Kissinger Transcripts: The Top Secret Talks with Beijing and Moscow* (New York: New Press, 1998), pp. 48–59.

81. Hersh, *Price of Power*, pp. 467–474; and Pran Chopra, *India's Second Liberation* (Cambridge, Mass.: MIT Press, 1974), pp. 212–213.

82. Georgi Arbatov records an incident three years later in which Brezhnev registered his strong disgust at the way the Americans had behaved during the Indian-Pakistani war; Georgi Arbatov, *The System: An Insider's Life in Soviet Politics* (New York: Times Books, 1992), p. 195.

83. "The Soviet Union's Hard Look at China," *Radio Liberty Dispatch* (Munich, April 12, 1972). See also Richard Anderson, Jr., *Public Politics in an Authoritarian State: Making Foreign Policy during the Brezhnev Years* (Ithaca: Cornell University Press, 1993), pp. 211–222.

84. Kissinger, *White House Years*, pp. 1099–1108.

85. Gaiduk, *Soviet Union and the Vietnam War*, pp. 231–233. See also Anne Gilks, *The Breakdown of the Sino-Vietnamese Alliance, 1970–1979* (Berkeley: Institute of East Asian Studies, 1992), pp. 71–91.

86. Nixon, *RN*, p. 589.

87. Kissinger, *White House Years*, pp. 1169–1176.

88. William Safire, *Before the Fall: An Inside View of the Pre-Watergate White House* (Garden City, N.Y.: Doubleday, 1975), pp. 435–436. See also Wicker, *One of Us*, p. 602.

89. Peter W. Rodman, *More Precious than Peace: The Cold War and the Struggle for the Third World* (New York: Scribner's, 1994), p. 127.

90. Nelson, *Making of Détente*, pp. 110–112.

91. Alexander L. George, "The Basic Principles Agreement of 1972: Origins and Expectations," in Alexander George, ed., *Managing U.S.-Soviet Rivalry: Problems of Crisis Prevention* (Boulder, Colo.: Westview, 1983), pp. 107–110.

92. Garthoff, *Détente and Confrontation*, pp. 175–177.

93. Ibid., pp. 179–185; Smith, *Doubletalk*, pp. 352–372; Elmo R. Zumwalt, Jr., *On Watch* (New York: Quadrangle, 1976), pp. 403–405. Secretary of Defense Melvin Laird's comment on this is particularly damning: "Short-term expediencies dominated the final stages of the SALT I agreements in 1972, when the urge to get an agreement at any cost became the chief end"; Melvin Laird, "America's Principled Role in World Affairs: A Realistic Policy of Peace and Freedom" in Robert J. Pranger, ed., *Détente and Defense: A Reader* (Washington: American Enterprise Institute, 1976), p. 108.

94. Joseph Alsop, "A View from the Summit," *Washington Post*, May 24, 1972. See also Hersh, *Price of Power*, pp. 531–535; and Safire, *Before the Fall*, pp. 435–436.

95. Hoff, *Nixon Reconsidered*, p. 203.

96. Nelson, *Making of Détente*, pp. 113–117.

97. Peter Flanigan to Richard Nixon, March 7, 1972, Box 10, Peter Flanigan Files, Nixon Papers. On Thursday, May 25, 1972, while at the Moscow summit, Haldeman recorded his expectation that "the Ag[ricultural] and Lend Lease [agreements would be signed on] Sat[urday]." Haldeman Handwritten Notes, Haldeman Files, Nixon Papers.

98. On the lend-lease dispute, see Flanigan to Nixon, May 23, 1972, Box 66, Trip Files, Central Files, Nixon Papers. On the interest rate issue, see Peter G. Peterson, *U.S.-Soviet Commercial Relations in a New Era* (Washington: Government Printing Office, 1972), pp. 18–19.

99. Safire, *Before the Fall*, p. 454.

100. Isaacson, *Kissinger*, p. 428.

101. *New York Times*, October 5, 1972.

102. Ibid., September 26, 1972.

103. I. M. Destler, *Making Foreign Economic Policy* (Washington: Brookings Institution, 1980), pp. 36–49. For context, see Marshall I. Goldman, *Détente and Dollars: Doing*

Business with the Soviets (New York: Basic Books, 1975), pp. 193–224; and Matusow, *Nixon's Economy*, pp. 222–229.

104. Presidential News Summaries, September 11, 12, and 19, 1972, Nixon Papers.

105. Joseph Kraft, "Russia's Wheat Steal," *Washington Post*, September 21, 1972.

106. Gaiduk, *Soviet Union and the Vietnam War*, pp. 241–242.

107. Kissinger, *White House Years*, pp. 1305–1406.

108. Victor Israelyan, *Inside the Kremlin during the Yom Kippur War* (University Park: Penn State Press, 1995), pp. 21–219; and Richard Ned Lebow and Janice Gross Stein, *We All Lost the Cold War* (Princeton: Princeton University Press, 1994), pp. 149–260.

109. Garthoff, *Détente and Confrontation*, pp. 360–403.

110. Mike Bowker and Phil Williams, *Superpower Détente: A Reappraisal* (London: SAGE Publications, 1988), pp. 97–167; and Paula Stern, *Water's Edge: Domestic Politics and the Making of American Foreign Policy* (Westport, Conn.: Greenwood, 1979), pp. 54–193.

111. Rodman, *More Precious than Peace*, pp. 163–182.

112. Garthoff, *Détente and Confrontation*, pp. 458–486. Kissinger's March 1974 discussions with Brezhnev in preparation for this summit are in Burr, *The Kissinger Transcripts*, pp. 217–264.

113. Garthoff, *Détente and Confrontation*, pp. 494–505.

114. Richard Nixon, *No More Vietnams* (New York: Arbor House, 1985), pp. 165–183.

115. Gerard Smith, *Disarming Diplomat* (Lanham, Md.: Madison Books, 1996), pp. 163–168.

116. Gideon Doron, "Peace or Oil: The Nixon Administration and Its Middle East Policy Choices," in Friedman and Levantrosser, *Cold War Patriot and Statesman*, pp. 119–137.

CHAPTER 7

The Foreign-Domestic Nexus in Gorbachev's Central and East European Policy

Egbert Jahn

THE TWO LEVELS IN THE ANALYSIS OF SOVIET FOREIGN POLICY

The two-level-game approach, or two-level foreign-policy analysis, represents a completely new view of the interaction between domestic and international policy.[1] It varies from the traditional theories that emphasize the dominance of either international relations or domestic politics, the domestic influences on foreign policy,[2] or the linkages between the national and international.[3] The benefits afforded by the new approach lie not in producing generalizations about the equilibrium between domestic and foreign policy, but in allowing more exact assessment of the relationship between the two. The approach is heavily oriented towards the actors and focused on the decision-making process. However, it first requires a precise analysis of the framework in which decisions are made by the domestic and foreign policy actors.

Robert D. Putnam, who introduced the approach in an article in 1988,[4] describes the two-level game as a metaphor; others call it a research technique, a theory, a model, or a concept. Here, "analysis on two levels" should be understood as a search for the empirical context of international occurrences that were preceded by substantial communication on the international and domestic levels.[5]

A question has been raised about whether the two-level-game approach can be applied to the Soviet Union. The answer is "yes," although the approach may require a certain modification or sharpening. Its application to various phases of Soviet foreign policy highlights a number of problems, because the domestic-policy level changed fundamentally several times, as did the political rules applying to this system.

When we speak of the Soviet system here, we mean the post-Stalinist authoritarian system that existed in 1956 to 1987/1988 and provided the framework for the first half of Gorbachev's foreign policy. In the Perestroika system, which only existed from about 1987 to the beginning of 1991, there were completely different actors and entirely dissimilar game rules than in the old Soviet system. Only a few generalizations about the Soviet decision-making process apply to the whole Gorbachev era. The analysis is made more difficult because the transition from the monopolistic authoritarian system to the increasingly pluralistic Perestroika system was not abrupt. Every so often new actors stepped onto the stage while others disappeared and, at the same time, the political "rules of the game" changed. We look first at the structures of the game at level II, as they emerged out of the Khrushchev and Brezhnev eras and still affected decision making during the greater part of Gorbachev's years in office.

In Socialist authoritarian regimes, the most important decisions are officially made by institutions that are "elected." However, votes of approval with ritual results of 100.0 percent or 99.9 percent do not correspond to the two-level-game concept of "ratification." Formal ratification of foreign-policy decisions, as a rule by 100 percent, is secured a priori.

Even in Western institutions, the ratification of an international agreement or the process of reaching a compromise is normally secured before a vote takes place. Creation of the necessary majority, which Putnam unfortunately calls "ratification," involves negotiating with members of, or at least the opinion leaders of, the government's party. This bargaining usually serves as a precursor to any formal votes.

The necessity of domestic negotiation presupposes a society in which there are particular interests, opinions, and specific decision-making competencies for organizations. In decision making, these differences must be coordinated and adapted to each other for a policy to take hold. Otherwise, the result is a nondecision or preservation of the status quo. Foreign-policy decisions are made by one or several governmental bodies as prescribed by the nation's constitution.

In a society of the Soviet type,[6] several of the prerequisites for domestic negotiation do not exist. At the same time, something akin to these prerequisites is required if the two-level research approach is applicable. It was not the goal of negotiations to establish a majority in a given assembly, because either no formal vote took place or a unanimous vote was expected. The content of the decision may have been unclear until shortly before the unanimous vote. This was sorted out in advance through informal bargaining among functionaries in the Communist Party, government, and society. Such negotiating on important foreign-policy decisions almost always took place, especially in the post-Stalin era. In some cases, it may have been much more intense than in the West. At the same time, these talks have been much more difficult for researchers to reconstruct than in the West.

The goal of the process in the Soviet system was not to create a voting majority in a democratically elected organization or in a non-democratic government organization such as the Supreme Soviet, since this existed in advance. Rather, it was the achievement of approval, or at least half-hearted agreement, or even silent toleration, of the Party leadership's decisions by politically relevant institutions or persons.

Seldom would one dare, even in the highest Party assemblies, to directly contradict the General Secretary. Disagreement would be expressed indirectly by referring to undesirable circumstances or suspected side-effects of a decision. Because political competition was not based on elections and there were no reliable public-opinion polls, collective opposition could not make itself felt in an organized and disciplined manner. It could only draw attention by withholding services, spontaneously expressing disapproval, and occasionally taking part in illegal actions and unrest. Domestically, the party feared not defeat in a decision or an election but the danger of rebellion. The actual or suspected conditions leading to a rebellion by the party bureaucracy, the military, the police, the workers in key industries, or ethnic or national movements all limited, in a vague manner, the domestic negotiating margins of the Soviet actor on the world stage.

The "rules of the game" at level II were not founded on a constitution or based on unambiguous and publicly known social conventions. Instead, informal but firm rules applied, predominantly in the Party machinery and, to some extent, in the machinery of the state and society. Scientists and politicians in the West attempted to familiarize themselves with these rules by means of Kremlinology based on piecemeal information and speculation.

In Western society, the state aggregates particular interests into a common interest and political will. Parties, along with other organizations or groups, are the legitimate representatives of particular interests and try to influence the general interest and common policy of the society. In the bureaucratic-socialist society, the equivalent institution was not the socialist state but the Communist Party. The state merely acted as the executor of class interests, as recognized and enforced by the Party. Party decisions were rarely direct mandates because they required a literal or slightly modified reiteration in a government body to become binding and receive validity. However, no will other than the Party's could be enforced. Accordingly, neither the head of government nor the prime minister acted as the political representative of the Soviet system, but the General Secretary of the Communist Party and his counterparts in other communist parties.[7] The political executive of the system was not the government but the Politburo, which made decisions binding for all government bodies. After the 27th Party Congress in 1986, the Politburo consisted of twelve members and seven candidates. At the pinnacle of the party machinery stood the General Secretary and nine Secretaries, two of whom were also Politburo members. This central Party machinery corresponded to a Western government in its functions. As a rule, however, it needed to transmit its decisions through the Soviet government machinery in over one hundred ministries.

The Central Committee (CC), which consisted of 307 members in 1986, "elected" the Politburo and the General Secretary. Composed of high functionaries from all areas of society, it primarily served to rubber-stamp decisions. Only during a crisis, when the Politburo was split or the General Secretary was weak, could the CC play a decisive role. According to Gorbachev's account, the 159 First Secretaries of the republics, territories, and regions, many of whom were also members of the CC, played a much greater role in the consultation process prior to Gorbachev's election than the remaining members of the CC.[8] Although the First Secretaries did not form their own assembly, they were occasionally invited to conferences. Even then the goal was not to achieve a voting majority but to more or less reflect or influence the mood.

In Marxist-Leninist understanding, the Party was responsible for aggregating the particular interests and the multiplicity of opinions in society. In so doing, the Party was not primarily concerned with the subjective interests of people, social groups, and classes. These could have been discovered through competitive elections, referenda, or opinion polls. Instead, the Party was concerned with the interests that could be discovered by applying Marxist-Leninist "scientific ideology." Opinions could be dismissed as mere prejudices, lacking enlightenment. In certain circumstances the Party needed to push through the "true" will of the people, based on "scientific" discovery, against the unenlightened, prejudiced views of the people. In this process, expressions of the subjective interests of the people were considered important but not politically relevant. If they did not correspond to "true, objective interests," they became future targets of scientific and especially ideological work.

The Party needed to pay much less attention to the, often unknown, majority opinion of the population than did Western politicians. The high status given to ideology in the work of the CC and the prominent standing of the CC Secretary and Politburo member in charge of ideology were founded on this understanding of politics. Mikhail Suslov was, for decades, considered the second most powerful man in the Soviet Union. After his death, Konstantin Chernenko and then, for a short time, Gorbachev were in charge of ideology. Their assignments included successful agitation and propaganda as well as education and training, even in the social strata and classes whose "objective interests" the Party purported to represent.

Discrepancies between the "objective interests" of the working classes and their subjective wishes were overcome in two ways. On the one hand, the Party sometimes separated itself from a previous understanding or interpretation. These discarded viewpoints would then be denounced as left- or right-deviant and a product of the concrete influence of a "handful" of mistaken people, thus protecting the authority of the Party as a whole. This occurred relatively seldom, however. More commonly, changes in direction or increasing discrepancies between sentiments in the population and Party ideology were cause for "increased ideological education." In fact, the "role of ideology" was conceived to be "growing," even under Gorbachev. It was never assumed that the workers comprehended their objective interests, that is, no longer needed to be educated about these interests.

It might seem that the Communist Party leadership did not need to consider the opinions and interests of the population and the Party because of the absence of competitive elections, votes, and public opinion. From this perspective, Soviet negotiators at international conferences were in a weak position, because they could not credibly point to internal pressures to strengthen their bargaining position. Of course, they would sometimes cite pressure from "the military" or from "hard-liners" to underpin an inflexible position. Gorbachev also made liberal use of the argument that he faced internal opposition to make his negotiating position credible. We now know, in many cases, that the pressure did not exist or that it could have been countered by the General Secretary's counter pressure, if he had been so inclined.

Nonetheless, the room for negotiations given the General Secretary was constrained in many ways by domestic politics. The Party leadership could not be assured of its continued dominance. It needed to satisfy important material as well as mental and psychological needs of society and its most important political components. Provision of real services was required to avoid risking unrest and rebellion.

Because the Party declared that historic progress and success would validate its rule, it also needed achievements. Ideology and propaganda could be used to celebrate fictional accomplishments, but the discrepancy between reality and fiction could not always be at the Party's discretion. The same mechanism was also at work within the Party and the Party leadership. Though corruption, Byzantine subjugation, and personal relationships all played an immense role in internal Party decisions, party functionaries also felt the necessity to legitimize Party rule through real services and accomplishments. Even the General Secretary faced these pressures. Because votes and public criticism did not serve as a correction, indirect forms of expressing disagreement took on an important role. General Secretaries could not ignore tense or volatile moods in the politically important institutions. The size of majorities was less important in assessing political constellations than the intensity of dissatisfaction among socially powerful minorities, the power apparatus, or key industrial sectors.

Negotiating political positions in the Soviet Union was less a bargaining process than consultation and the testing of opinions by the political leadership and the General Secretary. In such a process the General Secretary came to define the leeway for foreign-policy negotiations. He would assess this through his own perception of what the politically relevant actors would approve or tolerate.

The same things that make application of the two-level-game approach to the Gorbachev era difficult also make it particularly interesting. The "rules of the game" at level II were in constant flux, especially on initiatives by the main actor. This forces a shift in our research approach, away from a static model in which the actor operates on two given levels under broadly fixed rules and has only two interests: to be reelected or remain in power by some other means, and to achieve foreign-policy successes that serve to secure his position at home. During 1985 to 1991, Gorbachev and his close associates exemplified the political actor who not only wanted to find compromises between the given actors at levels I and II, but also to introduce completely new actors into level II and fundamentally change the rules of the game in domestic politics. Gorbachev's personal thought-process and consultation with his close associates concerned not only what was doable in the bargaining that took place but what was desirable from his perspective. And this was completely different in March 1985 than it was in March 1991.

The two-level approach must, in other words, take into account first the bargaining process at the level of the actor himself and then drastic changes in the "rules of the game" and in actors participating in the negotiating process.

INTERACTIONS BETWEEN PERESTROIKA AND THE POLICY OF NEW THINKING

"Perestroika," a Russian word meaning reconstruction or renovation, has entered languages around the globe and has, since 1987, become an accepted trademark for the reform policy that aimed at thoroughly changing yet stabilizing the Communist system. "Perestroika" also became the name of a short period of the Soviet Union's history, a period of failure inseparable from the leadership of the Communist Party of the Soviet Union (CPSU) General Secretary Gorbachev.

For changes in Soviet foreign policy under Gorbachev a separate trademark soon caught on: "New Thinking" (*novoe myslenie*). Gorbachev had used the term even before taking office as General Secretary in a speech before the British House of Commons on December 18, 1984.[9] However, it became a popular catchword only after "Perestroika." In general, "Perestroika" was used primarily for Soviet domestic politics and "New Thinking" for foreign policy.[10]

Gorbachev always emphasized the connection between Perestroika and New Thinking. However, New Thinking was not supposed to be limited to *Soviet* foreign affairs. Gorbachev and his followers believed that New Thinking about global affairs was essential in the case of the United States and all other countries.[11]

Gorbachev emphasized the need for changes in foreign policy by portraying the dangers of the nuclear age, environmental threats, and the growing social rift between industrial and developing countries. In other words, he referred to processes that were largely independent of a change in Soviet domestic policies. Internal reforms were justified by Gorbachev and his supporters by referring to declining economic growth in the Soviet Union and to socioeconomic and political crisis. Perestroika was repeatedly elucidated as a crisis-prevention plan for which there were no alternatives. And Perestroika was much more dependent on a changed foreign policy for its success than New Thinking was on Perestroika. This will become clearer in the following discussion.

First, Gorbachev's view of himself must be examined. In his book about Perestroika and New Thinking, Gorbachev declared:

True, we need normal international conditions for our internal progress. But we want a world free from war, without arms races, nuclear weapons, and violence; and not only because this is optimal for our internal development. It is an objective global requirement that stems from the realities of the present day.[12]

Here the use of a new foreign policy to make implementation of a new domestic policy easier was highlighted. Years later, Gorbachev and his associates still placed the emphasis on this:

The crisis situation in which the Soviet Union found itself at the time demanded decisive measures in all areas, a new quality of domestic politics, in theory and in practice. At the same time, it was clear that the completion of overdue tasks at the center of the country would be significantly more complicated, if not completely impossible, if we did not succeed at fundamentally, or at least, tangibly, changing the international situation, and containing the Cold War.[13]

At other places in 1987, Gorbachev commented that "neither the Soviet Union, nor its Perestroika pose any threat to anyone, except, perhaps, by setting an example—if someone finds it acceptable. Yet again and again we are accused of wanting to implant Communism all over the world. What nonsense!"[14] "Attempts at military dictation as well as at moral, political, and economic pressure are out of fashion today," he wrote, adding that "a correct understanding of Perestroika is also the key to comprehending the foreign policy of the Soviet Union."[15] Further on he notes, "The organic tie between each state's foreign and domestic policies becomes particularly close and practically meaningful at crucial moments. A change in the domestic policy inevitably leads to changes in the attitude to international issues."[16] In this case the priority of domestic politics is emphasized.

In his memoirs, Gorbachev portrays the connection in the following manner:

A number of factors had convinced me of the need for a serious re-examination of our foreign policy even before my election as General Secretary. I won't claim that I entered my new office with a detailed action plan in my briefcase, but I had a pretty clear idea of the first steps to be taken. Thus Perestroika began simultaneously in domestic and foreign policies, success in one area encouraging progress in the other, set-backs slowing down progress in both.[17]

Here, the interaction between domestic and foreign policy is underscored rather than the primacy of internal politics.

Especially in the last citation Gorbachev professes a close interdependence of foreign and domestic policies that he elucidates nowhere else. His books are not organized chronologically, but topically. The discussion of domestic policy is clearly separated from foreign affairs. In the portrayal of his own work in one area of politics, Gorbachev almost never refers to simultaneous successes or failures in the other area. There is little evidence on a case-by-case basis that the intimate dependence Gorbachev describes actually existed. The political dynamics in the separate policy fields were so strong that the claim of interdependence should not be taken too literally. In the end, Gorbachev celebrated increasingly impressive victories in foreign affairs and growing international recognition, whereas his standing in domestic politics waned drastically.

Thus the exact interactions between domestic and foreign policies need closer study. And though detailed analysis based on internal documents or even on public information about domestic and foreign-policy decisions is not yet possible, attempts can be made to sort out the structure of the interdependence during Gorbachev's rule and to work through the phases of the interrelationship.

There would seem to be three areas of interdependence. First, Soviet policy for decades held it all-important to maintain defense spending at a very high share of the gross national product. While this share stood between 1 percent (Japan) and 7 percent (United States of America) in Western society, the Soviet share during the Brezhnev era was calculated in the West to be 12 to 18 percent.[18] After 1991, numbers in the vicinity of 25 to 30 percent were mentioned in Russia.[19] If one wished to slash this defense spending in order to use the resources for capital goods and consumer products as well as services, then one needed a completely different foreign policy towards the West, the developing world, and the allies. Conversely, a change in foreign policy was not credible without drastic reductions in defense spending, lest it be interpreted as a temporary tactical maneuver.

A second area of interdependence between the internal and external involved the domestic socioeconomic system, the political system, and international economic relations. The broad separation of the world's socialist and capitalist economies was only tentatively bridged during détente. The separation was based, in part, on the tremendous differences in the two economic systems, such as in the quality and marketability of goods or the technical standards for products. However the West also consciously pursued a strategy of economic isolation based on security and alliance politics, on avoiding economic and political dependence furthering the competing system, and on the competitive interests of the Western industrial countries. This Western strategy was complemented by the socialist countries' fears of being dependent on the West and being subject to political blackmail, or being infected by the bacillus of market-economic ways and consumption standards. Such fears promoted the Soviet strategy of economic self-sufficiency and isolation.

With the transition to Perestroika and market socialism, the isolation of the Soviet economy from the world market was supposed to end. This was, of course, impossible without adaptation of the Soviet economic system to the dominant arrangements of the world economy, the free-market system. To increase trade with the West, to gain access to international economic organizations that were mostly dominated by the West, and to receive Western credit and aid, more than reform of the domestic economic system was needed. Cooperative foreign and security policies became imperative.

The third, and most decisive, area of interdependence between Soviet domestic and foreign policy was in ideology. Marxist-Leninist ideology broadly dictated the political thinking and behavior of Soviet politicians. This is in contrast to the Marxist-Leninist propaganda that expressed the ideology only selectively, in abridged form, or sometimes in an intentionally distorted form. However, the memoirs that appeared after 1991 and the documents that have become available show that leading Communists, including Gorbachev, were indeed Communists in the Marxist-Leninist sense of the word, not only pretending to be such. Of course, the mandated ideology, which in many ways also functioned as a national or social ideology, was not fully accepted by every Party functionary. Yet its applicability was defended by most out of conviction, making the discrepancy between individual consciousness and publicly-expressed ideological consciousness almost meaningless. Substantial changes in policy presupposed fundamental changes in the ideology, which needed to be laid out by the central authorities in charge of ideology. This remained valid until these authorities lost their Party-based authority, as happended progressively during Perestroika.

The ideological change under Gorbachev is fairly difficult to trace. For one thing, it was not a unique event but a prolonged process. Perestroika and New Thinking were much more than a change in direction, such as Khrushchev's in the 1950s. The two concepts were actually a call to action by thinking in a new and unconventional manner. In Brezhnev's day, individual scientists or journalists expressed unconventional views (with the approval of the censors) without presaging any changes in policy. The ideological transformation under Gorbachev also started in this manner. From the time Gorbachev spoke out against the Party's monopoly on the truth, articles appeared, even in official organs, with ideological views that anticipated a policy change in the Soviet leadership. At first Gorbachev saw this as a breach of the boundaries that the Party leadership had established at the beginning of Glasnost.[20] Gradually a public sector emerged that he was forced to respect as an independent factor in designing domestic and foreign policies. The rules of the game at level II had changed substantially by May 1989, when opposition views were expressed at the Congress of People's Deputies. Indeed, the representatives of public opinion were not only the reformers calling for liberalization and democratization. Critics of Perestroika quickly learned to use the new political means, and on occasion did so more effectively than the reformers. The publication, with support from the top echelons of the Party (presumably Ligachev),[21] of the attack on Soviet foreign policy by the chemistry teacher, Nina A. Andreeva, in March 1988 was an important turning point. From this time on, Gorbachev could no longer eliminate Party opposition to his policies through the old methods of democratic centralism and needed to accept it as a factor in politics and policy formulation.

Because of the importance of ideology, one of Gorbachev's early and central concerns was to staff the central offices responsible for ideology, and their dependent propaganda and agitation authorities, with people in his confidence.[22] The logic of the new official ideology had to be brought to bear in changing concrete thinking about policy. During Perestroika, revisions of ideology and policy stood in a permanent feedback loop, varying with the individual phases of the reform era.

One can assume that Gorbachev and his close associates had much more extensive reforms in mind than they dared to reveal in the first few years. They went beyond the current policies in their thinking during this phase. In the final phase the reverse was true; the thinkers spent more time reflecting than innovating. They needed to intellectually or ideologically process the political changes they had not anticipated. In addition, they needed to adapt to these changes if they were not prepared to forfeit their power. However, after Gorbachev's release from imprisonment following the coup in August 1991, the new environment of domestic politics no longer allowed them to adapt. Instead, they were placed on the back burner and then forced to step down despite the fact that the foreign-policy community would have preferred that they remain in power.

Important foundations for changes in ideology had been laid by earlier Soviet analysts, confronted with Western thought and their own empirical results.[23] Party functionaries with an ability to learn and politically active social scientists had done the preparatory intellectual work as early as the 1970s and, more intensively, in the early 1980s. These innovations escalated after Gorbachev empowered unconventional thinking in the name of Glasnost. There apparently was no blueprint for a revision of ideology on March 11, 1985; changes evolved from a process of learning that was initially slow to take hold but sped up quickly in 1987. After 1991, Gorbachev often mentioned that in reading earlier documents he was quite surprised at how much his own thinking had been shaped by old ideological clichés.[24] He does not claim that, in that earlier time, he already thought differently than his speeches suggested. He may have departed from his real thinking in some statements but the discrepancies were probably not large.

That the General Secretary did not speak for himself but was the voice of many different organizations and working commissions was suggested most poignantly by the Italian Eurocommunist Giancarlo Paglietta. Responding to three documents publicized almost simultaneously and to speeches made by Gorbachev during the 27th Party Congress in 1986, Paglietta remarked, "I have the impression that your Party has three General Secretaries at the same time. One has approved the new editorial version of the CPSU Program, a document which is permeated by views and attitudes from the past. Another gave the speech, which contained fresh ideas that aim at change. Finally, the third General Secretary prepared the resolutions, in reaction to the speech, for publication. These contain even more new material."[25] Thus Gorbachev, as an actor appearing on the public stage, had to be seen as a collective being. Analytically, it was extremely difficult to peel away the various elements to arrive at Gorbachev the person and his own views. The ideological differences between his pronouncements and those of the collective Party leadership were less significant at the end of 1986 than at other points like April 1985, January 1987, or even August 1991.

We can identify several fundamental and complimentary characteristics of the change in ideology from the time Gorbachev took office until the full flowering of Perestroika and New Thinking in 1987/1988. The most general and most significant is the transition from a primarily confrontational to an essentially cooperative way of thinking in domestic and foreign policy. Conflicts were no longer thought to be necessarily irreconcilable, and violence and force were to be avoided.

Soon after taking office, Gorbachev let it be known that he had given up the Marxist-Leninist model of progress. He no longer spoke of the different steps in the development of Socialism. Observers noticed that after his speech at the 27th

Party Congress he never again mentioned Communism[26]—in Communist ideology the stage beyond Socialism. By dropping the model of progress,[27] Gorbachev withdrew the ideological basis for the sociohistoric claim of Soviet superiority over other socialist countries. This new attitude had been expressed from the beginning with an offer to the People's Republic of China (PRC) to increase contacts, and it became politically significant when the Brezhnev Doctrine[28] was jettisoned. Abandoning the model of progress opened the door to massive criticism of Soviet history and failures. This set the intellectual scene for Perestroika, not just for an "acceleration" (*uskorenie*) of the developments and progress so far. Gorbachev's reconciliatory, cooperative stance,[29] and that of his supporters, was also evident in the effort to seek alliances even with the most dangerous political opponents. This led to rapidly changing coalitions with radical reformers and even with reform-delaying actors.

Gorbachev and his colleagues did not completely abandon the theory of class-struggle, but greatly limited it by emphasizing general human interests and the interdependence of countries and societies. This new ideological base-model, partly a Wilsonian idealism[30] inserted in the New Thinking, had a tremendous impact on domestic and foreign-policy conceptions. It removed the claim of the Party to leadership, its all-important justification as a class-party, and was a prerequisite for changing the Soviet concept of democracy so as to recognize different interests in society. In foreign affairs, it legitimized cooperation with even conservative governments in the West and developing countries. Previously, only collaboration with "realistic segments of the bourgeoisie," that is, those prepared for détente, was considered legitimate.

In addition to this idealistic component, New Thinking had an important element of realism. Class interests were not superseded by general human interest but by a new national interest in the Western sense. This conceptualization eventually made possible emphasizing ethno-national interests when speaking of the national interest.

The accent on the national or country's interests was the decisive ideological step in reducing the bloated and burdensome Soviet defense sector. Until Gorbachev, the world was understood in terms of a battle between global systems. Hence it was "the duty" of the Soviet Union to be militarily as strong as the opposing states combined. The goal was to be able to "defend" itself in a Third World War—"unleashed," of course, by the West—and possibly to achieve a "victory." This meant the Soviet Union needed the same number of nuclear weapons systems as the United States, Great Britain, France, and, possibly, China taken together. Any nuclear inferiority would be compensated for through superiority of conventional forces and offensive capabilities on the Eurasian continent.

With the emphasis on the "national interest" it became possible for Soviet security policy to free itself from its economically ruinous military spending. The arms race, President Reagan's Strategic Defense Initiative, and the decline in the Soviet Union's economic growth had glaring financial consequences. Reverting to "national interests," turning away somewhat from the "interests of the global system," allowed Gorbachev to swiftly attain foreign-policy successes and international recognition through unilateral arms reduction and arms-control agreements at a time when it was much more difficult to attain domestic victories. Gorbachev reduced Soviet foreign-policy burdens from global to Eurasian in scale and focus. What the "national interest" meant with respect to the allies in the Warsaw Treaty Organization (WTO) and the Council of Mutual Economic Assistance (Comecon) was less obvious.

PHASES OF DEVELOPMENT IN SOVIET DOMESTIC POLICY

Perestroika and New Thinking did not suddenly replace the old Soviet domestic and foreign policy. They were programmatically too immature in March 1985, though several of their ideological foundations were already in place. Subsequently, they were subject to strengthening and weakening on several occasions.

Moreover, an exact parallel between internal and external policies could not exist because the structure of international relations, the "rules of the game" for Soviet foreign policy, were altered far less during Gorbachev's time than the structure of Soviet domestic politics, where the rules and participants changed fundamentally. In international affairs, the system of states and power relationships stayed broadly stable, and in the most important states—the United States, Great Britain, France, Germany, Japan, India, and China—the same government party or coalition was in power in 1991 as in 1985. In some instances even the heads of government and foreign ministers remained the same. Only in the Soviet alliance system, as well as in Yugoslavia and Albania, were there dramatic changes, changes that culminated in the end of Communist Party dominance and the dissolution of the WTO and Comecon.

What phases can be identified in Soviet domestic and foreign policy during Gorbachev's time in office? Today, the years of this era are usually subdivided into periods during which Gorbachev pursued either a progressive policy (in the transition to a market economy, a constitutional state, and democracy) or a conservative policy. Gorbachev is seen as having allied himself alternately with the radical-reform elements and then with those seeking to stabilize the system.[31]

For the "Foreign-Domestic-Nexus" project, however, a different division into periods is necessary. The question is when and how the "rules of the game" at level II changed in the Soviet Union. With this in mind, it is possible to differentiate six stages in the run up to Perestroika, then Perestroika, and then the beginnings of its decline. These stages more or less followed each other historically, like phases of development. Still, their chronological demarcation can only be approximated, because some changes were still present as others began to dominate the scene.

The regimes of Brezhnev, Andropov, and Chernenko, as well as Gorbachev's early period as General Secretary were still in the authoritarian mold that Khrushchev had created. This system was defined by formal elections and, among the leadership groups, a complex balance-of-power defined by personal linkages and the special interests of the larger bureaucratic apparatuses (Party, military, KGB, defense industry, capital goods industry, consumer industry, unions, academy of sciences, etc.). The system hid divisions on policy and presented itself to outsiders as monolithic. Whereas some Western research, colored by notions of totalitarianism, emphasized the unified and homogenous character of Soviet politics, other Western studies, influenced by interest-group theories, attempted to identify the cleavages in Soviet politics and society.[32] The insights into Soviet politics that documents and memoirs since 1991 have made possible confirm neither approach.

Domestic and foreign policy in these years was indisputably shaped by the Party and was not questioned by any opposition. Its Politburo was neither a tight unit nor just the executive organ of an autocrat. But it was also not a forum with political divisions or representatives of interest groups. Its behavior had more to do with personal interests, and these led to utterly precarious alliances among its members. Apparently, political differences of opinion were almost never openly presented or discussed in sessions nor decided through formal votes. Instead, they came to a head, more often indirectly than directly, in talks among individual members or groups prior to formal group decisions. Differences of opinion seemingly had little to do with social interests. Usually they were more influenced by personal characteristics and mind-sets such as conciliatory or confrontational tendencies or sympathy or antipathy towards the leader. The successions to Brezhnev in 1982, Andropov in 1984, and Chernenko in 1985 were decided by such attitudes. These choices had nothing to do with being either for or against a policy of reform and little to do with coalition-building in the Politburo.[33]

All reformers first had long careers as integrated conservatives. Not a single one came to be Party leader with the charge of carrying out reforms. Whether the leader became a reformer or not depended on his personality and his perception of the need for change. Therefore, reformers and anti-reformers can be understood to be representatives of interest groups only in a limited sense. They did not owe their position to being institutional representatives of interest groups. Differences in the readiness to reform in the Communist countries of Eastern Europe depended somewhat on differences in the climate for reform, but decisively on the personalities in each Politburo. There was no functional equivalent of Gorbachev in the German Democratic Republic (GDR), Bulgaria, Romania, and probably Czechoslovakia, although there may well have been in Poland and in Hungary.

The first, unintentional, phase for what became Perestroika can be seen in the tone set by Andropov in 1978–1984 and in the slow intellectual emancipation from Marxist-Leninism of many institutes of the Academy of Sciences and several departments of the CC Secretariat (as well as perhaps the KGB) during the 1970s. Gorbachev owed his ascent to the Secretariat in 1978 and Politburo in 1979 to his loyalty to Andropov and Brezhnev.[34] In 1985 he was chosen not as a reformer ahead of rival candidates Grishin, Tikhonov, Romanov, Gromyko and Shcherbitsky, who were all conservative, but for his age and vigor. His electors in the Politburo and CC expected modest renovation but also continuity and no fundamental changes in the system.[35]

It is hard to overestimate the impact of Yuri Andropov as head of the KGB and in his short term as General Secretary. While not a reformer, he preferred Party functionaries with a certain independence, intelligence, and incorruptibility, with personal courage in the framework of Party loyalty, and with energy and vigor not impaired by corruption, illness, or alcoholism. On such criteria he promoted not only Gorbachev but also—partly at Gorbachev's initiative—Yegor Ligachev, Boris Yeltsin, and Nikolai Ryzhkov.

Gorbachev's period as substitute for Chernenko during 1984 was the first conscious preparation for Perestroika. Gorbachev assumed many leadership functions during the months when Chernenko was weak or ill and, every now and then, made his suggestions known.[36] Above all, he used the opportunity to inform himself of the manifold problems in many sectors and began building a staff of loyal associates.

Political change had been well prepared, but only in general outline, by March 1985. Apparently, the practical experience and problems of the following months led to a quick and intensive learning process that, by the fall of 1986 and especially after January 1987, made the beginning of Perestroika possible.

The conceptions of reform that Gorbachev's team held in March 1985 are difficult to reconstruct from published materials. However, they almost certainly went beyond the measures adopted in 1985 and 1986, which were preparatory and tactical. The political pronouncements and resolutions of the 26th Party Congress in February 1986 had characteristics of temporary compromises with conservatives in the Party leadership. The Party program was particularly rooted in the pre-reform era and was therefore almost forgotten only a short time later.[37] Gorbachev's speeches in 1987, as well as the book he published, became much more authoritative than the Party program.

Gorbachev and his associates later talked about their starting perspectives quite vaguely:

The concept of restructuring with all the problems involved had been evolving gradually. Way back before the April Plenum a group of Party and state leaders had begun a comprehensive analysis of the state of the economy. Their analysis then became the basis for the documents of Perestroika. Using the recommendations of scientists and experts . . . all the best that social thought had created, we elaborated the basic ideas and drafted a policy which we subsequently began to implement. . . . At the April 1985 Plenum Meeting, we managed to propose a more or less well-defined, systematic program and to outline a concrete strategy for the country's further development and a plan of action.[38]

Later, the reformers emphasized:

As one began to examine the problems of the Soviet Union at the beginning of the 1980s, one also dedicated a great amount of attention to the international sphere. Wide-ranging material came from the research institutes. . . . Individual foreign-policy scientists and specialists forwarded their thoughts and considerations to us.[39]

From the beginning, even before his election as General Secretary, Gorbachev dazzled observers with his public style—frequent speeches, a quick wit, avoidance of traditional clichés, handling problems directly, and approaching people openly. Nonetheless, he implemented the first changes in the old centralized style. Today, it is possible to view measures adopted in 1985 and 1986 as vital for subsequent reforms despite not being declared as such at the time. A huge change in cadres, for example, was justified as a necessary rejuvenation and accelerated continuation of existing policy, especially in the economy.[40]

Gorbachev and his associates like to describe his entire term of office from the first day to the last, as the era of Perestroika and New Thinking.[41] However, that he wanted to go well beyond traditional policy and to publicly portray it using American public-relations-style propaganda[42] did not become clear until the CC Plenum of January 1987. Only at that point did Gorbachev finally admit that he sought substantial changes in the economic system, the political system, and foreign policy, changes much more profound than earlier reforms under Khrushchev and Kosygin. Ironically, these innovations resembled the Reform-Communist efforts of the Dubcek era in Czechoslovakia[43] without the reformers wanting or being able to refer to the Czechs.[44]

In a systematic, theoretical sense Perestroika was an attempt at a Socialist reformation in socioeconomic sectors and at constitutional Communism in the political sectors.[45] Constitutional Communism can be defined as a one-party rule that introduced and adhered to the norms of a state based on written law and that tolerated a limited pluralism in opinion and public organization without permitting free elections. As in constitutional monarchies, there was no detailed theory and no unified system. Constitutional Communism was a pragmatic compromise during a short transition period from one system to the other.

For the transitions from the "administrative-command economy" to a "Socialist market-economy," from authoritarian one-party rule to constitutional Communism, and from Perestroika to the post-Communist system it is not possible to assign exact dates. Indeed, it is empirically difficult to determine exactly what system existed at any given time.

The most important initial step toward political reform was the encouragement given to criticism of existing deficiencies and the bureaucracy. In this context the practice of putting up more than one candidate for elections to the Soviets, a practice that had started earlier in other socialist countries,[46] created a choice not among different personal qualities but among different concepts of policy. The division of the CPSU was promoted by Gorbachev himself when in early 1987 he allowed Aleksandr Bovin to distinguish, for the first time, between the dynamic and active renovators and the conservative and passive brakemen of the Party.[47]

The strong conservative presence in the Party was a factor Gorbachev needed to take seriously when sitting at international negotiating tables. This was the case even though the conservative wing—like large parts of the military—was hardly represented in the highest leadership forums. On the other hand, possible rejection of an international proposal by conservatives in the Party could often be used by Gorbachev for leverage in negotiations with the West. Such a threat had much more weight and credibility coming from Gorbachev than Brezhnev or Khrushchev, because the West was interested in having Gorbachev's domestic position fortified through international accomplishments. Gorbachev's efforts to gain Western concessions, primarily in trade, were strengthened when the first rumors of a coup surfaced. The possibility of constrictions on Gorbachev's domestic negotiating margins improved his bargaining position abroad.

By 1987, Gorbachev's opponents were no longer only a "handful" of Politburo reactionaries but legions of bureaucrats in the Party and state apparatus. They were quickly joined by others who wanted a more radical Perestroika policy. There thus came into being an internal Party spectrum of brakemen, centrists, and radicals.

Moderate reformers such as Yegor Ligachev personified the Party conservatives while Boris Yeltsin epitomized the radicals and Gorbachev attempted to capture the middle. Though the moderates dominated the Party leadership and the conservatives maintained strong positions in the middle and lower Party bureaucracy, the radical reformers never held more than Yeltsin's seat among CC Secretaries. In fact, the radicals soon gave up the attempt at remodeling the Party from within and joined non-Party organizations and new parties. Yeltsin strengthened this tendency when he and the members of the "Democratic Platform" left the Party in spectacular fashion at the end of the 28th Party Congress in July 1990. Then in December Eduard Shevardnadze stepped down as foreign minister, and in July 1991 he renounced communism. This had the effect of pushing Gorbachev, once again, to the reform edge of the Party, just as the August coup later did. But even the conservatives could not fully escape societal movement toward a market economy and more democracy. By 1991, Party conservatism had very little in common with that of 1987 or 1984. The Communists who wanted to reestablish the centrally planned economy and one-Party rule became a marginal group that would eventually reconstitute itself outside of the Communist Party in several new fringe parties.

Perestroika drew to a close long before Gorbachev left office. In the socioeconomic area the end arrived with the abolition of Gosplan in the fall of 1990. In the political sphere, the beginning of the end came with abandonment of the Communist Party's claim to a privileged position in February and March 1990. At first, this did little to change actual power relationships and simply gave the opposition a moral boost. The party monopoly was only broken months later (on July 21, 1991), when Russian President Boris Yeltsin banned establishment of Party cells in government agencies and Russian firms. His lead was followed by Gorbachev on August 24, shortly after the coup.

Parallel to the fragmentation of the Party, a political public emerged composed of many informal groups. These groups were not established or approved by the Party or the police and did not meet the official registration requirements, but they were increasingly tolerated by the authorities. The initiative was taken by dissidents as well as by Party members but primarily by those who had not previously been politically active. Some of these informal groups evolved into political organizations and finally into parties. Numerous Party members or Party functionaries, not to mention clandestine KGB operatives, were active in non-Party organizations, especially the National Fronts. Among the milestones were the founding of the Baltic Peoples' Fronts in October 1987, the establishment of the "Memorial society" for the review of Stalinist history during 1988, and the screening of the Georgian film "Regret" and staging of the play "The Bolsheviks" by M. F. Satrov in 1989.

Thereafter, party pluralism and democratization in the Western sense took hold. The construction of non-Communist parties began with the creation of informal organizations and clubs in 1986–1988. It continued in mass movements and national Peoples' Fronts in the non-Russian republics (1988–1990), when political platforms within the CPSU and the first non-communist parties came into being.[48] The holding of elections repeatedly stimulated the process of party formation, especially the election to the Congress of People's Deputies in March 1989 and the elections to the Soviets of the Republics and the Territories in March 1990. Russia's first non-Communist party, the Democratic Union, was founded in May 1988, and rapidly split several times. More significant was the formation of an interregional group of representatives, composed of Communist and non-Communist Deputies, in May 1989. This group, with Boris N. Yeltsin and Andrei D. Sakharov as members, stood in clear opposition to Gorbachev's policies. In October 1990 a law on societal organizations was passed, legalizing the formation of independent parties. One result was a hodgepodge of dozens, later hundreds, of parties, most with a handful of members clustered around a prominent personality. The spectrum of groups relevant to any foreign policy negotiations had significantly expanded, well beyond the boundaries of the CPSU.

After May 1989, Gorbachev's bargaining position in domestic politics became much more complicated because he had to adjust to a broader distribution of power across society. He responded by strengthening government organs relative to the Party and by expanding his own prerogatives with the creation of the Presidency and his election to this office in March 1990. Subsequent to that date, power was increasingly transferred from the Politburo to a newly established Presidential Council. Nonetheless, Gorbachev retained links to conservative elements within the CPSU. In fact, he brought into leading positions all those who joined the coup against him in August 1991. Though the Party showed no inclination to defend the principles of Perestroika, Gorbachev, even after returning from imprisonment during the coup, held fast to his belief that it could be reformed.

The expansion of the domestic political spectrum had ambivalent effects abroad. In East-central and Southeast Europe, opponents of reform pursued a wait-and-see policy, gambling on Gorbachev's fall until their own sudden demise at the end of 1989. In the West, by contrast, some felt encouraged enough by the democratic changes in the Soviet Union to demand a more decisive reform course from Gorbachev. Others, however, feared that increasing polarization in the Soviet Union would benefit conservatives and continued to support Gorbachev until

December 1991. They practiced great restraint in their dealings with Yeltsin and the radical reformers in Russia and the other Republics.

In the end Perestroika lasted barely four or four and a half years, from January 1987 to July 1991. Indeed, Socialist system-reform and constitutional Communism emerged much earlier and therefore lasted longer in two other countries of the Soviet alliance system, namely Poland and Hungary.[49] However, there was no substantial Perestroika in the GDR or Czechoslovakia, nor in Bulgaria or Romania. There, authoritarian Party rule was directly replaced by democratization at the end of 1989 without an intermediate stage of Socialist reform or "liberalization." The adaptation of Perestroika rhetoric in several of these countries should not distort their true rigidity.

Perestroika rapidly lost support in the Soviet Union in the fall of 1990 after Gorbachev moved closer to those who wanted to slow reform. Mass defections from the Party, radicalization of the democratic and national movements, and the effective mobilization of opposing groups all undermined Gorbachev's power and hollowed out his reform program. Though the concept of Socialism became increasingly nebulous, Gorbachev was not prepared to promote the transition to pluralist democracy and to expose himself and his Party to free elections. When in December 1991 he stepped down from the office of President of a state that had already ceased to exist, few in the successor states lamented.

"FREE CHOICE," OR THE ABANDONMENT OF THE BREZHNEV DOCTRINE AS A DECISIVE STEP

The countries in the Warsaw Treaty Organization (WTO) and Comecon had a peculiar position in the international system. The ruling Parties there had not come to power through their own ability and remained dependent, until the end of their rule, on the military support of the Soviet army, despite periods of temporary popularity such as occurred in Hungary and Romania. This dependence was demonstrated in the GDR in 1953, Poland and Hungary in 1956, Czechoslovakia in 1968, and Poland in 1981, where the declaration of martial law by General Jaruzelski was the result of Polish decisions but under the threat of Soviet intervention.[50] In these four countries Soviet troops were stationed to reassure the Communist Parties and maintain Soviet control. There were no Soviet forces in Bulgaria and Romania, in part because no fundamental reform efforts developed within their Communist Parties but also because they were readily accessible.

For decades, the foreign policies of the allies mirrored that of the "leading" Soviet Union. Not until the short détente after 1963 did any of these countries, and especially Romania, begin to develop independent tendencies. When American-Soviet relations drastically worsened following the Soviet intervention in Afghanistan in 1979, the GDR, Hungary, and Czechoslovakia carefully developed independent foreign-policy initiatives. They did not, however, fundamentally challenge the conception of the "Socialist community of states" as a relatively closed alliance. According to a widely accepted view in the West, it remained until the end the "Eastern Bloc" or even an "external Soviet empire" with "satellite states" in which other than normal rules applied in international politics. Observers spoke of a collective "Socialist foreign policy" and assumed the applicability of the Brezhnev Doctrine, that is, that the "defense of socialism" through the use of force, even against a peaceful "counterrevolution," was the concern of all socialist states. This doctrine, underpinned by a detailed theory about "international relations of the new type" and the unique accomplishments of socialism, asserted the Soviet Union's right to intervene in any country that contemplated dropping Communist rule, Marxist-Leninist ideology, or membership in the WTO or Comecon. In this sense, Soviet bloc international relations bore a strong resemblance to Soviet domestic politics. A modification of the basic thrust of Soviet foreign policy had to have repercussions in the bloc, and domestic changes in the Soviet Union altered the political circumstances in those countries. The reverse held true as well; the Soviet leadership's toleration of antisocialist developments in the alliance had an influence on Soviet domestic politics.

The transformation in Soviet policy towards the bloc must be seen in the context of the entire Soviet foreign policy. The larger changeover and its stages are more difficult to map than the development of Perestroika or the New Thinking. Policies did not move at the same pace because they were driven by varied influences and governed by separate rules. Many foreign-policy innovations, like the withdrawal from Afghanistan or the international arms-reduction and arms-control measures, required months or years of negotiation and implementation, while developments in domestic politics escalated independently. For this reason, we cannot directly relate changes in foreign policy to specific phases of domestic development.

It is possible, however, to distinguish four stages of Soviet foreign policy under Gorbachev. Gorbachev took his first foreign-policy steps, leading the Soviet Union out of isolation, directly after taking office. As early as April 7, 1985, he declared a moratorium on deploying Soviet intermediate-range missiles, and he followed this up with further signals on arms-reduction policies. At the same time, Gorbachev initiated exchanges with American, West European, Indian, Chinese, Japanese, and East European governments aimed at eastablishing a new policy of cooperation based on equality. All this could be interpreted as tactical changes or attempts at attaining cheap propaganda successes. But noticeable from the outset was the new, more open, intelligent, even partly self-critical style. Also striking was that in practically all areas of foreign relations, Gorbachev arranged new negotiations at the state level as well as, where applicable, at the Party level. One could describe this first phase of Gorbachev's foreign policy as the resumption of cooperation and détente.

Just as in domestic politics, a comprehensive personnel change was a prerequisite for a profound transformation in foreign policy. On July 1, 1985, Andrei Gromyko was pushed out of the foreign ministry, which he had led since 1957, and replaced with the Georgian Eduard A. Shevardnadze, a regional Party Secretary with no foreign-policy experience. Thus was the way cleared for Gorbachev to take the new foreign-policy steps. There was also a thorough reorganization of the ministries and offices responsible for foreign affairs (Ministry of Foreign Affairs, Ministry for Foreign Trade, Defense Ministry, and Committee for State Security) as well as the Secretariat of the Central Committee.

Only in time did the new character of Soviet foreign policy, not just the rhetorical shifts, become apparent. Substantial innovations included the treaty banning intermediate-range nuclear missiles in December 1987, the first nuclear arms-reduction agreement since the beginning of the atomic age. This required revision of the ideological priority that had previously placed international class interests before national interest.

The really decisive change began in the summer of 1988, when Glasnost had made a broad spectrum of public criticism possible. In May, Viacheslav Dashichev published an article in *Literaturnaia Gazeta* in which New Thinking with regard to foreign policy was clearly expressed.[51] For the first time, Stalinist policy toward the West and toward Eastern Europe was fundamentally attacked. Indeed, the article stimulated a sharp public debate about the principles of foreign policy. Such discussions called the legitimacy of the "Socialist revolution" in East-central and Southeast Europe, and by extension, in the Baltic and Moldavia in 1940, into question. With the loosening of censorship and the extension of Glasnost, a critical discussion of Soviet history became possible, and this eventually forced publication of documents whose existence had long been denied in the Soviet Union. In this way Glasnost in domestic policy had direct consequences in foreign policy. On the other hand, an important impetus for the expansion of Glasnost came out of the linkage between domestic affairs and foreign policy, as when Soviet mothers began to publicly attack the brutal treatment of soldiers in the army and the cover-ups of their sons' deaths in the war in Afghanistan.[52]

The fundamental shift in Soviet foreign policy became apparent to the whole world not only in arms-control policy but through the withdrawal of Soviet forces from Afghanistan, announced in February 1988 and completed in February 1989. It was not coincidental that Gorbachev called the famous dissident Andrei Sakharov to tell him that his exile to Gorky (today, Nizhny Novgorod) was over when negotiations over the Soviet troop withdrawal had been initiated.[53] Sakharov had previously emerged as the severest critic of the intervention. His first public appearance at the forum "For a World without Nuclear Weapons, for the Survival of Mankind" in February 1987 lent Gorbachev's new human-rights and defense-cutback policies spectacular credibility. On that occasion Sakharov stressed the connection between foreign and domestic spheres by referring to the need to have foreign and security policies controlled by a critical domestic public.

Then came the regulation or at least dissolution of the superpowers' involvement in regional conflicts in South Africa, East Africa, and Central America. This reached a climax of sorts when Gorbachev and George Bush announced the end of the Cold War in December 1989 at Malta.

The next major change in Soviet foreign policy began in the summer of 1989 and became evident in the winter of 1989/1990 with the abandonment of the Brezhnev Doctrine. Under pre-existing policy the crumbling of Communist regimes in Poland, the GDR, and the other East-central and Southeast European countries should have triggered a military intervention. When it did not, it became clear that Marxist-Leninism and monopoly-rule of the Communists had been given up; the collapse of the WTO and the Comecon had become inevitable.

The last phase of Gorbachev's foreign policy was directly linked to domestic politics. The August 1991 coup against Gorbachev by officials he himself appointed had the effect of transferring power from the Soviet center to Russia and the other republics. At that moment, Russian, not Soviet, Moscow made the decision that the independence of the Baltic Republics should be approved and that relations with the WTO states should have a new foundation. In other words, New Thinking continued to be applied to the West and the rest of the world, even as Moscow made the transition from Soviet into Russian foreign policy. It was not until 1993 that Russian foreign policy assumed decidedly different traits as it was increasingly molded by geopolitical calculations and the desire to distance Russia from the West and exercise the independence of a superpower. Russian foreign policy towards the "near abroad," the other Soviet successor states, emerged explicitly in January 1992 and was already apparent in the second half of 1991.[54]

There were several connections between Perestroika and Soviet alliance policy. For one thing, Gorbachev and his colleagues saw certain foreign reforms, especially in the economies of Hungary, Poland, and the PRC, as models for Soviet policy. Then again, the promotion of extensive reforms in Eastern Europe was intended to reduce the subsidization of that area through low-priced Soviet energy exports and high-priced imports while at the same time stimulating development of new technologies from which the Soviet Union could also benefit. Finally, from successful reforms in Eastern Europe and the Baltic republics, Gorbachev expected to gain support for his own reform course against his domestic critics and Western critics of East-West economic cooperation. Gorbachev knew from the beginning that the old methods of "friendly" pressure could not be used to compel alliance members to adopt Perestroika. He had to leave it to these states and their ruling parties whether they wanted to follow Soviet policy (Czechoslovakia), refuse to do so (the GDR, Romania, and Bulgaria), or to take reforms even further (Poland and Hungary). Unfortunately, because of the uneven pace of reform in these countries it proved impossible to transform Comecon into a sort of East European Economic Community.[55]

For the West, Gorbachev's policies in Eastern Europe and in Afghanistan were credibility tests. Hence Moscow's altering its relations with its allies was an important component in the development of cooperative East-West relations. Moreover, the withdrawal from Afghanistan showed, for the first time, that the Soviet government was prepared to surrender control when it faced resistance from the majority of a people. Despite the fact that Afghanistan was not yet seen as a Socialist country, this move had powerful implications for Eastern Europe.

The new ideological formula Gorbachev used to justify his policy was called the principle of "free choice" in the development path. He intentionally did not speak of a right to self-determination, because in the Soviet tradition this concept was closely linked to ethno-national rights to secession.

It is not easy to pinpoint when this principle was first applied to Eastern Europe. In later years Gorbachev had a tendency to move up the dates of those decisions that promoted the end of Communist Party domination. In his memoirs, he claims that immediately after taking office he rejected the Brezhnev Doctrine, "which had never been officially proclaimed but which had in fact defined the USSR's approach towards its allies."[56] The occasion for this was a meeting, following Chernenko's funeral, with Party and government leaders from Eastern Europe plus Tikhonov, Gromyko, and Rusakov. There, Gorbachev says, he announced that he was in favor of "relations on an equal footing" and "respect for the sovereignty and independence of each country" as well as "all parties taking full responsibility for the situation in their own countries."[57] He also reports his impression that his partners did not take his words "altogether seriously."[58]

Perhaps Gorbachev did reject the Brezhnev Doctrine that quickly. Nonetheless, it took him several years to revise the ideological formula of socialist internationalism—the common duty to defend socialism and protect the socialist alliance, all of which was expressed in the Soviet readiness to intervene. Meanwhile, most political thinkers in the Soviet Union, Eastern Europe, and the West continued to assume that the Brezhnev Doctrine would still be practiced under certain circumstances. Only through many small steps was Gorbachev able to establish the fact that the Soviet Union was no longer ready to intervene with force and was not even prepared to meddle in the internal controversies of these societies.

In the summer of 1987, Gorbachev used the formula of free elections to justify the renunciation of a unified Communist world and to acknowledge that some peoples evidently did not want to follow the model of the socialist states.[59] For the Soviet Union and the world socialist system, however, Gorbachev still assumed that "the people" had freely chosen socialism and that this choice was irreversible. Not until the historical portrayal of "Socialist revolutions" was revised could the idea surface that those decisions had not been based on "free choice" and that a people might freely decide against the "real, existing socialism" that had hitherto been identified with "progress." This occurred in Poland in 1989 and completely surprised most Communists.[60] Gorbachev and his colleagues quickly began to alter their conception of socialism and progress. From this point on, developments in Eastern Europe had significant influence on events in the Soviet Union.

Personnel appropriate to a shift in relations with Eastern Europe were put in place early on. Gorbachev appointed his closest coworkers to this most delicate intersection of ideology and policy. In 1943 Stalin had formally dissolved the Communist International in deference to the Western powers, but in fact it was reorganized in the Central Committee as the Department for International Relations. After the crises in 1956 this had been subdivided and a special Department for Relations with the Communist and Workers' Parties of Socialist Countries created. It was headed by CC Secretary Konstantin Rusakov from 1968 to 1973 and again from 1977 to 1986. In February 1986, Gorbachev replaced him with a close confidant, Vadim Medvedev. Aleksandr Yakovlev was appointed CC Secretary for International Relations in general. Georgy Shakhnazarov was named Medvedev's deputy. All three belonged to Gorbachev's inner circle.

Though, according to Medvedev, Foreign Minister Gromyko handed only a few relationships over to the CC department for (parties in) socialist countries, under his successor Shevardnadze, relations between that department and the Foreign Ministry improved dramatically. A certain competition remained, since the Foreign Ministry was responsible for interstate relations and the CC Secretariat for inter-Party relations. However, the problems Gorbachev discussed with his East European specialists were the same whether they were meeting as Party functionaries or government office holders.

In dealing with the Eastern European leaders, Gorbachev encountered people who had been in top Party positions for decades: Todor Zhivkov of Bulgaria (1954–1989), János Kádár of Hungary (1956–1988), Nicolae Ceausescu of Romania (1965–1989), Gustav Husák of Czechoslovakia (1969–1987), Erich Honecker of the GDR (1971–1989), and Wojciech Jaruzelski of Poland (1981–1989). They were all over sixty, and several were more than seventy years old. With Jaruzelski, Gorbachev "formed a very close and . . . amicable relationship" and an intellectual understanding rare among politicians.[61] He considered him a devoted reformer who had saved Poland from possible Soviet intervention in 1981 by declaring martial law.[62]

Gorbachev also saw Kádár as a reformer, a man who in some respects had anticipated Perestroika and had the energy for further reform despite his age. Husák captured his esteem as well, while Honecker, Zhivkov, and, especially Ceausescu earned his disdain through their unwillingness to accept change.

The foundation of Gorbachev's policy towards East-central and Southeast Europe rested on the same notion as Perestroika: Only decisive reforms could save socialism from a crisis that would endanger its very existence. Conversely, Honecker, Zhivkov, and Ceausescu saw the danger to the Socialist order in Perestroika and gambled, quite openly, on the victory of Gorbachev's conservative opponents in the Soviet Union. As it turned out, Gorbachev's caution about getting involved in the domestic affairs of Eastern Europe prevented the Soviet conservatives from gaining real support from like-minded individuals in the region. It also helped that the conservative views of Honecker, Zhivkov, and Ceausescu differed considerably from each other.

From 1985 to 1988, Gorbachev saw the more radical reforms in Poland, Hungary, and the Baltic Republics, reforms inspired by his own Perestroika, as welcome political and moral support. These political and economic experiments were embraced as offering lessons for his own polices.

At some point in 1987–1988, however, developments in these countries went beyond what Gorbachev and the other Soviet leaders found desirable or tolerable. The date lies somewhere among three events: the first mass demonstrations against the Hitler-Stalin Pact in the Baltic in August 1987; the first negotiations between the Polish Minister of the Interior and Lech Walesa regarding a "round table" in August 1988; and the declaration of sovereignty by Estonia in November 1988. From this time on, Gorbachev faced not only the conservatives in the state and party organizations but also politically serious, mass reform movements that first demanded his resignation (or that of equivalent politicians in other countries) and finally called for an end to Communist Party rule. While these parties did not formally negotiate with him about domestic policy, they did force Gorbachev to compromise as a result of their demands. Hence Gorbachev could no longer act as a reformer, but increasingly had to react to developments he had no means to control. The Peoples' Fronts formed in October 1987 in the Baltic, and later in Ukraine and elsewhere, initially supported Perestroika and then quickly radicalized their demands, finally dropping the Perestroika slogan after violent incidents in Vilnius and Riga in January 1990. Starting in November 1988, when the parade of sovereignty declarations began, they demanded decentralization and ultimately, a confederalization of the Soviet Union. "Sovereignty" meant, in Soviet usage, simply a high degree of autonomy, of self-government, and of self-administration, but not independence. Lithuania was the first republic to declare itself "independent," on March 11, 1990, although it could not make this a reality until August 1991.

Gorbachev was responsible for one act of force that spilled much blood—the entry of Soviet troops into Baku in January 1990. Yet this incident was not especially controversial internationally, because it was considered to be a reaction to prior, civil-war-like disputes and blody pogroms in Azerbaijan. By contrast, forceful suppression of demonstrations in Tiflis in April 1989 and in Vilnius and Riga in January 1991, each of which cost several lives, provoked much criticism at home and abroad despite Gorbachev's claim that he had not ordered the actions himself. To be sure, he did approve them by his silence at the time. Nevertheless, none of these actions led to the restoration of the old order or the arrest of the more radical reformers. Gorbachev may have used repressive police and judicial measures to battle the radical movements and those questioning Communist control, but he never applied the Brezhnev Doctrine in his own country.

In retrospect, it seems clear that the transition from an active to a primarily reactive policy regarding Eastern Europe began with the unanticipated electoral victory of Solidarity in July 1989, which transferred all freely elected seats in the Polish Sejm and the Senate to the opposition. For a short time it appeared that the Brezhnev Doctrine would be implemented after all, as plans were considered in Poland to form a government without participation of the Communists. Under Soviet pressure, however, an all-party coalition was formed, with Tadeusz Mazowiecki becoming the first non-Communist Prime Minister in Eastern Europe. In Hungary, a round-table conference involving the Communist Party and the opposition agreed on a multiparty system in September, and the Hungarian Socialist Workers' Party was disbanded in October. In March and April 1990 the first Hungarian elections took place, from which a government without Socialist participation emerged.

Gorbachev, like Western leaders, could do little but watch as the Berlin Wall came down on November 9, 1989, and as Communist regimes collapsed in Czechoslovakia and Romania in December, and in Bulgaria during the same weeks. The politics that led to the reunification of Germany and to the dissolution of the WTO and Comecon had little in common with the original goals of Perestroika and New Thinking.

The end of Communist rule in Eastern Europe suggested that the Communist Party of the Soviet Union faced the same fate. Did events not prove conservatives correct in their claim that the "revisionism" of reform would lead to the end of Socialism? In mid-1990, debate raged in the Soviet Union over whether Gorbachev's policy had led to the loss of Eastern Europe and, especially, of the GDR. Defenders of Perestroika argued that the prevention of timely and consequent reforms by "dogmaticians" had been responsible for the downfall of the Socialist order. Besides, they said, Socialism had been forced on Eastern Europeans by Stalinist policies, whereas the Russians had achieved their revolution on their own. The purpose of the War for the Motherland was to free Europe from fascism, not to take Eastern Europe as a "war trophy." What is more, the changes in Eastern Europe and the unification of the two German states had freed the Soviet Union from an expensive economic and political burden. Now it was in the Soviet interest to "Finlandize" this area. Market economies and Western democracy in Eastern Europe, with neutral, Soviet-friendly foreign policies, could be reconciled with Soviet security interests.

In this manner, Gorbachev and his friends obscured the relevance of Eastern European experiences to Soviet domestic politics. The election successes of ex-Communists in Bulgaria and Romania suggested that Communist reform policies could be appealing in free elections; the electoral defeats of the Communists, first in Poland and then in Hungary, were explained as due to the specific conditions in those countries; the electoral defeat of the PDS-SED in the GDR was blamed on the Germans' demands for unification and the economic superiority and attractiveness of the Federal Republic. Interestingly, while Gorbachev's supporters emphasized the differences between developments in the Soviet Union and those in Eastern Europe, Soviet radicals were inspired by these events and saw them as a model for future changes in the Soviet Union, Russia, and the western republics.

Gorbachev held firmly to his belief in reforming the Communist Party until he was forced by Yeltsin in August 1991 to resign the position of General Secretary. Not until after the end of the Soviet Union in December did he break with Communist Socialism and engage himself in a social-democratic variety oriented towards Eduard Bernstein and a social market economy. Moreover, Gorbachev continued—and continues today—to insist that the Soviet Union was salvageable even after the August Coup. He blames Boris Yeltsin and his closest allies for bringing about the collapse of the country. He also contends that a progressive reintegration of the post-Soviet area, on the basis of a market economy and democracy, is politically possible and necessary.

CONCLUSION

This study is not a straightforward application of a two-level-game approach. Instead, it makes use of that approach to help clarify many aspects of the foreign-domestic nexus in the Gorbachev era. It also outlines important relationships on the domestic level, relationships that changed considerably during these years and thereby altered the game rules fundamentally. Mikhail Gorbachev grappled with the interactions between political developments in the foreign and domestic sectors that were clustered in three broad areas: defense and security, economic affairs, and ideology. He acted on the basis of what he *perceived* was the prime linkage: that ending the East-West confrontation would benefit domestic political reform (and vice versa) while releasing resources for a Soviet economic revival. And he correctly anticipated that domestic reform would, politically and ideologically, necessitate change in Eastern Europe and a sharp shift in the nature of Soviet-East European relations.

Nevertheless, things turned out badly for this leader. His great foreign policy successes did not translate into (or, in terms of game theory, were not reconcilable with) political or economic triumphs domestically. Dismantling authoritarian rule at home and relaxing Soviet control in Eastern Europe proved to be incompatible with saving Comecon, the Warsaw Treaty Organization, and socialist regimes. Instead, changes in each sphere provoked and reinforced changes in the others and soon pushed developments far beyond his capacity to manage or understand. In the end, socialism, the Soviet Union, and Gorbachev's political career dissolved, nearly simultaneously.

NOTES

1. The author wishes to express his profound gratitude to Carsten Baumann for translating this chapter from German into English.

2. See, for example, Seweryn Bialer, ed., *The Domestic Context of Soviet Foreign Policy* (Boulder: Westview Press, 1980) or Curtis Keeble, ed., *The Soviet State: The Domestic Roots of Soviet Foreign Policy* (Aldershot, England: Gower, 1985).

3. The trailblazer is James Rosenau, *Linkage Politics: Essays on the Convergence of National and International Systems* (New York: Free Press, 1969); see also Alexander Dallin, "Linkage Patterns: From Brest to Brezhnev," in Bialer, *Domestic Context*.

4. Cited as Robert D. Putnam, "Diplomacy and Domestic Politics. The Logic of Two-Level Games," in Peter B. Evans, Harold K. Jacobson, and Robert D. Putnam, eds., *Double-Edged Diplomacy: International Bargaining and Domestic Politics* (Berkeley: University of California Press, 1993), pp. 431–468. The article first appeared in the periodical *International Organization*, 42 (Summer 1988), pp. 427–460.

5. See Andrew Moravcsik, "Integrating International and Domestic Theories of International Bargaining," in Evans, Jacobson, and Putnam, *Double Edged Diplomacy*, pp. 3–42. Also see Peter B. Evans, "Building an Integrative Approach to International and Domestic Politics. Reflections and Projections," in ibid., p. 397.

6. This is a society based on the Soviet model with Communist one-party rule as it existed in the Soviet Union from the end of the 1920s or, at the latest, 1934 until the early phases of Perestroika. It applies to the Soviet Union progressively less after 1988.

7. It became accepted after 1977 to have the Party leader also act as the head of state, allowing him to sign international treaties. Gorbachev did not hold a government position until October 1, 1988, when he succeeded Gromyko as head of state. Even at this point, his role as Party leader remained paramount. This began to change with the creation of the office of President on March 15, 1990. Gorbachev held this office, even after he stepped down as Secretary General of the Communist Party on August 24, 1991, until December 25, 1991, when he transferred his remaining power to the newly elected President of Russia, Boris Yeltsin.

8. See Mikhail Gorbachev, *Memoirs* (New York: Doubleday, 1995), pp. 84–85, 163, 165–166.

9. Ibid., p. 161.

10. See, for example, Gorbachev, *Memoirs*, p. 401. The different titles of various language editions of Gorbachev's programmatic book in 1987 provide another example. The Russian edition had the title "Perestroika i Novoe Myslenie" and the subtitle "Dlja Nashej Strany i dlja Vsego Mira" (For Our Country and the Whole World). The English version carried the title "Perestroika" and the subtitle "New Thinking for Our Country and the World," while the German edition was titled "Perestroika. Die zweite russische Revolution. Eine neue Politik für Europa und die Welt" (Perestroika. The Second Russian Revolution. A New Policy for Europe and the World).

11. Accordingly, Gorbachev and his associates still propagate New Thinking today, while viewing Perestroika as an historic period that has ended. See Michail Gorbatschow, Vadim Sagladin, and Anatoli Tschernjajew, *Das Neue Denken: Politik im Zeitalter der Globalisierung* (München: Goldman, 1997), p. 9.

12. Mikhail Gorbachev, *Perestroika: New Thinking for Our Country and the World* (New York: Harper and Row, 1987), p. 11.

13. Author's translation of Gorbatschow, Sagladin, Tschernjajew, *Das Neue Denken*, p. 12.

14. Gorbachev, *Perestroika*, p. 130. See also p. 157. This is contradicted by other passages in which Gorbachev said that the "inevitable evolution of the world" will lead all people and nations to be convinced of the superiority of socialism, as on p. 151.

15. Ibid., p. 131–132.

16. Ibid., p. 132.

17. Gorbachev, *Memoirs*, p. 401.

18. *SIPRI Yearbook 1984. World Armament and Disarmament* (London: Stockholm International Peace Research Institute, 1984), p. 90.

19. Gorbatschow, Sagladin, and Tschernjajew, *Das Neue Denken*, p. 13.

20. Similarly in Gorbachev, *Memoirs*, pp. 208–211.

21. Nina Andreeva, "I cannot go against my principles," in *Sovetskaja Rossija* (March 13, 1988); see also Gorbachev, *Memoirs*, pp. 252–253.

22. For details, see Vadim A. Medvedev, *V komande Gorbacheva. Vzgliad iznutri* (Moscow: Bylina, 1994), pp. 26, 32, 37. In 1988, administration of ideology was so important that forcing Ligachev out of this job was considered a significant success for Gorbachev. See Gorbachev, *Memoirs*, p. 268.

23. On the most influential scientific institutes in foreign affairs, see Klaus von Beyme, *Die Sowjetunion in der Weltpolitik*, 2nd ed., (München: Piper, 1985), pp. 36–38. The book by Georgi Arbatov, *The System: An Insider's Life in Soviet Politics* (New York: Times Books, 1992), is quite revealing about the United States of America and Canada Institute.

24. Gorbachev, *Memoirs*, pp. 173–174, 241–242, 471.

25. Author's translation of Michail Gorbatschow, *Erinnerungen* (Berlin: Siedler, 1995), p. 286. For background on the documents, see Medvedev, *V komande Gorbacheva*, pp. 31–36.

26. Christian Schmidt-Häuer, *Michail Gorbatschow*, 5th ed. (München: Piper, 1987), p. 321.

27. On prerevolutionary history, Gorbachev in 1987 was still using the rough Stalinist schema of societies as slave-holder, feudalist, capitalist, and socialist. See Gorbachev, *Perestroika*, p. 151.

28. On the origin and significance of the doctrine, see Boris Meissner, *Die "Breshnew-Doktrin": Das Prinzip des "proletarisch-sozialistischen Internationalismus" und die Theorie von den "verschiedenen Wegen zum Sozialismus"* (Köln: Verlag Wissenschaft und Politik, 1969).

29. For an interpretation of Gorbachev's politics not as a domestic power play but a product of his own mentality, see Hannes Adomeit, *Imperial Overstretch: Germany in Soviet Foreign Policy from Stalin to Gorbachev* (Baden-Baden: Nomos, 1998), pp. 211–215.

30. Gorbachev never designated Woodrow Wilson as a role model. It was the *New York Times* editorial about his speech to the UN General Assembly on December 7, 1988: "Perhaps not since Woodrow Wilson presented his Fourteen Points in 1918 or since Franklin Roosevelt and Winston Churchill promulgated the Atlantic Charter in 1941 has a world figure demonstrated the vision of Mikhail Gorbachev, displayed yesterday at the United Nations." Gorbachev, *Memoirs*, p. 462.

31. Gerhard Simon and Nadja Simon, *Verfall und Untergang des sowjetischen Imperiums* (München: Deutscher Taschenbuch Verlag, 1993), pp. 36–37. Simon and Simon use this approach to differentiate nine periods during Gorbachev's time in power.

32. Pioneering at the time was the compilation by H. Gordon Skilling and Franklyn Griffiths, eds., *Interest Groups in Soviet Politics* (Princeton: Princeton University Press, 1971).

33. Gorbachev, *Memoirs*, pp. 137, 155, 166. In all three citations, Gorbachev stresses unanimity in the decision on a new General Secretary. This contradicts common Western presumptions; see, for example, Schmidt-Häuer, *Michail Gorbatschow*, p. 158.

34. Gorbachev, *Memoirs*, p. 5.

35. This according to G. V. Romanov, cited in Gorbatschow, *Erinnerungen*, p. 259.

36. Horst Temmen, ed., *Michail S. Gorbatschow: 'Zurück dürfen wir nicht'; Programmatische Äußerungen zur Umgestaltung der sowjetischen Gesellschaft* (Bremen: Temmen, 1987), p. 12.

37. The German publication of this program carried the misleading title "Das Aktionsprogramm Gorbatschows" (Gorbachev's Program for Action). Boris Meissner, *Das Aktionsprogramm Gorbatschows: Die Neufassung des dritten Parteiprogramms der KPdSU* (Köln: Verlag Wissenschaft und Politik, 1987).

38. Gorbachev, *Perestroika*, p. 27.

39. Author's translation of Gorbatschow, Sagladin, and Tschernjajew, *Das Neue Denken*, p. 12–13.

40. For details see Simon and Simon, *Verfall und Untergang*, p. 38–40.

41. Gorbachev's efforts to push the beginning of Perestroika back to his speeches at Konstantin Chernenko's funeral and the March Plenum in 1985 can be noted in Gorbachev, *Memoirs*, pp. 167f., 173, and in Gorbatschow, Sagladin, and Tschernjajew, *Das Neue Denken*, p. 25. See also the emphasis on the June Plenum 1987 as the beginning of substantial changes in economic policy in Gorbachev, *Perestroika*, pp. 84–85. Here he also wrote, "Perestroika is only just getting off the ground. So far we have only been shaping the mechanism of acceleration," (p. 64).

42. In this environment, as late as October 1986, it was possible for Chancellor Helmut Kohl to compare the propaganda techniques of Gorbachev with those of Goebbels and charge that Gorbachev was veiling conventional "totalitarian" politics. For Gorbachev's later judgment of his policies towards Bonn, see Gorbachev, *Memoirs*, p. 518.

43. See Zdenek Hejzlar, *Reformkommunismus: Zur Geschichte der Kommunistischen Partei der Tschechoslowakei* (Frankfurt: Europa Verlag, 1976).

44. A substantial comparison of Reform-Communism in Prague during the 1960s, the Solidarity Movement of 1980/1981, and Perestroika remains to be made. It is also unclear how much Gorbachev and others were interested in details of the reforms of the Dubcek era. According to his own account, Gorbachev had to avoid taking a stance on "Prague Spring" for a considerable time. See Gorbachev, *Memoirs*, pp. 482–483.

45. For a detailed account, see Egbert Jahn, "Das Scheitern der sozialistischen Systemreformation und des konstitutionellen Kommunismus. Ein Forschungsbericht über 'Perestrojka' und 'Neues Denken' in der Sowjetunion," in *Jahrbuch für Historische Kommunismusforschung* (Berlin: Akademie Verlag, 1996).

46. To compare with Hungary in 1970 and Romania in 1975, see Egbert Jahn, *Bürokratischer Sozialismus: Chancen der Demokratisierung?* (Frankfurt: Fischer, 1982), p. 174–175.

47. See Aleksandr E. Bovin, "Rezerv pamiati," in *Novoe Vremia*, Issue 5, (Moscow, 1987), p. 9.

48. For details see Galina Luchterhandt, *Die politischen Parteien im neuen Rußland: Dokumente und Kommentare* (Bremen: Temmen, 1993), pp. 15–29.

49. Even the economic reforms in the PRC had stimulating effects on Soviet Perestroika. See Gorbachev, *Memoirs*, p. 218.

50. See the detailed portrayal of the decision-making process in Wojciech Jaruzelski, *Mein Leben für Polen: Erinnerungen* (München: Piper, 1993), pp. 231–296.

51. Viacheslav I. Dashichev, "Vostok-Zapad: poisk novykh otnoshenii. O prioritetakh vneshnei politiki Sovetskogo gosudarstva," in *Literaturnaia Gazeta* (Moscow, May 18, 1988), p. 14.

52. For details see Manfred Sapper, *Die Auswirkungen des Afghanistan-Krieges auf die Sowjetgesellschaft: Eine Studie zum Legitimitätsverlust des Militärischen in der Perestrojka* (Münster: Lit-Verlag, 1994), pp. 132–133.

53. Ibid., p. 279.

54. See Adomeit, *Imperial Overstretch*; Kirsten Westphal, *Hegemon statt Partner—Rußlands Politik gegenüber dem 'nahen Ausland'* (Münster: Lit-Verlag, 1995); and on the case of Lithuania specifically, Gediminas Vitkus, "Lithuanian-Russian Relations in 1990–1995," *Untersuchungen des FKKS*, 12 (Mannheim: University of Mannheim, 1996).

55. See Christoph Royen, *Osteuropa: Reformen und Wandel. Erfahrungen und Aussichten vor dem Hintergrund der sowjetischen Perestrojka*, 2nd ed. (Baden-Baden: Nomos, 1990).

56. Gorbachev, *Memoirs*, p. 465.

57. Ibid.

58. Ibid.

59. Gorbachev, *Perestroika*, p. 12.

60. See Jaruzelski, *Mein Leben*, p. 326. Gorbachev does not depict his own reaction to the election results; see Gorbachev, *Memoirs*, p. 522.

61. Gorbachev, *Memoirs*, p. 485.

62. Ibid., pp. 478ff. See also Jaruzelski, *Mein Leben*, p. 290.

CHAPTER 8

Soviet Foreign Policy and the Gulf War: The Role of Domestic Factors

Galia Golan

INTRODUCTION

A two-level-game analysis uncovers the ways a leader, in struggling to achieve an international agreement, contrives to obtain terms acceptable to all the parties while building the political consensus inside his political system needed to get the agreement accepted. In seeking this, the leader can employ many tactics, as can the opponents of the prospective deal. This chapter traces Mikhail Gorbachev's struggle to reach agreement with the West, especially the United States, over what to do about Iraq's seizure of Kuwait. It outlines considerations that motivated Gorbachev, whose position was "dovish" in character—he was more eager for an agreement and more willing to make concessions to get it than many others in his government or the Soviet political elite.

The chapter also calls attention to ways in which, desiring an agreement, American leaders assisted Gorbachev in his domestic political efforts. Indeed, in terms of the adjustments suggested in the introduction to this volume, the chapter actually traces *two domestic political games, one within the government and the other between Gorbachev and the conservative opponents* of his policies. Thus, in a real sense, the analysis encompasses *a three-level game* (or even, if one differentiates the system and state, as I do, *a four-level game*). In doing so it highlights several points.

First, relevant win-sets are not shaped solely by the parties' interests and judgments on the issue at hand. They are strongly affected by where that issue falls within the broader political division on fundamental issues. Hence understanding the leader's efforts requires grasping the overall political context.

Second, this makes the framing of the issue at hand an important tactic in the multiple games, because the framing helps determine its relationship to the larger context. Thus if it becomes symbolic of larger issues and is approached on that basis, this affects the nature of the win-sets involved, the kind of effort the leader must put forth, and the chances for success. In this process the stature and leverage of the leader is not a constant. Hence, as the issue develops the leader's approach to it in search of an agreement must adjust to shifts in his or her personal political situation.

These elements are quite well displayed in the tangle of Soviet-Western interactions that swirled around the seizure of Kuwait by Saddam Hussein, the global political effort launched in response to it, and its culmination in the Gulf War.

Gorbachev's foreign policy with regard to the Middle East must be seen within the context of the priorities and circumstances of the period, both for the Soviet Union and the international system as a whole. Gorbachev had undertaken, as highest priority, the introduction of perestroika, that is, a reconstruction—increasingly comprehensive—of the Soviet economy, society, and political system. Perestroika was composed of reform and democratization of the domestic system together with what was called "new political thinking" for foreign policy. At one level, "new thinking" was intended to create an international environment that would facilitate the pursuit of perestroika. However, it was also a form of perestroika itself in that new thinking was intended by Gorbachev to shape an entirely new role for the Soviet Union in the world system. This role was to be based not on ideology or a zero-sum relationship between East and West but rather on adherence to universal values guiding states in an interdependent system in which conflicts were resolved by political means determined by a balance of interests. In short, the Soviet Union was to become a "normal" state of the enlightened world, shaping its foreign policies to suit its concrete domestic needs in keeping with universal values.

The pursuit of new thinking had to contend with both international and domestic factors. At the international level, the most important of these was skepticism abroad, particularly in the neoconservative American administration, with regard to the sincerity of the proclaimed new policies. Decades of Cold War suspicion and the widespread belief that Communism was immutable persisted in many circles in the West. Similar, possibly deeper, skepticism was apparent domestically among those elites and constituencies who supported perestroika. Cynicism, born of past tragedy and disappointment, was rampant within both the public and various elites who doubted Gorbachev's motives or believed the system (and the Party) to be ultimately implacable. At the same time, there was domestic opposition from powerful bureaucracies and interest groups. Vested interests more than ideology guided their attempts to sabotage perestroika in the hopes of preserving their power or privileged positions. The domestic struggle was waged against a backdrop of increasing political and economic dislocation and hardship within Soviet society, centrifugal (nationalist) tendencies and conflict, and disintegration of central controls and public order attendant upon—but also directly affecting—the attempt to implement perestroika.

THE SYSTEM-STATE LINKAGE

In formulating foreign policy, the Soviet leadership sought to respond to two sets of requisites with regard to the international system: what was needed from the international system for the Soviet state, and what was needed from the state in dealing with the system. In the first instance, Moscow needed a conflict-free environment so as to concentrate on domestic tasks and provide an international atmosphere conducive to economic cooperation. Actual assistance, in the form of aid, credits, and investment, was also sought in order to place the Soviet economy on a new market-based foundation and to cope with the costs, problems, and dislocations caused by the reforms (such as unemployment, breakdowns in supplies, and defense conversion). Gorbachev also needed success in the international arena to consolidate domestic support by demonstrating the benefits of perestroika and to weaken the opponents of reform.

To a large degree these requirements were dependent upon efforts by Moscow to demonstrate the sincerity, scope, and permanence of perestroika at home and new thinking abroad. To achieve this, it was incumbent upon Gorbachev to demonstrate the stability and effectiveness of his administration and leadership, progress in the introduction of reforms, and success in the implementation of changes and accords (such as the new arms agreements). Delays, impediments, or deviations from reform, not only in the economic sphere but in such areas as nationality rights (namely, the violent clampdown in the Baltics) impacted upon the state-system relationship.

It was also incumbent on Gorbachev to demonstrate Soviet willingness to cooperate in the peaceful resolution of regional conflicts. Withdrawal from the conflict in which the Soviet Union was most directly involved, in Afghanistan, was one of the most important pieces of evidence that Soviet foreign policy had changed. There was also an implicit international demand that Moscow support Western moves and comply with Western proposals as signs of the end of the Cold War and zero-sum perspectives.

Although Gorbachev tended to define the international system in terms of the West or the superpowers, there were other elements in the system that played a role in Soviet policies. In some cases, Soviet relations were affected, to a degree, by the broader system. For example, a spin-off from the new East-West relationship was the possibility of improving relations with states allied with the West such as those in the Gulf. Conversely, improved relations with a state like Israel affected prospects for better economic relations with the United States and Canada. The opposite—a deterioration in relations—also resulted in some instances, as in the effect of better relations with the West (and withdrawal from Afghanistan) on the attitude of certain Third World states such as Syria. Similarly, the collapse of the Soviet empire in Eastern Europe and of the Warsaw Pact had an impact not only on Soviet-Western relations but on the attitude of others toward Moscow.

STATE-TO-STATE RELATIONS

As in the general relationship between the Soviet state and the international system, in the state-to-state relationship with the United States Moscow was guided by its need for aid and support. Viewed as equally essential was Western and private business support. This dictated a policy of cooperation with the United States and compliance with American proposals, both to gain assistance and to create the basic essential credence in Washington with regard to new thinking. There was also a state-society element, as Moscow geared its policies also to convincing the skeptics and conservatives in America that Moscow was worthy of U.S. assistance and cooperation.

In addition, Gorbachev sought concessions, symbolic and other, from the United States to placate his domestic opponents and/or increase his autonomy vis-à-vis domestic opponents. It may even have been the case that some collusion was sought (and achieved) with Washington to intimidate Gorbachev's domestic foes by warnings about the price of failure to maintain a good relationship with America. For his part, President George Bush, once convinced that Gorbachev was sincere, sought to bolster Gorbachev's position and avoid the creation or aggravation of problems for the Soviet leader in his own country.

The effort by Moscow to maintain its great-power status led to what may have been an attempt to mask the actual asymmetry of the Soviet-U.S. relationship and Soviet weakness through a preference for multilateral, international frameworks. Similarly, a measure of criticism regarding American policies was occasionally employed, possibly to demonstrate Soviet strength despite its dependence upon American assistance, or possibly, out of actual opposition or concern over a war situation or the positioning of a massive American military force close to Soviet borders. Perhaps such criticism was also the result of concern over the effect these American moves might have in strengthening domestic opponents to perestroika and new thinking.

THE STATE-SOCIETY LINKAGE

With regard to the Soviet public, Gorbachev had the task of demonstrating the material benefits of perestroika (one reason the economic contribution of the West was vital). There was the very real problem of short-term economic hardships caused by perestroika, as well as the contradictions or expected contradictions resulting from the new policies, such as economic losses from lost arms sales presumably dictated by a new reliance on political resolution of conflict. A similar contradiction was apparent within the public. On the one hand, the public opposed involvement in overseas military actions and favored withdrawal from foreign endeavors as a drain on Soviet resources. Yet it retained a strong (and traditional) sentiment in favor of maintaining the country's status as a great power.

A related matter was the effort to reshape public opinion so as to counter the leader-as-dove dilemma: to prove to the public that there was still a *Soviet* foreign policy, independent and serving Soviet national interests (even though the latter remained undefined). Unlike the past, public opinion in the Gorbachev period became an important factor, in part because of its inclusion in perestroika. Various aspects of perestroika, in particular glasnost (openness, honesty), had opened the way to the articulation of public views. Also, one of the proclaimed reforms was a broadening of the foreign policy establishment and the creation of a popular role in, or control over, foreign-policy decision-making, be it through the elected organs of the state or other means. Although these changes were envisaged as part of democratization, they may also have been intended, at least in part, as a means of limiting and neutralizing the bureaucracies (e.g., the military-industrial complex) opposed to perestroika and new thinking.

THE INTRASTATE STRUGGLE

Many of the problems and issues arising in the state-society relationship were present as well in intrastate relations. In addition, certain elites and institutions sought to enlist, or exploit, public opinion in their opposition to perestroika. The regime had to counter—or placate—opposition from the military, the military-industrial complex, and Russian nationalists, to whom the costs of new thinking seemed too high. Added to these groups were the bureaucratic and conservative Communist opponents of perestroika.

At the same time, Gorbachev had to maintain the support of the pro-perestroika forces like the reformist elements of the CPSU, the intellectuals (in particular, academics and journalists), and new bodies in the emerging civil society. Institutions created or given new life under perestroika had to be taken into account, whether to elicit support or to counter their opposition. Among these were the Supreme Soviet and the newly created Congress of Peoples' Deputies, the international affairs committees of these bodies, the Supreme Soviet of the Russian Federation, and government ministries, primarily in Defense and Foreign Affairs.

The intrastate struggle was not just a two-way, vertical affair. It also consisted of competing elites, groups, and institutions, often allying among themselves as well as for or against the leadership of the state. At the same time, independent action by certain groups or elites included a foreign aspect, which in turn could affect the state's relations with others. For example, the shifting of military equipment beyond the Urals to circumvent the conventional arms accord, or contacts between conservative Communists and military groups with Iraq in violation of the anti-Iraq coalition's policy, were actions that impacted on foreign policy. And as already noted, in the area of system-state relations, state actions in relations with groups or institutions within society could impact on foreign relations, as in the case of the Soviet clamp-down in the Baltics.

MIDDLE EAST POLICY

As a result of the interplay of the various factors in the system, state, intrastate, and society levels, Gorbachev's Middle East policy, including his policy in the Gulf crisis, may be summarized as having been designed primarily to please the United

States and, secondarily, the supporters of perestroika, while undermining domestic opponents who also sought to enlist public opinion in torpedoing new thinking and perestroika itself. Washington's policy in the Gulf crisis and its attitude toward the USSR directly affected Gorbachev's relationship with both opponents and supporters of perestroika, while Gorbachev's effort to placate the opponents impacted on his policies during the crisis and, as a consequence, threatened to affect the relationship with the United States.

In terms of broad Middle East policy,[1] Gorbachev's effort to demonstrate to the West, particularly to America, the sincerity of new thinking and to forge a new place for Moscow on the world scene led to a number of changes. The Soviets abandoned their standard formula for a settlement of the Arab-Israeli conflict in favor of any accord acceptable to both sides and based on a balance of interests. This represented a virtual shift to neutrality. It was accompanied by a rapprochement with Israel (along with Egypt and the pro-Western, conservative states of the Gulf) and concessions with regard to Soviet Jews such as relaxation of restrictions on emigration and visits to Israel, freeing of Jewish religious and cultural life within the Soviet Union, and the elimination of official anti-Semitism. At the same time, assistance was withdrawn from Palestinian (and other) terrorism, and Moscow undertook to cooperate at the international level in the struggle against terrorism. It also formulated a comprehensive security proposal for the Middle East, and significantly reduced its military presence and arms deliveries there.

These moves were prompted by a combination of factors. Reduced arms supplies resulted from domestic perestroika, that is, the demand for profitability (hard currency payments) in foreign trade. The reduced military presence was also the result of the new, defensive military doctrine accompanying new thinking. Emigration of Soviet Jews, elimination of official anti-Semitism, and the freeing of Jewish life were all, in time, part of domestic perestroika (democratization). Yet they were also designed to meet Israeli demands and, even more importantly, the demands of Western Jewish business circles and the American government, which linked "most favored nation" (MFN) treatment to freedom of emigration.

It is far less clear to what extent these measures were also a response to pro-perestroika domestic lobbies *against* arms sales and Soviet military involvement abroad or *for* renewed relations with Israel and a balanced approach to the Arab-Israeli conflict. Various groups or individuals demanded these and other steps as confirmation of new thinking, and the implementation strengthened the supporters of perestroika, that is, Gorbachev's base. In Gorbachev's thinking, however, this may have been secondary to his interests in the international system and Soviet-U.S relations.

At the same time, an "ideological" factor cannot be overlooked. Gorbachev and his colleagues (Eduard Shevardnadze, Aleksandr Yakovlev) aspired to a fundamentally new policy for the Soviet Union, based on the concept of international interdependence and the universality of human values. New Thinking, on the Middle East, and as a whole, was both the product and the source of Gorbachev's interest in satisfying Western, especially American (and Israeli) demands.

Yet many of the above policies emerged only gradually while there were also contrasting policies that Gorbachev maintained to the end or almost the end of his rule, such as the continuation of arms sales, persistence in seeking an international Middle East conference, and refusal fully to renew Soviet-Israeli relations or permit direct flights for emigrants to Israel. Similarly, Gorbachev pursued what appeared to be a competitive policy vis-à-vis the United States with regard to the Iran-Iraq war.

Explanations may be found in the need to placate domestic constituencies, in particular the military-industrial complex. The military and the military-industrial complex were already suffering from perestroika and new thinking in the form of arms control agreements with the West, the new military doctrine, the impending collapse of the Warsaw pact, the reduction of the army, and defense conversion. For them, continued arms sales were imperative. Moreover, this constituency derived strength and legitimacy from continued, even increased, American arms supplies to the region. In addition, the power of nationalists, Arabists in the foreign policy establishment, and anti-perestroika elements of the CPSU may explain Gorbachev's reluctance to fully reverse policies on Israel and Jewish emigration. These "hesitations," however, were minor compared to the sea change Gorbachev introduced in policies toward Israel and Soviet Jews. In other words, external factors outweighed domestic constraints in determining the major elements and thrust of Gorbachev's Middle East policies.

In pursuing cooperation with Iran and in proposing an international peace conference for the Arab-Israeli conflict, Gorbachev was treading a fine line in an effort to respond to intrastate and societal interests without jeopardizing his central goal of Soviet-U.S. cooperation. The long (Muslim-inhabited) Soviet border with Iran as well as Soviet economic interests in the country may explain Gorbachev's policy there. But in both cases, another element must have been at play: the need to respond to opposition groups and public opinion with regard to Moscow's impaired global status. Concessions to the West, the decline of Soviet influence and prestige, and the shift to compliance with American positions regarding the Arab-Israeli conflict were to be compensated for by maintaining something of a Soviet role as a great power, ostensibly equal with the United States.

The very effort to convince the West of the sincerity of new thinking involved steps that subsequently necessitated potentially contradictory actions to placate the opposition created at home by the new foreign policy. In time this also led to a limited retreat on perestroika in domestic affairs in order to pacify public opinion and opposition groups. The latter were consistently strengthened by the general perception that Moscow had received too little return for great sacrifices in Soviet power and prestige. At no time was this pattern more evident than during the Gulf crisis of 1990–1991.

GULF CRISIS

From a broad two-level-game perspective, Gorbachev's handling of the Gulf War crisis, detailed in the rest of the chapter, can be summarized as follows. Initially, he sought international agreement on a response to Iraq in keeping with Soviet "new thinking" on foreign policy. In terms of his win-set, this was the best outcome. Success would have enhanced his and his government's international stature, reinforced his domestic support, and weakened the conservative opposition. Failing to achieve this, and with the United States leading the coalition toward war, he then desperately sought to broker a peaceful settlement of the crisis (the Primakov mission). However, his win-set, and that of his government, was much too large to provide the necessary leverage, because alignment with the West was deemed necessary at almost any cost, more important than a futile insistence on the peaceful resolution of disputes. Thus he was forced eventually to fall into line behind American policy. The difficulty at home was that the crisis unfolded against a backdrop of rising conservative pressure against his domestic reforms, with his opponents citing the Gulf crisis in seeking to undermine the entire reform effort. Thus he finished with no foreign policy success, just a painful demonstration of foreign policy impotence that confirmed the charges of the conservatives and that contributed to his rapid political demise shortly thereafter.

The Iraqi invasion of Kuwait occurred at a time of serious domestic difficulty for Gorbachev. The economic and nationalities problems had reached crisis proportions, the political sphere was sharply divided between conservative forces and democratic forces, and Gorbachev was attempting to juggle the two, keep the Union together, and nonetheless proceed with perestroika. Abroad, Gorbachev's foreign policies were seen as more successful. Indeed, the invasion came just as the Soviet and American foreign ministers were conducting cordial talks, discussing what was expected to be an important Gorbachev-Bush summit in Moscow in the winter. Domestically, however, Gorbachev's foreign policy was viewed with far less enthusiasm, as democrats sought greater domestic reform, conservatives (who opposed most of the foreign policy decisions) focused mainly on the possible breakup of the Soviet Union, and ordinary citizens were concerned with the social and economic deterioration of their daily lives. The Middle East, Iraq, Kuwait were far from their thoughts.

Moscow's official response to the Gulf crisis was in keeping with the international atmosphere Gorbachev had sought to create: a joint Soviet-American condemnation of the Iraqi move and agreement to suspend arms deliveries followed by adherence to the sanctions adopted by the United Nations Security Council. However, this was not an automatic stance. Mindful of the negative response that would come from conservative critics, Shevardnadze tried to avoid the imposition of strong measures against Iraq. The Americans, for their part, were intent upon gaining Soviet cooperation, fearful that criticism from Moscow would enable Saddam to play one superpower against the other or draw the wrong conclusions about the strength of the coalition against him. Secretary of State James Baker was willing, therefore, to temper language somewhat, though he was unwilling to permit any ambiguity in the signals to Saddam even for the sake of assisting the Soviet leadership in "selling" the package at home.[2]

The cooperative position adopted by Gorbachev was lauded by pro-perestroika forces in Moscow as a sign that the Soviet leadership had actually abandoned Cold War policies, not only because the position entailed superpower cooperation but because it represented opposition to an aggressor whose attack had been made possible by previous Soviet arms supplies and support. This view was shared by a large portion of the public: Thirty-eight percent of Russians polled believed that the Soviet Union was at least partially responsible for the Iraqi invasion because of past arms deliveries.[3]

Indeed, the crisis was utilized by the democrats for further condemnation of the ideologically motivated and military dominated policies of the past.[4] It was also used to promote demands for speedier, more thorough-going perestroika in such areas as democratization of decision making, greater access to and dissemination of information, parliamentary controls on the defense ministry and military-industrial complex, and, specifically, an end to what was viewed as the immoral practice of using arms supplies as an instrument of foreign policy (particularly because producing the supplies may not even have been profitable for the Soviet economy).[5]

On just what to do about this instance of Iraqi aggression, however, the democratic forces had more of a problem. Many maintained that the government was not going far enough; they demanded the withdrawal of all Soviet personnel from Iraq, abrogation of the Soviet-Iraqi treaty, and expulsion of all Iraqis training in the Soviet Union.[6] A minority called for Soviet military participation in the anti-Iraq coalition, not just political involvement.[7] They argued that the dispatch of even a symbolic military unit would demonstrate the fidelity of Moscow to the community of enlightened nations. Yet one of the central principles of new thinking was peaceful resolution (through political means) of disputes. For many democrats the use of force could not be condoned and Soviet participation in any military action abroad, even with volunteers, was rejected.[8]

Theory aside, there was also a strong isolationist sentiment. In large part this could be attributed to a "post-Afghan syndrome" after eight years of an unpopular war. It also reflected resentment over costly involvement in foreign ventures perceived as having served the interests of a particular elite at the expense of the average person's standard of living. No matter whom they blamed for the invasion of Kuwait or what they thought of Iraq, most people opposed any Soviet military involvement. In a poll taken in September, only 8 percent supported sending even a minimal Soviet force to the Gulf.[9]

Conservative forces seized upon these sentiments, hypocritically invoking the principles of new thinking to condemn the American buildup in the Gulf and what they claimed was the government's, namely Shevardnadze's, intention of committing Soviet troops. Thus they utilized the crisis for their own purposes. In addition to playing on isolationism and fear in order to weaken Shevardnadze and other Gorbachev associates, some conservatives, particularly in the military, pointed to the Western military buildup in the Gulf as proof that new thinking was unrealistic. Some claimed that Washington was massing forces near the Soviet

Union's sensitive southern border, redeploying NATO troops that could no longer be kept in Europe because of the ostensible end of the Cold War, and seeking to take over the Middle East.[10] Together with nationalists, conservative Communists, traditional Arabists and others, opponents argued that the government's support of the anti-Iraq coalition would harm Soviet interests in the region, particularly future (including economic) relations with the Arabs, while arousing the ire of 45 million Soviet Muslims. The bottom line was the blow to Soviet power and status incurred by supporting the Americans, one more in a series of blows that were weakening the Soviet Union domestically and internationally.

By late fall 1990, the campaign against perestroika began to bear fruit. An ultimatum by the military in October led to a series of domestic policy and personnel changes by Gorbachev, effecting both glasnost and economic reform and culminating in January with a violent crackdown in the Baltics by Soviet troops. In December Foreign Minister Shevardnadze resigned his position to protest these concessions to the Right, which he saw as substantially increasing the danger of dictatorship. Though the resignation was motivated in part by concern over Gorbachev's change in direction, Shevardnadze had been subject to almost continuous criticism from conservatives for his policy on the Gulf crisis, being accused of selling out Soviet interests to the benefit of the United States as well as a willingness to commit Soviet troops.[11] The deeper connections between the two—the strength of conservatism on the domestic scene and the events in the Gulf—were reflected in Shevardnadze's resignation.

In fact contradictions had already begun to appear in Soviet Gulf policy as a result of the domestic political clash and Gorbachev's concern over popular and elite opinion. Moscow had halted arms supplies to Iraq and joined the anti-Iraq coalition because, as senior Soviet Third World specialist Georgii Mirsky put it, the Soviet Union could not have disagreed with the United States on this issue of international law and order without risking the loss of "the trust earned in the West."[12] Marshal Sergei Akhromeyov gave a similar explanation:

If we argued before 2 August that there was a possibility of creating a global security system, this was based primarily on the agreement of the United States and the Soviet Union. And if the Soviet Union had not accepted the assessment concerning the [Iraqi] aggression and adhered to the decisions on sanctions, it would have been responsible for burying this system. It was a matter of principle, a very important one that concerned the further development of international relations.[13]

Yet Gorbachev made every effort to have the crisis resolved through broad international bodies, particularly the United Nations, so as to avoid the appearance of acquiescence to Washington.[14] (The use of the Security Council not only provided legitimacy for the Soviet role but also cover—abroad and at home—for the fact that the Soviet Union actually had very little power.) Still, it is revealing that Moscow dragged its feet and thereby delayed virtually every UN vote on the crisis, according its consent only reluctantly to the various resolutions, in particular resolutions 665 and 678, which provided for the use of force if necessary.

Moreover, at the same time, Gorbachev authorized seemingly contradictory diplomatic measures. Seeking to mediate a solution, the Soviets held talks in Moscow with Iraq, and Gorbachev's adviser (and top Soviet Middle East Expert) Evgenii Primakov was sent as a personal envoy to Iraq, ostensibly to negotiate the withdrawal of Soviet military experts.[15] In fact, Primakov journeyed to Amman, Cairo, Rome, Paris, and Washington after his trip to Baghdad in what was clearly an effort to mediate a solution independently from Shevardnadze's own efforts to demonstrate strict Soviet adherence to the anti-Iraq coalition. Positions espoused by Primakov contradicted those of Shevardnadze and hardly served the latter's purposes.[16] Shevardnadze reportedly asked Gorbachev to cease contact with the Iraqi leadership on the grounds that Primakov might give Saddam the impression that the coalition would not hold together. Moreover, just before Primakov's arrival in Washington with his plan to prevent an American move against Iraq, Shevardnadze informed Baker (via their aides, Sergei Tarasenko and Dennis Ross) that he did not approve of Primakov's mission, implying that he did not want Primakov's proposals taken seriously.[17] The Americans needed no such advice; they were not interested in concessions to Saddam Hussein in any form. But the incident did mark an unofficial U.S.-Soviet collusion unimaginable in the days before new thinking.

Primakov, himself, was not an opponent of new thinking; his motivation was probably dictated by an interest in preserving future relations with the Arab world as distinct from the priority Shevardnadze accorded to Soviet-American relations. His mission was meant to help Gorbachev both to placate the conservative opposition by creating an independent role for Moscow and to avert an unpopular military conflict that might strengthen the conservative opponents of new thinking and perestroika. Primakov was rumored to have ambitions to replace Shevardnadze, and this may also have had something to do with his initiatives.

Washington seems to have tried to assist Gorbachev in his domestic situation. At the September summit President Bush offered assurances that U.S. forces would not remain in the Gulf permanently and later, in connection with Soviet agreement to the Security Council resolutions on force, the Americans promised to give the embargo every chance to work first. At the summit Bush also provided a concession the United States had previously withheld: a promise that Moscow would be a full partner in future Arab-Israeli peace talks.[18] In addition, the Americans were probably instrumental in obtaining for Gorbachev the promise of $4 billion in credits from the Gulf states (Kuwait, Saudi Arabia, and the United Arab Emirates) upon the opening of Soviet diplomatic relations with Saudi Arabia and Bahrain. With these credits the Soviet leader could deflect criticism over economic losses incurred by opposing Iraq: the Iraqi debt to Moscow, revenues from commercial accords with Iraq, and future business with Baghdad.[19]

Finally, Bush sought to relieve pressures on Gorbachev when he told a news conference that America did not expect or seek a Soviet military contribution in the Gulf.[20] In fact, Washington had earlier suggested that Moscow send a contingent, apparently to relieve Soviet anxieties over unilateral American military moves. After the Soviets had rejected this, however, Washington seems to have concluded that it was more helpful to Gorbachev not to be confronted directly. Bush and Baker, moreover, had to contend with their own critics. Officials in the State Department, for example, opposed any Soviet military participation on grounds that U.S. policy had been striving for decades to keep the Soviets *out* of the Middle East.[21] Bush's statement denying any U.S. request for a Soviet contribution may also have been intended to undercut American opponents of Soviet-U.S. rapprochement, that is, those skeptics who demanded proof of new thinking in the form of active Soviet assistance in the crisis. These groups may have been aggravated by Primakov's mediating efforts, helping to prompt Shevardnadze's warning to Gorbachev and his request to halt Primakov's forays.

In November, concerned over public and congressional opposition to an American military move against Iraq, Bush sought a new Security Council resolution explicitly authorizing the use of force if necessary. The Americans believed that this would help keep their allies in the coalition. A major problem was finding a formula the Soviets could support without raising insurmountable opposition in Moscow and boosting the conservative cause there. The compromise, worked out mainly by Baker and Shevardnadze, employed the wording "all necessary means" instead of "the use of force" and included a time-table, that is, provided a deadline that gave Iraq another period of grace before action would be taken. Gorbachev reportedly asked the Americans to postpone announcing the Soviet agreement until after the Soviets had held one more meeting with the Iraqis in Moscow, obviously to avoid the appearance of following American dictates.[22] Even as the Americans acceded to Gorbachev's requests, and as Shevardnadze obtained the Soviet President's final agreement for resolution 678, Primakov was in New York trying to persuade the Americans to postpone the Security Council vote.[23]

American assistance, designed to help the Soviets provide the compliance Washington wanted, was not entirely sufficient. As conservative pressures grew in Moscow, Gorbachev began to renege on a commitment he had made to oppose Saddam's demands for policy linkages. From the early days of the crisis, Saddam had sought to condition withdrawal from Kuwait on Israeli withdrawal from the occupied territories and Lebanon. Instead the Soviets had agreed only to sequential linkage, an American proposal, that is, to work for settlement of the Arab-Israeli conflict *after* the Gulf crisis was resolved.[24] In December, however, Shevardnadze told Washington that Moscow was about to propose a resolution calling for an international conference on the Middle East, virtually accepting Saddam's linkage. After lengthy discussion the Soviets backed down, but part of the price required of the Americans was that they ignore other issues—inspired by Soviet conservatives—that were emerging. One was the Soviet military's attempt to undermine the recent accords on conventional forces in Europe (CFE) by transferring large amounts of heavy equipment eastward beyond the Urals so as to exclude them from the destruction required by the treaty.[25] Bush also found it necessary to offer certain benefits and incentives, agreeing to a summit in Moscow in February, extending up to $1 billion in credits, and making promises of other economic aid.

Though Bush continued to postpone completion of a trade bill that would include MFN, insisting upon a prior Soviet commitment regarding emigration, he did extend suspension of the restrictive Jackson-Vanik amendment for an additional six months. Basically Bush sought to provide what he considered necessary to help Gorbachev combat his domestic opposition without giving Moscow so much as to arouse suspicion among conservatives and skeptics in Washington.

On the whole, Gorbachev appeared to manage juggling conservative domestic pressures with his underlying interest in maintaining the new relationship with the West. Despite the delays at the UN and in talks with the Iraqis, Moscow finally supported and complied with Security Council resolutions; it also maintained its rejection of Baghdad's repeated proposals for linkage. Upon Gorbachev's orders the Soviet military provided the United States with technical information regarding Soviet weapons in Iraq's arsenal, even though, at the same time, at least one Soviet ship was intercepted bringing supplies to Iraq (via Jordan) in violation of the international arms embargo.[26] The sending of the ship was apparently carried out without Shevardnadze's (and probably Gorbachev's) authorization or knowledge. It was similar to steps taken by the Soviet military with regard to CFE, again without Shevardnadze's and perhaps Gorbachev's approval. In both cases, the military and military-industrial complex sought to undermine a policy they opposed and, in so doing, complicate state-to state and state-system relations.[27]

The ship incident occurred in January, and by then a decided shift in Gorbachev's position toward the conservatives had become apparent. This could be attributed to the resignation and replacement of Shevardnadze by a far less authoritative figure, professional diplomat Aleksandr Bessmertnykh, as well as to the approaching war and the actual hostilities in the Gulf. Yet it was, in fact, connected with far broader domestic developments, including further personnel changes, the reintroduction of a certain amount of censorship, greater leeway for the security forces (e.g., joint army-police patrols in over 400 cities), and most flagrantly, a violent crackdown on nationalists in Latvia and Lithuania.

It is difficult to gauge to what degree this further turn to the right—which brought about changes in Soviet policy regarding the Gulf War—was itself caused or at least assisted by the events in the Gulf. According to one observer the fate of perestroika domestically ("military reform and democratization as a whole") was actually being decided in the Middle East. The longer the struggle went on there, or if it "turned out not too successfully for the allies," the stronger the conservative forces would become in the Soviet Union. A swift and unconditional victory for the Americans, it was suggested, would permit Moscow "to come to grips with the army and the 'defense' enterprises, as [it had] before in the 1860s after the Crimean War."[28]

The domestic shift was reflected in Gorbachev's response to events in the Gulf. As one experienced Soviet commentator put it:

During the early stages of the conflict, observers noted the unprecedented fact that the Soviet Union, instead of opposing the West in the Middle East, showed awareness of the threat to world peace posed by the aggressor. . . . It turned out, however, that many influential forces in our country (the mighty military-industrial complex, above all) are displeased with such a policy. . . . Now Moscow qualifies its support . . . by ever increasing reservations. . . . Sympathetic neutrality towards the aggressor is getting ever more pronounced in Soviet foreign policy.[29]

This new stage in Gorbachev's policy on the Gulf was displayed in official comments and criticism, echoing statements by domestic conservatives (particularly in the military press and CPSU as well as the Soyuz group in parliament) that the United States was going beyond the mandate accorded by UN resolutions. In Washington for talks with Baker, Foreign Minister Bessmertnykh cautioned America against destroying Iraq rather than concentrating on the withdrawal of Iraq from Kuwait.[30] CPSU Politburo member Gennadi Yanaiev, whom Gorbachev had named vice-president in January (and who was later one of the plotters of the August 1991 coup attempt), had criticized the "flabby response" of Soviet policy in the crisis, and now, at the beginning of February, noted that though the Security Council had mandated only the liberation of Kuwait, the United States was bombing "peaceful targets in Iraq and not only in Kuwait."[31] This comment coincided with a Central Committee resolution calling upon Gorbachev to "take the necessary steps" to bring an end to the "bloodshed" in Iraq.[32] The following day Gorbachev issued a statement in which he spoke of what "appeared to be moves" by the coalition forces that "went beyond the mandate" given by the Security Council.[33]

Soviet democrats were not silent over this change in Gorbachev's policy. In an interview with CNN, Boris Yeltsin referred positively to the American's position in the war (just a few days after he had publicly called for Gorbachev's resignation).[34] The USA-Canada Institute (ISKAN) presented recommendations to the Supreme Soviet that Moscow join the war so as not to lose the opportunity to demonstrate the Soviet Union's loyalty to the international community or jeopardize the possibility of receiving needed assistance from the West. The conservative Sovetskaia Rossiya dismissed these fears: "As if the pitiful crumbs that our country received, and recently stopped receiving altogether, could create the impression that they [the Western nations] are ready to help seriously."[35] Yegor Ligachev, Gorbachev's powerful conservative opponent, expressed similar sentiments. As he put it, certain forces in the United States were "linking perestroika with the dismantling of socialism." From his point of view, Moscow was correct in refusing to participate militarily in the Gulf and should not have agreed to the UN resolutions on the use of force.[36]

Both the ISKAN proposals and Ligachev's comments were indicative of another element that had entered the public debate, the connection between domestic issues and policies, on the one hand, and relations with the international system, especially the United States, on the other. The Gulf War and Western aid were only part of the picture; American concern over Gorbachev's apparent turn to the right—in particular the crackdown in the Baltics—was woven into the already highly complicated domestic-foreign nexus. Shevardnadze's resignation had demonstrated the connection, as both Gorbachev and Bessmertnykh noted when the latter took office. Gorbachev spoke of the foreign policy tasks that had to be resolved against the backdrop of difficult domestic problems, particularly the possibility of a "deadlock of opposition."[37] Bessmertnykh, referring directly to the Baltic events, spoke to the Supreme Soviet about "an increasing intertwining of foreign policy and internal political processes," explaining that "if events in the Soviet Union assume a form that contradicts international standards and international law, foreign policy cannot be successful."[38] Meanwhile, a leading Gorbachev supporter, political commentator Nikolai Shishlin, warned: "We must realize that our internal decisions are totally bound and harnessed to the world's view of the Soviet Union—to the Soviet Union's international prestige—and to a confirmation of the Soviet Union's adherence to the policy of renewal which we opted for back in April 1985."[39]

Gorbachev and pro-perestroika forces were keenly aware not only of the impact negative domestic policies could have on relations with the United States, but that, for President Bush to maintain a friendly policy and provide assistance to the Soviet Union, he needed the support of the American public or at least of certain elites. Democratic *Literaturnaia Gazeta* explained that there were "two schools of thought" in the United States, for and against aid to the Soviet Union. And Bessmertnykh told the Supreme Soviet that although the American president was adopting a positive approach, "the US Congress, the press and certain segments of public opinion are reacting more strongly [i.e., negatively] to what is happening in our country." Thus, he said, he had been advised—when in Washington—to meet with American representatives and statesmen to "explain" domestic Soviet events.[40]

Many conservatives, however, rejected this linkage—and in language reminiscent of the pre-Gorbachev period. Complaining that the United States was trying to dictate to Moscow and blackmail it (by holding up aid; postponing the next summit), they charged Washington with meddling in the Soviet Union's domestic affairs.[41] These reactions related specifically to American complaints regarding the bloodshed in the Baltics. Projecting a mirror image of the Soviet situation onto the United States, many spoke of the growing influence of "hawks" in Washington, those who mistrusted the Soviet Union and wanted to restore the Cold War. It was, some claimed, to placate these groups that Bush now "overreacted" to events in the USSR and interfered in Moscow's internal affairs.[42] Dovish American opinion was also invoked as a motivating factor for the United States. By painting a dire picture of Soviet actions in the Baltics, Washington was said to be attempting to assuage its conscience and divert public attention from American atrocities against Iraq.[43]

In fact, the violent clampdown in the Baltics was causing Washington serious problems as Congressional and public circles demanded a strong U.S. response. Bush was concerned that a mild response or none at all might appear as American acquiescence in Moscow's methods. Yet too strong a reaction would encourage those in Washington already critical of Bush's "pro-Gorbachev" policy. Moreover, a strong response would run the risk of "ripping the Soviets out of the coalition."[44]

Indeed, Bessmertnykh reportedly told Bush in Washington that the Soviet Union's "ability to maintain its 'cooperative approach,' "—regarding Eastern Europe, German unification, and the Persian Gulf—"will depend on how the United States reacts to the trouble in the Baltics."[45] Bush in response concluded that Gorbachev's situation was truly most delicate, that is, that pressure would push him deeper into the conservatives' camp and further jeopardize perestroika—and along with it, Moscow's already precarious adherence to the anti-Iraq coalition. Therefore, the administration expressed its strongest warnings on the Baltics only privately (as in a letter to Gorbachev threatening to cut off economic assistance), tempering its language in public.[46] In the same vein, Bush's decision to postpone the scheduled summit because of events in the Baltics was presented to the public as the result of the complications created by the Gulf War and unresolved arms control issues.

To shore up the Soviet commitment to the coalition, the Americans not only accepted Gorbachev's assurances that the Baltic situation would be resolved peacefully but also provided renewed incentives for continued cooperation against Iraq by publicly reiterating the invitation to Moscow to become a partner in future Arab-Israeli negotiations.[47] Baker agreed to a joint statement on the Middle East that came exceedingly close to linkage of the two crises, only preserving the principle of sequential linkage in that it was geared to a post–Gulf War Middle East.

Conservatives in Moscow presented the American concession over the Baltics—a "deal" widely referred to in the Soviet media—as vindication of their position that a Soviet domestic matter had no place on the international agenda.[48] They rejected, however, any linkage with the situation in the Gulf (though they acknowledged that Washington's acquiescence had been born of America's need for Soviet support in the Gulf).[49] Instead they continued both their efforts to disengage the Soviet Union from the anti-Iraq coalition and their increasingly vituperative criticism of United States policy. These efforts included the use of official media and facilities, producing programs designed to win over the Soviet and even the American public. Support was accorded the popular antiwar protests in Western Europe and the United States while Moscow's international broadcasts, seeking to discourage American enthusiasm for the war, increasingly emphasized the enormous American casualties that would result.[50]

As conservative pressures grew, increasingly concentrating their attacks on the aggressiveness of the United States (and to some degree the impotence of the Soviet Union under new thinking), Gorbachev initiated steps that seriously threatened Soviet-U.S. relations. In early January he again dispatched Primakov to Iraq with a cease-fire plan and then hosted Iraqi foreign minister Tariq Aziz in Moscow in an effort to avoid the impending ground war. The Soviet leader was obviously concerned that he would not be able to withstand conservative pressures to abandon the anti-Iraq coalition in the event of a ground war. According to some observers, he also sought to prove that the Soviet Union still had a role to play on the international scene and to demonstrate his own abilities as the "peace maker."[51] Thus, by achieving an end to the Gulf hostilities and Iraqi withdrawal from Kuwait, Gorbachev could bolster his sagging prestige domestically. Presumably this is why Primakov's cease-fire initiative was referred to as the "Gorbachev plan." Gorbachev himself may have assumed (or been convinced by Primakov[52]) that the plan was close to being acceptable to the United States and particularly its West European allies, and that specific terms, such as the exact timing of the Iraqi withdrawal, could be quickly negotiated, eliminating the need for a ground attack.

Such domestically motivated moves constituted a dangerous gamble with regard to the American response and the future of the U.S.-Soviet relationship.[53] This relationship was critical to the fulfillment of perestroika (certainly this was how it was perceived by Gorbachev) and it was still in its formative stages. Fortunately, the Bush administration recognized once again that a publicly hostile response would drive Gorbachev more deeply into the arms of the conservatives and probably elicit Soviet obstructionism in the United Nations regarding the crisis and the postwar Middle East. Moreover, a hostile response would have strengthened American skeptics, not only discrediting the Bush-Baker policy toward Moscow but undermining future attempts to bolster Gorbachev and assist perestroika.[54] Washington, therefore, downplayed the Gorbachev plan publicly, calling it "helpful." At the same time, the Americans warned Gorbachev to desist from individual diplomacy and to support coalition efforts in the Security Council as well as on the ground.

After February 16, various military officials, including defense minister Dmitri Yazov, publicly criticized the Americans' initiation of a ground war, and the Foreign Ministry expressed "regret" over the missed opportunity for a peaceful settlement, as did Gennedi Yanaiev and the International Affairs Committee of the Supreme Soviet.[55] These first reactions placed the blame on the United States for rejecting the Soviet plan that, they claimed, would have opened the way for Iraqi withdrawal. By February 26, however, the official line, expressed by Gorbachev's spokesman Vital Ignatenko, was that "it was Saddam Hussein who missed the chance for peace."[56] Demonstrating Moscow's positive response to the Americans' warnings, he announced the Soviet intention to work "in accord with the United States in the Security Council," backing the demand that Iraq fulfill all twelve of the resolutions passed by the United Nations. Thus the Soviets came in line with the American position and did indeed cooperate fully with Washington in the subsequent activities at the UN.

The domestic debate over the Gulf crisis, however, continued well into the postwar period, the proponents of each point of view drawing different conclusions regarding the outcome of the war. This, too, was evidence of the impact of domestic concerns on attitudes towards the crisis. Conservatives, especially in the military, demanded both an enlarged Soviet presence in the Middle East to counter the American buildup and more resources to close the military-technology gap with the United States (demonstrated in the Gulf War) as well as limit the continued aggressiveness of Washington's foreign policy.[57] Conservatives campaigned for an "independent foreign policy"; liberals pointed to Soviet-U.S. cooperation in the Gulf crisis as a cornerstone of Soviet national interest.

Almost immediately after the war ended, Gorbachev shifted back in the direction of his liberal supporters and the democratic circles. He warned opponents that cooperation with the United States was vital and that the U.S.-Soviet relationship would not tolerate much strain.[58] He even subsequently reached an agreement with Yeltsin and resumed his pursuit of perestroika. Having lapsed in only a minor way in cooperating with the Western coalition—a lapse the United States largely chose to ignore—Gorbachev now expected Bush to deliver on the promises made to gain Soviet cooperation in the crisis.

Washington had already "delivered" its tolerance of the Baltic clampdown, and now it fulfilled its promise to bring Moscow into the Arab-Israeli peace talks. Gorbachev, for his part, and despite domestic demands for an independent foreign policy, accepted every aspect of the American position regarding an Arab-Israeli settlement (including abandonment of the demand for an international conference). The Soviets also assisted Washington in getting Syria and the PLO to accept American conditions for talks with Israel, at the same time introducing security proposals designed to satisfy Israeli concerns as well as to ensure stability in the region.

American behavior in the Gulf crisis and Gorbachev's mixed response were not the cause of the August 1991 coup attempt nor an immediate precipitant in the coup. Nevertheless, Gorbachev's foreign policy in general, and his support of the American-led anti-Iraq coalition, were among the contributing factors. The crisis brought Yazov and the highest levels of the military decisively into the opposition, in part because the large American force nearby could be perceived as a geostrategic threat to the Soviet Union. Without the war, Yazov might not have joined the conspirators, and without Yazov it is unlikely they would have attempted a coup. At the same time, Shevardnadze had been eliminated from the political scene because of the Gulf crisis, depriving Gorbachev of an important ally in the run-up to the coup (possibly even accelerating the plans of the conspirators).[59]

Moreover, the Soviet Union, and specifically Gorbachev, were humiliated in the Gulf War crisis. The lack of decisiveness, the fiasco of Gorbachev's (and Primakov's) efforts to prevent American military action, and the failure of the Soviet Union to act as a superpower (including its obvious irrelevance throughout the crisis) demonstrated the weaknesses of Gorbachev and his policies. While bolstering the conservatives, none of these developments strengthened Gorbachev with the democratic forces or the public. Indeed, they deprived him of the one area of success he had been able to offer, namely his foreign policy. In this sense, the Gulf crisis played a role in the shaping of the outcome of the coup: the demise of Gorbachev and his "replacement" by Yeltsin.[60]

The Gulf crisis represents an example of a foreign policy development that, though not the dominant issue in domestic policies, nonetheless fanned the domestic debate on perestroika and in turn was shaped by this debate and the fortunes of perestroika. Although American rhetoric was designed to assist Gorbachev domestically, Washington's actions strengthened the anti-perestroika forces, reducing the Soviet leader's ability to maintain his position as dove and pursue superpower cooperation to American satisfaction. In many ways, this interplay of domestic and international factors during the Gulf crisis was a precursor of foreign policy-making in post-Gorbachev Russia. Both the policy of the West (mainly the United States), and the conservative/democratic struggle in Russia remain the primary determinants of policy, while other factors (economic, ethnic, regional) are interpreted and variously weighed as a function of these determinants.

NOTES

1. For Gorbachev's Middle East policy, see Galia Golan, *Moscow and the Middle East: New Thinking on Regional Conflict* (New York: Council on Foreign Relations and Chatham House, 1992).

2. Michael Beschloss and Strobe Talbott, *At the Highest Levels* (New York: Little, Brown, 1993), pp. 247–248.

3. Twenty-four percent believed that there was no Soviet responsibility involved. (Radio Moscow in English, September 3, 1990.)

4. See for example, *Moskovskie novosti*, August 26, 1990; *Izvestiia*, August 24, 1990.

5. For discussion of domestic debate, see Galia Golan, "The Test of 'New Thinking': The Soviet Union and the Gulf Crisis," in George Breslauer, Harry Kreisler, and Benjamin Ward, *Beyond the Cold War: Conflict and Cooperation in the Third World* (Berkeley: Institute of International Studies, 1991), pp. 315–364. There was a debate about such sales, with elements of the military claiming that arms sales were 15 percent of Moscow's foreign currency earnings, whereas others argued that the program had been a giveaway since most Third World countries were unable to pay. Even Libya still owed the Soviet Union $2 billion, according to Radio Moscow, September 2, 1990.

6. For example, *Izvestiia*, September 5, 1990 (Aleksandr Bovin); *Literaturnaia Gazeta*, October 15, 1990 (Igor Belaiev).

7. Galina Sidorova, "The World Closes In," *New Times*, No. 36, 1990, pp. 4–5; *Moskovskie novosti*, October 14, 1990 (Alexei Arbatov called for at least volunteers); *Literaturnaia Gazeta*, October 10, 1990 (Belaiev).

8. *Izvestiia*, September 20, 1990 (Bovin); *al-Sharq al-Awsat*, August 19, 1990 (Shishlin); interview with Vladimir Lukin, "Force vs. Force," *New Times*, no. 3, 1991, pp.20–21.

9. Moscow television, October 2, 1990.

10. See, for example, statement by Warsaw Pact Commander Vladimir Lobov, *Izvestiia*, September 1, 1990.

11. Just before the January 15 American deadline for Iraq to withdraw from Kuwait, a Supreme Soviet deputy proposed disavowing Shevardnadze's agreement to the UN Security Council resolution on the use of force (*Literaturnaia Gazeta*, March 20, 1991). The Russian Congress of Deputies did pass a resolution against Soviet participation in a military force although earlier in the crisis it was more, not less, anti-Iraq than the Supreme Soviet in calling for abrogation of the Soviet-Iraqi treaty and other measures.

12. *Le Figaro*, August 16, 1990.

13. Interview in *l'Unita* (Rome), February 28, 1991.

14. He also made a proposal, supported by François Mitterand, that would have placed resolution of the crisis in the hands of the Arab states.

15. Primakov's official position at the time was member of the Presidential Council. He was sent to Iraq as "special Presidential representative."

16. Aleksei Vasil'iev reported in *Komsommol'skaia pravda*, February 16, 1991, that when Primakov was asked in the United States in October what he thought of the Security Council resolution favoring the use of "all means" against Iraq, he replied that he was opposed to it. Shevardnadze had authorized Soviet support for the resolution.

17. Beschloss and Talbott, *Highest Levels*, p. 274.

18. *Washington Post*, September 10, 1990 (joint statement and press conference after summit).

19. Iraqi debts to the Soviet Union, said to be anywhere from $5 to $20 billion, were most unlikely to be paid, and there was the loss from what would have been ongoing projects and commercial contracts, the most important of which were the tripartite oil deals that Moscow had with Baghdad. Iraqi oil imported to the Soviet Union was reexported to Bulgaria, Rumania, and India; the loss of this trade would cost the Soviet market 2 billion rubles in goods, according to K. F. Katushev, Soviet Minister for Foreign Economic Relations. Deputy Foreign Minister Belonogov gave the Parliamentary Committee on International Affairs somewhat different figures: a projected loss of over $800 million in trade with Iraq, of which $520 million would result from oil not supplied by Iraq for reexport to India, Bulgaria, Rumania, and other countries, and $290 million would derive from goods and services not supplied the Soviet Union. To this Belonogov added losses of $115 million in goods and $700 million in financial resources expected from Kuwait. The last referred mainly to a subsidy promised by Kuwait for the development of oil extraction in Siberia. Other Soviet economists added indirect losses, such as increased difficulties in obtaining Western credits, increased payments on the foreign debt, higher prices for foreign equipment, and reduced repayment of Soviet credits from Third World countries.

20. TASS, September 2, 1990.

21. Beschloss and Talbott, *Highest Levels*, p. 251.

22. Ibid., p. 285.

23. Primakov told the *New York Times* on November 15 that the United Nations should postpone a "use of force" resolution. According to Beschloss and Talbott (p. 285), Shevardnadze waited until he was in an airplane with Gorbachev before obtaining his consent to the final version of the resolution, so that Primakov could not interfere.

24. On the eve of the September Soviet-U.S. summit, Foreign Ministry spokesman Gerasimov explicitly ruled out linkage. The joint communiqué at the close of the summit spoke first of settling the present crisis and then of making security arrangements, adding that all "remaining conflicts in the Middle East and Gulf" should be resolved. (TASS, September 6, 1990, and *Washington Post*, September 10, 1990.) Primakov, however, did advocate linkage in his proposals to the White House (and France and Italy) in October.

25. Baker was reportedly angry when Americans arms negotiator James Woolsey raised the issue with Shevardnadze in Texas in December, commenting "Woolsey's screwed up. He's lost us about a day and a half's worth of work" (Beschloss and Talbott, *Highest Levels*, p. 292).

26. *Sovetskaia Rossiya*, August 25, 1990 and Beschloss and Talbott, *Highest Levels*, p. 274 (regarding Soviet assistance to the United States). The Soviet ship *Dmitrii Furmanov* was intercepted by American and Spanish ships on its way to Jordan with a military cargo, according to Soviet domestic radio, January 13, 1991 (FBIS-SOV, January 16, 1991, pp. 10–13). There were also reports—believed and critically cited by the democrats—that Soviet military advisers had remained in Iraq despite Moscow's claims that they had all left by January 9, 1991. Moreover, there were rumors of other

types of Soviet military aid (Reuters, January 25, 1991; *Liberation* (Paris), February 12, 1991; *Nouvel Observateur*, February 14, 1991).

27. Deputy head of the USA-Canada Institute, Viktor Kreminiuk, was later to explain that Soviet policies regarding the Gulf War "were not consistent because groups supporting new thinking diplomacy, and the right wing factions supporting the Hussein regime were confronted with each other. . . . The pressure of the right-wing factions . . . became an obstacle to the diplomacy of new thinking" (Shimbun, March 31, 1991 in FBIS-SOV, March 26, 1991, p.14).

28. Pavel Felgengauer in *Literaturnaia Gazeta*, quoted at length in *Izvestiia*, January 28, 1991.

29. Leonid Vasil'ev, "What Is Saddam Hussein Banking On?," *New Times*, February 12–18, 1991, p. 14.

30. *International Herald-Tribune*, January 28, 1991.

31. *Pravda*, August 31, 1990; *Sovetskaia Rossiya*, February 2, 1991.

32. *Pravda*, February 4, 1991. Democratic critics said this position, under the prevailing circumstances, would mean continued Iraqi occupation of Kuwait.

33. TASS, February 4, 1991.

34. *Sovetskaia Rossiya*, February 22, 1991, criticized Yeltsin's expression of sympathy with the American position for ignoring the suffering of the Iraqis, and compared his position unfavorably with that of Gorbachev.

35. February 22, 1991.

36. *Sovetskaia Rossiya*, February 6, 1991.

37. TASS, January 16, 1991, presenting Bessmertnykh to the Foreign Ministry staff.

38. Soviet television, January 15, 1991 and domestic radio, January 27, 1991 (FBIS-SOV, January 16 and 29, 1991, pp. 32, 7 respectively).

39. Moscow domestic radio, January 13, 1991 (FBIS-SOV, January 16, 1991, p.13).

40. Moscow domestic radio, January 16, 1991; Central television, January 15, 1991 (FBIS-SOV, January 16, 1991, pp. 32–34).

41. For example, *Krasnaia zvezda*, February 1, 1991; *Pravda*, January 29, 1991 and February 6, 1991.

42. For example, *Krasnaia zvezda*, February 1, 1991; *Pravda*, February 6, 1991.

43. One commentator (Evgenii Shashkov in *Pravda*, February 2, 1991) made a convoluted domestic-foreign policy connection when he claimed that the Baltic leaders tried to persuade the United States to postpone military actions against Iraq until the Lithuanian crisis was settled (presumably so that Washington would be free to pressure Moscow without having to worry about Soviet support against Iraq).

44. Comment attributed to Brent Scowcroft (Beschloss and Talbott, *Highest Levels*, p. 300).

45. Ibid., p. 324.

46. Ibid, pp. 319–320.

47. *Pravda*, January 31, 1991.

48. For example, TASS, February 1, 1991.

49. *Pravda*, February 6, 1991.

50. Radio Moscow World Service in English, February 21, 24, and 25, 1991, also with comments that the United States had gone beyond the UN mandate. Suddenly, on February 28, when the war ended, Radio Moscow World Service in English switched to praise of the "exceptional unity of the world community" in this "most just war" and added that in

fact the multinational forces did not go beyond the UN mandate (FBIS-SOV, February 22, 25, and 28, 1991).

51. Vyacheslav Dashichev in an interview in *Der Morgen* (Berlin), February 25, 1991. In answer to the question "Did Gorbachev try to get some relief in domestic policy by taking that political policy initiative?" Gorbachev's foreign policy adviser Dashichev answered: "A foreign policy success would certainly have improved the President's reputation at home and encouraged perestroika. Gorbachev has proven that he is an excellent tactician. He will not be hurt because his initiative was not successful. What counts is that he showed commitment to peace"(FBIS-SOV, March 1, 1991, p. 15).

52. An INTERFAX report (February 11, 1991) claimed there was dissent over the Primakov mission, with Foreign Ministry officials opposing. Those advisers who might have overruled Primakov, out of concern for relations with the United States or simply out of support for democratic reform, were no longer in Gorbachev's official circle of advisers, namely, Shevardnadze, Aleksandr Yakovlev, Vadim Bakatin, Leonid Abalkin, Stanislav Shatalin, Nikolai Petrakov. Rather, as pointed out by the press, Gorbachev was surrounded now almost exclusively by party and military bureaucrats, the KGB and Interior Ministry. (*Moscow News*, January 29–February 3, 1991; *Sovetskaia Rossiya*, February 2, 1991; *El-Pais* (Madrid) interview with Leningrad mayor Anatolii Sobchak, January 30, 1991 in FBIS-SOV, February 14, 1991, p. 6.)

53. That Gorbachev was aware of the risks involved was evidenced by the defensive explanation given in *Pravda*, February 11, 1991, to the effect that Washington had no objection to Gorbachev's sending a personal envoy, Primakov, to Saddam at that time. Later, however, a Moscow radio commentary said that the plan had met with "obvious irritation" in Washington (Radio Moscow, February 24, 1991 in FBIS-SOV, February 25, 1991, p. 4). *Izvestiia* (February 26, 1991) too, reported the negative response by various circles, the press, and even high officials (though not official representatives) in the United States, where "many people had doubts whether Soviet-US relations would be maintained at their now customary level after the war."

54. See, for example, William Safire in the *New York Times*, February 14, 1991. White House chief-of staff John Sununu reportedly said "Baker bends over backward to please the Soviets, and now the Soviets are bending over backward to help Saddam. That's just great!"(Beschloss and Talbott, *Highest Levels*, p. 335.)

55. TASS, February 24, 25, 1991; Moscow television, February 25, 1991 (FBIS-SOV, February 26, 1991). This was the same week the official disbanding of the Warsaw Pact was announced.

56. TASS, February 26, 1991.

57. For example, *Krasnaia zvezda*, March 14, 1991 (Air Force chief, Lt.Gen. Maliukov); *Trud*, April 2, 1991 (deputy head, Operational Strategic Research Branch of the General Staff, Lt.Gen. Shtepa).

58. Soviet domestic radio, February 26, 1991 (Gorbachev speech in Minsk in which he spoke of the "fragility" of Soviet-U.S. relations). Bessmertnykh took up the same theme in his press conference on the Gulf War, speaking of the "serious and damaging intrusion of subjective factors" into Soviet-American relations, and warning that "figures who deal with Soviet-American relations either from within—when they work on them—or from without—when they comment on them—should be guided primarily by considerations of high responsibility because Soviet-American relations, whether we like it or not, are a determining factor in the present international situation."(TASS, 28 February 1991.)

59. The coup actually occurred in two stages, the first of which was the June 1991 attempt to strip Gorbachev of his powers through parliamentary enactments. Though he defeated this effort, his isolation within the ruling circles was becoming evident at this time.

60. It might be argued that the Gulf crisis even played a role in the subsequent breakup of the Soviet Union by providing cover—and American tolerance—for the violent crack-down in the Baltics and by eliminating Shevardnadze from leadership circles, both developments reducing the chances of moderate solution to the nationality problem. Shevardnadze had a much better understanding of and more sympathy for the nationality issue than Gorbachev. He was decidedly opposed to the use to force in the earlier case in Georgia and, during the Gulf crisis, in the Baltics.

Conclusion

Keith L. Nelson

Clearly, despite a common allegiance to Robert Putnam's two-level-game theory, the authors of these chapters have employed a variety of approaches in attempting to ascertain the role of external and internal factors in specific foreign policy decisions. This variety is not simply a manifestation of the characteristics that typically differentiate the work of humanists and social scientists. Even among the historians as a group and the political scientists as a group there has been a wide range of concept and technique applied.

Of course, the scholars involved in this project have benefited from the questions that the Putnam model raises with regard to the influences playing upon leading statesmen. But our loyalty to Putnam's ideas was strongly qualified in the beginning by our loyalty to our subject. That is to say, we were driven primarily by our curiosity about the domestic side of the Cold War, not by a desire to test a set of social science hypotheses. Thus we chose not to "stretch the set of issues and countries that Putnam used to develop his original ideas," as did, for example, the authors and editors of *Double-Edged Diplomacy*,[1] but rather to stay with one set of nation-state relationships over an extended period of historical time. This decision had the obvious disadvantage of reducing the number of cultural contexts in which applications of the theory could be attempted. But it also presented us with an opportunity that the scholars of *Double-Edged Diplomacy* noted was missing in their own studies, namely, the chance to accumulate evidence on how historical change in the context of international politics has affected the nature of negotiating strategies.[2] By staying with the Soviets and Americans we have been able to hold the cultural factor constant as we carried out our "post-hole" excavations over time, maintaining a chance to see whether historical processes in these two steadily changing societies were altering the way in which their leaders came to international bargaining.

Granted, the matter of extended conflict and hostility does pose a special problem for Putnam's multilevel game theory. The Cold War was not an experience particularly conducive to creating negotiating opportunities for its principal adversaries. Yet even at its worst periods of antagonism there were at least implicit bargains to be struck between them, and in its waning years the need for new international arrangements was growing exponentially. Moreover, this particular set of nation-states offers interesting points of comparison in judging the appropriateness of any theory. Not only do we encounter here the contrast between politics and diplomacy in democratic and authoritarian societies, but we also deal with governments and economies that were constantly evolving, from Harding's minimal executive to Nixon's imperial presidency, from Stalin's brutal dictatorship to Gorbachev's perestroika, from Roosevelt's arsenal of democracy to Reagan's plunge into international debt, from Lenin's NEP to Khrushchev's spectacular space program. Finally, the nation-states allied with these protagonists present similar yet shifting challenges in developing generalizations. At the beginning of our story revolutionary Russia did not have formal alliances, and the Americans did not want any. In the Cold War of the 1950s both countries organized large blocs of states in which their own voices remained decisively dominant. By the 1970s and 1980s the relative decline of bipolarity meant that what we have called third-level (alliance) games became inescapably important to superpower domestic and foreign success.

A question that arose early for all of the authors of this volume has to do with how central to make the chief of government (CoG). Perhaps by privileging negotiations as subject matter we have unconsciously replicated a long-standing tendency of historians, especially liberal historians, to focus too much attention on the personalities of leading statesmen. Perhaps, if the truth were told, the Cold War was actually a clash/encounter of cultures and/or systems whose ebb and flow was largely independent of the individuals who held high office. George Kennan said as much in 1947 when he predicted that the tensions involved in Soviet Russia's relations with the West might take as long as fifty years to play themselves out and were largely independent of what we could do to alter them. This was "Primat der Innenpolitik" with a vengeance![3]

Yet it is hard to believe that the foreign policies of successive governments made no difference in their relationships, or that their initiatives were not an essential key in understanding the heating up and cooling down that went on in their respective societies as they projected hatred, fear, and sympathy to the outside. Obviously, it would be good to know more than we do about the psychology and desires of each leadership, just as it would be helpful to possess more in-depth analysis of what was driving the vested interests and the ordinary people of the country. Still, we do now have a great deal of the historical record, and, if we assume that men like Stalin, Brezhnev, Truman, and Nixon had at least some freedom to maneuver, it behooves us to attempt to examine what they did with the opportunity.

Did and does the autonomy of the CoG in negotiations change over time? There can be little doubt the answer is affirmative, although how much it changes depends on a myriad of factors including the health, age, and personality of the leader as well as the stage of his nation's development, the phase of his own tenure in office, and his relation to other actors such as his own bureaucracy or domestic constituencies. Second-term American presidents are notorious for their progressive loss of international leverage, and Patrick Morgan shows this to have been the case with Eisenhower in the late 1950s as the president struggled to have new negotiating positions taken seriously and found himself blocked by officeholders he had earlier appointed. Authoritarian statesmen, by contrast, are said often to accumulate power with longevity, but in the immediate aftermath of a revolutionary period (as, according to Jon Jacobson, in the Soviet Union of the 1920s) it may not be easy to amass the political insight or capital to develop a win-set with any prospect of negotiating success. Later, Khrushchev continued to be influenced by radical ideas, but, as Vladislav Zubok and Jasmine Aimaq point out, the greater social complexity of his day made his foreign policy much more vulnerable than Stalin's to conflicting pressures from domestic interest groups. Still later, Gorbachev was face to face with a civil society that literally required him to achieve withdrawal abroad as the price for moving the Soviet Union toward genuine reform. Both Egbert Jahn and Galia Golan emphasize the extent to which Gorbachev's foreign policy was seriously buffeted by domestic factors.

One of the great advantages of the CoG is his ability to establish the agenda of international negotiations, especially when he is in attendance (a practice that became frequent in the post-World War II world). President Nixon, we know, was adept at stipulating agendas. At the Moscow Conference of 1972 he was able to dictate the way in which economic issues were taken up, requiring, at an early stage, for example, a settlement of the age-old Lend-Lease controversy. He was also, of course, responsible for the fact that there were understandings on offensive weaponry as well as defensive. Brezhnev, at the same conference and despite American lack of interest, insisted on an agreement regarding the "general principles" of the superpower relationship. Khrushchev put Berlin on the agenda with Eisenhower at Camp David and with Kennedy at Vienna. "Ike" brought aerial inspections to the Geneva summit of 1956.

Not only do CoGs establish agendas, they also have a chance to manipulate "win-sets" in order to achieve agreements and the ratification of agreements. As our authors note, Soviet and American leaders did this in a variety of ways, especially toward the end of the Cold War, by enlarging the scope of bargaining, arranging side payments to affected groups, mobilizing those who stood to gain from agreement, and, if they thought it necessary, cloaking their negotiations in secrecy. Again the Nixon years come to mind, in the course of which we witnessed the president pay off labor unions to ship Soviet grain, fortify the generals' enthusiasm for SALT by preserving MIRV, and keep everyone in the dark regarding negotiations with China and the tactical intelligence he was providing Beijing. But John Kennedy too compensated the Pentagon, promising the Joint Chiefs of Staff future support in return for their endorsement of the partial test-ban treaty. And Eisenhower mobilized scientists against the bureaucracy to try to offset the latter's opposition to an earlier test ban. On the Soviet side, we know that Brezhnev paid a constant ransom to his military in the 1970s to ensure their toleration of détente. And Gorbachev, while cooperating with the United States in the Middle East, tried to play an independent role in Iraqi negotiations, largely with an eye to influencing what Soviet public and party would make of his New Thinking.

On the other hand, a CoG can also be driven to negotiate, or be constrained in negotiating by a bureaucracy, a legislature, public opinion, or foreign allies. This seems to be more often true in democratic societies, although it became common in the Soviet Union too, especially in the later years of its existence. Stalin had been forced to deal with the contending factions within the Communist Party in the 1920s, and most certainly he was concerned about the requirements of the Soviet industrialization process, but he was largely immune to pressure for negotiation from the public or from governmental institutions. (In other words, Stalin's constraints were to a very great extent self-imposed, although it is worth remembering that he faced what he saw as a hostile and dangerous world.) Such was much less the case with Khrushchev, who had to take popular demand for consumer goods and a plentiful food supply seriously (not to speak of widespread eagerness for a lessening of domestic terror) in addition to the often contradictory wishes of China and East European states. By the time Gorbachev reached the pinnacle of leadership, both the situation and the nature of his reform objectives compelled him to bargain and battle aggressively with the vested interests that stood to lose by change. Not the least of his dilemmas was coping with the Soviet public's obvious desire for an end to the war in Afghanistan. Nixon too had faced such a challenge, and American trauma resulting from the conflict in Vietnam was one of the primary reasons he had sought a new accommodation with the USSR and with China. Subsequently, in 1974, Congress helped to break down an agreement that public opinion had earlier made necessary, as the Jackson-Vanik amendment requiring enlarged Jewish emigration from the Soviet Union undermined and destroyed economic détente. Thus democracy can work both for and against international understandings.

Naturally, statesmen can respond to frustration creatively by claiming that their hands are tied (their win-sets narrowed) and by trying to drive a harder bargain. An excellent illustration of this was Khrushchev's insistence that his obligations to the German Democratic Republic required that the Berlin problem be settled by a set date. The tactic worked once by helping to push Western governments into the (ill-fated) 1960 summit conference. Later in the summer of 1961 it backfired on Khrushchev, provoking such a Western military buildup—and such a torrent of East German refugees—that he was forced into the embarrassment of building the Berlin Wall.

Alternatively, statesmen can collude with their negotiating opposites and try to help each other bypass the roadblocks that they confront at home or abroad. A good example occurred in 1990, when George Bush chose to ignore Mikhail Gorbachev's last-minute flirtation with Iraq's Saddam Hussein because he knew that the Soviet leader, whom Bush wanted to succeed domestically, desperately needed to create an image of effectiveness for himself with his own people.

Time and again, the leaders of the two superpowers faced problems in the negotiation or design of agreements when it came to blending short- and long-term considerations. Often these factors pulled in opposite directions, and sometimes the trend of events exacerbated this tension. This was particularly true when the short term considerations had to do with the leaders' personal values or particular interests, which, as Putnam's approach indicates, can differ a good deal from their goals as national leaders. This was apparent in Soviet foreign policy in the 1920s and again in the early postwar years, when the desire for the long-term benefits that good relations with the West could bring were not compatible with short-term domestic political/ideological concerns. Eisenhower built American strategic forces for the long haul, but he established an arms race and political momentum that he could not control in his last years in office. Nixon's dream of important short-term (first-term) political advantages in summit conferences and détente left the overall process of accommodation sorely vulnerable to reversal in later years. Gorbachev had important long-term ambitions for a rejuvenated Soviet Union, but the short-run effects of his agreements and policies raced far beyond his management—inside the USSR and in Eastern Europe—and brought his objectives, his state, and his career down in ruins.

What types of agreements are easiest to negotiate? Our evidence suggests that understandings are more readily achievable when the benefits of collaboration are obvious and the costs obscure. Or to put it another way, accommodations come easier when the benefits are concentrated and the costs diffuse. A plausible variation on this theme is that agreements are less difficult when they secure a mutual advantage or defuse a mutual danger, that is, when they do not attempt to exchange one thing for something different, and when they do this without robbing the parties involved of future options. Thus the quickest bargains may come in the realm of communications (shared intelligence), in arrangements such as the hotline agreement of 1962, which addressed a newly reinforced desire in both Washington and Moscow to know what the opposing leaders were thinking during serious crises. Economic matters are more challenging to arrange to mutual satisfaction, but at least such agreements do not usually foreclose long-term possibilities, and if they do, the obligations can be abrogated when it is advantageous to do so. Clearly, economic negotiations are facilitated when there is a matched and crying need on both sides, as in the 1970s when the Soviet Union's requirements for wheat and for technology encountered American eagerness to be rid of an increasingly negative balance of trade and costly agricultural surpluses.

Arms control and arms reduction agreements would seem the hardest to come by, not only because they commit a nation publicly against using certain kinds of force to defend itself or for bargaining, but also because they run up against a huge vested interest within the government, the defense establishment, whose special concern it is to maintain as much choice as possible among the tools of military power. Thus, as Victor Mal'kov shows, after World War II Stalin found it impossible to countenance an agreement that would deny him access to a bomb that he knew would become the paramount currency of future international relations. Subsequently Nixon could not bring himself to relinquish MIRV for fear of what the military and public reaction would be. One ironic conclusion, then, is that in pushing arms control to the forefront of superpower diplomacy, as Moscow and Washington did in the last years of the Cold War, statesmen intentionally or unintentionally may have been giving themselves the hardest negotiating nut to crack.

Two other thoughts are worth mentioning. Agreements on complex undertakings that involve large numbers of allies (systemic factors) would seem almost inevitably to be difficult to accomplish. This was certainly the case when the United States and the Soviet Union were trying to work out limitations with regard to the Mutual and Balanced Force Reductions (MBFR) in Europe during the 1970s. It was even truer ten years later, when Gorbachev was attempting to manipulate the East European Communist leadership into providing support for his policies of perestroika and opening to the West.

On the other hand, superpower agreements that do not require formal ratification, either by allies or a domestic legislature, are easier to achieve. Nixon's and Brezhnev's 1972 interim agreement on offensive weapons, for example, might never have been ratified at all if it had been a treaty. SALT II was rendered much more problematic by its treaty status, although of course the climate of opinion was also vastly different in the Carter years than in the Nixon. Still, in general it is much easier for a hawk (like Nixon) to have his arms treaties ratified, or informally accepted, than for a dove (like Carter), because neither Congress nor the public are as fearful that a hawk will be played for a sucker.

To conclude, one might ask whether, as some have suggested, the more formal and informal ties that exist between the negotiating countries, the more enhanced the possibility of synergistic diplomatic strategies? For the authors of this volume, I believe, the answer to this question would be an unequivocal yes. This is not to deny that there are occasions in any age, such as in the molten years before World War II, when the chances for unprecedented agreements are particularly favorable. Yet, on balance it would seem that the more connected the nations of the negotiators are, the more bargains are possible between them. That is why, as the Cold War wore on and as the Soviet and American communities learned more about each other and exchanged more goods and visitors, it became possible for them to escape the high tension of the early years. The leaders of both countries became better able to "role-play" and understand their opposites, and their peoples became better able to do this as well. They more easily developed empathy and enlarged their win-sets. In the end even Ronald Reagan proved unable to resist the urge to think of the Soviet Communists as fellow human beings.

So, as students of international relations, do we finish by thinking that domestic factors are more important than we previously had believed, or perhaps that they have become more important over time? Again, I think that our collective response would be yes, on both counts. They are more crucial to foreign policy than we had assumed, certainly in democracies but even in autocracies, where circles of influence are not quite so wide. Many of us had missed their significance, largely because we were caught up in the drama of interstate conflict and competition. Moreover, domestic factors are becoming increasingly important as societies become increasingly complex. The greater the intricacy of the social system, the harder it is to do foreign policy in isolation. However, it is also true that the more interconnected different societies are, the more domestic affairs are influenced by external developments. Public desires, corporate ambitions, and the like—all of these are steadily more impacted by what citizens learn and know of events abroad. There is a growing seamlessness to world history, even as leaders are forced by existing boundaries, constitutions, and institutions to continue playing games on several different levels.

NOTES

1. Peter B. Evans, Harold K. Jacobson, and Robert D. Putnam, eds., *Double-Edged Diplomacy: International Bargaining and Domestic Politics* (Berkeley: University of California Press, 1993), p. 398.

2. Evans suggests, for example, but has little evidence to demonstrate, that over the last five or six decades "the proliferation of transnational alliances and the increasing dominance of economic as opposed to security concerns have conspired, along with learning effects, to make synergistic strategies more prevalent." Ibid., p. 401.

3. Kennan's perspectives were and are essentially conservative. Obviously, radical historians also tend to reject the centering of attention on the leader.

Selected Readings on the
Foreign Policy–Domestic Affairs
Nexus

Allison, Graham T. *Essence of Decision: Explaining the Cuban Missile Crisis*. Boston: Little, Brown, 1971.

Almond, Gabriel. *The American People and Foreign Policy*. New York: Harcourt Brace, 1950.

Armstrong, John A. "The Domestic Roots of Soviet Foreign Policy." In Erik P. Hoffman and Frederic J. Fleron, Jr., eds. *The Conduct of Soviet Foreign Policy*. New York: Aldine, 1980.

Aspaturian, Vernon V. "Internal Politics and Foreign Policy in the Soviet System." In Aspaturian, ed. *Process and Power in Soviet Foreign Policy*. Boston: Little, Brown, 1971.

Bialer, Seweryn, ed. *The Domestic Context of Soviet Foreign Policy*. Boulder: Westview, 1980.

Cohen, Bernard C. *The Public's Impact on Foreign Policy*. Boston: Little, Brown, 1973.

Dallin, Alexander. "Soviet Foreign Policy and Domestic Politics: A Framework for Analysis." In Erik P. Hoffmann and Frederic J, Fleron, Jr., eds. *The Conduct of Soviet Foreign Policy*. New York: Aldine, 1980.

Evangelista, Matthew. "Domestic Structure and International Change." In M. W. Doyle and G. John Ikenberry, eds. *New Thinking in International Relations Theory*. Boulder: Westview, 1997.

Evans, Peter, Harold K. Jacobson, and Robert D. Putnam, eds. *Double-Edged Diplomacy: International Bargaining and Domestic Politics*. Berkeley: University of California Press, 1993.

Fearon, James D. "Domestic Politics, Foreign Policy, and Theories of International Relations." In Nelson W. Polsby, ed. *Annual Review of Political Science*, 1. Palo Alto: Annual Reviews, 1998.

George, Alexander L. "Domestic Constraints on Regime Change in U.S. Foreign Policy: The Need for Policy Legitimacy." In Ole R. Holsti, Randolph M. Siverson, and Alexander L. George, eds. *Change in the International System*. Boulder: Westview, 1980.

Goldmann, Kjell. *Détente: Domestic Politics as a Stabilizer of Foreign Policy*. Princeton: Center of International Studies, Research Monograph No. 48 (February 1984).

———, *Change and Stability in Foreign Policy: The Problem and Possibilities of Détente*. Princeton: Princeton University Press, 1988.

Halperin, Morton. *Bureaucratic Politics and Foreign Policy*. Washington: Brookings Institution, 1974.

Hanrieder, Wolfram F. *West German Foreign Policy, 1949–1963: International Pressure and Domestic Response*. Stanford: Stanford University Press, 1967.

Hughes, Barry B. *The Domestic Context of American Foreign Policy*. San Francisco: W. H. Freeman and Co., 1978.

Ikenberry, G. John, David A. Lake, and Michael Mastanduno. "Introduction: Approaches to Explaining American Foreign Economic Policy." *International Organization* 42 (Winter 1988): 1–14.

Jahn, Egbert. *Soviet Foreign Policy: Its Social and Economic Conditions*. London: Allison and Busby, 1978.

Katzenstein, Peter J., ed. *Between Power and Plenty: Foreign Economic Policies of Advanced Industrial States*. Madison: University of Wisconsin Press, 1978.

Kegley, Charles W., and Eugene R. Wittkopf. *Domestic Sources of American Foreign Policy: Insights and Change*. New York: St. Martins, 1988.

Keohane, Robert O., and Helen V. Milner. *Internationalization and Domestic Politics*. Cambridge: Cambridge University Press, 1996.

Kissinger, Henry. "Domestic Structures and Foreign Policy." *Daedalus* 97 (Spring 1966): 503–529.

Lake, David. "Powerful Pacifists: Democratic States and War." *American Political Science Review* 86 (1992): 24–37.

Lebow, Richard Ned. "Domestic Politics and the Cuban Missile Crisis: The Traditional and Revisionist Interpretations Reevaluated." *Diplomatic History* 14 (Fall 1990): 471–492.

Manning, Bayless. "The Congress, the Executive and Intermestic Affairs: Three Proposals." *Foreign Affairs* 55 (January 1977): 306–325

Milner, Helen V. *Interests, Institutions, and Information: Domestic Politics and International Relations*. Princeton: Princeton University Press, 1997.

Moravcsik, Andrew. "Introduction: Integrating International and Domestic Theories of International Bargaining." In Evans, Jacobson, and Putman, *Double-Edged Diplomacy*.

Peterson, S. *Crisis Bargaining and the State: Domestic Politics and International Conflict*. Ann Arbor: University of Michigan Press, 1996.

Putnam, Robert D. "Diplomacy and Domestic Politics: The Logic of Two-Level Games." *International Organization* 42 (Summer 1988): 427–460. (Reprinted in Evans, Jacobson, and Putnam, *Double-Edged Diplomacy*.)

Rosecrance, Richard, and Arthur A. Stein. *The Domestic Bases of Grand Strategy*. Ithaca: Cornell University Press, 1993.

Rosenau, James, ed. *Domestic Sources of Foreign Policy*. New York: Free Press, 1967.

———, ed. *Linkage Politics*. New York: Free Press, 1969.

Snyder, Jack. *Myths of Empire: Domestic Politics and International Ambition.* Ithaca: Cornell University Press, 1991.

Spechler, Dina Rome. *Domestic Influences on Soviet Foreign Policy.* Washington: University Press of America, 1978.

Vasquez, John A. "Domestic Contention on Critical Foreign Policy Issues: The Case of the United States." *International Organization* 39 (Autumn 1985): 643–666.

Verdier, D. *Democracy and International Trade.* Princeton: Princeton University Press, 1994.

Wallace, William. *Foreign Policy and the Political Process.* London: Macmillan, 1971.

Waltz, Kenneth. *Foreign Policy and Democratic Politics: The American and British Experience.* Boston: Little, Brown, 1967.

Zakaria, F. "Realism and Domestic Politics: A Review Essay." *International Security* 17 (1992): 177–198.

Index

About the Contributors

JASMINE AIMAQ received her Ph.D. in History at the University of Lund, Sweden, and has recently published *For Europe or Empire? French Colonial Ambitions and the European Army Plan*.

GEORGI ARBATOV, Emeritus Director of the Institute for the Study of the United States and Canada (ISKAN) in Moscow, headed that organization from its founding in 1968 until his retirement in 1994. During that period he was a member of the Academy of Sciences, the Central Committee of the Communist Party, and the Supreme Soviet. He is the author of several books and numerous articles, among them *The War of Ideas in Contemporary International Relations and The System: An Insider's Life in Soviet Politics*.

GALIA GOLAN, Jay and Leoni Darwin Professor of Political Science and Director of the Mayrock Center for Soviet and East European Studies at Hebrew University, Jerusalem, has published numerous studies within her field, including *Reform Rule in Czechoslovakia: The Dubcek Era, Yom Kippur and After: The Soviet Union and the Middle East Crisis, The Soviet Union and National Liberation Movements in the Third World, Moscow and the Middle East*, and *Gorbachev's "New Thinking" on Terrorism* (Praeger, 1990).

JON JACOBSON, Professor of History at the University of California, Irvine, is the author of *Locarno Diplomacy: Germany and the West, 1925–1929*, winner of the George Louis Beer Prize, and *When the Soviet Union Entered World Politics*.

EGBERT JAHN, Professor of Political Science and Contemporary History at Mannheim University and Director of the Department of Eastern Europe at the Mannheim Center for European Social Research, has written extensively on Czechoslovakia, East Germany, Russia, and other East European topics. Among his works in English are *Soviet Foreign Policy: Its Social and Economic Conditions* and "On the Future of Europe, East Europe, and Central Europe" in Ronald J. Hill and Jan Zielonka, eds., *Restructuring East Europe*.

VICTOR L. MAL'KOV, Professor of History at Moscow State University and a departmental chairman at the Institute of World History in Moscow, has published a number of books in Russian about the United States, including *Franklin D. Roosevelt: Domestic Policy and Diplomacy* and *The Manhattan Project: Intelligence and Diplomacy.*

PATRICK M. MORGAN, Professor of Political Science and holder of the Tierney Chair in Peace Studies at the University of California, Irvine, is the author of *Deterrence: A Conceptual Analysis, Strategic Military Surprise: Incentives Opportunities* with Klaus Knorr, and *Theories and Approaches to International Politics.*

KEITH L. NELSON, Professor of History at the University of California, Irvine is the author of *Victors Divided: America and the Allies in Germany, 1918–1923, Why War? Ideology, Theory and History* with Spencer C. Olin, and *The Making of Détente: Soviet-American Relations in the Shadow of Vietnam.*

VLADISLAV M. ZUBOK, a Senior Research at the National Security Archives in Washington, is author of *The Kremlin and the Berlin Crisis, 1958–1962* and, with Constantine Pleshakov, the award winning *Inside the Kremlin's Cold War: From Stalin to Khrushcev.*

ISBN 0-275-96636-4

9 780275 966362

HARDCOVER BAR CODE